EUROPE BETWEEN THE WARS

Europe between the Wars,

A political history

Martin Kitchen

LONGMAN
London and New York

Longman Group UK Limited,
Longman House, Burnt Mill, Harlow,
Essex CM20 2JE, England
and Associated Companies throughout the world.

Published in the United States of America
by Longman Inc., New York

© Longman Group UK Limited 1988

First published 1988

British Library Cataloguing in Publication Data
Kitchen, Martin
  Europe between the wars: a political
  history.
  1. Europe — Politics and government —
  1918–1945
  I. Title
  940.5'1   D727
  ISBN 0-582-01741-6   CSD
  ISBN 0-582-49409-5   PPR

Library of Congress Cataloging-in-Publication Data
Kitchen, Martin.
  Europe between the wars.

  Bibliography: p.
  Includes index.
  1. Europe — Politics and government — 1918–1945.
  I. Title.
  D727.K516   1988   940.5'1   87-3227
  ISBN 0-582-01741-6
  ISBN 0-582-49409-5 (pbk.)

Produced by Longman Singapore Publishers (Pte) Ltd.
Printed in Singapore.

Contents

List of Maps

Preface and Acknowledgements

In writing this book I have received a great deal of help for which I am deeply grateful. I should particularly like to thank Ronald C. Newton for his criticisms and suggestions, and especially T. R. Ravindranathan, particularly for his assistance in Chapter 4. A grant from the President's Research Fund of Simon Fraser University enabled me to complete the manuscript. I am alone responsible for the shortcomings of this book and for the opinions expressed below which, since the inter-war period was characterized by exceptional ideological frenzy, moral duplicity and an unimaginable level of systematic cruelty, are necessarily somewhat harsh.

For Ming Ming

CHAPTER ONE
The Peace Treaties

The peace treaties were hardly signed before they became the object of such vituperative criticism that even the victors began to wonder whether they might perhaps have been a trifle unfair. It soon became clear that they were unlikely to provide the framework for a lasting peace. They gave rise to such recriminations, resentments and misunderstandings that they contributed significantly to the outbreak of a new and more terrible war.

The most influential, brilliant, yet biased attack came from J. M. Keynes in his book *The Economic Consequences of the Peace*. It provided vicious portraits of the principal statesmen. The French Prime Minister, Clemenceau, obliged Keynes to 'take a difference view as to the nature of civilised man, or indulge, at least, in a different hope'. He saw President Woodrow Wilson as a foolish, misguided and essentially hypocritical presbyterian minister. In a separate essay he described Lloyd George as 'this siren, this goat-footed bard, this half-human visitor to our age from the hag-ridden, magic and enchanted woods of Celtic antiquity.' According to Keynes, the result of these three extraordinary men being closeted together for six months was a series of treaties which overlooked the really important issues of economic recovery, food, fuel and finance and concentrated on the political and territorial settlement. He also argued that the intolerable burden placed on the defeated Germans, as punishment for their misdeeds, would further exacerbate the situation.

The Germans claimed to have been swindled into agreeing to an armistice. They insisted that they had taken Wilson's Fourteen Points at face value and believed that they would be treated mildly by the Entente. In fact the German government expected a harsh peace and had no illusions about Wilson. Keynes was less realistic. He believed that the idealistic and high-minded Wilson had been forced by the wicked Clemenceau and Lloyd George to agree to a Carthaginian peace. The Germans did not know that the president was determined to punish them for their wrong-doings, but they had imposed the punitive Treaty of Brest-Litovsk on the Russians. They had done so ostensibly on the basis of the Petrograd Soviet's formula for peace without reparations and without indemnities, and claimed that the treaty was in accordance with the principle of the self-determination of peoples. They thus had first-hand experience of negotiating a vindictive peace while claiming to uphold lofty principles. During the discussions of the armistice proposals at the German High Command there was a unanimous conviction that the peace would be excessively harsh. Those who wished to use the crisis totally to discredit the majority parties in the Reichstag, and the entire system of parliamentary democracy, actually wanted the peace to be exceedingly harsh. They hoped that there would then be a powerful reaction against the Republic which had accepted such humiliation, and that this would unite the nation in its determination to undo the disgrace of November 1918.

It is hardly surprising that the peace treaties excited such passions, for they ended four years of unprecedented violence. Millions had died, ideologues had fanned national passions to terrible levels of mindless spite, and whole societies had become directly or indirectly involved. Within the objective limits of the time it had been a total war. The three major Entente powers were parliamentary democracies, whose inflamed electorates were in no mood for mercy, and who demanded of their leaders that the wicked should be struck down. The British General Election in December 1918 was punctuated by bellowings that the Kaiser should be hanged, that Germany should pay up, and that the lemon should be squeezed until the pips squeaked. In France, President Poincaré and Marshal Foch could count on the support of the Chamber of Deputies when attacking Clemenceau for what they felt to be his excessive leniency towards the Germans. Woodrow Wilson claimed to be unaffected by the opinions of the US Congress, but the mid-term elections resulted in his party losing control over Congress and ultimately to the rejection of the treaties by the Senate. There had been much talk of a 'democratic peace', and of 'open covenants openly arrived at', which would make the Paris Conference so different from the aristocratic and repressive Congress of Vienna. Few realized the harmful effects of uninformed and aggressive public opinion which had been aroused by years of war propaganda, and whipped up by the popular press, such as Northcliffe's dreadful *Daily Mail*.

Wilson's Fourteen Points, vague, impractical and largely unacceptable to his allies, were at least not seen as an agenda for the conference, but rather an outline of his lofty 'new order of things', to be guaranteed by the Covenant of the League of Nations. The president's vision of a world free from imperialism, restrictive trade practices and the domination and exploitation of ethnic minorities, was regarded as a hopeless pipe-dream by most European statesmen. They liked to think of themselves as hard-baked practitioners of *Realpolitik* while others, in fits of uncharacteristic moral indignation, denounced the Fourteen Points as a hypocritical cover-up for the mistreatment of American blacks, and as an attempt to render national economies defenceless against the domination of American capital. But most important of all, the Fourteen Points were completely at odds with the prevailing political climate at the end of the war. Treaties had already been signed which were in clear violation of both the spirit and the letter of the Fourteen Points. The Italians had demanded a high price for entering the war and had secured the promise of the south Tyrol, the Dalmatian coast and Albania, at the Treaty of London. The Japanese had gained British and French support for their extensive claims in China. Under the Sykes–Picot Agreement, Syria was to go to France and Palestine to Britain, a situation further complicated by the Balfour Declaration of 1917, which accepted the Zionist demand for a Jewish homeland in Palestine. Britain and France had made agreements with Romania and Greece, similar to those made with Italy, which were virtually impossible to reconcile with the Fourteen Points. The French government was also determined to gain a secure frontier on the Rhine, either by annexation or by the creation of a buffer state, and was not going to be deterred by the Fourteen Points from achieving this aim.

A further serious complication was the bolshevik revolution, which created the twin problem of security against Germany in the east and the containment of revolutionary communism. This strengthened France's determination to build up a strong Poland, which would include large tracts of German territory, so as to guarantee the enmity of the two states. A revived Poland would also separate Germany from Russia, thus making co-operation between these two pariah states exceedingly difficult. After the Treaty of Brest-Litovsk, the French recognized the Czechoslovak National Council as the government of the future Czechoslovak state, but it was several months before the British and Americans recognized the right of this new state to an independent existence. The Allies also accepted the demands of the Serbs, Croats and Slovenes to form a unified state with a constitutional monarchy, but this in turn was the cause of endless difficulties with the Italians, who insisted on their claim to the Dalmatian coast.

Probably the main reason for the widespread disillusionment with the peace treaties was that President Wilson's idealistic pronouncements had been a real inspiration to a war-weary Europe. Phrases such as 'the war to end wars' and 'the war to make the world safe for democracy' made it seem that perhaps, after all, the war had some meaning. His attacks on secret diplomacy, the suppression of ethnic minorities and on autocracy were widely applauded. It was devoutly hoped that the League of Nations would guarantee a lasting peace made possible by the removal of these major causes of war. To underline his commitment to these ideals, Wilson was the first president ever to leave the United States while in office and, to the amazement and disgust of not a few of his countrymen, he stayed in Paris for six months. Unfortunately, very few people studied Wilson's speeches, or even thought carefully about the implications of the Fourteen Points, and thus completely overlooked his repeated assertions that Germany had to be severely punished, and that the League of Nations would be designed as much to restrain Germany and secure the Entente as it was to provide impartial arbitration and justice. This conflict within Wilson's mind between his lofty idealism and his deep-seated loathing of Germany was ignored by even such shrewd commentators as Keynes, with the result that their subsequent disillusionment was all the more shattering.

The conference officially opened on 18 January 1919, but important discussions had already taken place, particularly since the arrival of President Wilson in the middle of the previous month. President Poincaré welcomed the delegates by pointing out that forty-eight years before, on the same day, the German Empire had been proclaimed after the defeat of France, and that the task before the conference was to 'repair the evil that it has done and to prevent a recurrence of it'. In fact the first major topic of discussion was not the fate of Germany but rather what to do with the bolsheviks. The French were determined that bolshevism should be crushed, whereas the British and Americans favoured mediation in the Russian civil war. Similar disagreements arose between Britain and France over support for Poland. The French wanted to strengthen Poland, but the British feared that Poland intended to grab as much territory as possible and present the conference with a *fait accompli*. Wilson, who felt that the Poles were mainly concerned to protect themselves against the bolsheviks, did not intervene in this argument.

The frontiers of the Eastern European states were to be settled by allowing each country to present their own case. These proposals were then referred to a committee of experts who made the final decisions. By far the most difficult case was that of Poland. While her case was discussed in Paris she was in conflict with all her neighbours, and was fighting Germans, Lithuanians and Ukrainians. The French and the Americans both favoured a large and powerful Poland, whereas the British tended to fear that if it were to absorb too many non-Poles the country might well prove to be the source of further conflict. There were also widespread fears that Polish activities against Germany might nurture the spirit of Prussian militarism, as well as undermine the authority of the Council. Whereas the United States and France were prepared to accept the Polish proposals for their own frontiers, Lloyd George objected vigorously that the inclusion of Danzig and Marienwerder could well lead to another war. Wilson replied that the Fourteen Points had guaranteed Poland access to the sea, and that in areas of mixed populations it was impossible not to disappoint those who found themselves in a minority. The British also felt that the Poles' loudly proclaimed anti-bolshevism was simply an excuse to annexe territory in Eastern Galicia. Lloyd George was opposed to Polish expansion eastwards as it still seemed probable that the Whites would win the civil war.

The British and Americans agreed that Eastern Galicia should come under the control of the League, but the French argued that it should become an integral part of the new Polish state. Clemenceau reluctantly agreed to a British proposal that Danzig should be a free city under the auspices of the League and that there should be a plebiscite in Marienwerder. The Galician question was not settled until 1923 when the Poles forcibly annexed the area. The British government still refused to accept French and American arguments that the Poles had a right to the province, and were only prepared to go as far as to concede a twenty-five-year mandate.

A further area of dispute in Poland was the Duchy of Teschen, which was divided by mutual agreement between the Czechs and the Poles. In November 1918 the Czechs drove the Poles out of their portion. They were then awarded East Teschen, which included the railway and valuable coal deposits. The Council suggested that there should be plebiscites in the Duchy, but they were never held. The

Teschen question was to provide Poland with a lasting grievance against Czechoslovakia which greatly increased the difficulties of building an effective defensive alliance in Central Europe against Germany's revisionist ambitions.

The Czechs appealed directly to the Entente, rather than attempting directly to forge their own destiny. Their claim to the Sudetenland, whose population was predominantly German, was based largely on economic rather than strategic arguments, although they did point out that the area was necessary for an effective defence against Germany. The Czechs got their way with little difficulty, largely because the statesmen at Versailles were very impressed by Benes and his colleagues, whom they found pleasantly reasonable and conciliatory in comparison with the Polish delegation. It was felt that the Sudeten Germans would be pleased that they had nothing further to do with their debt-ridden fatherland, and little concern was shown for the minorities in Carpatho-Ruthenia and in Teschen.

Wilson was particularly concerned about the question of the future of the German colonies. He felt that they should be administered as mandates of the League of Nations. Lloyd George supported the Dominions' claims to outright annexation of the German colonies, and told Wilson that he would not sign the treaty if the principle of mandates was adopted. Wilson was equally adamant, and announced that he would not be privy to the division of the world among the great powers. Lloyd George found a compromise solution to this serious breach between the British and the Americans, by proposing that there should be three different forms of mandates, and that the German colonies adjacent to South Africa, Australia and New Zealand should be given as mandated territories to those states. This was acceptable to Wilson since it upheld the mandate system and to the Dominions because they were easily persuaded that there was little real difference between a mandate and outright annexation.

There was also considerable dispute about the proposals for a League of Nations. There was understandable resistance to the idea that the Council of the League should consist only of the great powers. Opinions were divided as to how member states should be selected. The problem of the mandates also provoked further disagreements between Wilson and his more predatory partners who hoped to pick up the spoils of the German colonies. But the most important question of all was how the League was to enforce its sanctions. The French insisted that there should be an international force for this purpose, but Wilson argued that the United States' constitution gave Congress the right to declare war and to make peace and this right could not be alienated. The president sympathized with France's need to have guarantees against Germany, but felt that this could best be achieved by effective disarmament agreements and by conventional defence treaties. The question of a guarantee of racial equality, proposed by the Japanese delegation, was conveniently postponed. There was general agreement that Germany should be excluded from the League for the foreseeable future and a draft covenant was accepted, largely because all controversial issues were excluded.

From the outset of the conference it was obvious that one of the most difficult questions to resolve would be that of the future of the Rhine provinces. In December 1918, Marshal Foch had suggested that the Rhineland should be separated from Germany and garrisoned with French troops. This proposal was repeated at the conference. The British sympathized with France's need for security, but feared that too punitive a peace would fuel Germany's desire for revenge. They argued that a potential threat from Germany could be met by other and less disruptive means. Although President Wilson's aide, Colonel House, had some sympathy with the French point of view, the president insisted that the people of the Rhineland would have to be consulted, and that any solution would have to be based on the free exercise of the people's right to self-determination. The Anglo-American proposal that the left bank of the Rhine should be demilitarized was rejected by the French. Even the suggestion that the Rhine bridges should be held by allied troops, that the German army should be drastically reduced and that there should be an Anglo-American guarantee to assist France if she was attacked by Germany, was not enough to make the French change their minds. Clemenceau thought that the British and the Americans, with their obsession about disarmament and their distance from France, were in no position to offer immediate and effective help. But faced with the united opposition of the other two great powers, he eventually backed down. It was finally agreed that allied troops should occupy the Rhineland for fifteen years. There could be a phased withdrawal, provided that the Germans behaved themselves and observed the provisions of the treaty. Lloyd George felt that even this was going too far. He did not want France to become too powerful, nor Germany to be excessively humiliated. But Clemenceau, faced with the united opposition of President Poincaré, the military and the Chamber of Deputies, could not moderate his demands. Lloyd George therefore gave way, and in April the

Council of Four agreed to the demilitarization of the Rhineland and a fifteen-year allied occupation which could be extended if the Germans disregarded the provisions of the treaty.

There was general agreement that Germany should be disarmed, but considerable differences about how this should best be achieved. A Military Commission was formed to discuss this problem. It suggested that the General Staff should be abolished, that a military airforce, submarines, tanks and gas should be forbidden. The import and export of war materials and armaments should also be banned. The Navy was to consist of only 15,000 officers and men, six battleships, six light cruisers, twelve destroyers and twelve motor torpedo boats. Initially the French preferred a volunteer army on the grounds that an *armée de métier* would be a breeding ground for Prussian militarism. Eventually they accepted the British argument that a conscript army would make it more difficult for the Germans to build up a reserve army of men who had served short terms in the armed forces. It was finally agreed that the army should be restricted to 100,000 men who would be obliged to sign on for twelve years.

The British government supported Belgium's claims to Prussian Moresnet, Malmédy and Eupen, Dutch Limburg and Luxemburg and the internationalization of the Scheldt. This was partly out of genuine sympathy for 'gallant little Belgium', but also out of fear that a slighted Belgium would fall into the French orbit. The French resisted these claims, demanding a plebiscite in Luxemburg, knowing full well that it would go against the Belgians. The British had no sympathy for the Dutch, who had refused to surrender the Kaiser for war crimes and who had made a handsome profit from Germany during the war. The conference encouraged Dutch–Belgian discussions which eventually came to nothing. The French also refused to change their position, and the Luxemburg issue had to be dropped when a referendum in September 1919 showed an overwhelming majority in favour of preserving the status quo. Woodrow Wilson remained sensibly aloof from these Anglo-French wrangles. British sympathy towards Belgium did not extend to a willingness to guarantee her independence. In 1920 a Franco-Belgian alliance was signed with little enthusiasm on either side.

Italian demands for all the territory promised in the Treaty of London of 26 April 1915 were clearly contrary to the Fourteen Points and were bound to lead to serious difficulties between the Allies. The Italian foreign minister, Sonnino, provoked a cabinet crisis by insisting that Italy should claim Fiume and Istria in addition to the Dalmatian coast. Some of his colleagues suggested that the claim to the Dalmatian coast should be dropped and Fiume taken as compensation. Italian troops occupied Fiume, Valona and most of Albania and the government refused to consider any compromise. Although the British Foreign Secretary, Balfour, told Woodrow Wilson that 'a treaty is a treaty', most British officials had little sympathy for the Italians. They felt that their demands were excessive and they derided their contribution to the war effort. But as Lloyd George told the Italian Prime Minister, Orlando, the British government, although prepared to stand by the Treaty of London, could not support the Italian claim to Fiume which was not included in that treaty. The three western powers all agreed that Yugoslavia should keep Fiume, and the British delegation in Paris was strongly pro-Yugoslav. In January 1919 the Royal Navy stopped the Italians from sending troops to restore King Nikita to the throne of Montenegro, the officer responsible remarking that Montenegrins: 'Should be permitted to retain their inalienable right to murder each other, as and when they considered it necessary, provided that no inconvenience to the Allies is caused thereby.'

In order to postpone any unpleasantness over the Italian claims to Fiume, Balfour suggested that all questions pertinent to Germany should be discussed first. Faced with united opposition, Sonnino eventually gave way to this suggestion, but he did so with such ill grace that he was looked upon as a troublemaker rather than a victorious ally. When the question of Fiume was discussed in April the Italians refused to consider any compromises, including the suggestion that Fiume could, like Danzig, be internationalized and administered by the League. Orlando, spurred on by mounting nationalist sentiment at home, left the conference in protest, and only returned when Britain and France threatened to renounce the Treaty of London. Fresh rounds of discussions continued, but the Italians still refused to settle, prompting the Permanent Under Secretary of the Foreign Office, Sir Charles Hardinge, to remark: 'As much as I sympathise with Italy in every way, they are in my opinion, the most odious colleagues and Allies to have at a Conference . . . and "the beggars of Europe" are well known for their whining alternated by truculence!'

In September the Italian poet and proto-fascist, Gabriele d'Annunzio, seized Fiume with a handful of freebooters. Virtually bereft of American support the Yugoslavs were obliged by France and Britain to negotiate with the Italians over free-city status for the port. The Italians, increasingly embarrassed by d'Annunzio's antics, were now willing to talk. In 1920 Istria was partitioned and Fiume made a free city. Shortly afterwards the Italian army evicted d'Annunzio. This settlement did not last for long. In 1923 Mussolini sent the troops back again and annexed Fiume.

Although there was complete agreement among the Allies that Germany was solely responsible for the outbreak of the war, that complete restitution should be made and that German militarism was an absolute evil which had to be eradicated, they failed to reach any agreement on how Germany should be treated. Woodrow Wilson hoped that it would be possible to apply the Fourteen Points to Germany. The French, deeply concerned about their future security against Germany, wanted massive reparations, in spite of Wilson's assurances in his speech in February 1918 that there would be 'no annexations, no contributions, no punitive damages.' The British felt that French demands were dangerously excessive, but they too wanted their pound of flesh including the German colonies, control over the Middle East and substantial reparations. They were thus unable to play an effective role as mediators between what appeared to them to be Wilson's impractical idealism and France's unbridled greed. The French felt that the British were being typically hypocritical, the Americans that they were short-sightedly selfish and woefully lacking in the spirit of the new post-imperial age.

The Imperial War Cabinet's Committee on Indemnity reported that the total cost of the war to Britain was £24,000 million and that Germany should foot the bill. The French wanted compensation for the terrible losses they had suffered, but also wanted to use reparations as a means of keeping the Germans weak for years to come. From the outset, reparations were for them as much a guarantee of national security as they were compensation for past losses and wrongs. Wilson accepted the idea that there should be some compensation for damage done to civilians and their property, and even contributions towards disablement allowances and war-widows' pensions, but he was horrified at the magnitude of the sums proposed by his principal allies. France and Britain therefore found themselves lined up against the Americans over the question of reparations, but they also quarrelled vehemently between themselves about their relative shares of the amount Germany could be expected to pay. There was also bitter resentment at the size of the debt the Allies owed to the United States, a country which was scathingly described as the only one to have made a profit out of the war. It was suggested that if the Americans were prepared to cancel that debt it might be possible to be more magnanimous towards Germany and to live up to Wilson's lofty principles. Obviously the president would never have been able to get Congressional approval for such a scheme.

These differences of approach and opinion were reflected in the Reparations Committee. The French thought that the Germans should be made to pay $200 billion, the British put the sum at $120 billion, whereas the Americans thought $22 billion was the absolute maximum that could be expected. There were equally conflicting views as to how much Germany would actually be able to pay, and how these reparations payments should be divided between France and Britain.

Lloyd George was convinced that it was absurd to make demands on Germany which were in excess of her ability to pay, and he feared that excessive reparations would be harmful to British trading interests in Germany. Lord Northcliffe's *Daily Mail* and a number of Unionist MPs continued to stir up public opinion in favour of punitive reparations and the prime minister was placed in an exceedingly awkward position. Eventually he trounced the hardliners in the House of Commons, and the victory of some moderates in by-elections convinced him that he could afford to take a more moderate and reasonable stand in Paris.

The French Minister of Finance, Klotz, suggested on 28 March that the total sum of reparations should be assessed after the Peace Conference by a special Reparations Commission. There was general agreement to this proposal, but it still left open the question of whether that total should represent the amount which Germany owed in respect of the damage she had inflicted or whether it was merely an assessment of her ability to pay. The Americans felt that Germany should be forced to pay whatever she could over thirty years, but the French insisted that they should pay everything they owed, regardless of how long that took. Lloyd George supported the American position, but was determined that Britain should get her share of the reparations. He still had to look over his shoulder at his critics at home who kept up a chorus of denunciation of his excessive charity towards the Huns. Wilson threatened to leave the conference if the French did not moderate their stance, and demonstrably ordered the *George Washington* to get ready to sail from Brest. The French then agreed that reparations should be based on Germany's ability to pay, but this simply opened a fresh round of arguments about sums and payment schedules.

The postponement of the final figure for reparations was an uneasy compromise. It was too soft for the hard-liners and too harsh for the moderates. It led to years of wrangling on the Reparations

Commission, thus undermining allied unity and fuelling Germany's nationalist resentments.

Obviously no reparations or compensation could be expected from the Germans unless they were shown to be guilty. There was absolutely no doubt among the statesmen in Paris that this was indeed the case, and it was also generally agreed that leading Germans should be tried and punished for their crimes. It was not clear, however, how these war criminals should best be brought to trial, and a special commission was established to examine this problem. There were those, like Lloyd George, who felt that the Kaiser should be brought to trial and pay the penalty for the 'biggest crime in history', but Woodrow Wilson suggested that this would only serve to make a martyr of him.

The commission reported that German guilt was based on the flagrant violation of the 1839 treaty which guaranteed the neutrality of Belgium and by individual acts such as forcing young girls into prostitution and sinking ships by submarines. The debate about whether or not the Kaiser should be brought to trial continued, and when Wilson eventually came round to accept the arguments for a trial he questioned whether there would be enough evidence to secure his conviction. Lloyd George had little patience with this argument and said that the important thing was to send him to 'the Falkland Islands or the Island of Hell'. Then there was the question of whether the verdict should be based on a unanimous decision or by majority vote. Lloyd George did not trust the Japanese sufficiently to support the idea of a unanimous vote. For all these differences there was complete agreement that the Kaiser should be brought to trial, and the treaty stated that: 'The Allied and Associated Powers publicly arraign William II of Hohenzollern, formerly German Emperor, for a supreme offence against international morality and the sanctity of treaties.' The treaty also contained three mentions of German guilt: in the preamble and in the sections on reparations and sanctions.

As none of the war criminals were ever brought to trial, the war guilt clause only had importance in that it provided the legal basis for the collection of reparations. For this reason, and also because it was a point of national honour, it was seen in Germany as the most offensive and scurrilous section of the entire treaty. Not only was it felt to be grossly hypocritical, it was also denounced as illegal in that it was a violation of the legal maxim *nulla poena sine lege*. The accused were deemed to be guilty of crimes which had not existed in international law at the time they were said to have been committed. On behalf of the German government, Brockdorff-Rantzau demanded to see the evidence for German guilt, insisted that the war had been one of defence against Tsarist aggression and tyranny, and called for an impartial tribunal to investigate the origins of the war. The Allies had no patience with these arguments. They saw the invasion of Belgium as a crime, and argued that under case law all crimes should be expiated. In Germany the war guilt clause remains a highly emotional issue even to this day.

Neither Britain nor the United States had a coherent policy towards the new states in eastern Europe. Only France fully supported them and was determined that they should be economically viable and strategically defensible. There were suspicions, voiced most strongly by the Italians, that the French were attempting to recreate the Habsburg Empire with its capital in Paris rather than in Vienna. The Americans were in a quandary about how to reconcile the principle of the self-determination of peoples with the need for economic and strategic viability. The British were concerned about the inclusion of substantial ethnic minorities in the new states, but tended to side with the French, hoping to act as mediators, win influence in eastern Europe and promote their trade interests. They felt that this could best be achieved within a Danubian Federation, a kind of Habsburg Empire without the Habsburgs, but this scheme was completely at odds with the determination of the new states to preserve and strengthen their newly won independence. A further difficulty was that the Great Powers had virtually no troops in the area. The British withdrew their forces for service in the Middle East and the French maintained a very modest presence. The successor states promptly set about grabbing as much territory as they could, and these incessant border incidents prompted the Congress to issue a series of dire warnings, all of which were studiously ignored.

Romania had been promised a large chunk of Transylvania, the Banat and the Bukovina under the terms of the Treaty of Bucharest signed with the Entente in August 1916. The Allies now argued that since the Romanians had made an extremely modest contribution to the war effort these terms were too generous, adding that Serbia's claims to the West Banat were justified. The Romanians advanced well beyond the line approved in the Treaty of Bucharest and precipitated a crisis which helped to bring Bela Kun and the communists to power in Hungary.

With the communists in command of Hungary the question of the Romanian–Hungarian border became entwined with the question of halting the spread of bolshevism. Lloyd George and

13

Woodrow Wilson considered expelling Romania from the conference for violating the Treaty of Bucharest, but instead a blockade was imposed on communist Hungary. There were many supporters of the Romanian claims in the British Foreign Office, the French Chamber of Deputies and among staunch anti-bolsheviks such as Poincaré. It was debated whether to send a joint allied force to Budapest to overthrow the Bela Kun regime, but nothing came of it. Eventually the detestation of communism overwhelmed hostile feelings towards the Romanians, and the Congress virtually gave Romania *carte blanche* to oust the Hungarian communists. This they did, but then the difficulty was to get the Romanians out of Hungary and to stop them pillaging the country. The Romanian Prime Minister, Bratianu, insisted that Romanian troops would only leave Hungary if the powers agreed to the 1916 frontiers. Only after repeated allied threats, including that of breaking off diplomatic relations, did the Romanians agree to retreat behind the river Theiss.

On 25 November Sir George Clerk, on behalf of the Supreme Council, recognized the new Hungarian coalition government. The Hungarians bombarded the statesmen in Paris with a series of notes pleading for a reduction in reparations and that the territorial settlement should be less draconian. Count Apponyi insisted that the terms imposed on Hungary were far more stringent that those for any other defeated country and that having lost two-thirds of her population Hungary was in no condition to meet the allied demands. The British and Italian governments gave the Hungarians a sympathetic hearing, but they were not prepared to do much about it. The French were eager to get the Peace Conference over and done with, and the final Treaty of Trianon, signed on 4 June 1920, made a few minor concessions over reparations, but was otherwise virtually identical with the original conditions.

The Austrians, having lost their empire, felt that their only hope of survival was to associate with Germany. The British and Americans were sympathetic to this idea because they felt that this would water down the Prussian element in Germany, which was seen as the source of all evil. Furthermore, since the Danubian Federation was obviously a non-starter, it was felt that a federation of German states might be a workable alternative. France and Italy were utterly opposed to this idea, as were the successor states. They wanted the permanent separation of the two countries written into the treaties, the Allies undertaking to stop by force any move towards an *Anschluss*. In the end, the treaties did contain a reference to the possibility of revising this article, but it was generally assumed that once the Austrian economy was on a firm footing enthusiasm for union with Germany would wane. There were further revisions in the territorial settlement when Klagenfurt was returned to Austria after a plebiscite, having been seized by the Yugoslav army. The Burgenland was also given to Austria, largely to weaken a Hungary still controlled by the communists.

Reparations were demanded of Austria, and there was also a war guilt clause. The allied assertion that it had only been the German-speaking citizens of the Habsburg Empire who had supported the war was particularly resented, and the Austrians predictably denounced the reparations as wildly excessive and unrealistic. Only very minor concessions were made in the Treaty of St Germain, signed on 10 September 1919, and it was not until 1921 that it was agreed that the reparations demanded of Austria were greatly in excess of her ability to pay.

Of all the eastern European states, Bulgaria was the most detested by the Allies. They felt that Bulgaria was the Prussia of the Balkans, as the Greek Prime Minister Venizelos put it, and that she had consistently acted from the basest of motives. Having grabbed territory in the Second Balkan War of 1913, the Bulgarians had joined the Central Powers in the hopes of picking up some more spoils and had conducted the war in a brutal and cowardly manner. This detestation of Bulgaria was further strengthened by a desire to have the best possible relations with Bulgaria's traditional enemies, Greece and the new state of Yugoslavia. Once again the Italians were an exception. Determined to frustrate the Yugoslavs and the Greeks, they began to intrigue with the Bulgarians. The Americans, with their obsession about the self-determination of peoples, were also inclined to be more lenient towards the Bulgarians than either the British or the French.

In discussing whether western Thrace, most of which had been seized by the Bulgarians from the Turks in 1913, should go to Greece, the British and the French found themselves lined up against the Italians and the Americans. The Italians put forward ethnic and economic arguments in favour of western Thrace remaining part of Bulgaria. The Americans claimed that the loss of this territory would cause such resentment that it would prompt the Bulgarians to go to war once more. The British and the French insisted that Bulgaria should be punished and that Venizelos could not be expected to return to Athens empty handed. They challenged Italy's arguments by pointing out that Bulgaria would still have access to the Black

Sea and thus to the Aegean, since the Straits were to be internationalized. The Greeks were also the largest minority group in western Thrace. In the end it was agreed that western Thrace should be occupied by the Allies who then handed it over to the Greeks in 1920, much to the fury of the Bulgarians.

American requests that the principle of self-determination should be applied to Macedonia were squashed, for it would have led to an even greater state of chaos, and Yugoslavia and Greece retained possession of the territory they had won in 1913. Far more difficult was the problem of the southern Dobruja, which the Romanians had taken from Bulgaria in 1913. The Romanians were a minuscule minority, and the Americans insisted that the territory should be returned to Bulgaria. The British and the French stuck to the principle that an ally should not be obliged to give up territory to a foe, even though this might not seem equitable, or contribute to a lasting peace. This difficult question was shelved and the southern Dobruja was not even mentioned in the Treaty of Neuilly of 27 November 1919.

The Treaty of Neuilly left the Bulgarians bitter and resentful and a source of potential instability in the Balkans. But their rivals had been greatly strengthened. Romania emerged from the war with double the area and population, Serbia was transformed into Yugoslavia which was three times the size, and Greece had increased by 50 per cent. Bulgaria's economy was in ruins and was unable to meet the reparations payments demanded of it. With a ban on conscription Bulgaria had virtually no army to redress its grievances.

The future of the Baltic states was another issue which exacerbated the Anglo-French rivalry. Given France's predominant position in Poland, the British were determined to establish a counter-weight in the Baltic states. The immediate problem was that they were forced to rely on German troops to keep the bolsheviks out of the area. These did not prove very effective and the bolsheviks seized part of Estonia and occupied Latvia. A counter-offensive by counter-revolutionary forces, in which von der Goltz's German brigade played an important role, succeeded in forcing back the bolsheviks, but this did not solve the problem of the future of the states. The Whites, who were observers in Paris, insisted that the Baltic states should remain an integral part of a Russia freed from bolshevism. The Poles helped to drive the bolsheviks out of Lithuania, but then refused to leave Vilna. Von der Goltz overthrew the government of Latvia. A Baltic Commission was formed to deal with these problems and called for the withdrawal of the Germans and Poles and the formation of local armies under the supervision of the British Military Mission. The issue of future relations with Russia were settled when Yudenich's White Russian Baltic army was crushed by the Red Army in the autumn of 1919. German and Polish forces withdrew, and early in 1920 the Soviets recognized the independence of Estonia, Latvia and Lithuania.

Although there were a few enthusiastic advocates of a League of Nations in Britain they were regarded with suspicion in Whitehall, where the balance of power and the strength of the navy were seen as more reliable guarantees of peace and stability. But President Wilson's firm belief in a post-war world guaranteed by a League of Nations was shared by some influential figures, among them Lord Robert Cecil and General Smuts. Public opinion endorsed the scheme, and Lloyd George began to think that support for the League was a modest price to pay for the friendship of the United States and for calming his radical critics at home.

The French felt that the purpose of the League was to guarantee the peace treaties, save the world from aggression and enforce international justice. The Americans felt that this could best be ensured by general disarmament and by the application of sanctions against offending nations. This did not go nearly far enough for the French who wanted an international force, a proposal which Lloyd George found intolerable. He did not see why the League should have as its main function the protection of France against German aggression, and doubted that it would ever be able to create an effective international police force.

The French supported the plea by the smaller states that they be included in the Council of the League of Nations, for they felt that they would be more likely to resist German revisionist moves and had a bigger stake in upholding the treaties than had the great Anglo-Saxon powers. But the idea that the League should have real power, and should represent the interests of the smaller nations, was unacceptable to the British, and the Americans had serious reservations, particularly as it implied interference with the sacrosanct Monroe Doctrine. After much discussion it was agreed that the smaller states should be represented on the council, but it was left open how they would be selected. There was unanimity on one point: the League was designed primarily to keep down the Germans, and Germany was not to be admitted to the League until a vaguely defined period of post-war reconstruction was over. A French proposal that German war guilt should be written into the covenant of the League was rejected as being contrary to the spirit of 'union and concord between peoples', as the Portuguese representative rather sanctimoniously remarked.

Discussions over the League were also embittered by the growing naval rivalry between Britain and the United States. The British were furious that the American naval building programme aimed to create a fleet that was larger than the Royal Navy. The Americans said that they would agree to reduce the size of their navy when the League began to function properly, but as Lloyd George and most of his advisers doubted that it would ever happen, this was hardly consoling. The Americans agreed to a modification of their naval building programme when Lloyd George made veiled threats that he would oppose Wilson's attempts to uphold the Monroe Doctrine against any attempt by the League to interfere in Pan-American affairs.

At last a covenant was agreed upon, but it was a vapid document which avoided all contentious issues. But it went too far for those, like Lloyd George, who feared that the inclusion of the smaller states on the council combined with the obligation for combined action by members against any state which attacked another state, or which threatened aggression, would lead to the smaller states dragging the great powers into wars in which their interests were not at stake. Others, like the French, felt that these obligations were so vaguely defined as to be virtually valueless. The League of Nations was thus launched with little enthusiasm and the chances of success did not look bright.

Behind all the problems of the peace settlement was an inability to understand that the pre-war certainties had been destroyed. The statesmen in Paris were not short-sighted or stupid. A civilization had collapsed around them with such rapidity that they were left stunned and unable to fathom what was happening to them. The age of liberalism had gone, and the future was to be inherited by the dictators: single-minded and mean-spirited men whose utter contempt for liberal values was such that statesmen of a more traditional cast of mind were left totally perplexed. The awkward compromises they had made in the past were now regarded by many as crimes, rather than hallmarks of the diplomatist's art. The once honourable label of appeaser was thus to become a term of opprobrium.

Liberal principles were inevitably compromised in the peace settlement, even though most of the men responsible for framing the treaties had impeccable liberal credentials. In order to ensure that nothing so dreadful as the last war would ever happen again, they were determined that liberal democratic principles should apply throughout the world through the offices of the League of Nations. They seem to have believed that liberal principles were so self-evidently true, and that respect for the rule of law so widespread, that they would be willingly accepted. Unfortunately, there were states which felt that these apparently obvious truths were shams and delusions to cover up ruthless exploitation and repression. Even more serious was the contradiction within liberal thinking between a deep-seated revulsion against violence and the need to use force to uphold the law. Peace was the greatest virtue, therefore the use of violence to ensure the rule of law was something that the statesmen at Versailles had difficulty in accepting. Furthermore, for all the talk about the rule of law, each state was jealous to preserve its sovereignty and to hide from international scrutiny its own injustices and violations of the principles to which it paid lip service.

Those who were intent on destroying the peace settlement, headed by the dictators, were quick to use such contradictions against those who had designed it, and they did so with devastating effect. They were to score their greatest triumphs over the nationalities question. After all, if the liberal belief in the self-determination of peoples was correct, then the peace settlement was a gross injustice, and many well-meaning people agreed. If there was an injustice, or even a suggestion of injustice, then it should become the subject of negotiation and settled by compromise rather than violence. It did not matter that the percentage of people in Europe who were obliged to live in an alien land was a mere 4 per cent, nor that most of them were reasonably content until awoken to the horrors of their fate by unscrupulous demagogues. Nor was it of great importance that in a small area like Europe, with so many different languages and cultures, problems of this kind are inevitable. A matter of principle was involved which gave the liberal-minded statesmen a bad conscience, which in turn made them anxious to negotiate, thus undoing the peace settlement and handing over the initiative to those who were implacably opposed to everything it stood for.

If the rule of international law could not be upheld, and if the problem of the minorities could not be satisfactorily solved within the framework of the peace treaties, then how could the peace of Europe be secured? Those who felt that belief in the eventual efficacy of the League of Nations was a sad illusion reverted to traditional balance of power politics. But a key component in any effective containment of Germany was missing. The Allies were intervening in the Russian civil war and were determined to isolate the Soviet regime and to stop any expansion westwards. Russia was now as much an outcast as was Germany, but without the Russian alliance the Entente had to rely on the far weaker states of Czechoslovakia and Poland. But weak as any such alliance was bound to be, it was further enfeebled by rivalries between these two states and between the great powers, which in turn were largely the result of the peace conference.

Paradoxically, Germany in defeat was strategically greatly strengthened, despite all the endless complaints to the contrary. Russia was in a state of almost total chaos. Poland and Czechoslovakia could never play the role of Russia as a barrier to Germany's eastward expansion. France's economy had been devastated by the war. The Allies were totally unable to agree on a common policy, either on the nature of the peace settlement or on the means to uphold it. Germany was left as potentially by far the strongest state in Europe, and from the very beginning of the Weimar Republic it was determined not only that the peace settlement should be destroyed, but that the map of Europe should be redrawn so that Germany would be even more powerful than she had been in 1914.

Even the reparations fell far short of the 'Carthaginian Peace' which Keynes feared so much, and which he felt would force the Germans into the arms of the communists. The Germans refused to accept that they should pay any reparations or lose any territory, because they would not acknowledge the fact that they had actually lost the war. Keynes' *The Economic Consequences of the Peace* provided them with all the arguments they needed to devastate their critics and to prick the liberal conscience. The classic rebuttal to Keynes, Etienne Mantoux's *The Economic Consequences of Mr Keynes*, was not written until Germany was once more at war and France was on the verge of collapse. At no time were the reparations the sadistic and intolerable burden which the Germans complained about so stridently, and after 1921 they were reduced so that they were no longer a serious impediment to economic growth. Germany had the capacity to pay, but certainly not the will to make the sacrifices.

Ultimately no amount of revision would have satisfied the Germans and it is doubtful whether even a return to the status quo of 1914 would have been enough. Such an idea was unthinkable in 1919, for no one had the slightest doubts about war guilt and no politician would have survived if he had suggested that Germany should be forgiven. Once the western Allies began to doubt the settlement, to think of revising it, and even to suffer from feelings of guilt that perhaps it was too harsh and unfair, the whole system began to totter. The high ideals of those who believed that the peace settlement, and the League of Nations which was designed to uphold it, would secure a tranquil and just future proved to be illusions. But it was a noble liberal dream which lived on, tempered with a gradual sad realization that men's dreams, however noble and exalted, have to be mixed with a cold realism if they are not to be shattered. But the vanquished saw none of this. They felt that they were being monstrously punished for a crime they had not committed. They were incensed by the way they were judged and found guilty and by the terms of the *Diktat* which was imposed upon them. They felt that the ideals of the League of Nations were mere cant and that the entire system had to be destroyed. Thus, in the name of righting wrongs, unimaginable crimes were committed. The path from Versailles to Munich was a short one, the way evened by the contradictions inherent in the peace settlement.

CHAPTER TWO
Economics: Inflation and Depression

Although economic historians will doubtless continue to debate the long-term effects of the war, particularly the question of whether or not it was directly responsible for the great depression, there can be no doubt whatever that its immediate effects on economic and social life were profound and shattering. The most obvious and immediate of these consequences was the terrible loss of life.

About 60 million Europeans were mobilized during the war and of these about 8 million were killed, 7 million were permanently disabled and 15 million seriously wounded. Obviously it was the younger men who suffered the most. In Germany 40 per cent of those killed were between the ages of 20 and 24 and 63 per cent between 20 and 30. Only 4.5 per cent were over the age of 40. There were also social disparities among these figures. Skilled workers, many of whom were exempted from military service, suffered the least. The middle class, which in all the belligerent countries provided the bulk of the officer corps, suffered the heaviest casualties.

Although the statistics are far from satisfactory, it has been estimated that Germany lost 15.1 per cent of its active male population, Austria–Hungary 17.1 per cent, France 10.5 per cent and Britain 5.1 per cent. Many of those killed left widows and orphans. 1.4 million Frenchmen died. There were 680,000 widows and, because of a remarkably low birth rate, the relatively small number of 760,000 orphans. In Europe as a whole there were about 4.25 million widows and possibly as many as 8 million orphans.

A sharp increase in the civilian death rate resulted from malnutrition, poor sanitary conditions, deprivation and the terrible epidemic of Spanish influenza. The infant mortality rate, a good indication of the general level of health, sharply increased in 1918. About 5 million civilians died from these war-induced causes. Population was further affected by the sharp decline in the birth rate during the war years. In 1916 the French birth rate was half that of 1913, and the German birth rate fell by the same percentage by the following year. If the birth rate had remained at the 1913 level the population of Germany would have increased by 3.7 million, that of France by 911,000 and of Britain by 776,000.

In the pre-war years there were slightly more women than men in Europe, and this tendency was accentuated as a result of the war. By 1921, 52.4 per cent of the German population was female. In France the figure was 52.5 per cent and in Britain 52.3 per cent. By 1921, 36.8 per cent of the women in France were single, an increase from 31.3 per cent in 1911. In part this was due to an increase in the divorce rate due to the strains of long separations during the war and a loosening of moral standards in the post-war world. In Germany the divorce rate more than doubled by the early 1920s, and much the same is true of France and Britain.

There was thus a slight increase in the older age groups and in the proportion of women. Slightly more women than before the war were in managerial and professional positions, but this certainly did not amount to anything like a revolution in the status of women. Men were doctors and women were midwives, and enterprises run by women were certainly less important than those run by men. The percentage of women working in industry declined markedly after the war and men returning from the front went back to their old jobs and the women found work in the service sector and in agriculture. These industrial jobs had changed as a result of mechanization and rationalization which made it even more difficult for ex-servicemen to adapt to civilian life. The war had also greatly speeded up the process of urbanization and it was in the cities that the social changes and tensions provoked by the war were most noticeable.

In spite of the dreadful and needless loss of life in the war it would be a serious mistake to attribute the shortcomings of the inter-war period to the absence of the 'lost generation'. According to this myth the intellectual elite was destroyed in the war and only the mediocre were left behind to become the second-rate politicians, unimaginative entrepreneurs and hide-bound bureaucrats who were unable to surmount the successive crises and who were directly responsible for another world war. It is true that the young men of the elite suffered the worst casualties, but if 2,680 Oxford graduates were killed it should also be remembered that 14,650 (80%) of those who served also survived. In brutal economic terms, since the period was one of high unemployment it can be argued that these heavy losses in fact alleviated the situation for all the wastage of the skilled, the intelligent and the enterprising.

The war had also caused unprecedented material destruction. In France 250,000 buildings were destroyed and a further 500,000 damaged; 6,000 square miles were devastated and this area accounted for 20 per cent of the country's agriculture, 70 per cent of its coal production and 65 per cent of its steel. It has been estimated that the total value of property losses in the war was $30,000 million. Germany suffered the least and only lost about $1,750 million. Such figures can be deceptive. In terms of dollar value countries like Poland did not fare so badly, but 11 million acres of agricultural land and 6 million acres of forest were devastated, 60 per cent of the cattle stock was killed and 1.8 million buildings destroyed. The destruction throughout the rest of eastern Europe and the Balkans was on a similar scale, and in Russia the loss of life and property in the war and the civil war beggars description.

The cost of four years of near total war was staggering, amounting to 6.5 times the total national debts of the world from the end of the eighteenth century until 1914. Of the total $260 billion the Allies owed $176 billion. Most of these costs had been covered by deficit financing and current revenue had only been sufficient to meet a minute fraction of the total expense. This resulted in an enormous increase in the money supply and gold and silver reserves dwindled. Most of the belligerent countries abandoned the gold standard and their currencies rapidly depreciated. Inflation inevitably rose sharply, but in most countries it was not totally unmanageable by the end of the war. Forceful government policies could have curbed the chronic inflation of the immediate post-war years.

Although the central powers did not suffer much material damage during the war they were made to pay heavy penalties under the terms of the peace treaties. Germany, for example, lost about 15 per cent of her pre-war capacity, all her foreign investments and 90 per cent of her mercantile fleet. The territorial settlement caused a number of severe dislocations and the total sum of reparations payments, although unspecified, was widely regarded as an intolerable burden. The Treaty of Versailles was undoubtedly harsh but it was hardly responsible for all of Germany's economic difficulties.

The effects of the peace settlement were also severe on Austria-Hungary. Agricultural production had fallen by 53 per cent and by 1919 Austria was virtually starving. The country only had 6.5

million inhabitants, but of them 615,000 were civil servants who had once run an empire of 52 million. The received wisdom of most Austrians was that this pathetic remnant of a once great empire, starving and cut off from its traditional sources of raw materials and traditional markets, its financial institutions denied easy access to most of their investment outlets, was incapable of survival. Hungary, which lost substantial territories to Romania, Yugoslavia and Czechoslovakia, fared no better.

Territorially the big winners were Poland, Czechoslovakia, Yugoslavia and Romania but all these states suffered from serious difficulties and deprivations and faced the problem of integrating their territories into single viable economic entities. Even the neutral countries, where many substantial fortunes had been made during the war, suffered from severe shortages, sharp rates of inflation, and high unemployment. Two countries profited enormously from the war – the United States and Japan. The former had converted a net debit of $3,700 million, exclusive of inter-governmental debts, into a net credit of about the same amount. Industrial production had been boosted by allied demand for American goods, and the United States had also granted enormous credits so that by the end of the war it was second only to Britain as a creditor nation. Japan had played only a minor role in the war and had achieved a spectacular increase in industrial production. Between 1913 and 1918 Japanese exports increased threefold.

Even the United States and Japan suffered from the effects of the economic dislocations of the war. The Americans had to find work for 4 million ex-servicemen, and farmers were seriously affected by the fall in agricultural prices which had become enormously inflated during the war. The export of industrial goods from the new world to the old was only possible if the Americans were willing to grant substantial lines of credit, and businessmen were often so taken by the slogan 'business as usual' that they seemed blind to the fact that the world had changed radically as a result of the war. Even the Japanese suffered initially from the shrinkage of world trade and from the effects of domestic inflation.

As earnestly as all the European states wished to get back to business as usual, this proved singularly difficult. The gold standard had been abandoned, currencies had depreciated at widely different rates and reconstruction and the restoration of world trade was not possible without a stabilization of these currencies. With massive debts, reparations and dislocations caused by wartime destruction and the re-drawing of the frontiers of Europe, the task of currency restoration was made exceptionally difficult and governments, seeing certain short-term advantages, were often reluctant seriously to tackle the problem of inflation.

The war resulted in a greatly increased demand for iron, steel and coal and the engineering and shipbuilding industries thrived. Once the war ended this resulted in serious problems of excess capacity for it was impossible to maintain such high levels of demand. Much the same applied to raw materials and to agricultural products. Both sectors had expanded enormously as a result of the increasing pressure of demand. When demand dropped there was no market for the excess production of Cuban sugar, Malayan rubber, Bolivian tin or North American grain and as a result prices dropped, incomes fell and with them the demand for European manufactured goods. Import substitution, which began as an exigency of war, continued into the post-war period leading to the erosion of the commanding position of such industries as dyestuffs in Germany or cotton in Lancashire. New technologies similarly undermined traditional industries. Synthetic nitrates spelt the end of the Chilean nitrate trade and oil replaced coal as a basic fuel. Innovative technologies seized the opportunities offered during the war, but they were bitterly resented and resisted by the traditional sectors, resulting in serious problems of adjustment to a technologically-based economy. Most statesmen were every bit as conservative as these hide-bound businessmen so that many of the opportunities to create a new, modern and dynamic economic order were lost in a determined effort to restore a world that had gone for ever.

A good case can be made that this world was on the way out in any case, and that the war merely speeded up the process. Free trade was giving way to protectionism, and markets were dominated by cartels and combines. The purchasing power of European currencies was bound to change and at different rates, since the performance of national economies differed widely. Not even the magic gold standard could have maintained the remarkable stability of exchange rates indefinitely. State intervention in the economy in the pre-war years was already extensive and the outline of what Hilferding was to call 'organized capitalism' was already clearly visible.

Massive expenditure on unproductive and destructive goods and services is characteristic of all wars and inevitably leads to inflation. The inflationary effects of the Great War were however unprecedented and the experts failed to gauge the enormous pent-up demand that would be released once rationing, quotas and controls were removed. Europe was short of raw materials, capital and consumer goods. There was a shortage of shipping and most road and railway systems were working well below capacity. Efforts by the Supreme Economic Council, the European Coal Commission and the the Meulen Plan to overcome these shortages were far from successful. The frantic search for raw materials fuelled inflation, made recovery even slower and led to further currency depreciation. Between 1919 and 1920 continental Europe imported $17.5 billion worth of goods, and only exported $5 billion. Governments did little to close this widening gap and frantically tried to meet excessive debt payments by dumping large amounts of currency on the speculative market and by negotiating short-term loans from increasingly reluctant creditors. Businessmen wanted the irksome wartime controls dropped, governments aquiesced and inflation rates rose still further. By 1920 prices in Britain were three times the 1913 level, in Germany they had risen five times. In eastern Europe the situation was catastrophic. Prices in Austria were 14,000 times the pre-war level, in Hungary the multiplier was 23,000, in Poland 2.5 million, and Russia 4 billion.

Early in 1920 the post-war boom slackened. It was first noticeable in those countries where industrial recovery was the most rapid. Taking manufacturing activity as 100 in 1913, the United States had reached 122, Japan 176, Britain 93, France 70 and Germany 59. Business activity slackened noticeably in the United States in January and in March the Tokyo stock market collapsed, the price of basic commodities such as rice falling drastically. Throughout Europe prices fell, unemployment rose and production was cut back. Only those countries whose currencies were virtually valueless were able to maintain production rates since their export prices were attractively low. The depression was more rapid and severe in the United States in 1920–21 than it was in the great depression of 1929, but mercifully it was relatively short-lived.

There is much uncertainty among economic historians why prices fell so dramatically. The argument that it was the supply side which was the main cause is not particularly convincing. The price of raw materials did fall, but only after the prices of industrial goods had begun to drop, and there was no real reason why cheaper raw materials should have caused an industrial recession. There is some evidence of consumer resistance forcing down prices, but this was hardly enough to have had such a dramatic effect. Far more important were the severe deflationary policies of the governments of the United States and Britain. They were determined to balance the budget, reduce military expenditure and restrict credit. Such measures, coming at a time when a downswing in the world economy had already begun, greatly exacerbated its effect. Other countries such as Austria, Hungary, Poland and Russia, but most notably Germany, preferred an inflationary policy.

The fall in commodity prices made it increasingly difficult for debtor countries to meet their obligations to their creditors, assuming that they seriously intended to do so, and the problem of inter-allied debts and reparations became even more intractable. The severe deflationary policies of the United States government resulted in a sharp decline of exports to that valuable market and there was a severe dollar shortage in Europe which could only partly be counteracted by the sale of gold reserves, which in turn postponed the stabilization of the European currencies. The problems of the European national economies were compounded in that they had contracted debts at a time when prices were high and were having to pay them off when prices had fallen by an average of 40 per cent. Attempts to increase production to meet these debt payments tended to push prices down still further.

When the depression began, little had been settled about the reparations Germany were to pay, beyond an interim agreement that she owed £1,000,000,000 on account. At the Spa conference in July 1920 it was agreed that France should take 52 per cent of the total reparations, the British Empire 22 per cent, Italy 10 per cent and Belgium 8 per cent. In April of the following year the Reparations Committee decided that Germany was to pay a total of 132 billion gold marks, about £6,600,000,000. The allied governments knew perfectly well that this was an unrealistically vast sum and therefore in effect postponed indefinitely the payment of two-thirds of this amount by allowing that this fraction of the total should only be collected when Germany clearly demonstrated an ability to pay.

The Germans were to pay 2 billion gold marks per annum, but very shortly informed the commission that this was impossible. Inflation in Germany had been fuelled by the government's refusal to raise taxes on incomes and company profits during the war, and had been increased by the cost push of labour which had managed to gain higher wages and shorter working hours in the period immediately after the war. The basic problem was how to allocate the burden of reconstruction, reparations and restocking. The right-wing parties would not accept higher rates of taxation and the left would not agree to deflation. Given a succession of weak coalition governments nothing could be settled. Erzberger's efforts to sort out the finances and to increase taxation failed and he fell to an assassin's bullet. Revenues were hopelessly inadequate and domestic debt rose alarmingly. The lowering of import costs as the mark recovered was now reversed as payments in kind became increasingly difficult. Gold and foreign exchange reserves became depleted and the mark began a rapid slide downwards against the major currencies.

The British were prepared to accept a two-year moratorium on cash payments from Germany, but the French would not agree, seeing no reason why the Germans should not pay for the war they had started and began to think in terms of 'productive guarantees', by which they meant the occupation of the Ruhr, in order to ensure that the reparation payments were made. Thus, when the Germans applied in July 1922 for a two-year moratorium on cash payments the French and British governments were unable to agree on a common policy. The Germans tried again in November, hoping that it might be possible to convince the Allies that a moratorium was essential for the stabilization of the mark. Again the French refused. In December Germany was unable to make the required deliveries in kind and on 11 January 1927 the French and Belgians marched into the Ruhr.

Before the occupation of the Ruhr the Reichsbank had been frantically printing money to meet the need for foreign exchange and to maintain the liquidity of the banking system. This continued after the occupation, for the government adopted a policy of passive resistance and the strikers had somehow to be paid. The result was a total collapse of the currency which obliged the government to call off passive resistance and to create a new currency, the Rentenmark.

The Reparations Committee appointed two sub-committees to examine the problem of reparations, and in April 1924 they accepted the recommendations of the committee chaired by the American general, financier and later vice-president, Charles C. Dawes. The Dawes Plan left unchanged the total amount owing by Germany, for any reduction would have been unacceptable to the French, but drastically reduced the amount of the annual payments from an initial 1,000 million gold marks to 2,500 billion in 1929, by which time ironically it was estimated that the German economy would have fully recovered. To help Germany get back on her feet a loan of 800 million gold marks was offered.

Initially the Dawes Plan worked remarkably well. The annuities were paid on time, the new mark was remarkably stable and the French were no longer able to dominate the Reparations Committee and unilaterally extort payment from the Germans. But much of this was done with borrowed money, most of it in the form of short-term loans. Between 1924 and 1930 Germany borrowed about 28 billion marks abroad and paid 10.3 billion marks in reparations. Far more money went to Germany after the Great War than was to be advanced under the Marshall Plan. This was inviting future trouble, for even had there not been a depression in 1929 it is inconceivable that loans on this scale, greater than the amount paid in reparations and sufficient to meet the interest payments on earlier debts, could have continued indefinitely. Such loans encouraged the Germans to import goods and reduced the propensity of the lending countries to buy German goods. The ready availability of capital in Germany stimulated the domestic market at the expense of exports. As it was the effects of the depression were greatly magnified by the degree of dependence of the German economy on such large amounts of short-term loan capital.

Compared with the problem of reparations the question of inter-allied war debts was relatively minor, but it did give rise to a number of difficulties. Of a total of about $23 billion, which excludes the Russian debt, about half was owed to the United States. Britain was in debt to the United States for $4.7 billion but was owed $11.1 billion by other countries and was thus a net creditor. France owed the United States and Britain $7 billion but had only loaned $3.5 billion and was by far the largest net debtor among the Allies, hence her determination to extract as much as possible from the Germans.

A number of British statesmen took up the suggestion, advanced by Keynes, that all debts should be cancelled, but the United States would not agree, insisting quite correctly that they had been contracted in good faith and that the Allies had a legal obligation to repay the money advanced to them. The Americans would not agree to a scheme to redistribute the debt among the Allies which was put forward by Sir Josiah Stamp, and the proposal to link reparations with the inner-allied debt and make the Germans pay the Americans directly was also rejected. Britain and France made some concessions to their debtors and pointed out that they only needed the money to pay the Americans. Gradually the Americans began to reduce their demands, and by 1926 the debt owed by France and Belgium was reduced by 50 per cent, Italy's debt by 80 per cent and Britain's by 30 per cent. The Allies were given up to sixty years to repay their remaining debts and the interest rate was very low.

Since the Americans insisted on being paid in gold and dollars and the creditor countries did not want payment in kind, for fear that it would harm domestic industry, the major problem was to find the currency to pay these debts. In practice the creditor countries loaned money which was then returned via the European Allies to the United States. It was an absurd situation which collapsed as soon as American credit dried up after the Wall Street crash. By 1931 the Americans received only $2.6 billion from the Allies out of a total debt of $12 billion and these payments were amply covered by the reparations paid by Germany which in turn were only a fraction of the amount originally demanded. The French got more than three times the amount from Germany than they paid to the Americans. Britain alone ended up as a net loser in this transfer of reparations and war debts.

Although it was widely felt that 1925, the year of Locarno, was a watershed year in which Europe entered a period of prosperity, the extent of that recovery should not be exaggerated. Manufacturing output had only regained the 1913 level, and in the countries of eastern Europe it had not even done that. In Germany it was still 10 per cent below, in Britain and France only 10 per cent above. Unemployment was a persistent and serious problem. In Britain 1 million workers were without jobs throughout the period and unemployment never fell below 9 per cent. In Germany the situation was even worse. In 1926 18 per cent of the workforce was unemployed, and three years later, when the depression had not yet begun to have a serious impact on the economy, there were 2 million unemployed. In Scandinavia more than 10 per cent were unemployed in the late 1920s. Throughout Europe unemployment figures remained persistently high even in periods of relative prosperity.

This high level of unemployment was due in part to the deflationary policies adopted by many governments, to the rationalization and concentration of industry and to the decline of the agricultural sector. Furthermore, population was rising faster than the rate of growth, thus pushing up the levels of unemployment. Recovery was also impeded by unstable currency rates, speculation on future exchange rates and by supply-side deficiencies which made it exceedingly difficult for countries whose currencies had depreciated to profit from increased exports. Low exchange rates made it all the more difficult to buy the equipment and raw materials needed for reconstruction on foreign markets and shortage of domestic capital was a further inhibiting factor. In such a situation the only alternatives seemed to be either a ferocious dictatorial command economy such as that in the Soviet Union or to go cap in hand to the richer nations. The Stalinist model held few attractions and the private sector was very loath to lend money to such dubious prospects as the eastern European countries. Creditor nations such as the United States and

Britain were equally unenthusiastic and the League of Nations only stepped in during crises, offering reconstruction loans to Austria in 1922, Hungary in 1924, and to Bulgaria and Estonia in 1926.

France hoped that her substantial foreign debt could be paid off by extracting reparations from Germany. But neither the extent of the debt nor the amount of reparations were determined until the Dawes Plan and the agreements with the United States and Britain in 1926. With a high rate of inflation investors were reluctant to renew their government bonds, it was impossible to balance the budget and there was little incentive to save. Between September 1924 and July 1926 there were ten successive ministers of finance none of whom were able to take effective action or to win the confidence of financiers who preferred to invest abroad. The franc fell from 18.5 to the dollar at the end of 1924 to 49 on 21 July 1926. Poincaré reversed this trend with a strict deflationist policy which was acceptable to the bankers who were relieved that the era of the *cartel des gauches* had come to an end. They were busy repatriating their funds when the British economy began to get into serious difficulties as a result of the return to the gold standard and the subsequent General Strike. Even with these difficulties some sectors of the French economy had done well. The export trade had prospered in the early 1920s and since these exports were mostly sent to the richer countries and were often non-essential items which were less affected by price fluctuations, they were not seriously hurt by the stabilization of the franc, for at 25 to the dollar it was still overvalued. The Bank of France's holdings of foreign exchange increased from £5.3 million in November 1926 to £120 million by the end of May the following year as speculators assumed that there would soon be a revaluation. Moreau, the Governor of the Bank of France, began to convert sterling into gold at such a rate that it seemed that Britain might be forced off the gold standard. American intervention helped defuse this dangerous situation, but suspicions lingered on, justifiably as it turned out, for the British had no inkling of the extent of France's forward claims on gold.

Behind these disagreements was a profound difference over the question of the stabilization of currencies. It was generally agreed that stability had to be restored to exchange rates, but there were widely differing opinions on how best this could be done. Sir Charles Hawtrey, the Treasury's official guru, believed that the stabilization of prices could be achieved by international credits which, although inflationary, would counteract the effects of the business cycle. This view was widely accepted and the stabilizationists included such prominent figures as Moreau, Keynes, Louis Rothschild the Austrian banker, Benes and above all Benjamin Strong, governor of the Federal Reserve Bank. The Americans favoured massive international loans as a means of encouraging American exports, increasing employment and strengthening the mighty dollar, even though many of these loans were as wildly speculative and morally dubious as the worst Wall Street speculations which were roundly condemned by the same officials who supported them.

Part of the stabilization programme involved a return to the gold standard, but it was not the traditional one whereby a customer could demand gold from the central bank in exchange for a note. With the exception of the United States, where at least in theory it was possible to demand gold dollars until 1933, and also Sweden and the Netherlands, it was a 'gold bullion standard' whereby the central banks held gold ingots and excluded the public from their dealings. Other countries adopted a 'good exchange standard' whereby the exchange rate was fixed by dealing on foreign exchange markets to maintain a constant exchange rate with another currency which was on the gold standard. This combination of credit expansion and the refusal to allow the public to have any influence on the determination of value by buying gold if they so desired, was condemned by monetarist economists like Hayek and von Mises and also by bankers like Hjalmar Schacht, who resented the excessive powers of men like Strong and Montague Norman of the Bank of England.

Moreau agreed with Schacht and objected strongly to a system which made the dollar and sterling the only first-rate currencies and which enabled Strong and Norman to meet behind closed doors and make decisions which drastically affected the world's economies. Such a system robbed the other countries of true financial sovereignty, and since it was designed to take care of the selfish interests of the Americans and the British it was bound in the long run to fail.

In the late 1920s it seemed that the system was working very well. World trade expanded at an unprecedented rate. Prices remained stable and economists announced that they had at last found the philosopher's stone. Yet beneath the façade there were serious problems. There was no international agreement over stabilization so that it was carried out in a piecemeal and haphazard fashion, as a report of the League of Nations was later to point out. Some currencies were overvalued, others undervalued, as they responded to speculation and political pressure rather than to a serious assessment of realistic parity values. The high elasticity of money and credit with respect to interest rates was a major cause of instability. Perhaps most important of all was the staggering increase of American productivity – 43 per cent between 1919 and 1929 – which was not offset by lower prices and thus concealed a mounting rate of inflation. At the same time consumers were unable to sustain the boom, for even in the United States wages were too low for the artificially high prices which were the result of the stabilization programme. Countries on the gold exchange standard had substantial indirect claims on gold by holding other currencies similarly linked to the gold centres. Thus if one such currency got into difficulties it could cause a domino effect. There was also a tendency for countries on the gold exchange standard to make massive claims on gold in the hope of converting themselves to the bullion standard as the French were to do in June 1928. The Germans also converted their foreign exchange reserves into gold. The over-valued pound was constantly threatened, thus putting more pressure on Britain's gold reserves and making her the most vulnerable point in the entire system. Britain's sterling liabilities were dangerously in excess of her gold reserves, while in the United States the situation was the exact reverse. As a result there was neither the necessary degree of co-operation between New York, London and Paris, nor a determined effort by the United States to take over the commanding role played by Britain before the war. Paris rivalled London, and the alliance between New York and London began to crumble. The world's monetary system was thus without effective leadership. The situation was further complicated by the frequent disparity between the exigencies of domestic economic considerations and the need to maintain external equilibrium. Thus at times it was desirable to raise the discount rate to stop the outflow of specie, but to do so was unacceptable because of the domestic political repercussions of a deflationist policy.

In Europe the prosperity of the the period from 1925 to 1929 was unevenly distributed. Those countries which were already advanced industrial states benefited from the enhanced productivity brought about by new technology and organizational techniques. The predominantly agricultural countries of eastern Europe and the Mediterranean had to face the twin problems of a growing population and the stagnation of the agricultural sector. In the more advanced countries the prosperity of these years was based on prior investments; profits from new investments were uncertain and there were already signs of a certain decline in the rate of expansion. Production rose satisfactorily, but it was not matched either by an adequate rate of investment nor by sufficient rise in wages to sustain further growth. Industrial development was also uneven. The traditional industries such as cotton and iron and steel either declined or registered very modest rates of growth. Britain's cotton exports, faced with growing competition from Japan, India and China, declined to half the pre-war level. The steel industry suffered from problems of over production, although in Germany, France, Luxemburg and Belgium impressive growth was recorded. The German steel industry was reorganized with the formation of the Vereinigte Stahlwerke in 1926 and five firms now produced 75 per cent of the country's iron and steel. The industry had used the opportunities afforded by inflation and reconstruction for modernization and improvement. The French also built successful modern plants in Lorraine. But such successes only exacerbated the problems of over production in Europe.

Starting from a modest base, the increase in the production of motor cars in Europe was an impressive 12.7 per cent per year. Prices fell by about a third, and although the motor car was still essentially a luxury item in Europe it was no longer only affordable by the rich. The electrical and chemical industries thrived, as did petroleum products. Economies of scale reduced the price of domestic electricity which, as it reached an increasing number of homes, stimulated the demand for electrical appliances. The mass production of cheap radio sets was a typical growth industry. Investment was increasingly directed towards the manufacture of consumer items such as radios, motor cars and electrical appliances, for it seemed that the substantial middle–class market was secure and that expansion was assured. This resulted in unfortunate distortions in the growth rates of different sectors of the economy. Something of a 'scissors crisis' existed between the less technological industries such as agriculture and the extraction of raw materials which were hurt by falling prices and the more advanced sectors which were able to maintain prices at artificially high levels. The exponential growth of the motor car industry, of petroleum products and of the electrical industry, a growth that looked as if it would continue for a long time to come, was so impressive that it was easy to overlook the serious problems of stock–piling in agriculture and underemployed resources in the iron and steel industry.

By 1928 there was a widespread feeling that the question of reparations needed to be examined afresh since most experts felt that the payments demanded of Germany under the Dawes Plan were excessive, even though the German economy had made impressive advances. The Agent General for Reparations, S. Parker Gilbert, felt that the Germans were borrowing far too much money to pay for reparations. The French hoped to link the question of reparations with that of war debts and therefore welcomed the proposal to hold a conference.

Under the chairmanship of Owen D. Young, an American, even though the United States did not take an official part in the conference, a committee of experts met in Paris in February 1929 charged with finding a 'final and definitive settlement' to the reparations problem. After several weeks of preliminary and inconclusive discussion the German representative, Hjalmar Schacht, was understood to demand the return of the German colonies and the Polish Corridor without which, he claimed, the country would never be able to pay the full amount of reparations. The French responded to this impertinence by threatening to withdraw their deposits in Germany and undermine the mark. It is still uncertain quite what happened, but there can be no doubt at all that relations between France and Germany became very strained and co-operation between their central banks came to a sudden halt. Schacht eventually signed the report of the committee, claiming that Germany's weakness in the face of these French threats gave him no alternative. The plan did not please the British Chancellor of the Exchequer, Philip Snowden, who objected to the division of reparations. This led to an ugly confrontation between Snowden and the French Minister of Finance, Chéron, at a conference on the plan at The Hague in August 1929. Snowden called Chéron's views 'ridiculous and grotesque', an expression which apparently is even more insulting when translated literally into French. A run on the pound, probably caused by an increase in the Federal Reserve discount rate, was blamed on the French. The Bank of England felt obliged to raise interest rates to support sterling, a move that contributed to the collapse of Wall Street.

The Young Plan, although utterly unacceptable to the German right, further relieved the burden of reparations. As with the Dawes Plan, payments were to begin low and to gradually increase. The annuities were divided into a compulsory section and an optional amount which did not have to be paid if Germany found herself in financial difficulties. A $300 million loan was granted to get the plan started. The Reparations Agency was disbanded and French troops were withdrawn from the Rhineland.

The Young Plan loan did not seem as attractive to American investors as did the Dawes loan. A substantial part of the American part of the loan had to be discounted and was bought up by the French. Short-term funds went from New York and London to Paris. The market became increasingly strained, and the Americans were particularly concerned about the gold drain. As the speculative fever on Wall Street increased these short-term funds were withdrawn from Europe, the cost of short-term loans increasing dramatically in New York to cover security transactions. In 1928 the Americans invested $1 billion in Europe, but in 1929 this fell to $200 million.

Long before the Wall Street crash the German economy was in serious difficulties. Lockouts in the Ruhr in late 1928 resulted in a fall in output. An extremely severe winter caused widespread hardship. Interest rates were increased, inventories grew and there were 2 million unemployed. A number of firms collapsed and there was a startling increase in the number of bankruptcies. In August 1929 the Frankfurt Insurance Company crashed with serious repercussions throughout the financial world.

It was the problem of unemployment which precipitated a political crisis. As unemployment figures rose, the deficit of the Unemployment Insurance Fund grew alarmingly. The Social Democratic government suggested that the contributions of those still fortunate enough to be working should be increased by 4 per cent. This proposal was unacceptable to the trades unions and to the German People's Party which represented the interests of the goverment workers whose tenured positions were not threatened by unemployment. The government coalition collapsed and the new government was formed by Brüning who was determined to follow a policy of rigorous deflation. New taxes were imposed and economies made in an attempt to balance the budget. It was hoped that wages could be forced down at the same rate as prices thus restoring profits and paving the way for recovery. This proved to be serious delusion. Unemployment shot up, the political cirsis deepened and foreigners withdrew their capital as fast as they could. The more nationalistic Brüning's policy became and the more he denounced the Young Plan the faster these foreign funds were repatriated.

The German government, like those of the other European manufacturing countries, tried to protect their own farmers from the competition of imported produce, the price of which was rapidly falling. The agricultural countries responded by raising their tariffs on industrial goods. Soon there was a full-scale tariff war with many states imposing import restrictions to save their hard-pressed markets.

By 1931 the average tariff rates of fifteen European nations rose by 64 per cent above the 1927 level. At the same time frantic efforts were made to increase exports in order to reduce unemployment and restore the balance of trade. Obviously these measures were contradictory and self-defeating, and whereas it was relatively easy for governments to reduce imports it was virtually impossible to increase exports when the trading partners were determined that this should not happen. In this struggle the agricultural countries of eastern Europe suffered the most. They had been severely hurt by a world wide 'scissors crisis', beginning in the 1920s, which saw a drastic fall in the price of raw materials and agricultural products as the terms of trade increasingly favoured the industrial nations. This situation was exacerbated by higher output. Stocks piled up and prices continued to fall, so that after 1929 there was terrible poverty amidst relative abundance. Since these eastern and southern European countries were international debtors the situation became critical, for they had to increase their exports to meet their payments. The more they tried to increase their exports the faster prices fell and they were trapped in a vicious spiral.

In Germany the agrarians were protected against the effects of the depression and the disparities between agricultural and industrial prices by protective tariffs, cheap credit and subsidies in the form of the *Osthilfe* which was financed largely from a tax on industry. Brüning was determined to make sure of support on the right for fear that the Nazis would make further gains from among the nationalist parties, but measures such as the *Osthilfe*, tax exemptions to large industrial enterprises such as the electrical combine AEG, naval rearmament, the moves towards a customs union with Austria and the continued attacks on the Young Plan, counteracted the attempts to cut back government expenditure, infuriated foreign investors and worsened the financial crisis. The Brüning government tried to counter the effects of the financial crisis by strengthening the control of the economy by the state. Three-fifths of bank capital was directly controlled by the state, intervention was institutionalized by the creation of the *Akzept* which channelled the funds of its investors into banks and industry. New forms of currency such as the *Askimark*, the *Effektenmark* and the *Registermark* were created to extend government control over virtually all foreign transactions. By the end of the 1930s these elaborate forms of exchange controls, credit restrictions and clearing systems amounted to little more than the old-fashioned barter of foodstuffs and raw materials for manufactured goods and Germany was not alone in encouraging such practices. By 1937 almost 75 per cent of European trade was on a barter basis.

In such a situation German banks were in an alarmingly precarious position. Their liquidity was dangerously low, as was the ratio of their capital to their deposits. Share prices were falling rapidly and the situation was hardly improved when the banks began to buy up their own shares in an attempt to halt this downward movement in prices. The Reichsbank was losing gold at an increasing rate and a $125 million loan in October 1930 brought only temporary relief. As prices fell profits declined and securities continued to plummet. The banks found it increasingly difficult to collect on their loans. Throughout Europe bankers came to the unfortunate realization that they had lent too much money and at too high a risk. At the end of 1930 two French banks failed and there was yet another political scandal when government officials were implicated in some shady dealings. France, like Switzerland, Italy, Belgium and Holland, was slow to experience the full effects of the depression and clung to the gold standard. This proved to be a distinct disadvantage, for prices were far too high, and with the devaluation of the dollar in 1934 capital began to leave Paris in alarming quantities in search of bargains in New York and London. High domestic prices and a chronic deficit obliged successive French governments to protect agriculture against foreign competition and to force down industrial prices to encourage exports. In spite of unacceptably high levels of unemployment these governments were all deflationist, although only Doumergue and Laval were confirmed advocates of the utmost restraint. These policies failed in France as elsewhere. Industrialists preferred to cut back production rather than reduce prices, and the guaranteed minimum prices in the agricultural sector resulted in a continuation of uneconomic levels of production. Thus the disparities between the agricultural and the manufacturing sectors continued, in spite of policies designed to overcome them. Nor could governments overcome the problem of the deficit. The depression inevitably resulted in a fall in revenue as tax receipts dwindled and the demand for social services, particularly unemployment benefits, increased. These had to be maintained at an acceptable level, not only for obvious political reasons, but also because they were an essential means of sustaining demand.

In May 1931 Austria's most important bank, controlled by the Viennese Rothschilds, closed its doors. The Credit Anstalt had taken over the Bodencreditanstalt in 1929 which in turn had absorbed the Unionbank and the Verkehrsbank only two years previously. This move meant that the Credit Anstalt accepted such a large number of loans that about two-thirds of Austrian industry was either directly or indirectly controlled by the bank. Accumulated losses became so high that the National Bank of Austria and the House of Rothschild rushed to its assistance. News of this rescue operation resulted in a run on the bank, particularly by foreign investors. The Bank of International Settlements organized a modest loan, but this was soon exhausted and had to be renewed, the French making the loan conditional on the Austrian government dropping its plan for a customs union with Germany. Montague Norman, the Governor of the Bank of England, gave the Austrians a $7 million loan for one week to tide them over and as a rebuke to the French for mixing finance and politics. The French responded by converting large quantities of sterling into gold and the pound came under heavy attack.

The situation in Austria had an immediate and drastic effect throughout central Europe. German depositors hastily removed their money from the big banks, and foreign investors prudently looked around for safer havens for their money. Soon it was reported that the big retail chain, Karstadt, was in difficulties and that the Nord-stern insurance company appeared to be on the verge of collapse. Within a few weeks the Reichsbank lost almost 2 billion Reichsmarks in gold and foreign exchange as foreign investors became alarmed at both the economic and political instability of the country. On 20 June 1931 President Hoover announced a moratorium on all inter-governmental debts. The French, who stood to lose the most from the moratorium, objected strongly but were forced to give way under American pressure. On 6 July they agreed to the moratorium, and on the following day the important textile firm, Nordwolle, which had gambled on a rise in world prices, collapsed obliging its principal creditor, the Danatbank, to close its doors. The president of the Reichsbank, Luther, went cap in hand to London and Paris, but unable to give the French the political guarantees they demanded, which included strict adherence to the Treaty of Versailles, he returned to Berlin, his mission a failure. Attempts to force the mergers of the Danatbank and the Dresdner Bank and the Dresdner with the Deutsche Bank failed and a rush on the banks had to be stopped by a 'bank holiday' which lasted for three weeks. The bank rate was raised to 15 per cent and the rate on commercial loans to 20 per cent.

It was agreed that a foreign loan was essential to save the situation, but the French still insisted on a political guarantee and the

Americans, faced with a serious budgetary deficit, would not consider a fresh loan of the magnitude deemed necessary. Montague Norman sourly remarked that the Bank of England had already loaned as much as was 'convenient'. Eventually it was agreed to extend the existing loan for a further three months and a standstill agreement on the withdrawal of foreign debts was reached. The Brüning government took vigorous action to improve the position of the German banks by converting their long-term loans into discountable state paper, by guaranteeing deposits and by forcing the major banks to reorganize or merge. The state invested heavily in the banks so that by the end of 1932 64 per cent of the capital of the big banks was held by the state. At the same time strict foreign exchange controls were imposed and payments of foreign debts were henceforth made where possible with blocked marks.

Many European bankers now found their German credits blocked and therefore began to sell sterling in order to replenish their gold reserves. The Bank of England pushed up the discount rate, but was constrained by the fear of further unemployment from pushing the rate up high enough to attract large quantities of gold. The Labour government wanted to borrow money abroad to keep the pound on the gold standard, but the Bank of England insisted on a severe deflationary policy which would include a cut in the dole in order to impress foreign bankers. A foreign loan was forthcoming but attached to it was a demand that the British government should exercise the economies outlined in Sir George May's report published in July which attacked the Labour government's expenditures on social welfare programmes. The Labour party split on the issue of a 10 per cent cut in the dole and Ramsay MacDonald formed a National government which convinced the bankers that the orthodox had triumphed over the ideologues of the Labour Party. The loan was thus forthcoming, but a few days later there was a protest against pay cuts in the Royal Navy by personnel at the base in Invergordon. This relatively trivial incident was greatly exaggerated to the point that it seemed that the Royal Navy was in full mutiny and the British Empire was about to collapse. The Bank of England began losing gold at an alarming rate as investors panicked and the central banks of the smaller European states withdrew their funds. On Saturday 19 September the Bank of England advised the government to go off the gold standard. This startling move was announced on the following Monday.

The pound depreciated rapidly and holders of sterling began to fear that it would collapse. The British government did little to ease the pressure and refused to undertake any exchange guarantees. By the end of the year the pound was 30 per cent below par. The Scandinavian and east European countries followed Britain in abandoning gold. France, Holland, Switzerland, Belgium, Italy and Poland formed a gold bloc, settling accounts between themselves in gold but refusing to export gold outside the bloc. The Germans refused to devalue, fearing the political reaction in a country traumatized by the experience of 1923. German economists who argued that a devalued mark would help exports and create jobs were howled down, not only by fervent nationalists but also by the doyen of social democratic economists, Rudolf Hilferding. Germany avoided the worst consequences of an over-valued currency thanks to the standstill agreement but German exports fell even faster than the drop in world trade. The United States, which also remained on the gold standard, faced similar balance of payments problems. The gold bloc countries began to dispose of their dollar assets thus draining gold from the Federal Reserve and the authorities responded by raising interest rates which increased the deflationary pressure.

At the Lausanne conference in June 1932 reparations virtually ended with the 'sale' of 3 billion marks worth of German war debt by the Bank for International Settlements. But Brüning had already been dismissed by Hindenburg '100 metres from the finishing line'. His successors, Papen and Schleicher, both favoured a reflationary policy but they had no time for such measures to have much effect and they were overwhelmed by a political crisis for which they could find no solutions.

As each nation tried as best it could to deal with the problems of the depression the world became increasingly divided, and the monetary and commercial barriers designed to protect each country or group of countries served to increase the effects they were designed to counteract. By 1932 there was a widespread conviction that only an international agreement on tariffs, trade and credit would ameliorate the situation. There was a general agreement that there should be a tariff truce and an effort to secure an all-round reduction in tariffs and the restoration of the free exchange of goods and services. This would of necessity be coupled with the abolition of exchange controls, a restoration of predictable exchange rates probably by a return to the gold standard at lower rates of convertibility, a stabilization of world prices, the settlement of international debts and a concerted effort to stimulate employment. The matter became all the more pressing when the United States abandoned the gold standard, thus making stabilization the main concern of the international banking community.

The world economic conference met in London on 12 June 1933. It was a distinguished gathering of prime ministers, foreign secretaries and bankers which soon reached an agreement on stabilization. It was agreed that the dollar should be fixed at $4.00 to the pound and 0.04662 to the franc with a 3 per cent fluctuation permitted either side of these prices. When news of the agreement was leaked to the press stock and commodity prices began to fall. President Roosevelt, who was on a sailing holiday, rejected the $4.00 exchange rate as 'a purely artificial and temporary experiment affecting the monetary exchange of a few countries only'. The president's statement, which used quite unnecessarily harsh language, effectively destroyed the conference. The countries of the British Empire huddled together and formed the sterling area. The gold bloc strengthened its defences. Nazi Germany took further steps along the road to autarchy.

Economists continued to dispute whether the Roosevelt administration really knew what it was doing when it went off the gold standard and then torpedoed efforts at stabilization, and whether or not the effects of these moves were beneficial. Whatever the answer to such questions, by the middle of 1933 the world was beginning slowly to pull out of the depression. The United States began a gradual recovery. The sterling area looked after its own interests with some success. Germany and Italy continued along their independent, selfish and ultimately dangerous paths. The gold bloc was stuck with grossly over-valued currencies and sank rapidly into even deeper depression. The poor countries of Europe had continued problems servicing their debts, but there was a modest increase in industrial production and in exports in most countries.

The gold bloc was formally constituted when President Roosevelt refused to go along with the stabilization proposals of the London conference. It was a desperate defensive measure based on the vain hope that rigorous deflation would result in satisfactory trade balances and adequate gold reserves. The result was an over-valued currency, over-priced goods and a decline in exports. Thus at a time when world trade was beginning to expand French exports continued to fall. At home real prices declined but this was ignored by those whose pensions or incomes from government employment had been cut by the governments determined to balance the budget. Between 1930 and 1935 French pensioners' real incomes rose by 46 per cent, government employees' by 18.9 per cent and workers' average wages by 18.5 per cent. Unemployment was relatively low, because foreign workers who were no longer required were simply deported. But there was widespread social unrest since most people imagined that they were being called upon to make great sacrifices, simply because they had fewer francs in their pockets.

The Belgian government, prompted by a group of economists from the University of Louvain, decided to devalue the franc by 28 per cent. This was done in March 1935 and the effects were immediate and salutary. Prices went up, exports recovered, and the gold reserves improved. In spite of this success the French grimly defended the franc as if, as Flandin patriotically and unwisely said, it were the fortress of Verdun. This view was shared by the communists who felt that an over-valued franc was in some mysterious way advantageous to the French workers, and this view acted as an important restraint on those socialists in the Popular Front government who were considering devaluation. The Matignon accords which awarded wage increases, reduced working hours and granted holidays with pay resulted in higher prices. Exports did not recover from the effects of the strikes which the accords had brought to an end. Political uncertainty led to a decline in the stock market, in further price increases and in the flight of capital. In October 1936 the government bowed to the inevitable and suspended convertibility. Devaluation came too late and was insufficient to remedy the situation. The franc could only be maintained at its new level by massive purchases and in November 1938 it had to be devalued once again by Daladier so that one pound sterling was now worth 178 francs. The rate before 1936 had been 75.

The first French devaluation was supported by the Tripartite Monetary Agreement with the United States and Britain which was soon joined by Belgium, Holland and Switzerland. It was a very limited agreement, and was certainly not a viable alternative to the gold standard, but it did keep exchange rates from fluctuating wildly outside the gold support prices agreed upon for each country. The signatories did not agree to do anything very much except to pay lip service to the principle of co-operation to maintain exchange rates. As such it was a step forward in the direction of accepting the need for international agreements on trade and finance which previously had been thought to be essentially national concerns.

By the summer of 1936 production and prices, which had been rising steadily for some two years, moved up sharply, particularly in the gold bloc where the effects of devaluation accentuated this upward movement. The Tripartite Agreement did much to restore confidence in currencies and investors began to sell their gold and buy securities, particularly in the United States. Gold sales were on such a scale that there was widespread concern that the price of gold might go down, and this triggered off a fresh round of dishoarding. In fact the gold price held steady, but as large amounts of gold were bought in London and then sold in New York the arbitrage discount had the effect of pushing up the exchange rate of the pound and therefore tempting hoarders to 'sell on the London market. The American authorities were at a loss to know what to do to stem the 'gold avalanche' and ended up doing nothing. Many economists feel that nothing was probably the best thing to have done, and was certainly better than some ill-considered measure the likes of which had caused such havoc in 1933.

1937 saw a marked recession in the United States caused by inventory accumulation, tighter money and a change in fiscal policy designed to deal with a serious deficit. This did not have a significant effect in Europe and mainly hurt the poorer countries. Throughout Europe the security markets fell in response to the collapse of prices on Wall Street. In part this was due to large-scale rearmament programmes, before Munich in the case of Britain, afterwards in that of France. Germany began full-scale rearmament and a policy of autarchy in the summer of 1936 with the bombastic announcement of a four-year plan under Hermann Goering which included such ambitious projects as the mass production of artificial rubber and petroleum and the exploitation of low-grade domestic iron ore designed to overcome the chronic shortages of foreign exchange. By now most countries subscribed to some form of Keynesianism, but as an increasing amount of government spending was going into armaments it proved impossible to come to any international agreement on public works, raw materials and the co-ordination of counter-cyclical policies. Europe was far too busy preparing for a war to take much notice of such well-meaning and intellectually rigorous proposals as the Van Zealand report on trade which was published in January 1938. Even had this not been the case it is unlikely that the United States would have given the leadership any such system would have required, for the American leadership was so lacking in understanding of the international monetary system that the Treasury Secretary, Henry Morgenthau, made the amazing proposal that the Soviet Union should join the Tripartite Monetary Agreement. It was the war which finally forced upon the United States the realization that as the world's richest and most powerful nation it had play to a true leadership role. This it was to achieve in such measures as Lend Lease, Dumbarton Oaks, Bretton Woods and the Marshall Plan. Without the war it is difficult to imagine that American attitudes would have changed so dramatically.

CHAPTER THREE
Collective Security, Disarmament and the League of Nations

In the introduction to his diaries, published in 1929, Viscount D'Abernon, the father of the Treaty of Locarno, wrote that the lesson of the post-war years was not 'negative and minatory, but positive. It is not a recital of unfortunate events which led up to a great catastrophe. It is the narrative rather of a historical period in which immense progress has been made towards pacification, and during which the international suspicion diminished, and the cause of co-operation between nations appreciably advanced.' Such optimism was widespread among European statesmen on the eve of the great depression, for it seemed that Locarno and the entry of Germany into the League of Nations was at least a partial realization of Lloyd George's extravagant claim in the House of Commons on 11 November 1918 that the last great war had been fought.

Such talk was more than an outburst of emotional rhetoric deemed suitable for armistice day, it was an expression of a widely held belief that the world was entering a new age in which international anarchy would be overcome by the creation of an effective organization that would ensure peace. The League of Nations was an international parliament with a constitution which was intended to solve all disputes between nations in a rational spirit. Its inauguration was seen by many as a momentous event, as significant in its own way as the great revolutions in England, America and France. Lloyd George's motion that the peace conference in Paris should be regarded as the first meeting of the League of Nations was passed, and a committee chaired by the American president was appointed which quickly came up with the text of a Covenant. An assembly of all the member states, each with one vote, was to meet yearly. Britain, France, Italy, Japan and the United States were to have permanent seats on the Council of the League. The Assembly could then elect four, and later six, further members of the Council. Belgium, Greece, Brazil and Spain were elected to the council. The founder members of the League were the thirty-two allied powers and thirteen neutral states. Russia was not included, for the League had been formed in part as a direct response and challenge to Lenin's appeal for a new world order based on bolshevik principles. States could join the League if their admission were approved by a two-thirds majority.

The Covenant was full of worthy sentiments but was necessarily vague. It was agreed that armaments should be reduced 'to the lowest point consistent with national safety' and that the League should 'take any action that may be deemed wise and effectual to safeguard the peace of nations'. A Permanent Court of International Justice was to be established. Should any member state of the League 'resort to war in disregard of its Covenants' the other member states were to impose sanctions, first in the form of a complete trade embargo and then the Council was to recommend the appropriate military action. The League also addressed such international problems as health, drug trafficking and prostitution. The former colonies of the defeated states were to be placed under the 'tutelage' of the advanced nations 'which should be exercised by them as Mandatories on behalf of the League' These tutor states were to send yearly reports on their pupils' progress towards the time when they would be able to 'stand by themselves under the strenuous conditions of the modern world.'

It is easy to point out the weaknesses of the League and to laugh at its antics in the spirit of two masterly contemporary novels, *Clochemerle* and *England, Their England*. Many diplomats felt that it was an absurd attempt to avoid the unpleasant realities of diplomacy and asked what would ensure that the Covenant would not, like other treaties, be broken. Military men scoffed at the ridiculous notion that war could be outlawed by international conventions, and warned that it would create a dangerous and misleading sense of security. The League had no armed forces to enforce the Covenant. The defeated powers denounced it as nothing more than an attempt to give some moral authority to a blatantly unjust treaty, and the mandates were similarly derided as hypocritical attempts to disguise old-fashioned colonies. They detested the League because they were convinced it was what the French hoped it would be – an international agreement to uphold the peace, subjugate Germany and contain Soviet Russia. Clemenceau and Foch knew that the League could not coexist with the revisionism of the defeated states and the revolutionary pretentions of the Soviet Union, and probably sniggered when Lord Curzon, with characteristic pomposity, announced in the House of Lords on the occasion of the first meeting of the Assembly in Geneva in November 1920. 'The world's great age begins anew; the golden years return!'

President Wilson, seriously impaired after a series of strokes, refused to consider any of the compromises necessary to ensure ratification of the Treaty and forced Henry Cabot Lodge and the 'Strong Reservationists' to vote with the 'Irreconcilables' against the Treaty and against American membership in the League.

The Soviet Union was determined to destroy the world that the League hoped to uphold. Attempts were made to spread the revolution to Germany, Hungary, Austria, Finland, the Baltic States and Poland. In March 1919 the Third International was founded as the 'general staff of the revolution'. Lenin announced that as soon as the Soviet Union was strong enough it would destroy capitalism throughout the globe and his comrades denounced the League as an imperialist front intent on the destruction of the first workers' and peasants' state. But all these revolutionary dreams proved illusory, even though the American journalist Lincoln Steffens told Bernard Baruch, in a phrase that is as memorable as it is inane, 'I have seen the future – and it works!' Trotsky, who had announced that a socialist state did not need a foreign policy, was soon proved wrong, for the Soviet Union found that since its revolution was not an exportable commodity it had to live with its neighbours. Revolutionaries had to become statesmen and the ideologues, after a few dialectical gymnastics, came up with the notions of peaceful coexistence and socialism in one country. All this was very perplexing, for this combination of peaceful coexistence with the pursuit of the long-term goal of world revolution involved a degree of duplicity, mendacity and confusion which diplomats found singularly difficult to comprehend. Was the Soviet Union really a revolutionary state, or was it pursuing traditional tsarist and imperialist goals? Was its much vaunted anti-imperialism simply a clever way to extend Moscow's control by their direct influence over movements of national liberation and of anti-colonialism? In 1921 when the Red Army marched into Mongolia ostensibly to set up a revolutionary peoples' government it seemed elsewhere to be simply the brutal exploitation of the weakness of the Chinese government, and whatever the motives, they were irreconcilable with the Covenant of the League of Nations. This revolutionary-imperialist policy, brutally

49

applied against the Georgians, was used to extend Moscow's influence in Afghanistan and Persia and was effective in getting Batum from the Turks. It did not work against Finland or the Baltic states where local resistance to bolshevism was strong and where there was powerful support from the interventionists. Nor did it work against the determination of the Poles to defend their country and it could not stop Bessarabia going to Romania. Moscow was never able to accept these defeats and even prepared to sign a pact with the Nazis to get these lost territories back in the Russian empire. For the moment the Soviet Union was exhausted, its economy in ruins, its future uncertain, but this very uncertainty was disturbing, and even if the country was only a shadow of its former greatness, it was still a powerful factor which could not be ignored.

The League had to function without either the United States or the Soviet Union and could therefore only guarantee the status quo as long as Britain and France were strong enough to resist those who were bent on revision. Outside Europe this was not possible and in Europe serious differences between London and Paris on the implementation of article 10 of the Covenant on the territorial integrity of member states, and the growing feeling that the peace settlement had been harsh and unjust, meant that the League was far from being the creature of the victors, as so many of its critics insisted it was. The League was created in the belief that the principles of liberal democracy would be generally accepted throughout the world and was powerless to deal with states which despised such ideals. The revolutionary activities of the Comintern so terrified the parties of the moderate left and centre that they sought alliances with the right and with the armed forces. The extremes on the left and the right kept up a raucous campaign against the League whose moderate supporters had little influence on public opinion. Faced with an ineffectual League, an isolationist and indifferent United States and an isolated and aggressive Soviet Union, the revisionist states were encouraged to pursue an active policy. The situation was further complicated by the fact that at the time of the first meeting of the League so many European borders were still uncertain. Poland did not have a recognized eastern border, the frontier between Russia and Finland was undecided as was the future of the Baltic states. Throughout central and eastern Europe boundary commissions set about the difficult task of redrawing the map of Europe and the inhabitants of the plebiscite zones had yet to determine their future.

The important coal mining region of the Saar was to be administered by the League for fifteen years and its future decided by a plebiscite. Ninety per cent demanded return to Germany in 1935, a major triumph for Hitler. The plebiscite in Schleswig, held in 1920, resulted in a division of the duchy between Denmark and Germany. Plebiscites in Allenstein and Marienwerder were equally decisive and these Prussian districts, with the exception of a few Polish villages, returned to Germany. The plebiscite in Upper Silesia was a far more sensitive issue. About 60 per cent of the votes went to Germany, 40 per cent to Poland, but the votes were very unevenly distributed, resulting in a confusing patchwork of Polish and German areas. The League commissioners were unable to agree on what to do and the adjudication by the League Council was most favourable to the Poles and therefore caused bitter resentment in Germany.

The plebiscite in Upper Silesia did not reflect very favourably on the impartiality of the League, but the administration of the Saar and of the free city of Danzig was conducted with admirable fairness and efficiency. In Upper Silesia an Arbitration Commission effectively upheld the rights of minorities and did much to lessen the animosities between Germans and Poles and to minimize the injurious effects of partition on the Silesian economy.

In 1920 the division of Europe between revisionist and saturated states and the inability of the League to provide an effective alternative to traditional balance of power politics were not matters of particularly great concern. Those states that were hostile to the League and to the peace settlement, among them Germany, Russia, Hungary, Italy and Poland, were still too weak to do much beyond grumbling, although Russia and Poland went to war over their common frontier. Poland made substantial gains, although it did not achieve its goal of the frontiers of 1772 and a federation with the Ukraine. The Poles also seized Vilna, which had been made capital of Lithuania, by a *coup de main* organized by General Zeligowski in flagrant violation of armistice terms, but which was accepted by the Allies in 1923. The French government supported Poland's expansionist ambitions and thus found itself once again in violent disagreement with the British who did not. In February 1921 a Franco-Polish alliance was signed which included a secret military convention. The French sent large quantities of military material to Poland, but in spite of this lucrative trade the alliance was not universally popular in France. Many suggested that a belligerent country such as Poland which was on singularly bad terms with both Russia and Germany might well prove to be a tiresome liability.

Hungary was less successful in its attempts to undo the Treaty of Trianon. Allied pressure forced the Hungarians to abandon their attempt to seize Slovakia and the Romanians resisted invasion in the summer of 1919. The country was a monarchy without a king and in 1921 Charles IV made his two abortive attempts to regain the crown of Saint Stephen much to the embarrassment of the Hungarian government. The first time he was politely asked to go away, and the second time he was unceremoniously arrested and handed over to the Allies who packed him off to Madeira where he died shortly afterwards. As his heir, Otto, was only eight years old there was little likelihood of the threat of the restoration of the Habsburgs, which has caused so much anxiety among Hungary's neighbours, troubling the region for some years to come.

Fear of Hungarian revisionism resulted in the formation of the Little Entente between Czechoslovakia, Romania and Yugoslavia in a series of alliances in 1920 and 1921. This alliance system was extended with the conclusion of the Romanian–Polish pact in March 1921, which was directed against Russia, and a Polish–Czechoslovakian neutrality pact in November. From the outset the Little Entente was closely linked to France although there were no formal diplomatic ties until the Franco-Czech alliance of January 1924. France sent weapons and military missions to the Little Entente and there was a clear understanding that all four states would work together to uphold the treaties. France was now committed to defend Poland against both Germany and Russia, to thwart Hungary's revisionist ambitions and to support Yugoslavia against Italy. France thus undertook not only to be the principal guarantor of the Treaty of Versailles but also of the entire peace settlement. With her enormous power and prestige this did not seem to be an overly ambitious undertaking in the early 1920s and she presided over a Holy Alliance *redivivus*, but without a convincing surrogate Metternich.

This soon proved to be a delusion as Germany gradually undermined the treaty while the Western Entente of Britain and France, supported by Belgium and sometimes by Italy, was unable to agree on a common policy towards Germany. It soon became evident that France needed the full co-operation of another great power if the treaties were to be upheld. The Little Entente was effective in containing Hungary, but it was no substitute for Russia or the United States if the revisionist ambitions of an economically and militarily revived Germany were to be frustrated. Nationalist feelings ran so high in France that no politician could consider reaching an accommodaton with Germany by direct negotiations or within the framework of the League. Therefore France had no alternative but to attempt to weaken Germany as much as possible by insisting on the strict application of the terms of the Treaty of Versailles.

Since Britain rarely supported France in this endeavour the Germans flouted the disarmament and reparations clauses of the treaty from the outset, and skilfully put a rift between France and Britain at every opportunity. In April 1920 the French occupied Frankfurt am Main and the neighbouring area in retaliation for German military action against opponents of the Kapp putsch in the Ruhr which violated the demilitarization clause of the treaty. The British protested vigorously against this action by France, but the French responded by threatening to occupy the Ruhr if the Germans refused to meet their treaty obligations. The Spa conference in July 1920, called to discuss the implementation of the peace treaty, was the first at which the Germans met the Allies on equal terms, but the results were inconclusive. The Germans blandly informed the Allies that the German army was still 200,000 men, twice the amount allowed by the treaty, and that they had three times the permissible number of machine guns and six times the number of artillery pieces. When the Allies threatened to occupy the Ruhr in order to put pressure on the German delegation Hugo Stinnes, the coal and steel baron, roared: 'If black troops – those worthy instruments of Allied policy – are used for this purpose, the feelings of every white man will recoil, nor will the Allies get any coal.' With the Russians advancing towards Warsaw the British suggested that German disarmament should be slowed down and it was also agreed that the coal shipments would be reduced. Germany refused to carry out the revised disarmament provisions and did not meet their reparations payments so that in March 1921 allied troops occupied Düsseldorf, Duisberg and Ruhrort. The Schedule of Payments was presented to Germany on 5 May 1921 which in effect reduced the reparations debt to 50 billion gold marks on which 5 per cent interest was to be paid and 1 per cent amortization. The first billion marks were to be paid by 31 August 1921. The German government was given a week to reply, failing which the Ruhr would be occupied. Germany had no alternative but to agree and paid on time, but then paid nothing for the next three years.

French instransigence and German diplomatic skill placed an intolerable strain on the Franco–British alliance and therefore strengthened Germany's bargaining position. France, by insisting that the Council of the League should deal with the reparations question rather than the Reparations Commission, gave the whole issue far greater publicity than it would otherwise have been afforded.

There were now open differences between heads of government on the Council, rather than between experts on the commission, which served to emphasize the weaknesses of the Entente. Without the support of the United States, Britain was in no position to change France's policies towards Germany and the most Lloyd George could do was to act as a restraining influence. An endless series of conferences on reparations resulted in payments in kind, principally coal and timber, being constantly reduced, to the increasing frustration of the French who, as the economic sanctions against Germany became less effective, fearing isolation attempted to strengthen their relations with the states of eastern Europe and also with Britain.

There were alarming differences between Britain and France at the Washington Conference in late 1921 and Briand suggested to Lloyd George that an Anglo-French alliance was the best way to settle outstanding differences between the two countries for Briand was becoming increasingly concerned about France's isolation. Nothing came of this scheme. Briand resigned, having been charged with showing excessive deference to the British. Poincaré demanded a precise guarantee of direct military assistance in the event of war with Germany, but Lloyd George would offer nothing but vague promises in return for substantial concessions from France. Poincaré saw this as further evidence of British untrustworthiness and would not pursue the matter.

By this time Lloyd George was in serious political difficulties at home and he hoped that the forthcoming conference at Genoa would be such a success that he could come home in triumph. The agenda was very ambitious. It was hoped that a solution could be found to the problem of German reparations and that the Americans would reduce or even write off allied war debts. Soviet Russia was to be admitted to the community of nations. The world economy would be set to rights by tackling both debts and inflation and by taking bold measures to stimulate international trade. The conference was a failure. The French would not deal with the Russians unless they recognized the debts they had repudiated. The Americans did not go to the conference. The only event of note was a treaty signed between Germany and the Soviets at Rapallo, a resort close to Genoa, on 16 April 1922 in which the Germans recognized the Soviet régime and repudiated all debt claims, insisting that the Russians should not compensate any others. Russia in return waived any right to reparations from Germany. The Allies were extremely angry about the Treaty of Rapallo and it was rumoured that it included an agreement of military co-operation. In fact a few weeks previously the Germans and Russians had already concluded an agreement on military, economic and political co-operation which enabled the Germans to build most of the weapons they were forbidden by the Treaty of Versailles on Soviet territory. After Rapallo there was no chance of the Genoa conference achieving any positive results and outstanding problems were referred to a committee of experts in The Hague. They were equally unsuccessful. Lloyd George returned to London, his hopes of a settlement shattered and the French were more determined than ever after Rapallo to make the Germans pay in full.

Rapallo was a triumph for German revisionism. General von Seeckt gloated that Poland, 'one of the strongest pillars of the Versailles settlement', would, with the help of the Soviet Union, soon disappear from the map of Europe, France would be drastically weakened and Germany recover her 1914 boundaries. Chancellor Wirth told Brockdorff-Rantzau, who was sent as ambassador to Moscow, that Poland had to be 'finished off', and also talked to Chicherin, the Soviet foreign minister, about the frontiers of 1914. Some German politicians wanted to go further than that, insisting that the frontiers of 1914 had not been sufficient to guarantee the security of the Reich. In France reaction was prompt and harsh. At Bar le Duc on 24 April Poincaré denounced the Rapallo Treaty and warned that France had the right, the means and the will to intervene militarily if the Germans did not meet their obligations under the Treaty of Versailles. This speech was reported favourably in the French press. In Germany public opinion was unenthusiastic about the treaty, fearing that the Russians had tricked the German delegation. In spite of emphatic denials that there were any military clauses in the treaty the rapprochement between Germany and the Soviet Union was similar in effect to German policy in Morocco before the war. Maltzan, the architect of Rapallo, was a great admirer of Kiderlen and like him hoped to divide the Entente. The calculation proved once again to be false. Britain would not support an aggressive French policy in the Ruhr and Poincaré's speech was strongly criticized by Lloyd George and by the British press, but the British government was very concerned about the obvious anti-Polish and revisionist thrust of the Rapallo Treaty and there was no doubt that Britain was now at least more tolerant of France's intransigent attitude, and there was no danger at all of the Anglo-French Entente falling apart. Lloyd George was perfectly correct when he said in 1929 that if there had been no Rapallo there would have been no occupation of the Ruhr.

In July 1922 the Germans asked for a moratorium on reparations payments until the end of 1924. The French would not consider such a suggestion unless they were given some secure guarantee that the debts would eventually be paid. The British government was far more conciliatory, feeling that Germany badly needed a breathing space and pressed the Germans to join the League of Nations in the hope that this would convince the French that Germany was prepared to accept the responsibilities which membership implied. The German government demanded such absurd conditions before considering application for membership of the League that Poincaré was given a welcome opportunity to veto the proposal.

The British government tried to find a solution to the problem of reparations and allied war debts by issuing the 'Balfour Note' in August 1922 which suggested that the British would only demand payment from their debtors equal to the amount they owed to the United States. This was an ill-advised move. The Americans were predictably annoyed at being held solely responsible for these problems and the French pointed out that there was a great deal more involved in reparations than mere money. The reparations crisis became increasingly serious at a time when the British government was absorbed with the problems of Greece and Turkey and the Chanak crisis. Lloyd George resigned, to be succeeded by the 'unknown Prime Minister', the Canadian-born Bonar Law, who felt that since Germany would not pay reparations and since there was little that could be done about it, the wisest policy was to do nothing. This was unacceptable to the French when it was put forward as official British policy at the Paris conference on reparations in January 1923. They knew perfectly well that such a suggestion would mean the end of reparations. By this time the Germans were hopelessly behind in the shipment of timber and coal. The Reparations Commission, by a vote of three to one, officially declared Germany to be in default and on 11 January 1923 a small contingent of French and Belgian troops entered the Ruhr to protect a group of technicians who were to ensure that the Germans handed over the goods they owed. The British government, although strongly opposed to this action, wished to avoid a breach with France and therefore permitted the use of the railway which ran through the British zone without which the occupation could hardly have taken place. This policy, described by the British representative on the Reparations Commission as 'surly neutrality', irritated the French and encouraged the Germans to be more obdurate.

Passive resistance, which resulted in the Ruhr closing down, was a disaster for Germany, except for those whose debts were wiped out by the destruction of the currency, but it also meant that there was precious little for the Allies to collect. The Belgians and the Italians saw little point in continuing the occupation, but the French believed that were they to admit defeat the entire Versailles settlement would be called into question. The British profited from the situation since they no longer faced any competition from the Ruhr, exports increased dramatically and unemployment dropped. In August Stresemann formed a national government which decided to stop passive resistance and set to work to restore the currency. The British and Americans strongly supported this initiative and put financial pressure on France to end the occupation. Poincaré had to give way, and the French attempt to sponsor separatist movements in the Rhineland failed even more dismally than in 1919, for the leadership was pathetic and without any popular support. The French joined the Dawes committee on the revision of reparations payments and thus acknowledged that the policy of force had been a mistake. At the elections in May 1924 Poincaré was defeated by Herriot and the Radicals who were anxious to come to a settlement with Germany.

The Dawes Plan could not be implemented without some substantial revisions of the treaty and therefore a major international conference was held in London in July and August 1924. Britain's first Labour Prime Minister, Ramsay MacDonald, used his charm and administrative ability to mediate between France and Germany and scored a major personal success. He was justly proud of what he described as 'the first really negotiated agreement since the war'. The London conference brought substantial benefits to the Germans. The military occupation of the Ruhr was to end within a year, the economic effects of the occupation ceased immediately. The Reparations Commission was stripped of most of its powers, and it became virtually impossible to impose sanctions on Germany if the reparations were not paid in full and on time.

The net result of the occupation of the Ruhr was thus a substantial revision of the Treaty of Versailles. France now realized that her security could not be made dependent on rigorous single-handed enforcement of the peace settlement. Herriot was convinced that France needed the support of other states, particularly Britain, and therefore enthusiastically supported the draft 'Treaty of Mutual Assistance' which was presented to the League Assembly in September 1923. It was proposed that in the event of war the Council would determine which country was the aggressor within four days and that all member states would then be obliged to give military assistance against that aggressor. Britain, the Dominions, the Scandinavian states and Holland were determined to resist making such a binding commitment and the proposal was rejected.

MacDonald was anxious to find an alternative to the draft treaty and did not wish to appear as the wrecker of a popular measure to preserve the peace. He understood French fears of Germany but felt that they were unfounded. He was therefore prepared to offer guarantees which he was convinced would never have to be put into effect. He was the only British prime minister to go to a meeting of the Assembly, and along with Herriot secured the unanimous acceptance of the 'Geneva Protocol'. This was an ingenious attempt to strengthen the covenant by combining compulsory arbitration, disarmament and further guarantees of the frontiers of 1919. Although the Geneva Protocol was a somewhat toothless document it was widely criticized. In Britain the Conservatives campaigned against the protocol in the 1924 elections, which they won. The new foreign secretary, Austen Chamberlain, formally announced the rejection of the protocol in March 1925.

France's hard-line policy had failed in the Ruhr occupation and the Geneva Protocol had been rejected. In both instances in seemed that the British had been the principal villain of the piece. In January 1925 Stresemann proposed a Rhineland pact by which Germany would guarantee the existing borders in the West, renounce war with France and agree to submit any disputes with Poland over the eastern frontiers to arbitration. This was essentially a repeat of proposals made in late 1922, but at that time the French government rejected them out of hand on the grounds that with France poised to strike to collect reparations, the Germans stood to gain far more from such an undertaking. For two years Germany persisted with these proposals, but the issue of reparations and then of disarmament, which the Inter-Allied Military Control Commission (IMCC) was vainly trying to force upon the Germans, prevented any progress. Stresemann made every effort to stop the investigations by the IMCC which reported that the Germans had made a whole series of infractions. The January proposals were thus an attempt to avoid further criticism from the IMCC by shifting the argument from one over disarmament to consideration of a Rhineland pact which Stresemann hoped would secure the evacuation of Cologne without too scrupulous attention being paid to the disarmament issue. Stresemann's hope was that the French would see a Rhineland pact as a better guarantee of their security than the disarmament of Germany and the occupation of the Rhineland, particularly in the absence of an Anglo-French military alliance. Given that the German army refused to co-operate with the IMCC there was no other way for Stresemann to get the Allies to agree to the evacuation without which Germany was not a fully sovereign state. Furthermore a Rhineland pact was greatly preferable to an Anglo-French military alliance and a continuation of the attempt to enforce even the modified terms of the treaty. Stresemann also needed a success to counter the many critics of his fulfilment policy and to survive as foreign minister. He therefore threatened to sabotage the Dawes Plan if the Allies would not begin to withdraw their troops from the Rhineland.

Austen Chamberlain favoured an Anglo-French entente, but the pro-German ambassador, D'Abernon, wanted to avoid any such commitments and with sovereign disregard for government policy he proposed to Stresemann a modified version of the 1922 multilateral non-aggression pact. Stresemann endorsed the proposal, which he assumed had been initiated in Whitehall, and used D'Abernon rather than the German ambassador in London to follow it up. Chamberlain was deeply suspicious. He felt that Stresemann was trying to wreck the Anglo-French alliance and was attempting to secure the evacuation of the Rhineland on the cheap. He therefore told the German ambassador that the proposal was premature and inappropriate.

Within the Baldwin government Balfour did not share Chamberlain's enthusiasm for a military alliance with France; indeed he felt that the French obsession with security was 'intolerably foolish' and that 'They are so dreadfully afraid of being swallowed up by the tiger, that they spend all their time poking it.' Churchill, Birkenhead, Amery, and Curzon agreed with Balfour that an Anglo-French military alliance was undesirable and felt that some sort of regional arrangement involving Germany would be the best solution provided it was postponed to a time when France was in what Churchill described as a 'much better state of mind'. With the rejection of the Geneva Protocol Chamberlain agreed to Churchill's proposal to suggest to Herriot the possibility of a pact that would include Germany. Chamberlain saw this as a possible alternative to the Anglo-French alliance, but Baldwin gave way to the 'anti-French' group who would consider no such commitment until the Treaty of Versailles had been substantially revised and the French had been made to make major concessions. Austen Chamberlain stood his ground and threatened to resign if the British government was not prepared to guarantee the security of France before the

Treaty of Versailles was revised. At this Baldwin gave way, promising his foreign secretary that he would bring the Balfour group into line and Chamberlain realized that a Rhineland pact was the only way in which the Anglo-French alliance could be held together. Although Chamberlain was the strongest advocate of a close alliance with France he rejected the suggestion that Germany should be kept in 'abject inferiority and subjection' and fancied himself as a 'moderator and conciliator'.

Having agreed to accept the Dawes Plan and to end the forcible extraction of reparations, the French were prepared to support in principle the idea of a Rhineland pact. The major concerns of the French government were that Cologne should not be evacuated before the Germans complied with the disarmament clauses of the Treaty of Versailles and that the security of Czechoslovakia and Poland would be properly safeguarded. Stresemann was determined to avoid any formal recognition of Germany's eastern borders and repeatedly made it clear that the Rhineland pact excluded any renunciation of the use of force in the east.

Negotiations continued throughout the spring and summer and finally, in October, Chamberlain, Briand and Stresemann met at Locarno. They were eventually joined by Mussolini who zoomed up Lake Maggiore in his speedboat with characteristic bombast, much to the disgust of the Belgian foreign minister, Vandervelde, who was revolted at having to be associated with the fascist murderer of his socialist comrade Matteotti.

The Locarno Treaty proper presented few problems. The Franco-German and the Belgo-German frontiers were guaranteed, Stresemann having first hoped to avoid any formal acceptance of the border with Belgium. It was agreed that Germany should join the League of Nation with a permanent seat on the Council and would be exempted from complying with article 16 of the Covenant, which called for sanctions against aggressors, on the questionable grounds that the country was disarmed and dangerously exposed to invasion. The real reason was that Germany wanted to avoid taking any step that might be interpreted by the Soviets as hostile to their interests. Indeed Stresemann skilfully used the threat of a closer relationship with Russia to win concessions from the French and British. Violations of the Rhineland pact were to be determined by the League Council, but since this required unanimity and since the Germans now had a seat on the Council, this made the pact virtually useless. The French tried to get out of the impasse by securing an agreement that 'flagrant military violations', which meant the movement of troops across frontiers or into the demilitarized zone, would involve an automatic response without the Council first having to meet.

The arbitration treaties between Germany and France, Belgium, Czechoslovakia and Poland were effectively sabotaged by Stresemann. Briand and Chamberlain tried to get him to guarantee Germany's eastern frontiers, but he would not agree to any such undertaking. The most he would do was to state that the frontiers should not be altered by force, but he refused to put his signature to this promise. He managed to stop the French from giving a guarantee to the arbitration treaties between Germany and Poland and with Czechoslovakia. The treaties neither accepted the frontiers nor were they non-aggression pacts. Indeed when Chamberlain informed the House of Commons that Germany had renounced the use of force in the east he was promptly told by Berlin that this was not the case. The French could not get the British to guarantee the eastern frontiers and Chamberlain told the British Ambassador to France, Lord Crewe, that the Polish Corridor was not worth 'the bones of a British grenadier'. In such circumstances all Briand could do was to reaffirm France's alliances with Czechoslovakia and Poland, although they had been significantly weakened.

France could no longer attack Germany in the west in the event of a German invasion of either of her eastern allies, unless Germany first attacked France. If the French went to the aid of these allies as a response to what they deemed to be a 'flagrant military violation' they could be branded as aggressors and face intervention from Britain in support of Germany. Most important of all, the treaties distinguished clearly between Germany's western and eastern frontiers and the British, by guaranteeing one set but not the others, showed that they regarded the eastern frontiers as far less important and implied that they were not going to do much to defend them. Locarno created the impression that the Versailles Treaty was binding in the west, although Stresemann immediately called for the return of Eupen and Malmédy from Belgium, but that it was open for revision in the east. It was widely felt that the Locarno agreements had given Germany the go-ahead to revise the eastern settlement and Stresemann told a delighted German audience that once the French troops left the Rhineland nothing stood in the way of Anschluss with Austria and the recovery of territory lost in the east.

In spite of the fact that Stresemann had achieved a major revision of the hated treaty and had made sure that Cologne would be evacuated, that the IMCC was rendered impotent and that no mechanism was left to enforce what remained of the Versailles settlement,

Locarno was far from popular in Germany. Most nationalists found it intolerable that Germany had agreed to the western boundaries, and Stresemann could not answer his critics without seriously compromising Briand and even Chamberlain. The more he was criticized at home the more concessions he wrung from the Allies; among them were the speeding up of troop withdrawals and the further reduction of the IMCC.

That Locarno was greatly to strengthen a determinedly revisionist and bitter Germany by reducing the possibility of a two-front war and weaken France and her eastern European allies was almost totally overlooked in 1925. The champagne, the sunshine, the boat trips on the lake, the bonhomie between the statesmen, the acceptance of Germany as an equal member of the community of nations and the Nobel peace prize for Austen Chamberlain, Briand and Stresemann, were what really counted. The much vaunted 'spirit of Locarno', *L'esprit de Locarno* and *die Locarnogeist*, were, as a French diplomat asserted, enough to save the situation for years to come. The British government had given a guarantee to the French which they were convinced would never have to be honoured. The French, even though military talks with Britain were contrary to the treaty, also believed that the Entente had been strengthened and that detente with Germany would make military assistance from Britain unnecessary. In 1925 Germany was in no position to even contemplate attacking France and the French had come to the realization that a repeat performance of the invasion of the Rhineland would be a disaster. Thus neither side made any significant concessions. The three powers had their reasons to be satisfied with their work, but these reasons were very different. The French believed that they had guaranteed their security. Britain believed that they had given the French sufficient reassurance so as not to be tempted to act as foolishly as they had done in 1923. Germany saw the way open to revision of the eastern frontiers, eventually by force if necessary.

The settlement of the Greco-Bulgarian frontier dispute of October 1925 by the determined action of the Council greatly enhanced the prestige of the League, as did their intervention in the dispute between Turkey and Iraq, and they were even able to make a modest contribution to lessening tension between Lithuania and Poland over rival claims to Vilna. But when the question of German admission was raised in February 1926 it provoked an unbecoming wrangle that did much to tarnish this shining image. When the German application for membership of the Council was presented Spain, Brazil and Poland also applied and China and Persia announced that, if the number of permanent seats on the Council was increased, they wished to be considered. Austen Chamberlain supported the Spanish claim, and Briand favoured Poland. As both Spain and Brazil were non-permanent members of the Council they voted against any proposal which did not include their own claim. The squabbles went on throughout the summer until it was agreed that Germany should have a permanent seat, and that three further temporary seats should be created and that the states occupying these three seats should be eligible for re-election by a two-thirds vote of the Assembly. Spain threatened to leave the League, and Brazil actually left. Stresemann used the crisis to get some further concessions from the Entente, but was for once firmly told by Austen Chamberlain not to haggle. On 10 September 1926 the Germans took their seat in the Council with much pomp and circumstance and Briand gave a rousing speech calling for peace and disarmament.

Germany now had a permanent seat on the Council and the 'Locarno tea parties' continued, as the great powers fixed things in private meetings while the council debated trivial issues at inordinate length. The League Council appeared to many of the smaller states as a reincarnation of the Holy Alliance with Stresemann as its Talleyrand. The first and most mysterious of these 'tea parties' was in fact a luncheon attended by Briand and Stresemann at Thoiry. No record was kept of the meeting, but it would appear that Stresemann renewed the German claim to Eupen and Malmédy, and also demanded the return of the Saar, the evacuation of the Rhineland and the abolition of the IMCC. The French government, in spite of the financial difficulties they were facing, was not prepared to make such drastic concessions and probably realized that Stresemann's promise to commercialize some or even all of the reparations bonds was too impractical to be taken seriously. Nor was the meeting without its moments of tenseness, such as when Briand complained about the number of para-military organizations in Germany. But to the world outside it was all conviviality, rabbit stew, a glowing communiqué, and another refreshing draught of the Locarno spirit.

Thus on the one hand the League seemed to have been taken over by the great powers and was increasingly falling prey to the secret diplomacy which it was supposed to supplant. On the other hand many agreed with Austen Chamberlain that Locarno was 'the real dividing-line between the years of war and the years of peace' and that international prospects were encouraging. This ambivalence can be seen in the attitude of the Soviet Union which denounced the League as an association of imperialist states but which also co-operated to a greater or lesser extent with its humanitarian and economic organizations and showed some interest in its attempts to promote disarmament. The Soviet Union also signed a treaty of neutrality and non-aggression with Germany on 24 April 1926 in order to strengthen Rapallo and to counteract what they feared was the anti-Soviet thrust of Locarno. This suited the Germans admirably for it emphasized the anti-Polish and revisionist element of the relationship with the Soviet Union and it was hoped that the Soviet connection could also be used to extract further concessions from the Entente.

Mussolini had joined in the Locarno meetings so as not to be left out of such a publicized gathering of statesmen, and to stay on relatively good terms with Britain, but he was concerned that the agreements would encourage German revisionism in Austria and lead them to press their claims to the South Tyrol. In this he was at odds with his own foreign office who wanted harmonious relations with Germany and even a 'Balkan Locarno' which would ensure that Yugoslavia and France would not combine against Italy. Mussolini would have none of this. He was determined to continue with his anti-Yugoslav policy which he underlined by signing the Treaty of Tirana in November 1926 which further increased the dependency of Albania on Italy. In Tunis, Syria, Egypt, and Turkey Mussolini came up against the great power interests of Britain and France. He had learnt in the Corfu crisis of 1923 that although he could win considerable concessions from the great powers, there was a limit to their tolerance and he had not been able to remain in possession of this relatively insignificant island without the consent of the British government. France tolerated a whole series of irritations from the Italians but Mussolini was in no position to follow in Caesar's footsteps and fight his own Gallic war, the more so since he realized that the many differences between Britain and France were differences of opinion rather than fundamental clashes of interests and that the alliance would hold in the face of an Italian aggression which seriously threatened either power's vital interests.

Mussolini therefore had to content himself with modest gains in Libya between 1923 and 1928, in Somaliland in 1924 and from 1925 Italian influence in Abyssinia steadily increased with London's blessing. In the Balkans he made similarly modest progress. Fiume was annexed in 1924, but neither this action nor the Treaty of Tirana were significant steps towards the realization of his grandiose imperial dreams. They also speeded up the process of completing the negotiations for the Franco-Yugoslav Treaty of November 1927, by convincing Briand that Italy could not be included in any Balkan pact. Mussolini set about destroying the Little Entente by signing a treaty of friendship with Romania in September 1926, by offering diplomatic and economic support to Bulgaria and by signing a treaty of friendship with Hungary in April 1927. The attempt to create an Italian sponsored alliance between Hungary, Romania and Bulgaria in 1927 failed, in part because of Romania's distrust of Hungary's ambitions in Transylvania. Mussolini had to make do with a military alliance with Albania, signed with King Zog in November 1927 which reduced the country to the level of an Italian protectorate.

The effect of Mussolini's policies was to draw the states of the Little Entente closer together and increase the apprehensions of the Greeks who set about improving relations with their neighbours, in spite of some troublesome disputes over frontiers. Mussolini made few gains apart from strengthening his hold over Albania and he became more involved with the problems of Bulgaria and Hungary. The lesson of this frustrating experience was that a revisionist policy could only work in co-operation with a great revisionist power such as Germany; but until 1936 Mussolini was fearful of Germany's ambitions in Austria and the South Tyrol and also was suspicious of Germany's intentions in the Balkans. Eventually he felt that the loss of an independent Austria was a worthwhile price to pay for the booty that could be picked up alongside an actively revisionist Germany. Mussolini had announced that Locarno was merely an armistice, and that it would not be followed by peace but by a renewal of hostilities. The experience of the 1920s did much to determine that in a future war Italy, obviously too weak to go it alone in spite of all the bombast, would follow in Germany's footsteps.

If Mussolini's attempts to revise the peace settlement were unsuccessful during the Locarno years, Poland's efforts to strengthen it fared no better. Relations with Czechoslovakia were improved, since both states feared that Locarno would encourage Germany's revisionist ambitions in the east. Poland signed a treaty with Romania in 1921 and it was renewed in 1926, but this precluded any improvement of relations with the Soviet Union for it accepted Romania's right to Bessarabia. Poland's efforts to create a Scandinavian Locarno and a Baltic pact came to nothing. Germany and the Soviet Union had a common interest in revising the Polish frontiers, although they were somewhat suspicious of each other's intentions. France was becoming increasingly disenchanted with the Polish alliance, whereas

Britain had long since reached the conclusion that there was little that could be done to stop Germany.

Stresemann did not rely on Soviet support to achieve his eastern ambitions, but preferred to work on the British to encourage the French to give way over the Rhineland and disarmament, but Austen Chamberlain frequently found Stresemann tiresomely importunate, whereas he held Briand in great respect. This personal preference reinforced the underlying imperatives of British policy. When forced to choose between Germany and France, Britain would opt for France. But in the Locarno years it seemed unthinkable that such a choice would ever have to be made. Furthermore, in the late 1920s the British government was not particularly concerned with Germany. There were far more important issues such as the Far East, the Soviet Union and the Geneva disarmament talks. France could not afford the luxury of ignoring Germany. They knew that the Rhineland would eventually have to be evacuated and therefore in 1927 began construction of the Maginot Line. This strengthened the resistance of those military men who argued that it would be madness to evacuate the Rhineland before the Maginot Line was completed and Briand was obliged to put up a stronger resistance to Stresemann's demands for withdrawal of the IMCC and of the occupation troops.

The IMCC, which had never been an effective organization, was withdrawn in 1927 and in the same year the occupation troops were reduced by 10,000 men to 60,000. Stresemann complained bitterly that this was a totally inadequate gesture of conciliation and that it was incommensurate with the sacrifices he claimed that Germany had made at Locarno; but Chamberlain and Briand resisted all such attempts to split the Entente. New opportunities for Germany were offered by the proposal to take another look at reparations and to settle the question once and for all, and also by a new shot of the Locarno spirit in the form of the Kellog-Briand Pact. Stresemann announced that he would only accept a new reparations settlement, however favourable to Germany, if the immediate evacuation of the Rhineland was guaranteed. Since the Rhineland was to be evacuated in any case in 1935, Briand had a very poor hand to play against Stresemann who liked to boast of his Metternichian skill in the use of finesse.

In April 1927 Briand, prodded by some distinguished Americans, suggested to the American government that they should sign a pact renouncing war as an instrument of policy. Since it was virtually inconceivable that France and the United States would go to war it was simply seen as a means of bringing the two countries closer together. The United States Secretary of State, Frank Kellogg, after much prevarication and with little enthusiasm, took up this suggestion, but proposed that all the countries in the world should be invited to sign the pact. The vacuous text of the pact was finally agreed upon and signed by the United States, Britain, France, Germany, Italy, Japan, Belgium, Poland, Czechoslovakia, the Dominions and India at a imposing ceremony in Paris. It was widely heralded as the beginning of a golden age of peace, and the United States was welcomed back from isolation. In fact it amounted to little more than what an American senator contemptuously called an 'international kiss'. Since it involved no contractual obligations most of the states signed the pact with the exception of a few Latin American states which objected to the United States declaration that the pact did not cover infringements of the Monroe Doctrine. It was soon violated by both Italy and Japan, but as the pact of Paris merely declared that war was sinful nothing could be done, and the Covenant of the League only had woefully inadequate means of punishing states for fighting certain sorts of wars. The British government proposed that the Covenant and the Pact should somehow be combined, suggesting that sanctions should be imposed on any state violating the Kellogg-Briand Pact. Although supported by the French this proposal was resisted by the Japanese and Scandinavian governments, the discussions dragged on, the British government fell and the international climate changed. By 1930 the optimism of the Locarno years was beginning to diminish and the vision of a golden age of peace began to fade.

Meanwhile, in August 1929, Britain, France and Germany, who had just agreed on the Young Plan for reparations, although there were serious differences as to how the plan was to be implemented, met with Italy, Japan and Belgium at The Hague for a conference claiming to mark the 'final liquidation of the war'. The dominant figure at the conference was the Chancellor of the Exchequer in the Labour government, Philip Snowden, who without troubling about diplomatic niceties, demanded and secured a revision in Britain's favour of the percentages of the reparations payments made at the Spa conference of 1920. This made him immensely popular at home but did nothing to improve Anglo-French relations. The Foreign Secretary, Arthur Henderson, ignored Briand's insistence that French troops in the Rhineland should remain for at least another year and announced that the British troops would be home for Christmas. Briand found himself faced with what almost amounted to an

Anglo-German front and was obliged to agree that the Rhineland should be evacuated by the end of June the following year.

Stresemann died in October 1929 aged fifty-one. He had achieved much for his country, greatly reducing reparations, securing the evacuation of the Rhineland and reasserting Germany's position as a state of influence and importance. But strident agitation against the Young Plan by the nationalist right showed that Stresemann's moderate revisionism was unacceptable to an influential section of German opinion. Almost 6 million voted against the Young Plan in the plebiscite sponsored by the Nationalists and Nazis. Briand could now no longer control Germany by the provisions of the peace treaty and therefore proposed a European union which he hoped might provide an acceptable means of ensuring a peaceful future for Europe. Whilst the European governments discussed this idealistic proposal, the news broke that Adolf Hilter's party had won 107 seats in the Reichstag elections of September 1930. The League Assembly tactfully appointed a committee to examine Briand's plan and nothing more was heard of it. At the end of the year the Preparatory Commission for the Disarmament Conference produced its draft convention which indicated that there was unlikely to be much progress on that front. As the depression deepened international tensions increased. The peace settlement which had fallen into such ill repute had been effectively dismantled, but there seemed to be nothing to take its place, and the optimism of the Locarno years, which had been in part founded on the unwarranted assumption of continued prosperity, was now being gradually replaced by resentment, by talk of crisis and even of another war.

The Soviets, fearing that the upsurge of rabid nationalism in Germany would put an end to co-operation between the two countries, began to improve relations with western Europe, signed non-aggression pacts with their neighbours, including Poland, and prudently moved their armaments factories behind the Urals. They had every reason to be concerned. All the German political parties demanded the end of reparations which, with sublime disregard for the facts, were held to be responsible for the depression. Most of them wanted massive rearmament, which they somehow imagined could be achieved without increasing the deficit, demanded frontier rectifications in the east, the return of the colonies and Anschluss with Austria. With allied troops in the Rhineland the Germans had to exercise some caution and moderation in their demands. Now there were no restraints as politicians outbid one another to win the nationalist vote. In Geneva the foreign ministers of Germany and

Poland, Curtius and Zaleski, had a heated exchange over the rights of the German minority in Poland from which it was clear that Germany regarded Poland with obsessive hatred and would never be satisfied with the status quo. The launching of the pocket battle-ship *Deutschland* by Hindenburg was a dramatized to show Germany's determination to be a major naval power once again, for the ship was superbly designed, combining tremendous firepower with exceptional speed, although it was just within the limitations set by the peace treaty.

In March 1931 funds were voted for a sister ship and plans made for a third. With deliberately provocative timing the German government announced on the following day that they intended to negotiate a customs union with Austria, a move clearly intended by Brüning as the first step to an Anschluss and to a major revision of the eastern settlement. The French government exploited Austria's financial difficulties over the Credit Anstalt to force them to back away from the project, and the Court of International Justice at The Hague ruled that the proposal was a violation of the Geneva Protocol of 1922 whereby the League had salvaged the Austrian economy. The German government refused to accept this ruling and continued to demand the customs union. Although the economic crisis was deepening and protests about the reparations burden became ever more shrill, the government pushed ahead with its rearmament programme. The Hoover Moratorium did nothing to improve the situation for the simple reason that reparations were never the root of Germany's financial difficulties.

On 2 February 1932 the Disarmament Conference began at Geneva. The moment was hardly auspicious. The Preparatory Commission had sat for five years and had been unable to come up with a satisfactory draft convention. Japanese troops were marching through Manchuria and the League was unable and unwilling to do anything to stop them. Germany was demanding equality in arma-ments with the other great powers, and the French were bound to resist any such moves. This situation was to become even worse when Papen replaced Brüning as Chancellor in May 1932 and attempted to win over the nationalists by a more strident approach to international politics. The president of the conference was Arthur Henderson, but as the government had resigned he was no longer foreign secretary. He therefore officiated as a private individual and was in no position to give the conference the direction it so badly required.

The conference was soon bogged down in interminable arguments over the definition of offensive and defensive weapons and on methods of verification. Germany withdrew from the conference, protesting that either the other powers should disarm down to their level, or they should be allowed to rearm up to theirs. Since this was irreconcilable with France's need for security this suggestion resulted in a deadlock which was only partially overcome when Britain, France and Italy granted Germany 'equality of rights in a system which would provide security for all nations'. It was hoped that this formula would reconcile France's need for security with Germany's demand for equality. The Germans, who had won a significant concession, returned to the conference. The conference dragged on, Hitler was appointed Chancellor and in October 1933 the Germans once again withdrew from the conference and also from the League. The French flatly refused to consider Hitler's proposals for fixing the relative strengths of the armed forces of Germany and its neighbours and the conference gradually fizzled out. Hitler could claim that he had been forced to rearm because of the French refusal to disarm; the French that they could not disarm as long as Germany continued to pose such a threat to their security.

In 1932 disarmament was not a high priority for most governments. They were far more concerned with economic matters, particularly what would happen when the Hoover Moratorium expired in July. It was generally felt that the German reparations debt would have to be cancelled, but the French still hoped to get something in return for this. But the Germans saw no reason why they should guarantee the territorial status quo in return for a concession which the Allies were bound to make. Britain and Italy felt that the reparations should be cancelled, but the most the French would concede was that they should be reduced. Although Britain called for a meeting of the Young Plan countries at Lausanne in January, it was not until June that the conference was able to convene. After much acrimonious debate it was agreed that the Germans should pay one final reparations bill of £150,000,000 in 5 per cent government bonds.

It was soon revealed that this was little more than a publicity stunt designed to placate French opinion. The Allies agreed that they would not discuss the allocation of this lump sum, nor would they ratify the agreement until the Americans cancelled or reduced their war debts and the moratorium was to remain in effect until the Lausanne agreements were ratified. All this was of little account for the Germans thought it was outrageous that reparations had not been cancelled outright and they had no intention of paying. The Allies realized that the money could not be collected, certainly not after Hitler became chancellor. The Lausanne Convention was never ratified, but it made no difference. Reparations were dead. The Germans had paid a total of 20 billion marks, roughly what they owed up to the middle of 1921. That the country was crippled by reparations was a persistent myth, but in fact the reverse was true. Germany was strong enough to refuse to pay and was able to win substantial concessions for paying those modest amounts that the Allies were able to extract from them. The American debt was never cancelled. One by one their creditors defaulted, the Treasury calculating the amounts owing and the accrued interest with increasing frustration as the prospects of payment grew ever more remote.

The governments of Europe viewed Hitler's appointment as chancellor with considerable alarm, for he seemed determined to destroy what little remained of the Versailles settlement. His first moves in foreign policy were therefore designed to reassure his neighbours. He promised not to revise the treaty by force, was careful not to antagonize the British by getting involved in another naval arms race, signed a Concordat with the Holy See and repeated the pacific platitudes of Geneva while preparing for war if neccessary. The Soviet Union was not taken in by this masquerade and began to look for allies against Hitler by joining the League, preaching collective security and vowing to defend bourgeois democracy against the threat of fascism, a policy whose most notable achievements were the alliances with France and Czechoslovakia in 1934.

The Little Entente was deeply concerned by developments in Germany and improved military liaison between member states and was justifiably alarmed at an Italian proposal for a four-power pact with Germany, Britain and France, which made provision for a revision of the peace treaties, presumably in the east. The French managed to revise the draft so that it became totally innocuous and even Hitler was prepared to sign this worthless document. Poland resented the fact that they had been excluded from the pact, felt that France might well abandon its eastern allies in a real crisis, and began to think of coming to an understanding with Germany in a desperate attempt to preserve the status quo.

Mussolini was far from delighted to see a rival fascist as chancellor of Germany. In spite of assurances to the contrary in *Mein Kampf*, he believed that Hitler had designs on the South Tyrol and therefore was determined to keep the Germans out of Austria, a country which under Chancellor Dollfuss was rapidly becoming a client state of Italy. Such were Mussolini's concerns about Austria that he began to consider a rapprochement with France who, even though Italy had been the most persistent and tiresome of the revisionist powers, were sufficiently concerned about the potential danger from Nazi Germany that the Foreign Minister, Barthou, went to Rome to see if some common ground could be found. Eastern Europe proved to be the major obstacle, for as long as Italy's allies Austria and Hungary were bitterly opposed to the Little Entente, no progress could be made towards a Franco-Italian understanding.

The Little Entente was divided over these moves. Czechoslovakia would be in serious danger if Germany occupied Austria, but Yugoslavia had no desire to see Austria dominated by Italy. Romania was too distant to have strong feelings either way. In October 1934 King Alexander of Yugoslavia went to France to argue his case against Italy. He was welcomed in Marseilles by Barthou but both men were gunned down by a Croat terrorist as they drove away from the harbour. The Yugoslavs were convinced that the Italians were behind the assassination but the French, anxious not to prejudice their negotiations with the Italians, helped to persuade the League Council to condemn the Hungarian government for a degree of complicity with the murders. The French were annoyed by the Yugoslavs' persistent suspicions of Italy and pushed ahead with their approaches to Rome, particularly after the murder of the Austrian Chancellor, Dollfuss, by Nazis in July 1934. In January 1935 Barthou's successor as French Foreign Minister, Pierre Laval, went to Rome to sign a series of agreements by which both powers agreed to co-operate in the face of any threat to the independence of Austria and to put a halt to German rearmament. Agreement was also reached on outstanding issues between the two countries in North Africa, and Laval gave an ambiguous assent to Italian ambitions in Abyssinia. This last agreement was kept secret and caused considerable embarrassment later, the French insisting that they had only been referring to economic interests, the Italians that they understood that France was indifferent to the prospect of an Italian conquest of Abyssinia. No records were kept of these conversations, but their effect was undoubtedly to encourage Mussolini's ambition to conquer Abyssinia. The net effect of the Rome agreements was to weaken the Little Entente and to place further strain on Franco-Polish relations, Poland being drawn closer to Germany. Little was gained in return, apart from vague expressions of concern about German intentions towards Austria.

Britain supported the French initiative to bring Italy over to the side of those states which were apprehensive about Germany, but was unwilling to make any continential commitment. In April 1935 the three powers met at Stresa to reaffirm the Locarno and the Rome agreements and to issue the rather empty warning that the signatories would resist 'by all practicable means any unilateral repudiation of treaties which may endanger the peace of Europe'. A resolution was drafted for presentation to the League Council condemning Germany's recent violations of the Versailles Treaty which, although it passed unanimously, did nothing but annoy the Germans and provide excellent material for Goebbels' propaganda ministry.

The Stresa Front was in part a response to Hitler's announcement in March 1935 that he would create a German air force and introduce compulsory military service which would result in an army of some 550,000 men; it therefore caused a sensation when the British government announced that they would accept Hitler's offer to limit the German navy to 35 per cent of the Royal Navy in all types of ship. Hitler believed that it was possible to have good relations with Britain and there were many in Britain who, in spite of their revulsion at the brutalities of the Nazi régime, were basically sympathetic to Germany, disliked France and had no desire to make any new commitments to European security and felt that even Locarno was an unnecessary burden. Barthou's policy of co-operation with the Soviet Union and Italy against Germany was most unpopular in Britain. The British government obliged the French to make a number of concessions on the issues of German rearmament, which Flandin and Laval were more ready to make than had been their predecessors, Doumergue and Barthou. The Franco-Soviet alliance was extremely unpopular in Britain particularly among the pro-German right, but also on the left who felt that it was provocatively anti-German and in the general staff, who had nothing but contempt for the Soviet military. The German government was skilful in playing on this strong anti-Soviet feeling in Britain and Hitler gave a major speech in the Reichstag on 21 May 1935 in which he was most conciliatory, proposing mutual arms limitations and the outlawing of the bombing of civilian targets which was a particular concern in Britain.

In June 1935 Ribbentrop, as Hitler's ambassador extraordinary, travelled to London and concluded the naval agreement by which the German claim to 35 per cent of British naval strength was accepted, 45 per cent in the case of submarines rising to 100 per cent if there was a threat from Russia, along with an exchange of naval information. The French were horrified and protested that the naval pact was contrary to the Stresa agreements, but the British government ignored these objections and unkindly signed the pact on the 120th anniversary of the Battle of Waterloo. In Britain the naval agreement was seen as a triumph of common sense and pragmatism. Disarmament talks had failed, France had refused to negotiate and Germany had accepted British naval supremacy. Only a few mavericks like Winston Churchill protested. In France the agreement was seen as betrayal, the British unilaterally condoning the violation of the Treaty of Versailles. The Italians, whose relations with Britain were strained over Abyssinia, condemned the pact, largely in order to preserve their entente with France. In spite of such protestations they were not unhappy at this revision of the peace settlement. The Soviets saw the pact as confirmation of their worst suspicions that the British government was plotting to let the Germans loose against them. Hitler's 'happiest day in his life' was indeed a triumph. Britain had condoned a repudiation of the peace treaty and had allowed a four-fold increase in the German navy. Discord had been sown between Britain and France and further strain placed on relations between France and her eastern allies. But Hitler exaggerated the importance of the agreement. It did not lead to the alliance with Britain for which he hoped, and it strengthened his mistaken view that bluster and intimidation were inevitably successful in diplomacy.

In October 1935, after lengthy preparations, the Italians invaded Abyssinia. The French government, still angry over the naval agreement between Britain and Germany, was sympathetic to Mussolini who could count on its support against Germany in Austria and against the British in East Africa. The British government, which had substantial economic interests in and territorial ambitions towards Abyssinia, had sent Eden to Rome to settle differences over Abyssinia, but the mission had been a failure. The French had refused to support Britain against Italy and had no desire to risk the Franco-Italian alliance for the sake of British colonial ambitions. The British replied by warning Laval that if he did not co-operate against Mussolini they might withdraw from the continent, protected by the Anglo-German naval agreement. This threat did make France slightly more heedful of the need to make some concessions to the British.

Although the British and French governments agreed that war with Italy should be avoided at all costs, the British government brought the question of Abyssinia before the League Council, largely to placate public opinion on the eve of a general election, fully expecting that sanctions against Italy would be so limited as to have no effect. Britain thus posed as the champion of collective security while continuing to negotiate a compromise settlement with Italy. This created a difficult situation, for the smaller states were pressing for oil sanctions and Mussolini had warned the British that if they supported these sanctions he would order air strikes against the Mediterranean fleet which could well lead to a war which the service chiefs insisted Britain was in no position to fight. The British government therefore wanted to negotiate a settlement to the Abyssinian crisis before sanctions were imposed. This policy was strongly supported by the French, Laval warning the Italians that he would resign if they did not accept the British proposals and that France would go to Britain's aid if the Italians attacked the Mediterranean fleet.

In December the foreign secretary, Sir Samuel Hoare, travelled to Paris and worked out the details of a plan with Laval whereby Italy would annexe a substantial part of the fertile plains of Abyssinia, the emperor would remain with his mountain kingdom and be given a corridor to the sea to the port of Assab in Eritrea. The British government accepted the Hoare–Laval Plan, but public opinion was outraged at a government elected on a platform of support for collective security giving way to brutal aggression against a backward, impoverished and innocent nation. Hoare had to resign and was succeeded by Eden. The plan showed that Britain and France's support for collective security was a sham and the League was further discredited. The Stresa Front was in ruins. Britain had backed down when threatened by Mussolini and had shown extraordinary ineptitude throughout the crisis, lacking any consistent policy except a desire for peace at almost any price. In May 1936 the King of Italy was proclaimed Emperor of Abyssinia, and in July Britain proposed that sanctions against Italy should be lifted. The League Assembly passed the motion unanimously. The Emperor Haile Selassie, whom Britain, France and the the League had been unable to save, settled into exile in Bath. Mussolini boasted that the 'greatest colonial war in all history' was the foundation stone of a new Roman Empire and the Italian people rejoiced at such a splendid victory and at the glittering prospects which lay before them.

CHAPTER FOUR
The Soviet Union

One power was conspicuously absent from what the Germans contemptuously described as the 'Paris suburban treaties'. Russia was not invited to attend the Peace Conference and although the powers spent a great deal of time discussing what would be done about the problem of Russia, nothing could be decided. There was full agreement that the Bolsheviks were a singularly undesirable bunch of terrorists and murderers who had taken Russia out of the war and therefore deserved no place among the victors. Their dictatorial methods were condemned by an alliance which claimed to have been fighting a crusade for democracy. The repudiation of all foreign debts and the seizure of foreign property without compensation was denounced as a crime against the sanctity of contract and of private property. Nowhere was this feeling stronger than in France, for Frenchmen had invested enormous sums in Imperial Russia and small investors who had bought their few francs worth of Saint Petersburg municipal bonds loudly demanded their money back. There was also the reasonable fear that the revolution would spread westwards, controlled and manipulated from Moscow.

Allied intervention in Russia had begun in March 1918 when the British landed in Murmansk under the pretext of protecting military supplies from falling into the hands of the Germans. The French and Americans followed suit. In the following month the Japanese landed a force in Vladivostok and were soon joined by the British and Americans. In July British, American and French detachments were sent to Archangel. But a more serious threat to the Bolshevik regime was the Czech Legion, consisting of prisoners of war and deserters along with members of the Czech brigade which had fought with the tsarist army. The Bolsheviks had given the Czech Legion permission to leave Russia via Vladivostok from whence they intended to go to fight on the Western Front. The French suggested that the Czechs should embark at Archangel so as to get to the front quicker. Rumours spread among the Czechs that the Soviets were out to disarm them, Sporadic violence broke out between Czechs and Reds whereupon Trotsky ordered that any Czech found with arms should be shot. By June the Czechs were in open conflict with the Red Army. There was now widespread hope among the Entente that the Czechs, aided by anti-Bolshevik Russian soldiers, might be able to overthrow the Bolshevik regime and that all that needed to be done was ensure that they were adequately supplied and equipped. Large-scale intervention by the Allies could thus be avoided. By July 1918 the Bolsheviks found themselves in such a precarious position that Lenin took the extraordinary step of asking the Germans for help against the interventionists. Ludendorff's demand that German troops should occupy Petrograd put an end to this unwise proposal. The Allies were fully engaged in the ferocious summer campaign on the Western Front and were in no position to intervene effectively in the Russian civil war. The immediate danger to the Bolshevik regime from the Allies therefore soon appeared to be exaggerated.

With Germany defeated there were powerful voices urging full-scale intervention in Russia to put an end to Bolshevism and to stop this virus spreading into central Europe. But Churchill and Foch, who headed this campaign, were hopelessly out of touch with the realities of the situation. There was precious little money left to pay for an extensive campaign in Russia, there was widespread war-weariness after four terrible years of slaughter, and public opinion was strongly opposed to intervention. Both President Wilson and Lloyd George had strong political objections to intervention, many of the allied troops in Russia openly sympathized with the Reds, and the French sailors in Odessa mutinied. By the autumn of 1919 all allied troops were withdrawn from Russia except for some Japanese and Americans who stayed on in Vladivostok.

Allied intervention was half-heated and ineffectual and its only significant effect was to strengthen the hold of the Bolsheviks. They were able to show up the Whites as mercenaries and lackeys of the imperialist powers and thus appeal to Russian national sentiment. The Allies accorded partial recognition to Admiral Kolchak, the most successful of the anti-Bolshevik leaders, who had established a government in Siberia and was advancing into European Russia. Similar support, both verbal and material, was given to other White leaders. Attempts were made to negotiate an end to the civil war with a conference on the Prinkipo Islands and a mission by William Bullitt to Moscow, but both were failures largely because of the disingenuity of the Allies and the Bolshevik's resolute refusal to be swindled. With Denikin controlling southern Russia and the Ukraine, Yudenich advancing from the Baltic and Kolchak from Siberia it seemed that the Bolsheviks would soon be toppled and Russia could be welcomed back into the community of nations.

These hopes soon proved to be illusory and by the end of 1919 the White armies had been decisively beaten. This was due in large part to the utter failure of the Whites to co-ordinate their strategy and to agree upon a basic political and social programme. The White armies lacked popular support, found it increasingly difficult to get recruits and were plagued by massive desertions. But the decisive factor in the civil war was the Red Army which Trotsky as Commissar for War had converted from a somewhat ramshackle collection of Red Guards units into a highly organized, professionally trained and strictly disciplined regular army. None of this could have been possible without the support given by the peasants to the Bolsheviks. They had no desire to fight and bitterly resented the Bolsheviks requisitioning their produce, but they had been given land under the Bolshevik redistribution policy and knew that this would be taken away from them if the Whites were victorious. The peasants had no great love for the Bolsheviks, but they certainly preferred them to the Whites.

The experience of the civil war had profound and lasting effects on Soviet society. It did much to strengthen and institutionalize the authoritarian tendencies which were already firmly implanted in a regime supported by a minority of the Russian people and which depended for its continued existence on workers and peasants who had little sympathy for reasoned debate or liberal tolerance. The Red Army was by far the largest, best disciplined and most efficient organization at the Bolsheviks' disposal, and it provided the basis for the administration of all areas under their control. The 'All Russian Extraordinary Commission for Struggle Against Counter-Revolution, Sabotage and Speculation', or Cheka, which had been formed shortly after the revolution, got into full swing during the civil war. There was much for the Cheka to struggle against, for the Whites were guilty of the widespread use of terror and the growth of the Cheka's extraordinary powers was at least in part a response to this violence. It soon became a fearful instrument of terror, making almost 100,000 summary arrests of suspects of whom more than 8,000 were shot without trial. The experience of the intervention strengthened the tendency to see the world in Manichaean terms: heroic revolutionaries locked in a battle to the death with imperialist reactionaries; of the new and the good against the old and the bad. The terror, violence and revolutionary zeal of the civil war years were at least open and unashamed, in marked contrast to the bureaucratic, faceless, cynical brutality of the Stalin era. To the countless victims of the period such fine distinctions made no difference.

In March 1919 the Communist International was formed in Moscow at a hastily improvized congress to co-ordinate the efforts of the radical left to overthrow bourgeois democracy, undermine the Second International, end intervention and concentrate all efforts on establishing the dictatorship of the proletariat throughout Europe. The Comintern, with Zinoviev as president and Radek as secretary, was devoted to the defence of the Soviet Union and the spreading of the revolution: two aims which in 1919 were wholly compatible. Its executive committee, the IKKI, was to become known as the general staff of the world revolution and it was some years before it degenerated into a mere tool of Soviet foreign policy.

The civil war was nearing its end when the Poles attacked the Ukraine and were soon in possession of Kiev. The counter-attack by the Red Army was enormously successful and the Poles were quickly pushed back to the border. Lenin, possibly persuaded by the rhetoric of the second congress of the International which was held in July 1920 and which became intoxicated with the vision of world revolution, argued in favour of crossing the border and marching to Warsaw. Trotsky and Radek urged caution, pointing out that the Poles would be most unlikely to welcome the Red Army as liberators from serfdom and the domination of capital and would join a national crusade against the instrument of old- style Russian imperialism. Lenin as usual prevailed, thus making the worst miscalculation in his career. The Red Army marched triumphantly to the Vistula, but Pilsudski organized a spirited defence against the invaders who in turn were swiftly routed. In October 1920 an armistic was signed which left the border well to the east of the Curzon Line which had been internationally recognized as the frontier between the two states. In addition to this military defeat there was the humiliation of the slow realization that hopes for a European revolution were ill-founded and that a substantial segment of the working class did not see Russia as its revolutionary homeland.

Internally there was mounting unrest particularly among the peas-antry, caused by the disruptions and dislocations of the economy during the civil war.

When the Bolsheviks seized power they had no clear idea how they intended to organize the economy. Lenin and Trotsky wanted to tread cautiously and argued that it was best to preserve the essentials of a capitalist economy and to control and direct it in the interests of Soviet power. The more radical wing of the party, whose spokesman was Bukharin, insisted that the building of a strictly socialist economy should be a priority. The result was a compromise, but one which could not possibly survive the ravages of a civil war. On 28 June 1918 industry was nationalized, marking the beginning of the period of 'War Communism'. In part this was a response to the spontaneous seizure of factories by workers who felt frustrated and even betrayed by the Bolsheviks. After all, the peasants had been given land immediately after the revolution, but the industrial proletariat, in whose name the revolution had been carried out, had got precious little. It has been estimated that three-quarters of the factories nationalized in June had already been taken over by the workers. The Bolsheviks were thus recognizing something which had already happened, and were anxious to preserve the allegiance of a class without which they could not possibly survive. For the first eight months the regime survived economically from day to day, the Supreme Council for National Economy (Vesenkha) having none of the authority which its grandiose title suggested. By the summer of 1918 the economy had collapsed, there was widespread hunger, chronic shortages of raw materials and industrial production was grinding to a halt. In such a situation feeding the population became the first priority.

Just as the nationalization decree was a response to the workers seizing the factories, the land decree had been a recognition of the peasants' right to the land they had already seized. The land settlement partially satisfied the peasants, but this substantial increase in the number of small-holders and drastic reduction of the average size of the landholdings was economically inefficient as well as being contrary to socialist policy. All land had been nationalized in the decree of 8 November 1917, but the peasants were granted the use of their land and the distinction between use and ownership, which was confirmed in the law of 9 February 1918, meant absolutely nothing to them. They avoided the state grain monopoly and sold their produce on the black market in an attempt to get a reasonable price. Food shortages grew worse when the Germans requisitioned grain from the Ukraine after the Treaty of Brest Litovsk, and became chronic with the onset of the civil war. If they traded on the black market the peasants were branded as speculators, and when they cut back production that would simply be requisitioned they were punished as saboteurs. The few communes and collective farms that were started up during the civil war were idealistic experiments by enthusiastic communists, but they did not make a significant contribution to an increase in production and were viewed with horror by the peasants who saw them as the unpleasant shape of things to come. The alliance between the Bolsheviks and the peasants which had made the revolution possible was rapidly falling apart. It was said that the peasants loved the Bolsheviks who had taken the land away from the landlords, but loathed the communists who believed in the collectivization of agriculture and who requisitioned their crops.

The use of the machine gun as an instrument of agricultural production was a complete failure and the chronic food shortages that resulted caused a flight from the towns as people desperately looked for food. Workers who stayed behind frequently went on strike to protest against the shortages of food. At times it seemed that the Russian proletariat would either disappear into the countryside or revolt against the Bolsheviks. Lenin began to talk of the need for strict control of labour, extolled 'Taylorism' (American production techniques which had previously been denounced as the apotheosis of capitalist brutality and degradation) and took to quoting from 2 Thessalonians that he who did not work should not eat. Factory committees were condemned for putting the selfish needs of the few above the interests of the class as a whole. The trades unions became instruments for the disciplining of the labour force, for improving production, regulating wages and stopping strikes.

With the increasing shortages of manufactured goods, the breakdown of the transportation network and the lack of food, even for those who worked, money ceased to have any value and barter was virtually the sole means of exchange. Some Bolsheviks looked upon this chaos and called it socialism. Money, they claimed, had 'withered away' and the economy was passing through a phase of the 'revolutionary disintegration of industry'. The capitalist market economy had been destroyed and had been replaced by socialist planning and rationing and any teething problems were regrettable but inevitable. Others saw 'War Communism' as a series of improvised stop-gap measures designed to overcome the immediate problems caused by revolution and civil war. They saw the withering away of money as rampant inflation, and failed to find anything revolutionary about the disintegration of industry. As long as the workers and peasants were prepared to accept nationalization, centralization, the control of labour, the elimination of money and the requisition of foodstuffs as sacrifices that had to be made the Bolsheviks saw no reason to change their policies, and tended to make a virtue out of necessity. But the people could tolerate these deprivations no longer. There were widespread peasant revolts and strikes, and in March 1921 the sailors in Kronstadt, who had been among the staunchest supporters of the Bolsheviks, revolted against these harsh political and economic controls and called for power to be given back to the Soviets.

The cost of the civil war in human terms had been horrendous. It has been estimated that some 8 million people died, 7½ million from hunger and disease. The cities were half empty and many of the specialists and intellectuals who were desperately needed to build the new society had fled the country. The only people who seemed to thrive were the notorious 'bagmen' who brought food to the towns which they sold for vast profits. The Bolsheviks, who always looked to the history of the French revolution for parallels, were terrified at the prospect of widespread *Jacqueries*. When it took 50,000 Red Army soldiers to suppress the peasant revolt in Tambov and with Nestor Makhno holding out against the Bolsheviks in the Ukraine, their worst fears seemed to be confirmed. At the party's tenth congress in March 1921 the first decisive steps were taken to dismantle the system of War Communism, most notably by replacing the requisitions (*prodrazverstka*) by a tax in kind. This relieved the immediate danger of the peasant uprings spreading but it did not satisfy the workers who resented the dictatorship of the commissars, mourned their comrades in Kronstadt and resented the decision to give back the small factories to private entrepreneurs. Their frustrations swelled the ranks of the Workers' Opposition who called for workers' control of production and a purge of non-proletarian elements from the party.

Although Lenin was opposed to the restoration of private trade, arguing that it would be a fateful step back from the socialist goal, he once again accepted its spontaneous revival and shied away from using further violence and contented himself with the satisfaction that the 'commanding heights' of the economy were still firmly under state control. On the critical issues of the trades unions, the congress reached a somewhat unsatisfactory compromise. The Workers Opposition was beaten back, but so was Trotsky's attempt to turn the unions into 'productions unions'. The unions were to be non-party organizations which were not instruments of the state, but something ominously termed 'proletarian compulsion' could be used when necessary.

The resulting 'New Economic Policy' (NEP) was every bit as improvized as War Communism. It was a response to mounting disaffection with a system that no longer seemed justified once the civil war was over. On the other hand Lenin was deply concerned by the vehemence of the debates at the congress and was determined that there should be less discussion and more action. Thus although the New Economic Policy saw a liberalization of the economic sphere it also saw a strengthening of the dictatorship. Having defeated Trotsky and the Workers' Opposition, Lenin pushed through a resolution forbidding factions and factionalism within the party and strengthened his hold over the central committee. Lenin's justification for this action, which he described as a temporary measure, was that during a retreat discipline was particularly necessary. It was not only the party which was disciplined. Shortly afterwards some 2,000 Mensheviks were arrested, the following year some right-wing Social Revolutionaries were tried and executed and leading Mensheviks and Cadets were deported. Far from being temporary, these measures, along with the new practice of sending dissident elements to remote parts of Russia so that they would be away from the centre of power, were to become commonplace under Stalin's dictatorship.

For most Russians NEP was a tremendous relief after the violence and deprivations of the civil war. Although the harvest of 1921 was a disaster owing to widespread drought causing millions to die of starvation, the harvests of the next two years were exceptionally good. The peasants had enough to eat and the richer peasants, the Kulaks, prospered. In the towns there was a return to former ways. The markets were busy, night clubs reopened as did the churches, the arts flourished in an atmosphere of experiment and excitement, and the elegant middle class was again to be seen in the theatres and concert halls. But none of this helped the industrial workers, and the Bolshevik revolutionaries began to ask themselves whether the revolution had lost its vigour and sense of direction. Lenin did not make the situation any easier by making contradictory statements about NEP, at times referring to it as a serious defeat, at other claiming that it was a viable interim policy that was likely to remain in force for a long time.

In the final months of his life Lenin became increasingly concerned, as did most of the old revolutionaries, with the problem of bureaucracy. The Bolsheviks had felt it necessary to use as much of the old tsarist administration as they could, and they needed the skilled experts of the old regime to run the country. Lenin knew that revolutionary zeal was no substitute for experience and expertise, but he also feared that these representatives of the old regime might be tempted to sabotage the attempt to build socialism and try to control and direct inexperienced communist administrators. The Bolsheviks believed in organization and administration and had no sympathies for conventional ideas of democratic control, but they believed that any such bureaucratic apparatus should be responsive to the needs of the revolution. They therefore saw the organizations of the Communist Party as the best possible antidote to the moderating and conservative effects of the administrators and experts they had inherited from the tsars. Lenin himself had serious doubts that the Russian workers had the necessary culture to fulfil this role, and for all his reservations about the old bureaucracy he still believed it to be superior in every respect to anything that semi-literate party activists could achieve. Within the party the feeling was quite different. There were those who believed that revolutionary zeal and impeccable proletarian lineage was enough and that the belief in training and expertise was essentially a bourgeois prejudice. This belief was often a rationalisation for the desire for powerful and influential jobs for the boys: rewards for years of sacrifice for the revolution, or opportunities for rapid and comparatively effortless promotion. Many workers on joining the party left the factory bench and were given positions within the party bureaucracy where their lack of education and training was hardly noticeable and which provided them with power, influence and material comforts. This gradual growth in the size and importance of the party, along with administrative changes which gave far greater powers to the Politburo, which initially only had five members, gave enormous power to the General Secretary, and Stalin was to use this with exceptional skill to establish his dictatorship.

Lenin's health had been precarious since 1921 and in May 1922 he suffered a stroke which left him partially paralysed. His right side was permanently paralysed after a second stroke in December 1921 and he lost his speech as the result of a third stroke in March 1923. After his second stroke Lenin dictated his testament in which he expressed many of his fears and forebodings about the system which he had created. Lenin was concerned that Stalin had accumulated too much power as General Secretary, was furious that he had been rude to his wife, Krupskaya, and felt that he should be removed from the post of General Secretary. But he also had serious reservations about all the other members of the Central Committee. He repeated his concerns about the growth of bureaucracy in the state and in the party, and feared that the alliance between the workers and peasants, on which the revolution was based, might soon break down.

While Lenin lay dying, agonizing about these problems for which he more than any single man was responsible, a fierce power struggle took place within the Politburo. Zinoviev, Kamenev and Stalin joined together to combat Trotsky who weakened his position by attacking the party for its increasing bureaucratic and conservative nature. Stalin thus had little difficulty in mobilizing the party against Trotsky and made sure that he had virtually no support among the delegates to the XIII Party Congress in 1924. Although there was much talk of collective leadership the purge of Trotsky's supporters was carried out in the name of support for the 'Central Committee majority'. Lenin's ban on factions thus enabled Stalin to outmanoeuvre his most serious rival. Trotsky's proposals to militarize labour meant that he could get very little support from the workers of Petrograd or Moscow, and just at the time when the triumvirate launched their attack on him he fell ill. He was sharply criticized in the Politburo, attacked by Stalin in *Pravda*, and by Zinoviev in the Communist International. Accepting defeat, Trotsky left for the Caucasus to recover his health. Shortly after the Party Congress condemned him for his opposition to the leadership Lenin died. Lenin might possibly have supported Trotsky against these attacks and without his support Trotsky was doomed.

The dead Lenin became the object of such veneration that the firm foundations of the cult of the personality were laid. Petrograd was renamed Leningrad, Lenin thus being made the direct heir of Tsar Peter. Stalin, who still remained a shadowy figure in the background and who appeared somewhat insignificant besides the flamboyant and absurdly vain Zinoviev and the weak but intelligent Kamenev, spoke in sycophantically modest terms of his humility in the face of the towering example of the late lamented leader and set about recruiting 240,000 new party members from the working class in the 'Lenin Enrolment'. In this much trumpeted reform of the party to honour the Great Leader, the General Secretary saw to it that unreliable elements were purged and that only those who were loyal to him were admitted. The small elite and revolutionary party of Lenin had now been transformed into a mass party whose function was to run the affairs of a great state and whose members did not wish to place their prestige and their privileges in jeopardy by rashly criticising the leadership. Meanwhile Stalin could bide his time, waiting for the moment to become the sole legatee of the embalmed corpse in the Lenin mausoleum.

To show that he was fit for this role he delivered a series of staggeringly crude and jejune lectures which were published as 'On the Foundations of Leninism'. Intellectuals in the party took no notice of this effort to tend the sacred flame, but it was soon to become the bible of the less sophisticated party members and established Stalin as the leading expert on the new orthodoxy of 'Leninism' which had to be defended against all manner of hideous heresies. At a party meeting in May 1924 Trotsky sat in silence while Zinoviev and Kamenev insisted that Lenin had been quite wrong in suggesting that Stalin should be removed from his post, and the attempt by Lenin's widow to get the will read aloud was defeated and the document was merely circulated among leading party members. Stalin thus avoided the humiliation of having Lenin's harsh criticism broadcast to the party congress.

Trotsky tried to fight back, aiming the brunt of his attack against Kamenev and Zinoviev, blaming them for not wanting to seize power in October. He now became the object of a flood of vituperative articles and speeches, Stalin remaining largely silent, anxious to appear a moderate in this increasingly unseemly squabble. Zinoviev argued that Trotsky should be expelled from the party, but Stalin and his supporters felt that for the moment it was enough to relieve him of his duties as Commissar for War.

The struggle against Trotsky was conducted against the background of growing dissatisfaction in party circles with NEP. Activists viewed with alarm the restoration of many features of a capitalist system which included not only the privatization of sectors of industry, the acceptance of the profit motive, the decentralization of planning and such obvious signs of bourgeois degeneration as the return of prostitutes to city streets and the servility of tip-hungry waiters. Some began to feel that the revolution had done little but help to enrich the 'Nepmen' who dominated the retail trade and prospered greatly. For most Russians these were welcome signs that things were returning to normal, but there were serious economic problems of which the most critical was the steady rise in agricultural prices relative to industrial prices. Industry was desperately short of capital and was selling on a declining market. Prices were cut still further, wages fell, and unemployment began to cause concern. Former managers of industry were given their jobs back, granted many privileges and often admitted to the party. Thus for many workers NEP seemed to be an almost complete restoration of the bad old ways of pre-revolutionary capitalism. The trades unions were as much instruments of production as they were organizations for the protection of the interests of the working class; and the workers were further disciplined by the traditional threat of unemployment.

Industry banded together in trusts determined to overcome the collapse of prices which took place in 1922. Wholesale syndicates were formed to artificially inflate prices and by 1923 this resulted in a 'reverse scissors' crisis in which industrial prices outstripped agricultural prices; the widening gap appearing on a graph, in Trotsky's vivid analogy, like the opening blades of a pair of scissors. The scissors began to close in late 1923 thanks to an excellent harvest which brought general prosperity. Prices of certain basic commodities were fixed in an attempt to overcome some of the worst features of NEP, and the industrial workers were appeased by promises of higher wages. But this industrial recovery was one-sided and a matter of concern to many Bolsheviks. Recovery had been largely confined to the consumer industries, and heavy industry was lagging badly behind, and although one risked being branded a 'Trotskyite' for saying so, it was generally agreed that socialism would be built on the foundations of heavy industry. But for the moment all seemed to be well for the crisis had been overcome. If it was regrettable that the Nepman and the Kulak prospered, it could be pointed out that the free market principles of NEP had been curtailed by price controls and the economy was growing steadily. The central issue of the relationship between the market and state control of the economy was still unresolved and could hardly be settled within the framework of NEP, particularly while the struggle against Trotsky, the most outspoken advocate of heavy industry, was still being waged.

The harvest of 1924 was not particularly good and agricultural prices began to shoot up again. This triggered off a fresh round of debates within the party. Most Bolsheviks felt that NEP should be continued and that the peasantry should be helped since the economy was so dependent on agriculture. Preobrazhensky, a leading economist, put forward an alternative scheme which he called 'primitive socialist accumulation' whereby the peasantry should be exploited in order to provide the capital needed for industrial expansion. This view was strongly attacked by his co-author of 'The ABC of communism', Bukharin, who believed that the peasants should be encouraged to 'get rich' and that this wealth could then be filtered by less ferocious means into industrial investment. To Preobrazhensky this was a betrayal of socialism, but Bukharin replied that his views were nothing but an intellectual justification of Trotskyism.

Stalin was careful not to get too closely involved in this debate, but since further concessions were made to the peasantry in 1925 it was generally assumed that he sided with Bukharin. This impression was heightened in the ensuing struggle between Bukharin and Zinoviev. In September 1925 Zinoviev published a scathing attack on Bukharin for his pro-Kulak policy, for his 'get rich' philosophy and for his refusal to see NEP as anything but a retreat. At the same time Zinoviev attacked Stalin for his ideas on 'socialism in one country' which he saw as a betrayal of socialist internationalism. At the XIV Congress in December 1925 Stalin gave somewhat lukewarm support to Bukharin and thus secured the defeat of Zinoviev who in turn was supported by Stalin's other rival, Kamenev. Stalin followed up this victory by a massive attack on the Leningrad party organization which was the basis of Zinoviev's power. The operation was entirely successful and Zinoviev was left without support.

Zinoviev and Kamenev, although they had been outspoken opponents of Trotsky, now found themselves in the same camp. They agreed with Trotsky that industralization must come before the enrichment of the peasantry, and they also agreed that Stalin had become far too powerful. Stalin had little difficulty in routing the resulting 'United Opposition' in the summer of 1926. Zinoviev was dismissed from the Politburo and Kamenev lost all his offices. Soon afterwards Trotsky lost his seat in the Politburo. Pressure on the opposition was kept up. They were threatened with expulsion from the party, denied access to the press and their meetings were disrupted by hooligans. In 1927 Trotsky and Zinoviev were expelled first from the Central Committee and then from the party. Trotsky was exiled to Alma Ata in Kazakhstan near the Chinese border, Zinoviev and Kamenev to the less distant town of Kaluga.

The left opposition could be destroyed so easily because it was out of touch with the mood of the vast mass of the Russian people. After the terrible experience of the Great War, the revolution, the civil war, famine and almost complete social disruption they wanted peace and quiet. If the Russia of NEP was not the socialist paradise which some had dreamt of, it was at least a society in which most people felt that they were better off than they had been for years, and there were hopeful signs that further improvements were just around the corner. Stalin had been very skilful in not associating himself too closely with Bukharin. He had attacked his unfortunate 'get rich' slogan and differed with the opposition only on the matter of the timing of the industrialization drive. Once he believed that the industrial sector was strong enough to take on the peasantry he had no hesitations whatsoever in unleashing the day of reckoning with the peasants, which all Bolsheviks knew in their heart of hearts had to come. Poorer peasants loathed the Kulaks, workers detested the bourgeois specialists and managers and the Nepmen were seen as seedy parasites. Behind all the ominous talk of 'Thermidor' was a determination in certain circles that the revolution should push forward to make the sufferings of the past worthwhile and also to open up positions of power and influence to those who felt that they had been cheated. It was precisely these elements which Stalin was able to mobilize in his bid for absolute power.

By 1927 the wealthier peasants were prospering, but there was very little that they could buy with their money. It was therefore advantageous for them to hoard their produce, for money had little value and withholding commodities from the market pushed prices up still further, guaranteeing even greater profits at some future date. The Central Committee now began to denounce the Kulaks in terms very similar to those that had been used by the United Opposition and even declared war on the Kulaks. On the other hand it was admitted that the Kulaks were by far the most efficient producers because of the larger scale of their farms and therefore had to be encouraged. Stalin did not agree. He felt that the answer lay in collectivizing the smaller peasants, thus forming larger and more efficient units of production, although he initially suggested that this should be done by gentle persuasion rather than violence. There was a widespread feeling that something drastic needed to be done because the Soviet Union was in the middle of a war scare which may or may not have been deliberately manipulated by the party. Whatever the case, it served to heighten the crisis and the peasants were even more reluctant to bring their goods to market. The opposition were now branded as traitors who were prepared to stab the country in the back just at the moment when the enemy were at the gates, and the crisis was used to justify the requisition of foodstuffs by force just as had been done during the period of war communism.

Discontent on the land was rife and powerful voices were raised in defence of the peasantry. Among the most important were Bukharin, who was leader of the Comintern as well as editor of *Pravda*, the trades union leader Tomsky, and the titular head of the Soviet government, Rykov. A compromise was reached in the summer of 1928 between Stalin and this opposition group. It was admitted that excesses had taken place, prices were allowed to rise somewhat and assurances were given that future grain collections would be conducted with due regard to 'revolutionary legality'. But at the same time it was made clear that the industrialization programme would push ahead and that food would be provided for the cities by whatever means were deemed necessary. The result was that the peasants became even more adept at concealing their produce, the criminal code was used to enforce requisitions by the so-called 'Urals-Siberian method', and without coercion no produce was delivered up at all because of a thriving black market. Bread rationing now had to be imposed in the cities and the countryside was plunged into a crisis which seemed to many to be the first stage of a peasants' revolt.

Although the right opposition continued to urge caution and conciliation there was a widespread belief that NEP had failed. All agreed that large-scale production was the answer to improved agriculture, and that without an increase in agricultural production industry would not be able to expand. Most now felt that the hated Kulak was incapable and unwilling to fulfil this role, and that the answer lay, as Stalin had tentatively suggested in the past, in the creation of co-operatives from the lands of the smaller peasants. Agriculture would be industrialized, industry supplying the machinery that was needed and the collective farms would feed the industrial workers. The socialist policy of collectivization and mechanization would end the hoarding, speculating and the social and economic disparities on the land, thus enabling industry and agriculture to move forward in harmony.

The first five-year plan had been discussed at the XV Congress in 1927 at a time when Stalin had decided that the conciliation of the peasantry was no longer necessary or desirable, and perversely when the attack on the Trotskyite–Zinovievite opposition, the group which was associated with speedy industrialization, was at its height.

The five-year plan was not only opposed by the right opposition on the grounds that its goals were set too high and the pace was too frantic, but also by the non-party experts and managers who were happy with NEP and did not want to see any changes. In March 1928 a spectacular public trial was held of fifty-five engineers and managers from the coal mines of the Shakhty area in the Don basin. The accused confessed their guilt in lurid terms, claiming that they were saboteurs hired by foreign powers. Eleven of the accused were condemned to death and five were executed. A mass purge of other such experts was not possible simply because they were badly needed if the five-year plan were to succeed, but the Shakhty trial was a foreshadowing of larger and more gruesome show trials. Stalin however was quite prepared to destroy these 'bourgeois technical experts' at the first possible opportunity for he was determined not only to industrialize as quickly as possible, but to do it in a way which seemed to be revolutionary and proletarian. The cost of this revolution was of little concern to him, but the means employed were vital.

The way was thus prepared for the five-year plan by direct confrontation with the peasantry, by cowing the suspect bourgeois experts and also by the increased exploitation of labour. Given the chronic shortage of capital, productivity had to rise faster than wages, and it was hoped that this could be achieved by strict discipline, rationalization, by non-monetary rewards such as the adulation afforded 'Heroes of Labour' and by requiring workers to sacrifice their Saturdays as 'Communist Saturdays' when they worked without pay. At the same time real wages fell, either by the refusal to allow increases at a time of inflation or by fixing 'norms', a useful euphemism for the despised capitalist exploitative system of piece work. This direct exploitation of the working class necessitated a curtailment of the authority of the trades unions which under NEP had secured some benefits for the workers and were not simply coercive organizations. It was thus no coincidence that Tomsky was a leading member of the right opposition.

This right opposition was never more than a minority of the Politburo and proved far easier to destroy than had the left opposition of Trotsky and his allies. The right felt that the pace of industrialization was far too hectic, that agriculture had to be greatly improved before industrial production could be significantly increased, and perhaps most important of all they believed that NEP was Lenin's true legacy and should not be drastically changed either in its economic or social aspects. Although Bukharin was a skilled polemicist and published his ideas in an important article in *Pravda*, the opposition was never properly organized. Its centres of power were within the trades union movement and the Moscow party organization. Stalin had no difficulty in purging the Moscow party, leaving the task to his trusted henchman Molotov. Kaganovich, another of Stalin's more ruthless supporters, was entrusted with the task of destroying Tomsky. This did not prove too difficult as Tomsky resigned his position as president of the central council of the trades unions and as a further protest did not attend the final session of the trades union congress in December 1928. That was the effective end of his career. Bukharin was destroyed in 1929, denounced by Stalin as a 'right opportunist' and 'capitulationist'. An attempt by the right to link up with the remnants of the left opposition against Stalin, whom Bukharin described to Kamenev as a reincarnation of Genghis Khan, was a complete failure. Kamenev had never been a resolute man and was now broken, and Trotsky from his place of exile said: 'With Stalin against Bukharin? Yes. With Bukharin against Stalin? Never!' Although the attack on the right opposition was at first kept from public scrutiny, partly because Bukharin enjoyed a certain popularity, by the end of 1929 they were forced to recant in the pages of *Pravda* and they were left without power or influence. Their policy of caution and consideration for the peasant had no appeal whatsoever to the party activists who now dominated Soviet society and who saw in the plans for forced industrialization further opportunities to advance their careers. Stalin's control over the party was thus based not simply on his ruthlessness and his skill in manipulating a vast bureaucratic apparatus, it was also a result of his being able to give the party what it wanted and to offer glittering prospects of a new and more thoroughgoing socialist society.

The five-year plan was first discussed in March of 1926, but the final draft was not approved until the party conference of 1929. Its emphasis was on the production of iron and steel. An agreement was reached with Ford to build cars and trucks, and particular emphasis was placed on tractors which were needed for the collectivization programme and also because the factories could be relatively easily converted to military production, particularly of tanks, should the need arise. Armaments played an important part in the plan, although this aspect was rarely discussed in public. But it was not until the second five-year plan that they assumed overriding importance. Steel was the magic word, symbolic of strength, of industry and even of socialism. Stalin, the 'Man of Steel', became the high priest of this new cult to which everything had to be sacrificed.

For all the careful preparation of the plan it contained a number of serious weaknesses and false assumptions and failed to make room for unpleasant contingencies. It was assumed that there would be no serious disruption of agriculture and that crops would at least equal the average of the previous few years. The catastrophic effects of collectivization were therefore not foreseen, even if a crisis had been predicted as the result of a natural crop failure. It was assumed that individual productivity would rise faster than wages and that the costs of production would therefore go down. In fact the desperate shortage of capital plus the increased demand for labour resulted in the wage bill rising twice as fast as productivity. It was further assumed that there would be an increase in the volume of world trade when in fact the five-year plan coincided with the great depression. It was further estimated that defence expenditures would decrease when in fact they were greatly increased after the Japanese invasion of Manchuria in 1931. The obsession with steel was such that it was forgotten that steel production was dependent on adequate transportation, on the supply of raw materials and on fuel. Production targets were constantly changed upwards and even the title of the plan was a misnomer, for it was finished after four years.

The exact achievements of the first five-year plan are difficult to assess because the statistics are highly questionable and prices are misleadingly quoted in 1926–27 roubles, without making allowance for the high rate of inflation during the period of the plan. Nevertheless, progress was spectacular and existing industrial enterprises greatly improved their output. New cities such as Magnitogorsk and Komsomolsk were built, the Dneiper dam was completed largely thanks to American expertise, new industrial centres were built and existing ones expanded. Little of this had an effect on the first five-year plan, but production was to come on stream in the second plan. For all the exaggerated claims and dubious production figures the results were impressive, particularly at a time when the capitalist world was suffering the worst effects of the depression. Blinded by the results as they were presented in official propaganda, few questioned the human costs of this impressive advance and Soviet planning seemed to be a model for the rest of the world. The five-year plan seemed to provide a blueprint for a better society, free from the dislocations of the anarchy of capitalist production and from the misery of unemployment.

Undoubtedly the greatest disaster during the period of the first five-year plan was in agriculture. Industrial workers suffered many of the frightful effects of a totalitarian regime devoted to increasing production at any cost, but the peasantry fared even worse. The plan did not foresee any sweeping changes in agriculture during the next five years and an excellent harvest was predicted for 1929. The problem remained one of collection rather than of actual production. High quotas were imposed, particularly on the Kulaks, and brigades of officials were sent to the countryside to ensure that everything was collected in excess of the amount needed for the peasant's own consumption. This was done with considerable brutality, the peasants being fined, imprisoned and driven from their land. A state of class war existed in the countryside. Party officials began to press for an increased rate of collectivization although they assumed that it would still be voluntary and that it would take a considerable time to complete. Peasant resistance to collectivization increased their determination to press ahead, even without the consent of the peasantry. It was still undecided what to do with the Kulaks. Some argued that their expertise was needed to make the collective farms efficient, others claiming that as class enemies they would sabotage any efforts to socialize agriculture. It was not until the end of 1929 that Stalin made the ominous announcement to a conference on agriculture that the Kulaks had to be 'liquidated as a class', and it was not a very big step to set about liquidating them as people.

In the winter of 1929–30 hordes of workers, party activists and agricultural specialists, backed up by units of the Red Army, descended on the countryside to force the peasants into collective farms. The Kulaks had their property confiscated and were driven off the land. Any peasant who resisted collectivization was instantly branded a Kulak and suffered the same fate. Those who were responsible for the collectivization campaign had precious little experience of agriculture, no understanding of the peasant mind and were armed with vague and often contradictory instructions. The result was unimaginable chaos and brutality. Peasants slaughtered their livestock rather than surrender them to the Kolkhoz. Many officials of the collectivization programme were murdered by outraged peasants. The collectivizers soon forgot that the programme had been intended to be voluntary and something approaching a civil war raged throughout the countryside.

It soon became obvious to all but the blindest advocate of collectivization at any cost that there would have to be respite if the crops were to be sown in the spring. In March 1930 Stalin published an article entitled 'Dizzy with Success' in which he blamed subordinate officials for the excesses of the programme, called a halt to further collectivization and allowed most collectivized animals, except those which had belonged to the villainous Kulaks, to be returned to their owners. The peasants reacted to this step back by withdrawing from the collectives in large numbers so that within a short space of time the number of collectivized peasants halved. The retreat was a necessary move and it saved the spring sowings. Excellent weather conditions resulted in a record crop in 1930, but this was only a temporary respite. Once the harvest was in the collectivization programme began again with a vengeance, party activists stung by what they felt were Stalin's unjust criticisms pushed ahead and met with very little resistance from a demoralized peasantry. The harvests of 1931 and 1932 were disastrous but foodstuffs were collected regardless of the need to provide animal feed; as a result vast numbers of animals were slaughtered, causing severe shortages in the following years. Even in the most prosperous agricultural regions there was widespread famine from which millions of peasants died. In December 1932 internal passports were required for the peasants so that they were unable to leave the land even though they were starving to death. Yet in spite of these restrictions 9 million peasants left the land to work in the industrial labour force during the period of the first five-year plan. On the whole it was the younger and more vigorous peasants who took this step, thus further weakening the rural economy. The result was probably the greatest social upheaval in Russian history. Rural life was transformed and there was a massive migration to the industrial centres. Such a change was truly revolutionary.

Collectivization was thus a human tragedy and an economic disaster. The specialists needed for collectivization simply did not exist, for the Soviet state had neglected to train sufficient numbers of agronomists, veterinarians and engineers that were essential if collectivization were to be successful. The Kulaks, who were by far the most experienced and productive farmers, had all been slaughtered or driven off into exile and were thus not even given the chance to contribute to the collective farms. For all the talk of the industrialization of agriculture the tractors and machines which alone would have made the huge collective farms viable were not yet built. Ideologues of the class war in the countryside armed with a few quotes from Marx, Lenin and Stalin, were in no position to undertake such a radical transformation and their frustrations were vented in outbreaks of violence and blind rage at what Marx had called the 'idiocy or rural life'. NEP had failed in agriculture and was irreconcilable with the socialist transformation of society, but the collectivization programme was an even greater disaster. The peasants who had seen the Bolsheviks as the architects of the revolutionary land settlement now regarded them as despots determined to destroy their way of life and to restore the full horrors of serfdom. The rift between the town and the countryside, which socialists had always tried to overcome, was now almost complete.

Planning for the second five-year plan had begun before the disastrous effects of collectivization were known and the goals set were absurdly optimistic. In 1933 it had to be completely rewritten in view of the fact that growth rates had slowed down dramatically and some important sectors of the economy were in fact stagnating. In an attempt to overcome some of the disastrous social effects of the first five-year plan a greater emphasis was placed on living standards and on consumer industries, but once the plan came into effect these goals were hastily revised and heavy industry once again became top priority. In large part this was due to the perceived need to increase the strength of the armed forces to meet the threat from Japan in the east, and after Hitler's victory in January 1933, from Germany. Defence expenditure increased from 1,421 million roubles in 1933 to 17,481 million roubles in 1937, or from 3.4 per cent of the total budget to 16.5 per cent. But however much the plan was changed and however exaggerated some of the claims made for it, it was still a most impressive performance. The huge new industrial centres which had been built in the first plan now came into production and the Soviet Union was transformed into an industrial giant with a vast armaments industry without which the Nazi onslaught in 1941 could never have been resisted.

The second five-year plan marked a retreat from some of the fervent excesses of the first plan. As early as 1931 Stalin had spoken out against 'vulgar egalitarianism', thus paving the way for the introduction of wage incentives and large disparities in wages and salaries. Faced with the results of the startling ineptitude of ill-trained party zealots, Stalin also suggested that bourgeois experts were needed after all. Such moderation was a direct response to glaringly obvious shortcomings in the first plan, but it was also further rejection of the needs and aspirations of the working class who were seen not as the self-conscious makers of history or as those in whose interests the revolution had been carried out, but rather as mere means of production. The new working-class hero was not the revolutionary and the militant but Stakhanov, a dim-witted-looking miner who hacked fourteen times more coal than was required by the norm. Detested by his fellow-workers for making possible an even greater exploitation of labour, he was also symbolic of a new

individualism and of the collapse of the legendary proletarian solidarity which at least in theory had been a basic tenet of all marxism.

In 1937 industrial growth slowed down significantly. In part this
was due to a marked reduction in the rate of industrial investment
caused by a greater emphasis on stockpiling arms. But a more
significant cause was the disastrous effects of the great purge.

Between the trial of the Shakhty engineers in 1928 and the beginning of the great purge there were a number of trials in which the
prosecution learnt some valuable lessons. The trial of the 'industrial
party' in 1930 was a complete farce as some of the more ominous
of the co-conspiritors were in fact dead. This did not stop some of
the accused from being condemned to death, although the sentences
were later commuted. In the following year there was a widely
publicized trial of Mensheviks accused of being pessimistic about the
prospects of the first five-year plan. In 1933 eighteen engineers
working for Metro-Vickers were accused of sabotage, six of whom
were British citizens. The need for foreign experts, a degree of
concern for public opinion abroad and singularly unconvincing
evidence for the prosecution resulted in light sentences. The trial of
the Bukharinite M. N. Ryutin in 1934 started off a mass purge of
right-wing elements in the party which resulted in several hundred
thousand expulsions and the exile of leaders such as Zinoviev and
Kamenev; but it should be pointed out that for Stalin distinctions
between left, right and centre were of little significance. It would
seem that Stalin believed that Ryutin was out to murder him, but
his colleagues on the Politburo did not share the view that political
opposition necessarily took the form of a desire to physically exter-
minate the opponent.

In December 1934 Kirov, the Leningrad party boss, was
murdered outside his office. The murderer, Leonid Nikolaev, was
arrested, tried *in camera* and executed within the month. It was said
that Nikilaev had been previously associated with Zinoviev. All this
was most fortunate for Stalin. Kirov was his most likely successor,
enjoyed a degree of popular support and had expressed some
concerns about Stalin's dictatorial methods and the excesses of the
five-year plan. At the same time it gave him the opportunity to settle
his accounts with the Zinovievite opposition. Stalin profited so much
from the murder and reacted so quickly afterwards with extensive
amendments to the criminal code that it seems quite probable that
he was responsible for the murder. Large numbers of left opposition-
ists, including Zinoviev and Kamenev, were imprisoned and further
sinister changes were made to the criminal code including the noto-

rious article 58 on counter-revolutionary activities. The death sentence could now be applied to twelve-year-old children and the families of those proclaimed guilty could be punished regardless of whether they had any knowledge of the criminal activities committed by a family member.

Whilst Stalin carefully set the stage for the great purge the new constitution was proclaimed in 1936. It was largely the work of Bukharin, and with its guarantees of freedom of speech, religious toleration and the right of the republics to secede from the Union it was celebrated as the most democratic constitution in the world. All this was a sham and there was an all-round retreat to a more repressive society. The Soviet Union had been widely admired for its enlightened attitude towards sexual morality and as the only country where homosexuality was not a criminal offence it was particularly admired by those who were persecuted for such proclivities. In the 1930s all this changed. Divorce was made considerably more difficult, abortions were made illegal and homosexuals were prosecuted. Then in August 1936 the first of the great show trials began.

The principal 'mad dogs' whom the prosecutor, Vyshinsky, demanded should be shot were Kamenev and Zinoviev who were forced to confess that they had organized the murder of Kirov and that they would have killed Stalin as well had they had the chance. Behind these representatives of the left opposition hovered the sinister shadow of Trotsky who was denounced as the master mind of these murderous plots.

There was to have been a second great trial that year of Bukharin, Rykov and Tomsky along with other members of the right opposition, but the charges were dropped for lack of evidence. Tomsky committed suicide and Bukharin and Rykov refused to confess to crimes of which they were innocent. The NKVD chief, Yagoda, was dismissed, probably for failing to secure these confessions, and was replaced by the even more murderous Ezhov. Most important of all, Bukharin was able to secure a majority in the Politburo which threw out the charges against him and his associates. This only postponed his fate since those who voted for Bukharin were all later to be executed.

In January 1937 Radek, Sokolnikov, Pyatakov and Serebryakov, all of them prominent Bolsheviks who were accused of being the ring-leaders of the 'anti-Soviet Trotskyite centre', were brought to trial and accused of being the agents of Germany and Japan and attempting to sabotage Soviet industry on behalf of their foreign masters. The accused were either shot or died shortly afterwards in prison camps.

This absurd vision of a vast fascist plot to destroy the Soviet Union in which leading Bolsheviks were implicated got completely out of hand in the summer of 1937 when the military leadership was brought to trial on charges of conspiring with the Nazis. Although such evidence as there was against them had been fabricated in Berlin, and it seems highly unlikely that Stalin was not aware of this, the result was an incredible slaughter of the senior officers of the armed forces. Marshal Tukhachevsky, the outstanding Soviet strategic thinker, who had incurred the wrath of Stalin as early as 1920, was murdered and of the five Soviet Marshals only Voroshilov and Budenny survived. All eight admirals were killed, as were all eleven deputy commissars of defence and seventy-five out of eighty members of the Supreme Military Council. Almost all corps and divisional commanders were executed and 221 out of 397 brigade commanders. It is impossible to tell whether, had these executions not taken place, the Red Army would have been more effective against the Germans in 1941, but there can be no doubt whatever that the armed forces suffered terribly. The men who stepped into their shoes were mostly second-rate, lacking in intellectual curiosity or any understanding of modern mobile warfare. A group of unimaginative hacks took the place of these highly professional, skilled and experienced officers, and it was impossible to replace the 35,000 executed officers without a certain drop in standards.

The last of the great show trials was held in March 1938. This time it was the turn of the right opposition who had so narrowly escaped in 1936. These included Bukharin, Rykov and Yagoda, the latter to be destroyed by the instrument which he had done so much to perfect. To make doubly sure of their conviction, Vyshinsky accused them of forming a bloc of right-wingers and Trotskyites. Although this was sheer fantasy and Trotsky had nothing but scorn for Bukharin's position, death sentences were meted out to most of the accused. At the end of the year Ezhov was replaced by Beria as head of the NKVD. He was to finally settle accounts with Trotsky who was murdered in Mexico in August 1940.

Those who escaped the death penalty were sent off to labour camps in remote regions. In what David Rousset has described as the *univers concentrationnaire* there were some 6 million inhabitants by 1937. The social upheaval caused by the purges resulted in a social revolution which transformed Russian society. There was a vast increase in the size of the bureaucracy which was now staffed by ill-educated, rapacious and power-hungry people who were ideally suited to indulge in the cult of the personality. They owed every-thing to Stalin. They could blame all the shortcomings of the system they served on the vile machinations of the armies of saboteurs and agents of foreign powers who were being unmasked in the show trials. They were also delighted to see the high and the mighty fall, and joined in an unseemly scramble for power and influence. As one after another of the old leadership was removed there was increas-ingly less room for manoeuvre to those who stayed behind, and Stalin found it correspondingly easier to assert his unchallenged control over the state apparatus. But the new ruling class which emerged was anxious and unsure of its position. Stalin showed no compunction in liquidating a number of his prominent followers. His henchmen knew that they too could be easily deposed and Stalin deliberately fostered such feelings of insecurity to strengthen his absolute dictatorship.

In 1930 Trotsky wrote: 'Of course the fundamental difficulties of socialist construction lie beyond the will of the leadership. They are rooted in the impossibility of building a socialist society in a back-ward country, an extremely backward one.' As early as 1921 Lenin had written that this small Russian proletariat 'owing to the war and to the desperate poverty and ruin, has become declassed, i.e. dislodged from its class groove and has ceased to exist as a prole-tariat'. In the place of a developed proletariat through whose liber-ation, according to classical marxist theory, the whole of society could become liberated, we find a massive bureaucratic apparatus whose bosses were, where possible, of proletarian origin, but which was essentially alienated from and inimical to the true interests of the working class. Where Marx and the young Lenin had talked of the withering away of the state the Soviet Union saw an extraor-dinary hypertrophy of the state apparatus and in a strange mockery of Marx this immense superstructure determined and shaped the infrastructure. Lenin and Stalin, far from being in the direct line of succession to Marx as was so loudly claimed, in fact turned him on his head.

Trotsky once wrote: 'Essentially the revolution means the people's final break with the Asiatic, with the Seventeenth Century, with Holy Russia, with icons and cockroaches.' Stalin's Russia reverted to many of these earlier forms. He saw himself as heir to Ivan the Terrible and to Peter the Great, and like Tsar Peter he created a new ruling class which forced through industrialization and further exploited the peasantry. Sharp differentiations of rank and status were emphasized by the reintroduction of uniforms and medals. In spite of the degree of dependence on the West for the technology needed for industrialization Russia again turned inward, became deeply suspicious of the foreign and the modern and became, in short, increasingly 'Asiatic'. Around the cult of Lenin and Stalin there arose a new secular religion with its mummified holy relics and its icons and which demanded extraordinary sacrifices and acts of faith from its followers. Stalin's revolution created a great modern industrial state, but in other respects it was profoundly reactionary, reverting to older forms and modes of thought although at the same time faithfully carrying out Lenin's legacy. Those who argue that Stalin betrayed Lenin fondly imagine that NEP was something other than an admission of defeat, that it was a Leninist blue-print for socialism. Had Lenin lived it is possible that the regime would not have been quite so capricious and brutal, but the experience of war communism, even when allowances are made for the exigencies of the civil war, shows that this may be simply a matter of giving Lenin the benefit of the doubt. It is obvious that the *smychka* – the alliance between the workers and peasants – which was tenous at the best of times, was bound to be broken at some time if the Bolshevik vision of socialism was to be realized. In this sense the alternative programme of Bukharin, even if it had worked in economic terms, was irreconcilable with the creation of this form of socialism. The resulting non-capitalist party-dominated monolithic state seemed a cruel betrayal of the idealism and the unselfish vision of many of the revolutionaries, but it was a society which was still able to call upon those utopian aspirations without which any society, revolutionary or not, will atrophy. Stalinist Russia was still a country which millions felt was worth fighting and dying for, and Stalin's industrial revolution, violent, harsh but relatively brief when compared with the historical experience of the advanced capitalist countries, provided the weapons to do the job.

CHAPTER FIVE
Eastern Europe

Several new nation states were created in eastern Europe at the Paris Peace Conference. They were based on the Wilsonian premise that the self-determination of peoples offered the best assurance of international peace and progress, provided that self-determination was combined with a democratic system of government. But it soon became apparent that strict observation of this principle would result in the creation of states that would not be viable, and as a result Czechs and Slovaks constituted only 65 per cent of the population of Czechoslovakia. Even defeated and truncated countries, like Hungary and Bulgaria, still had 10 per cent of their populations made up of ethnic minorities.

POLAND

Poland, with a population of 30 million, was the largest and strongest of these new nation states and yet Molotov described it as 'the monstrous bastard of the Peace of Versailles', John Maynard Keynes said it was 'an economic impossibility whose only industry is Jew-baiting' and Lloyd George complained that giving Upper Silesia to Poland would be like giving a clock to a monkey. The problems of Poland sprang in large part from the fact that before 1914 the country had been partitioned between the Russian, Austro-Hungarian and German empires, and the republican leaders disagreed over which of the former partitioning powers would make the most useful ally.

The republicans were divided into two main camps and by 11 November 1918 there were two Polish governments. The leading politician in Congress Poland was Roman Dmowski, whose National Democratic Party supported the Russian war effort in the hope that France and Britain would induce St Peterburg to establish an autonomous reunited Poland at the end of the war which would be under Russian protection. He was opposed by Jósef Pilsudski who, from his exile in Austria, considered Russia the main enemy and who formed a Polish Legion in Galicia to fight on the side of the Central Powers. When the German army occupied Congress Poland they established the so-called Regency in Warsaw which amounted to little more than a puppet government designed to recruit Poles for the German army. Pilsudski protested against this sham and refused all further co-operation with the Central Powers, whereupon he was promptly dispatched to a prison in Magdeburg. One of his lieutenants, Jósef Haller, made his way to Murmansk and thence to France, where he formed a new Polish Legion under his command which fought with considerable distinction for the allied cause.

Dmowski and Pilsudski were remarkably contrasting characters. Dmowski was a *petit bourgeois*, he was dispassionate, conservative, and a Russophile who rejected the great Polish uprising of 1863 as a monumental blunder. Pilsudski, on the other hand, was a nobleman, a Russophobe and a passionate patriot in the classic Polish romantic tradition who thought that the 1863 revolt was one of the proudest chapters of Polish history. He had begun his political career in a terrorist organization which plotted the assassination of Tsar Alexander III, for which association he was sentenced to five years exile in Siberia in 1887. Lenin's older brother was one of the leaders of this group and was executed for his role in the plot. Pilsudski later became a leader of the Polish Socialist Party (PPS) and crossed swords with Rosa Luxemburg and the Social Democracy of the Congress Kingdom and Lithuania.

After the armistic Pilsudski was released from prison and the Regency Council, which had been established under the auspices of Germany and Austria-Hungary in 1916, invested him with full powers. In the meantime the Allies recognized the Polish National Committee in Paris under Dmowski's leadership. Pilsudski as head of state controlled the army, the administrative machinery and the police, but Dmowski had the ear of the victorious Allies in Paris. He therefore promptly set about defaming Pilsudski as 'pro-German' and, to make doubly certain that the Allies would distance themselves from him, suggested that he was infected with bolshevism. Pilsudski realized that he needed the co-operation of his opponent in order to obtain economic assistance and diplomatic recognition for Poland from the Entente, and therefore attempted to negotiate a truce. He sent a letter to 'Dear Roman', who, fully aware of the strength of his position, refused the invitation to join forces with him. The deadlock between these two men was finally ended by the famous pianist Jan Paderewski who secured the recognition of Pilsudski as head of state and Pilsudski, in his turn, appointed Dmowski and Paderewski as official Polish delegates to the Paris Peace Conference.

Elections for the *Sejm* were held on 26 January 1919, the first universal, equal, secret and direct parliamentary elections in Polish history. The following month Pilsudski placed his dictatorial powers at the disposal of the *Sejm* and announced that henceforth he would adhere to strictly democratic principles. Parliament in turn reaffirmed his appointment as head of state and supreme commander of the armed forces, with the proviso that he and his cabinet were henceforth responsible to the *Sejm*. It was now widely believed that Poland was firmly established as a democratic state.

This infant democracy was immediately faced with a series of wars. The Ukrainian war lasted from November 1918 to July 1919, the Posnanian war with Germany from December 1918 to June 1919, the spasmodic Silesian war from August 1919 to July 1921, the Lithuanian war from July 1919 to October 1920, the Czechoslovak war from January 1919 to July 1920 and, most important of all, the Soviet war from April to October 1921. These 'nursery brawls', as Norman Davies calls them, were a result of territorial disputes arising out of the peace settlement. Poland did not become involved in the Allied intervention in Russia as Pilsudski's government was more afraid of the Whites than the Bolsheviks and had hoped that it might be possible to form a federation of Poland, Lithuania, Byelorussia and the Ukraine in which Poland would play the dominant role. Pilsudski believed that without such a federation Poland would be unable to preserve her independence from Russia and Germany and hoped to exploit the civil war and Allied intervention to achieve this aim. In the process he almost lost the whole of Poland to the Soviet Union, and the Red Army, which had driven Pilsudski's troops back to the gates of Warsaw were defeated at the last moment at the battle known as the 'miracle on the Vistula'.

The political life of the country was dominated from the outset by the rivalry between the National Democrats, also known as the

Endeks, and Pilsudski's supporters. This was compounded by the bitter personal rivalry between Pilsudski and Dmowski. Over the years their political and ideological differences faded into insignificance, but their mutual animosity persisted. The National Democratic Party, the party of the middle class, was nationalist, conservative and anti-Semitic. As the largest single party in the constituent assembly they dominated its proceedings. Throughout the inter-war years the party was supported by the Catholic Church which had played such an important role in the nationalist movement, particularly in the western part of the country. Poles in the west remained loyal to the party after the war and therefore the socialist and peasant parties were unable to make much headway in that region.

Even before the Great War the Polish socialist movement was split into two factions: the Social Democracy of the Kingdom of Poland and Lithuania (SDKPiL), which was led by Rosa Luxemburg and which considered a social revolution to be the prerequisite for a truly independent Polish nation, and the moderate and nationalistic Polish Socialist Party (PPS) which was led by Pilsudski and to which the majority of socialists belonged. After 1918 Pilsudski and a number of his followers renounced socialism. A Polish Communist Party was formed in 1918 from the SDKPiL and left-wing elements of the PPS, but throughout the interwar period it was little more than an insignificant sect which was unable to make any headway against the traditional antipathy of Poles for Russians. The party was also proscribed by Pilsudski.

The peasant movement was also divided, the Polish Populist or Peasant Party being split into the 'Piast' and 'Liberation' factions. By 1925 there were ninety-two registered political parties in Poland, of which thirty-two were represented in parliament. In such a situation it was almost impossible to form a stable government and by the time Pilsudski executed his coup in May 1926 there had been fourteen different cabinets.

After much bitter wrangling a new constitution was finally adopted in March 1921. It was admirably democratic, vesting most political power in the lower house, the *Sejm*, and the authority of the president was drastically curtailed. The National Democrats, having played the predominant role in framing the constitution, were determined to restrict Pilsudski's power as much as possible. Pilsudski bitterly denounced the constitution, which was based on that of the Third Republic in France, saying that he had no intention of becoming a bird in a golden cage. He retired from public office to his estate at Sulejowek, near Warsaw, which soon became a hotbed of conspiracy and intrigue against the *Sejm*.

The Polish economy was in a terrible mess as a result of three partitions, the effects of the war and the chronic economic disruption of eastern Europe. At independence there were six currencies in circulation and a common currency had to be created. There were no government agencies to serve the whole country and no established financial institutions designed to meet the needs of the new state. There were no direct rail links between Warsaw and a number of provincial centres, for the railways had been built for the convenience of the partitioning powers. Thus there were fifty railroad lines from Austrian and German Poland which ended at the frontier of Russian Poland, but there were only ten lines which operated on the other side of this border. It was only in 1927, with the opening of Gdynia, that Poland finally secured its own seaport.

Economic development had been very uneven. Apart from Upper Silesia and a few scattered areas in Congress Poland, with their textile, coal and metallurgical industries, the infant Polish Republic was still largely rural. More than 70 per cent of the population made their living from agriculture. Even the traditional Polish markets for industry and agriculture were disrupted by the establishment of new borders in western and central Europe. The huge Russian market remained closed to Poland although large numbers of extremely backward peasants were incorporated within the eastern borders. As the Red Army retreated after the Miracle on the Vistula they took with them vast quantities of industrial machinery and rolling stock, none of which was ever returned. As a result of the endless small wars, Poland lost more than 50 per cent of its bridges, 60 per cent of its railroad stations, almost 50 per cent of its locomotives and 20 per cent of all buildings. Inflation was an acute problem. In November 1918 nine Polish marks would buy one American dollar, by the end of 1923 the exchange rate was 2,300,000 : 1. As elsewhere, many lost their savings and there was a consequent increase in social and political polarization. The blame for this unfortunate situation was often placed on a discredited parliamentary regime which was under constant attack from both left and right.

In such a situation the new democratic constitution was unlikely to work effectively. Between the promulgation of the constitution in March 1921 and Pilsudski's coup in May 1926 the country was permanently on the verge of civil war. This became apparent from the first elections for the first Legislative National Assembly in November 1922. None of the political parties was able to gain a clear mandate. Of the 444 seats in the *Sejm* the National Democrats and their allies won 126, the Right Centre 44, the Centre 88, the Left 98 and the National Minorities, a bloc of fringe parties, 89. The parties favoured by Pilsudski – the Democratic Union and the State Associations in the Eastern Marches – failed to win a single seat. As a presidential candidate Pilsudski was vigorously opposed by the right and championed by the left, but he refused to allow his name to be put forward. After five acrimonious ballots Professor Gabriel Narutowicz was elected president of the Republic on 14 December, but two days later he was gunned down by a nationalist fanatic and minor painter at the Warsaw Gallery of Fine Arts whilst chatting to the British ambassador. Narutowicz had won the election thanks to the support of the minority groups and this sealed his fate, for he was denounced by the right as the creature of the lesser breeds and particularly of the Jews. Pilsudski's followers felt that the assassination offered an ideal opportunity to deal with the National Democrats once and for all, but the leadership of the PPS was not yet ready for armed insurrection. The Speaker of the *Sejm*, the Piast-centrist Rataj, was able to surmount the crisis by urging compromise. He negotiated a non-party government under General Wladyslaw Sikorski, a legionary who had quarrelled with Pilsudski but who had still managed to remain on fairly good terms with him. Stanislaw Wojciechowski, a former socialist, was elected president with the backing of the left and the centre who united against the threat from the right.

In May 1923 a new cabinet was formed under the leadership of Wincenty Witos, the leader of the Piast wing of the Peasant Party. The Piast had been associated with the left, but in order to form this government Witos had to appeal to the right and play down the programme of land reform. This alienated the left wing of the Piast which, under the leadership of Jan Dabski, founded another Peasant Party closely associated with the Liberation faction in its opposition to the National Democrats. This split within the Piast was one of the major reasons for Witos' resignation in December 1923. Unable to control the galloping inflation, incapable of dealing with the wave of strikes and riots and without a viable majority, he was forced out of office. Once again the Pilsudski faction wanted to strike against the right but was unable to gain sufficient support from the other parties for such a move. Their position had been greatly weakened, for during his seven-month tenure of office Witos had purged the army of most of Pilsudski's supporters and Pilsudski resigned his posts as Chief of the General Staff and president of the Supreme War Council.

There followed another extra-parliamentary government under Wladyslaw Grabski whom parliament invested with exceptional powers. Grabski's major achievement was to bring inflation under control. On 14 April 1924 the mark was replaced by the gold guilder (*zloty*) and the day after this currency reform the Bank of Poland was established. The immediate results were impressive. There was a decline in unemployment, a gradual inflow of foreign capital and a short period of internal peace. But in late 1925 Germany reneged on her trade treaty with Poland and increased the tariff on Polish coal, the nation's main export. This triggered off a trade war between the two countries. By mid 1924 the *zloty* fell to half its original value and a fresh round of hyper-inflation was on the horizon.

On 20 Novmeber 1925 the Grabski government was replaced by the coalition cabinet of Count Aleksander Skrzynski. This broadly based government included the National Democrats and the PPS and in an effort to appease Pilsudski a number of his followers were restored to their leading positions in the army. But the economy went from bad to worse and by the end of 1925 a third of the labour force was unemployed. An American specialist, Edwin Kemmerer, advised the finance minister, Jerzy Zdoziechowski, to adopt a strongly deflationary policy which initially met with some success. The PPS denounced this policy as harmful to the workers and small farmers, withdrew its two ministers and went into opposition. The unemployed rioted in Lublin and elsewhere and the Skrzynski cabinet fell on 5 May 1926.

By now it seemed to most Poles that a coup was inevitable and the only real question was who would lead it: Dmowski, Sikorski, Pilsudski or someone else. When the Skrzynski government fell the president recalled the discredited Witos to form a new government. Since Witos' centre-right government of 1923 had failed so miserably this was a senseless decision which so infuriated Pilsudski and his followers that the long-awaited *coup d'état* was carried out between 12 and 15 May 1926. He was supported by all the parties of the left – the socialists, the parties of the poor peasants and even the communists – all of whom saw Pilsudski as the only alternative to home-grown fascism. There was little opposition to the destruction of the democratic state, since Pilsudski enjoyed a reputation for being incorruptible and had considerable influence in the army. But within a few months it became clear that far from being the champion of the left, Pilsudski was looking for support on the right, in spite of his lifelong opposition to all political factions associated with the industrialists and the landowners.

Unlike most dictators, Pilsudski had little interest in the details of government. In spite of his references to the 'prostitute *sejm*' he pretended that Poland was still a democracy and appointed his own creatures as prime ministers and presidents. Although he had considerable knowledge and understanding of foreign and military affairs he was bored with economic and domestic matters. He had no clear ideology or programme and contented himself with vague talk of restoring Poland's moral health and giving the nation a place in the sun. His opponents condemned such cliché-ridden pronouncements as charlatanism and one of his closest associates, Ignacy Daszynski, asked him during the coup where he was going. His reply was a simple 'I do not know'. To his supporters such vagueness was proof of his level-headed pragmatism.

Having refused the presidency, Pilsudski operated from behind the scenes and the only office he held continuously from May 1926 until his death nine years later was that of minister of war, although he served as prime minister between October 1926 and June 1928 and between August and December 1930. He rarely bothered to attend cabinet meetings and delegated official duties to his subordinates. The day-to-day business of government was left to such politicians as Professor Kazimierz Bartel, the leader of the small Labour Party in the *sejm*, who served as prime minister on two occasions between 1926 and 1930. Initially Pilsudski did not have a political organization of his own and when he established one in March 1928 its title reflected his extreme antipathy towards party politics. No dictatorship ever came up with quite such a remarkable name for the government party as the 'Non-Party Bloc for Co-operation with the Government' (BBWR). It was made up of a disparate collection of his acolytes who called themselves the 'Improvers of the Republic', breakaway factions of the Piast and Liberation parties, a splinter group of the PPS and several conservative factions, including one representing big business interests. The Bloc had no more of a clear cut programme than did their leader and was held together solely by his authority and prestige.

The early years of the Pilsudski regime were ones of relative affluence. The currency was stablilized, there were major infrastructural investments including the building of a modern port at Gdynia, which had been a sleepy seaside resort, and the construction of a

massive fertilizer plant as part of a programme to modernize agriculture which, in the event of war, could be converted to produce
ammunition. The constitution of 1921 was not openly flouted and
the only amendment was in August 1926 which gave the president
certain special powers. Unlike most dictatorships, there was a
considerable degree of personal and political freedom in Pilsudski's
Poland, at least until 1930. No political party, with the exception
of the communists, was banned; arrests were infrequent and the press
was usually left alone.

Cracks began to appear in the system as early as 1928. Once the
left began to realize that Pilsudski had no intention of supporting its
programme it began to criticize his semi-autocratic rule and to
clamour for a truly democratic parliamentary regime. Although the
BBWR emerged as the largest parliamentary group in the elections
in March that year, the left also increased its strength at the expense
of the centre and the right. The government interpreted these results
as a victory, but the left accused Pilsudski and his supporters of using
pressure tactics and the illegal use of state funds for electoral
purposes. In the spring of 1929, Gabriel Czechowicza, the finance
minister, was impeached for withholding information from parliament on certain expenditures. It soon became clear that he had done
so under instructions from Pilsudski who had disbursed these funds
during the electoral campaign. Pilsudski stoutly defended his finance
minister and called the proceedings against him 'ritual murder'. The
verdict against him was inconclusive, but the episode was considered
to be a defeat for the regime. The next eighteen months saw a
struggle for control between the Pilsudski faction and a centre-left
coalition consisting of the Piast, the Liberation, the Peasant Party,
the PPS and some other smaller groups. Pilsudski's response was to
dissolve parliament on 30 August 1930. Prior to the elections in
November the Marshal arrested a large number of opposition politicians, denouncing them as 'scoundrels'. They were mistreated,
humiliated and kept in prison until the elections were over. This
assured the regime a majority in the new parliament which eventually passed an authoritarian constitution in 1935. Having
triumphed over parliament Pilsudski assumed the prime ministership
for the second time on 25 August, but soon gave the post to one
of his creatures, Walery Slawek.

Pilsudski paid a high price for this victory. The arrests and
mistreatment of the opposition alienated even some of his staunchest
supporters including the leader of the BBWR, Tadeusz Holowko.
He now had to rely on the support of the army to maintain his

position and the situation was best summed up by Maria Dobrowska, the poet and former admirer of the Marshal: 'The moral links between the government and the majority of the population were shattered. From now on, all attempts to restore them, however well intentioned, turned out to be in vain.'

After 1930 the Pilsudski regime, known as the Sanacja (return to [political] health), came to be dominated by a inner circle of advisers and cronies. There were dubbed the 'colonels', many of whom had served in the Legion, and important offices of state were rotated among them. The old Marshal was now sick and worn out and rarely participated in the running of the government and seldom attended cabinet meetings.

Perhaps it was Pilsudski's unwillingness to direct the government which accounts in part for its lacklustre performance in the 1930s. Rigid deflationary policies, which were particularly hard on the workers and peasants, did much to protract the depression almost until the outbreak of the war. In foreign affairs, Pilsudski believed that the Soviet Union was a greater threat than Nazi Germany and imagined that Germany's bellicose proclivities could be channelled in the direction of Austria, Czechoslovakia and the Soviet Union without Poland being in any way threatened. Thus when Hitler made friendly overtures to Poland, Pilsudski willingly negotiated a non-aggression pact with Nazi Germany in January 1934.

Pilsudski died in May 1935. One month before his death the temporary absence of opposition deputies from the chamber was used as an opportunity to vote in a new constitution. Parliament's powers were curtailed, those of the president and the cabinet greatly enhanced. The 'colonels' exploited this new constitution to strengthen their hold over the country. A new electoral law restricted the franchise, prompting the opposition parties to boycott the elections of 1935 and 1938. In the elections of 1935, for example, less than 50 per cent of the eligible voters participated, as opposed to 75 per cent in 1930. The 1930s also saw the rise of the radical right and particularly of anti-Semitic organizations in Poland, fuelled by the economic crisis and emulating similar movements elsewhere in Europe. To many on the right fascism seemed to offer the only solution to the aimless drift of the government. In order to counter this threat from the extreme right and to regain some of its lost popularity, the government intensified its nationalist rhetoric. After the 1935 elections a 'non-party' *sejm* was established and the BBWR was abolished as redundant. Colonel Adam Koc created a new mass organization, the Camp of National Unity (OZN), early in 1937 which was based, according to a leading spokesman, on the principles of nationalism, social justice and organization. Unlike the BBWR, which had made no distinctions among Polish citizens, the OZN was openly anti-Semitic although it discouraged physical violence against Jews. It was hoped that forced mass emigration would provide a solution to the 'Jewish problem' and it was only the outbreak of the war which averted the passing of anti-Jewish legislation on the Nazi model.

In the post-Pilsudski period the two dominant political personalities were Ignacy Moscicki, the President of the Republic, and Eduard Rydz-Smigly, the supreme commander of the army. Neither had anything like the prestige of Pilsudski and merely headed factions within the government, the president preferring a return to constitutional rule and Rydz favouring a strengthening of the dictatorship. This dispute remained unresolved when the outbreak of war made the entire issue superfluous.

In foreign policy Jozef Beck tried to maintain a balancing act between Germany and the Soviet Union. He tried to cultivate relations with Germany without becoming involved in anti-Soviet campaigns like the anti-Comintern Pact of November 1936. This attempt to be friendly to Germany without appearing to be hostile to the Soviet Union was a disastrous failure. By the time it was repudiated in early 1939 it was too late, and Poland was soon to fall prey to both powers.

HUNGARY

On 16 October 1918, the Hungarian prime minister, Sándor Wekerle, formally dissolved the union between his country and Austria. A week later the Wekerle cabinet, long associated with the detested war and the equally unpopular Habsburg regime, resigned. Ten days later Count Mihály Károlyi assumed the post of prime minister and less than two weeks later, on 13 November, Charles IV of Habsburg was deposed and Hungary proclaimed a republic.

Károlyi was an aristocrat who held progressive views. Before the war he had advocated Hungary's withdrawal from the Dual Alliance with Germany, he proposed a more tolerant policy towards the country's minorities. He was strongly opposed to the war and even supported the Entente and Wilson's Fourteen Points and he therefore imagined that he would get lenient treatment from the Allies. On

24 October 1918 he established a National Council, consisting of his own radicals and the Social Democrats, and while this was not an elected body, it was accepted by the majority of Hungarians as a more legitimate reflection of the needs of the country than was the discredited parliament, which had been chosen on an extremely limited franchise (in 1914 less than 10 per cent of the population had the vote) and which represented the interests of the aristocracy and the wealthy.

Károlyi's first act as prime minister was to distribute his vast estate of 50,000 acres among the peasants. He then laid plans for a radical land reform. In December the franchise was extended to all men over twenty-one and all women over twenty-four. To appease the national minorities he appointed Oszkár Jászi, the leader of the bourgeois Radical Party, as minister of nationalities. Jászi, later to become a professor at Oberlin College, was an advocate of land reform and political democracy and was an impassioned opponent of the pre-war Magyarization policy. Since the Hungarians made up less than 50 per cent of the population in pre-war Hungary the problem of the nationalities was particularly pressing and Jászi was almost the only politician whom they trusted.

Károlyi's efforts to appease the nationalities came to nothing. It was far too late for conciliation and they were exhorted by their fellows in Serbia, Romania, Croatia and Bohemia to join their respective nation states which were in the process of formation in east-central Europe. The prime minister's faith in the Allies was misplaced and they made plans to deprive Historic Hungary of vast tracts of land. The chief of the Allied mission in Budapest, the French Colonel Vyx, handed Károlyi a note from the Paris Peace Conference on 20 March 1919 demanding the establishment of a depopulated neutral zone in the south-eastern part of the country in order to create a buffer area between the Hungarian and Romanian troops stationed along the demarcation line. This proposal for a neutral zone was part of Marshal Foch's suggestion for an anti-Soviet crusade which would involve Romanian troops which he had presented to the Peace Conference in February. The proposal was rejected but the section on a neutral zone in Hungary was accepted along with the idea that the population, which was almost exclusively Hungarian, would have to be evacuated.

No Hungarian politician was prepared to accede to such a demand. The Allies continued the blockade after the collapse of the Habsburg Empire and the chronic economic situation continued to worsen. Returning prisoners of war were extolling the virtues of the revolution in Russia. Since the Allies paid no heed to his entreaties and allowed his country to be dismembered by the secession states, Károlyi had no alternative but to resign. He handed over power to a new government called the Revolutionary Governing Council, a coalition of the social democratic left and communists, and then left the country. The social democrats had no desire to join with the communists, but they were bereft of western help and latched on to communist promises of Russian assistance. Károlyi gave up the reins of power believing that this popular revolutionary government was in accordance with the people's wish, and was determined not to stand in the way.

On 21 March the Hungarian Soviet Republic was proclaimed and it was to last until 4 August. Its guiding spirit was Béla Kun, a journalist and former prisoner of war in Siberia, who headed the Republic's Council of People's Commissars. The Soviet Government got off to a very bad start. It alienated the peasantry by nationalizing the land rather than redistributing it. The nationalization programme was carried out with such fanatical zeal that it covered all aspects of economic life, even the barber's shops. All industrial enterprises employing more than twenty-five workers were also nationalized. A proposal to deport all priests and memebrs of religious orders to Austria alienated the faithful. Soviet Russia, involved in the life and death struggle of the civil war, was unable to send the help which it had promised. The reign of terror instituted by the Police Commissar, Tibor Szamuely, lost the regime its remaining support. The Soviet offensive against Slovakia was halted by the intervention of the Allies and Béla Kun began a campaign against Romania which ended with the mass desertion of his troops. As has been observed by the socialist Lajos Kassáks in his reminiscences, the political inexperience and constant ideological hair-splitting of Kun and his followers made matters worse:

> The intellectuals who joined Kun before the dictatorship have become confused and enmeshed in their contradictions. They were philosophers, poets and aesthetes who stepped into the healthy storm of revolution, but they could not take the continuous fights, attacks and retreats, and at the end they sullenly slipped back to the lukewarm bottomless mud of their doctrinaire fixed ideas. Dangers abounded outside, but they gathered . . . in one of their rooms in the Soviet House and endless, bitter debates began. There was György Lukács, the former Heidelberg philosopher, Jósef Révai, former bank clerk and aesthete . . . Ervin Sinko, the young Christian Tolstoyian writer, . . . and Elena Andreevna Grabenko, Lukács' Russian wife. There were also scatterbrained ideologues. Quotations from Hegel, Marx, Kierkegaard,

Fichte, Weber, Jean Paul, Hölderlin, and Novalis were flying in the air.

Béla Kun fled with his associates to Vienna on 4 August and immediately afterwards Romanian troops entered Budapest. For the next quarter of a century the socialists and communists were virtually excluded from the political life of Hungary.

This brief Soviet regime had a great influence on the subsequent course of Hungarian history. The ruling classes were unable to come to terms with the humiliation they had suffered, and refusing to believe that their workers and peasants would start a revolution on their own, they began to look for a scapegoat. The Jews filled the bill admirably and were denounced as war profiteers and bolshevik agents. It was constantly underlined that most of the leading revolutionaries, including Béla Kun, were Jewish. This upsurge of virulent anti-Semitism was most unfortunate because the pre-war oligarchy had taken great pains to assimilate the Jews into Hungarian life and most Jews had responded favourably to this Magyarization policy. Anti-Semitism was now respectibly patriotic and, with the advent of the depression, became increasingly widespread.

During the last stages of the Soviet regime the counter-revolutionaries were active in Vienna and in south-eastern Hungary, particularly in the French-occupied cities of Arad and Szeged. In April the first of the anti-bolshevik committees was formed. The Vienna committee was formed by Count István Bethlen and those in Hungary by Miklós Horthy, a former admiral in the Austro-Hungarian navy and a former aide-de-camp to the Emperor Franz Josef. These committees were composed largely of representatives of the old oligarchy: aristocrats, army officers, civil servants and the like. When the Romanians left Budapest in November 1919, Horthy entered the capital, hanged many workers and communist sympathizers, instituted pogroms and set the stage for a ruthless and protracted white terror. The Allies were anxious to find a suitable government in Hungary to formalize the new frontiers, which had been in *de facto* existence since the signing of the armistice, and to which the Soviet regime with its appeals to Hungarian nationalism would never agree. Consequently as soon as Horthy arrived in Budapest the Allies recognized the counter-revolutionary regime of Károly Huszár, which was backed by the admiral's troops.

Elections for a national assembly were held in January 1920. Although they were ostensibly held according to the new universal suffrage with secret balloting, the continued white terror made a

mockery of the whole enterprise. The socialists boycotted the elections and the communists were proscribed from participation by
special legislation. The largest number of seats (seventy one) were
won by the Smallholder's Party led by István Szabó and the Christian National Union, made up of various right-wing groups,
obtained eighty-one seats. These two groups formed a coalition to
form the new government.

Hungary did not become a republic; instead it remained a
kingdom, although no one knew who was to be the king. The
oligarchy, which had made a remarkable comeback, was divided on
the question of a Habsburg restoration. This became apparent when
King Charles attempted to regain his throne in April and again in
October 1921. On the first occasion Horthy, who had been elected
Regent of the Kingdom, and the prime minister, Count Pál Teleki,
persuaded him to leave the country. On his second attempt Charles
landed in an airplane in western Hungary and found some local
support. After a few skirmishes the unfortunate ex-emperor was
packed off into exile to Madeira. The higher nobility and the tradi-
tionalist Catholics were predisposed to a Habsburg restoration,
whereas the gentry and the protestants tended to be opposed. Few
favoured a republic. In October 1922 Charles died and the issue lost
its immediacy. Hungary remained a kingdom without a king until
the collapse of the Horthy regime in 1944.

The peace treaty, which was signed with Hungary at Trianon on
4 June 1920, was a disaster for the country. By its terms Hungary
lost 70 per cent of its pre-war territory and 60 per cent of its population. This meant that more Hungarians now lived outside Hungary
than within its borders. Large areas which were mainly inhabited by
Hungarians were attached to the newly established states of Czechoslovakia, Romania and Yugoslavia. With the exception of Yugoslavia these states had actively participated in crushing the Hungarian
Soviet Republic and all three were determined to uphold the peace
treaties. To make matters worse the nationalities policies of these
states were even more oppressive than that of the Hungarian
oligarchy before the war. Thus for Hungary revision of the Treaty
of Trianon became the paramount political issue of the inter-war
years. The Horthy regime exploited to the full this sense of national
humiliation. The slogan *Nem, Nem, Soha* ('No, No, Never'),
denouncing the hated treaty, was repeated *ad nauseam* at political
rallies, in the classroom and from the pulpit for the next twenty
years. In addition the treaty required Hungary to pay an unspecified
amount in reparations, and restricted the armed forces to 35,000

officers and men, to be deployed only for maintaining internal order and for defending the frontiers.

From 1920 to 1944 Hungarian politics was dominated by the right either of the Horthy or the National Socialist variety. The Horthy right permitted a parliamentary system of sorts to survive, sometimes allowed the trades unions to function and although it was anti-Semitic it did not go as far as the National Socialists in demanding the physical extermination of the Jews. In the 1920s the Horthy right was omnipotent. The office of Regent vested Horthy with immense powers: he was commander-in-chief of the armed forces, he could dissolve parliament at his discretion and could appoint and dismiss the prime minister. Every member of the armed forces was required to swear a personal oath of allegiance to the Regent. He could veto legislation, and it was virtually impossible to remove him from office. Horthy, a man of limited intelligence, was surrounded by odious sycophants who penned such official paeans as:

> Our gloriously ruling Great Lord, the Regent, His Serene Highness, the Hero Miklós Horthy of Nagybanyá, came among us as if hurrying into our midst from the ranks of heroes eternally galloping along with Prince Csaba [Attila the Hun's favourite son and legendary ancestor of the Magyars] on the path of the warriors high up in the sky to lead his forlorn race in the most terrible hours of its downtroddenness and inhuman trials.

When Count Teleki resigned in April 1921, Horthy appointed the former leader of the anti-Kun forces in Vienna, Count István Bethlen, as prime minister. A Transylvanian Calvinist, scion of a distinguished landowning family which had played a significant role in Hungarian history, Count Bethlen dominated Hungarian politics for the next ten years and enjoyed the support of the big landowners and capitalists. Although he detested the Treaty of Trianon as passionately as the most rabid National Socialist, he knew that no revision was possible for the foreseeable future. He also realized that the first priority had to be an effective economic and political consolidation. He succeeded in bringing inflation under control, built new factories, managed to attract large amounts of foreign capital and stabilized the currency with the introduction of the new *pengö*. The textile and chemical industries grew rapidly and industrial production more than doubled during the Bethlen years. But the Bethlen achievements stood on shaky foundations. Despite the rapid growth of industry and foreign trade, 75 per cent of exports were in agricultural commodities, primarily wheat. These exports were the lifeline of Hungary's industrialization drive, for they were used to finance the purchase of raw materials and machinery required by industry. Any fluctuation in the price of wheat on the international market therefore affected Hungary profoundly. When wheat prices fell Hungary had to rely increasingly on foreign loans and by the time Bethlen resigned in 1931 the aggregate foreign debt had reached a catastrophic level.

Bethlen's main political support came from the nationalist factions. In 1922 he merged them with the Smallholder's Party to organize a government bloc called the Christian and Bourgeois Party of Smallholders and Agrarians, later rechristened the United Party. By this time the Smallholder's Party had lost all its earlier radicalism, although its leader, István Nagyatádi Szabó, a wealthy peasant, still advocated land reform. A paltry amount of land was transferred to the peasants in accordance with Szabó's proposals, but after his death in 1924 there was no further attempt at land reform and the semi-feudal system of the countryside continued unabated.

Bethlen also made his peace with the socialists in a secret agreement in which he granted an amnesty to the socialist leaders, permitted them to organize, gave the trades unions the right to collective bargaining and returned their funds which had been confiscated. In return the socialists promised to desist from anti-national propaganda, to support the government's foreign policy and to restrict trade union activities to strictly non-political matters. They also agreed to confine their propaganda to the cities by leaving the peasants and landless labourers alone and to abstain from organizing the civil servants, railway and postal workers. Both parties honoured this agreement until the collapse of the Horthy regime.

Bethlen introduced a new franchise which was first used in 1922. It supplanted the sham universal suffrage of 1920 and the electorate was now reduced to less than 30 per cent of the population as a result of various educational and residential qualifications. While secret balloting continued in the towns, it was not permitted in the countryside. The open balloting in the country districts meant government-backed violence and intimidation. The police kept the opposition elements away from the villages. The net result was the virtual disenfranchisement of the rural masses and the United Party had no difficulty in securing the absolute majority.

Having satisfied his ambition to return Hungary to the tutelage of the pre-war 'historic classes', Bethlen turned his attention to foreign affairs. The country joined the League of Nations, toned down its anti-Semitism to appease foreign financial interests and secured a 'reconstruction loan' from the League. Good relations were established with Austria and a treaty of friendship was signed with Italy in April 1927 in spite of Mussolini's complaints about 'Hungarian feudalism'.

The great depression ruined Bethlen's system. Wheat prices collapsed, Czechoslovakia renounced its trade treaty with Hungary in 1930, the collapse of the Austrian Credit Anstalt, which was closely linked to the major Hungarian banks, occurred in the following year and rising unemployment caused widespread unrest. Bethlen resigned in August 1931 but his successor, Count Gyula Károlyi, proved ineffective and in September 1932 Horthy appointed the minister of war, General Gyula Gömbös, prime minister.

Gömbös, the son of prosperous peasants of German origin, had served as a captain in the Austro-Hungarian army during the war and was one of the prime movers of the anti-bolshevik forces at Szeged. He belonged to the extreme right and greatly admired Hitler and Mussolini. He had worked closely with Horthy to overthrow the Soviet Republic and the two men were on close personal terms. He had two guiding political principles: a fanatical detestation of the Habsburgs and an equally rabid anti-Semitism. He managed to convince himself that the Hungarians were the victims of a Habsburg–Jewish conspiracy and felt that Bethlen's policies were hopelessly liberal. In 1927 he had founded the Party of Racial Defence to propagate his anti-Semitism, but in the following year he returned to the Bethlen fold and was rewarded in 1929 with the ministry of war.

His appointment as prime minister was due to Bethlen and Károlyi's failure to rescue Hungary from the clutches of the depression rather than any positive virtues and abilities of his own. He was endorsed by the civil servants, junior army officers, students and some businessmen, all of whom hoped that he would introduce fascism to Hungary. His followers were encouraged by his debut. He made bombastic speeches from balconies in the Mussolinian manner. He spoke frequently on the radio, cultivated the press and choreographed elaborate patriotic parades. He produced a National Work Plan, consisting of ninety-five points, in which he promised everything to everyone: land and tax reform, liquidation of agricultural debts, cheap loans, employment opportunities and the restoration of the secret ballot. But it soon became glaringly obvious that Gömbös lacked the necessary traits for a fascist dictator. Much as he longed to emulate his beloved Mussolini, Horthy had no intention of becoming a second Victor Emmanuel. Consequently Gömbös was unable to do away with parliament and the 'historic classes' blocked his schemes for land reform. Bethlen continued to wield considerable authority behind the scenes and Gömbös had only a limited voice in the selection of his cabinet. To the astonishment of his followers he abandoned his plans for a resolutely anti-Semitic policy and announced that he had changed his mind about the Jewish question.

The Gömbös regime introduced no major reforms, but it changed the political environment. Bethlen's aristocratic *de haut en bas* style was replaced by the demagogy of Gömbös who attempted to create a fascistic regime. With the aid of 'vanguard fighters' he sought to organize a fascist party and a special labour section of the government party was created to indoctrinate the proletariat with the virtues of fascism. Gömbös created special departments for the press and propaganda, introduced censorship and founded cheap newspapers to disseminate his ideas. He created a network of spies, tapped telephone lines, tampered with the mail and infiltrated his own creatures into the army and the civil service.

His foreign policy was based on the principle of international fascist solidarity. He was the first foreign statesman to visit Hitler, contacting him secretly one week after his appointment as chancellor. In June 1933 he visited Hitler in person and laid the foundations for the close alliance between their two countries which was formalized in the treaty of 1934. He also took an early opportunity to visit Rome where Mussolini loudly denounced the Treaty of Trianon, much to Gömbös' delight. Differences between Italy and Germany over Austria made it difficult for Gömbös to perform a balancing act between the two countries, but he tried desperately to act as a mediator. With the formation of the Rome–Berlin axis in 1936 his dream of an alliance between his two heroes, Mussolini and Hitler, became a reality.

During the Gömbös years a large number of small fascist groups sprang up in Hungary inspired by the example of Italy and Germany. In August 1938 the two largest of these groups, led by Count Sándor Festetich, scion of a famous landowning family, and Major Ferenc Szálasi, whose father was Armenian and whose mother was of Slovak-Magyar origin, united to form the Hungarian Nazi Party, the Arrow Cross. Szálasi was a confused ideologue whose incoherent ideology was a mishmash of racist and authoritarian notions. The two guiding principles of the Arrow Cross were anti-Semitism and land reform and the movement won substantial support from army officers, students, unemployed workers and landless peasants.

Shortly before his death in March 1936 Gömbös persuaded the Regent to dissolve parliament and call new elections. His radical right supporters had a majority in the new parliament and Gömbös began once again to talk about land reform and the introduction of fascism into Hungary. The landowners were horrified, denouncing the prime minister's 'social demagogy' and deploring that their estates had become the 'permanent target of every land-hungry nobody and pauper'. The landowners were supported by conservatives such as Bethlen and Horthy, and were it not for the fact that Gömbös obviously did not have long to live, the regent would probably have removed him from office.

Kalmán Darányi, a somewhat obscure conservative, succeeded Gömbös as prime minister. He agreed with the landowners that a traditional conservative policy at home was the wisest course, but although Bethlen and his followers were becoming increasingly concerned about the obvious aggressiveness of Nazi Germany, the inexorable logic of the revisionist position forced all Gömbös successors to follow in Hitler's wake. Darányi was at first hesitant to get too close to Germany but he soon overcame this reticence. In November 1937 he agreed to participate with Germany in the dismemberment of Czechoslovakia and early in the following year he announced plans to introduce anti-Jewish legislation.

Horthy dismissed Darányi in May 1938 for making overtures to the Arrow Cross and on the recommendation of Bethlen he appointed an outstanding economist, Béla Imrédy, who was considered liberal and pro-British, in an effort to improve Hungary's relations with the west. However, it was under his prime ministership that the first anti-Jewish measures were passed which limited Jewish participation in certain professions to 20 per cent. Curiously enough this move was supported by several Jewish leaders on the grounds that it was the best way to avoid even harsher measures. After Munich, when Hungary was given the southern strip of Slovakia which was populated largely by Magyars, Imrédy became an unabashed supporter of Hitlerite Germany. In January 1939 he took Hungary into the Anti-Comintern Pact and in the meantime introduced even more drastic anti-Jewish legislation which deprived a large number of Jews of any possibility of earning a living. With this measure he hoped to curry support from Nazi Germany and to increase his popularity at home, but it provoked a strong reaction from traditional conservatives. His opponents produced some embarrassing evidence showing that this stalwart anti-Semite had a Jewish grandmother, and his efforts to defend himself were undignified and absurd. His credibility destroyed, he was dismissed by Horthy in February 1939.

Imrédy was succeeded by the relatively liberal and western-oriented Count Pál Teleki, who had been prime minister from 1920 to 1921. But he did little to reverse the policies of his predecessors. Imrédy's anti-Jewish legislation was passed in May 1939. He was anxious to remain on friendly terms with Germany, but he also wanted to keep out of the war. He managed to do this for two years, but when Horthy decided to allow German troops to cross through Hungary to invade Yugoslavia he committed suicide on 2 April 1941. The following day Horthy appointed László Bárdossy as prime minister and it was he who took the fatal decision to declare war on the Soviet Union in June as a consequence of which the Regency was to be destroyed and Hungary became a communist dictatorship.

CZECHOSLOVAKIA

Unlike Poland and Hungary, or the other countries in east–central Europe and the Balkans, Czechoslovakia functioned reasonably successfully as a democracy during the inter-war period. In fact, it was the only truly democratic nation in the area, showing reasonable respect for parliamentary procedure, individual liberties and the rule of law. The major problem was how to accommodate the different nationalities and to overcome the cultural, social and economic differences among these groups. The Czech areas of the Habsburg empire were highly developed and contained a number of industries, such as the Skoda works which supplied the Austro-Hungarian army with most of its weapons. Rapid industrialization brought a considerable improvement in the living standards of the Czechs in the second half of the nineteenth century. Between 1850 and 1910 the population of Prague increased four-fold to over 600,000 and that of Pilsen from less than 10,000 to over 100,000. This migration of peasants to the urban centres altered the traditional features of many cities. The towns with their bourgeois German culture became increasingly Czech in many respects. Prague was the classic example of this development. While the older industries such as glass and textiles were still controlled by Germans, Czech financiers played a significant role in the development of heavy industry. Emil Skoda became the major arms producer in the Habsburg Empire. Tomás Bata's shoe and leather company, established in Moravia, became the largest of its kind in the world. By the turn of the century the Czechs were no longer the serfs of their German overlords. There was now a substantial Czech bourgeoisie and the Czech industrial proletariat began to be seen as a threat to the privileged position of German industrial workers. The Germans were still the dominant group, but the Czechs were beginning to catch up. They developed a rich cultural and intellectual life with their own university and a national theatre.

The development of Slovakia did not follow this pattern. Having been under Hungarian rule since the tenth century, it never achieved an independent status. The ruling class consisted largely of Hungarian landowners, and the cities were predominantly German or Jewish. Industrialization had hardly had any impact on this traditional culture. The Slovaks were largely illiterate peasants: R. W. Seton-Watson estimates that of a population of 2 million there were probably no more than 1,000 educated Slovaks. This backwardness was compounded by the hold over the population exercised by a poorly educated and ferociously reactionary Catholic priesthood who denounced all aspects of modern life as the works of the devil. A Lutheran minority formed something of an intellectual elite which was receptive to modern ideas and who identified with Czech culture and aspirations.

While there had been a number of attempts to forge ties between the Czechs and Slovaks on the basis of their common Slav heritage, the two groups had never thought of an independent Czechoslovak state before 1914. The most that the Czechs hoped for was a status similar to that of the Hungarians after the *Ausgleich* of 1867, and few of their leaders wanted a complete break with the Habsburgs. The Slovaks lacked any coherent idea of nationhood and were unable to think of anything beyond the termination of the Magyar influence. This they hoped to achieve under the unfortunate Franz Ferdinand, the victim of Sarajevo, who as heir to the throne and sympathetic to the Slavs was on singularly bad terms with the Hungarians.

The war and the subsequent collapse of the Austro-Hungarian Empire created a totally different situation and made possible the formation of a Czechoslovakian state. Until the war was almost over the independence movement was the concern merely of a handful of political emigrés led by Tomás Masaryk, the son of a Slovak coachman from Moravia. As a professor of philosophy at the Czech University of Prague and a deputy in the Austrian *Reichsrat* he was well known in western intellectual circles. Czech, Slovak, Romanian, Serb and Croat students flocked to Prague to sit at the feet of this venerated master. Until the outbreak of the war Masaryk believed in the sanctity of the empire but, with the Habsburg's playing second fiddle to the Germans, his views changed radically. He wanted no part in an Austria which had become little more than a vehicle for German expansionism into eastern Europe, but he still had no idea what sort of Czechoslovak state he wanted. At first he leaned towards a monarchy with a Russian, Belgian or Danish prince on the throne, but during his exile in the west he and his associates settled on a democratic republican solution.

Masaryk spent most of the war years in England while his lieutenant, Edvard Benes, an obscure thirty-year-old university lecturer, directed the daily operations of the newly established Czechoslovak National Council in Paris. At first these exiles had almost no access to the upper echelons of the British and French governments and their cause was promoted by several pro-Czech intellectuals, including Wickham Steed, the influential foreign editor of *The Times*, R. W. Seton-Watson, a British expert on central Europe, and Ernest Denis, a professor at the Sorbonne. The Entente powers at this stage had no desire to break up the Austro-Hungarian Empire and were unwilling to hear Masaryk's case.

During 1917–18 the situation changed dramatically. Masaryk created the Czech Legion from former prisoners of war in Russia and it captured the Trans-Siberian Railway and thus was an important factor in the Russian civil war. Wilson's Fourteen Points obliged the Entente to change its attitude towards the future of the Dual Monarchy and thanks to the persuasive skill of the National Council the idea of a Czechoslovak state gradually became more palatable to the Allies. By September 1918 the Austro-Hungarian army was in full retreat on all fronts and the Emperor Charles' frantic attempts to preserve the empire were too little and too late to have any effect. On 18 October Masaryk, who was in Washington, proclaimed the independence of Czechoslovakia and nine days later Count Gyula Andrássy, the son of the architect of the Dual Alliance of 1879, accepted the terms of an armistice. On 28 October the National Committee, now in Prague, proclaimed the independence of the 'historic lands of Bohemia and Moravia' and on the following day the Slovak leaders announced their decision to unite Slovakia with Bohemia and Moravia to form the Czechoslovak nation.

In the new state only 65 per cent of the population were Czechs and Slovaks. The 3 million Germans were a majority in many of the frontier areas. The 700,000 Hungarians wished to belong to an independent Hungary. 75,000 Poles were the object of constant Polish government propaganda and the 460,000 Ruthenes clamoured for autonomy. Although Masaryk had made a number of commitments to the Slovaks, including the establishment of a separate diet, the use of Slovak in government and schools and an autonomous administrative and judicial system for Slovakia, for a number of reasons these promises were never fully implemented and the Slovaks complained that they were treated as second-class citizens.

The National Assembly, with its seat in Prague, was selected by the executive committees of the various political parties. Karel Kramár, the leading politician in Bohemia and leader of the National Democratic Party, served as prime minister until July 1919. Kramár, a passionate nationalist who was married to a Russian, had been condemned to death by the Austrians during the war and hated the bolsheviks and the Germans with equal intensity. Benes was appointed foreign minister, an office which he held for seventeen years, and Masaryk was welcomed home as president on 21 December 1918.

The government's first priority was to tackle the economic difficulties of the republic. Alois Rasin, the highly gifted minister of finance, established a stable new currency, the Czech Crown. Rasin was murdered in January 1923 by a deranged young bank clerk of communist persuasion, but fortunately his successors were talented men such as Dr Karl Englis, a professor of economics at the newly established Brno University. Kramár also introduced a Land Control Act which limited individual holdings to a maximum of 150 hectares (370 acres) of arable land or 250 hectares (618 acres) of land in general. This destroyed the vast estates of the aristocracy but most of these new allotments were far too small to be economically viable. There was also considerable resentment that although some German and Hungarian peasants received land, most of it went to Czechs and Slovaks. The Sudeten Germans claimed that the land reform was a scheme to repopulate the non-Czech areas with Czechs, but the government insisted that its objective was to create a substantial class of small-holders who were loyal to the republic and avoided the thorny issue of whether particular groups had been unduly favoured.

The first general elections were held under the new constitution in April 1920. The socialist parties won 136 of the 281 seats, and the leader of the Czech social democrats, Vlastimil Tusar, became prime minister. He immediately came under fierce attack from the right by Kramár's National Democrats, from the centre by the Agrarians and from the left by the bolshevik wing of his own party. He

125

favoured a flexible policy towards the Sudeten Germans, but got no thanks from that quarter and was criticized by a majority of the Czechs for his moderate attitude towards the German question. The left wing of the social democrats tried to drag the entire party into the Third International but having failed it constituted itself as the Czech Communist Party (KSC) under Bohumir Smeral. It remained a small and fanatical clique until 1925, content to indulge in thunderous and self-righteous denunciations of the bourgeois state and all its ways, its unique distinction being that it was the only political party in which all the ethnic groups were represented.

Internecine warfare among the social democrats forced Tusar to resign in September 1920. Two months after his resignation the communists and social democrats began an unseemly squabble over the ownership of the People's House in Prague which housed the party secretariat and printing press. This infantile brawl, which eventually resulted in an abortive general strike, further discredited the left.

Following Tusar's resignation, Masaryk appointed a caretaker government, the 'cabinet of experts' under Dr Jan Cerny, which proved to be suprisingly long-lived, surviving until September 1921. Cerny's government remained in office largely because the various party leaders were unable to agree on a satisfactory coalition government. Eventually a second 'cabinet of experts' was formed under Benes. This resulted from the formation of the *Petka*, a broadly based five-party coalition, consisting of the social Democrats, the National Socialists (not to be confused with the Nazis), the Agrarians, the Populists (Catholics) and the National Democrats, which controlled Czech politics during the inter-war years. The *Petka* covered an ideological spectrum ranging from Catholicism to moderate marxism and represented the interests of such diverse groups as farmers and bankers, workers and industrialists but which excluded the national minorities, the Slovak autonomists and of course the extreme left, and the Agrarians, who stood for land reform and represented the interests of both the rural poor and the middle class. In 1922 the Czech Agrarians were joined by the Slovak and Ruthenian Agrarians and the leader of the united party, Antonin Svehla, was appointed prime minister in October and remained in office until November 1925, the longest lasting Czech government in the inter-war years. It achieved a number of striking successes The Social Insurance Law, which was not in fact passed until after the government fell, was the most progressive of its kind anywhere in the world. Agricultural and industrial prices were stabilized and unlike Poland, Romania and many other countries, the army was brought under strict civilian control.

The government collapsed because the coalition began to fall apart over the Social Insurance Law. The Agrarians were only prepared to support it if they were given high protective tariffs on agricultural produce, but the two socialist parties would not agree, since this would inevitably lead to an increase in the price of food. Another bone of contention was that the Populist Party opposed the participation of President Masaryk and several ministers at a ceremony in July 1925 honouring the martyrdom of John Hus at the stake in 1415. The papal nuncio, Francesco Marmaggi, scandalized by this encomium to a notorious heretic, left Prague in protest and the government countered by breaking off diplomatic relations with the Vatican.

In the elections of November 1925 the social democrats lost ground, winning only 29 seats in the Chamber of Deputies as opposed to 74 in 1920. The communists did remarkably well, gaining 41 seats and becoming the second largest party after the Agrarians with 46. Since none of the parties wished to form a coalition with the communists, Svehla again formed a government. From 1922 to 1925 he ruled with the backing of the socialists, then from 1926 to 1929 he ruled in opposition to them. Briefly out of office from March until October 1926 due to ill health, Svehla formed a third cabinet which included the German Agrarian and Christian Social Parties and which led to a considerable improvement in relations between Czechs and Germans.

The elections of 1929 resulted in an improvement in the social democratic standings to 39 seats and a drop in the communists' to 30. The Agrarians remained the largest party in the Chamber with 46 seats. Little attention was paid to the fact that the Nazis won 7 seats. A new centre-left government was formed which was joined by the German social democrats. It remained in office until 1932.

This government had to deal with the severe problems of the depression which were compounded by Czechoslovakia's economic links with Austria and Germany, two pivotal centres of the crisis. Unemployment was chronic in the industrial areas and the government's strict deflationary policies made matters worse. The devaluation of the Crown in early 1934 did something to ease the situation, although recovery was painfully slow.

The more backward parts of the country such as Slovakia and Ruthenia suffered the most from the depression, thus further exacerbating ethnic unrest and social tensions. According to one estimate, during the winter of 1932–33 a third of Slovakia's population had no regular income. Protectionism helped the better-off Czech farmers, but it did nothing for the large numbers of landless labourers and forestry workers in Slovakia. In such a situation it was hardly surprising that the Slovak nationalist movement made substantial progress. In 1928 Professor Voytech Tuka, a leader of the Slovak People's Party, published an article in which he argued that the Czecho-Slovak union of 1918 contained a secret clause limiting its effectiveness for ten years and, since the Czechs had not given the Slovaks their autonomous rights as they had promised, he argued they could secede from the union. Tuka was arrested and placed on trial for treason. It was shown that he had received financial support from Hungary and he was sentenced to fifteen years imprisonment. His disgrace did much to dampen enthusiasm for Slovak national independence but the worsening economic situation in the early 1930s caused a resurgence of demands for autonomy and even for total independence. The Slovak People's Party then began to co-operate with other nationalist movements, particularly with the Germans.

The Sudetenland had also been deeply affected by the depression, light industries such as glass and textiles being particularly hard hit. The consumer-oriented industries of the area were all dependent on the dwindling export market. The tourist trade was adversely affected by the severe exchange controls imposed by the Nazis. Although most of the political parties of the Sudetenland identified with their Czech counterparts the Sudeten-German Nazis exploited the economic and social crisis to serve the aims of their masters in Berlin.

During the 1920s the Nazis had little influence in Czechoslovakia and in the 1930s their success depended on the progress of the Hitlerite movement in Germany. By 1931 the Prague government felt obliged to ban Nazi uniforms and in 1932 several leading Nazis were arrested on charges of plotting a coup. The Nazis felt obliged to make a duplicitous profession of their loyalty to the Czech state and they were ordered by their German comrades to cool their ardour. But this setback was only temporary and the movement continued to grow. Then in February 1913 the vast majority of the parties in parliament voted to suspend the parliamentary immunity of the Nazi deputies. Afraid that the government would proscribe them entirely, the Sudeten Nazis disbanded the party and went underground. This had little effect on their popularity and by the end of 1933 the German ambassador, a man not particularly sympathetic to their cause, estimated that about 2 million of the 3 million Sudeten Germans were Nazi sympathizers.

In 1934 the party regrouped under the leadership of Konrad Henlein, a thirty-five-year-old gymnastics instructor, to form the *Sudetendeutsche Heimatfront* which absorbed the old Nazi Party and amalgamated it with extreme right-wing groups, fascist as well as nationalist. In spite of some singularly unconvincing rhetoric to the contrary, the Home Front was indistinguishable from the Nazi Party and received substantial financial support from the Reich. From the outset it was an instrument of German foreign policy, although at times it was in danger of being overtaken by its more unruly and fanatical members.

The party, renamed under government pressure to become the Sudeten German Party, received 60 per cent of the German vote in the elections of 1935. It now became the second largest party in parliament next to the Agrarians. The enduring economic crisis and the continuing series of successes in German foreign policy kept Henlein and his party in an aggressive mood and the last four years of the unfortunate republic's existence was dominated by the German question and its impact on international affairs.

The Czech government tried to resist German expansionism through a series of foreign policy initiatives. It signed a pact with the Soviet Union in 1935 and tried to consolidate its relations with France. But with a rapidly worsening situation following extensive German rearmament, the reoccupation of the Rhineland and the annexation of Austria, all these efforts came to nothing. The government made major economic and political concessions to the Sudeten Germans, but Hitler was never interested in compromise and his 'irrevocable decision' to destroy the republic made any such effort utterly pointless. Pressured by Britain and France to give way to Germany's demands, the Czechs were forced to capitulate and the Sudetenland was handed over to Germany after the Munich Conference. The Poles and Hungarians soon fell on the hapless country. Slovakia became a nasty puppet state of Nazi Germany and the Czechs suffered the miserable fate of living under the savagely repressive regime of the hideously inaptly named Protectorate of Bohemia and Moravia.

Czechoslovakia continued to function as a democracy until the bitter end. Its success story as the only 'enduring European democracy east of the Rhine' was not accidental. With its relatively high level of economic development, its reasonably prosperous peasantry, the flexibility of *Petka* rule and the constitutional-parliamentary orientation of its leadership – all helped to preserve democracy in Czechoslovakia. The ultimate failure of this experiment in democratic rule was not the result of internal weaknesses: it was caused by superior and ruthless Nazi power and the unwillingness of the western powers to come to the rescue of a state which was far worthier of defence, and would have been far more easily defended than was Poland. Munich thus proved to be not only morally dubious but also militarily and politically disastrous.

CHAPTER SIX
Italian Fascism

On 2 August 1914 the Italian government announced that it would remain neutral, for the conservative Prime Minister Salandra hoped that what he termed Italy's 'sacred egoism' could be satisfied by negotiating substantial concessions from the Central Powers. When the Germans suffered their first reverses the nationalists, intoxicated by visions of territorial aggrandizement, began to press for war. The editor of the socialist daily newspaper *Avanti*, Benito Mussolini, true to the spirit of the resolutions of the Socialist International against war at Stuttgart in 1907 and Basel in 1912, denounced both the German aggressors and the Anglo–French imperialists and announced that the only war for socialists was that between the bourgeoisie and the proletariat. But in October his astonished readers were treated to outspoken denunciations of the neutralists as traitors and cowards. He was obliged to resign from *Avanti*, and shortly afterwards started a new paper called *II Popolo d'Italia*, which was financed in large part by French money with substantial contributions from the other Entente powers.

The Socialist Party remained resolutely neutralist and still paid lip service to the idea of revolution, but unity had been destroyed as many activists were attracted by the prospect of channelling their revolutionary energies into the glorious struggle against German imperialism and militarism. The split within the Socialist Party between those who harboured vague but passionate longings for action in a 'revolutionary war' and those who clung to neutrality was symptomatic of a profound division within Italian society. Conservatives tended to sympathize with the authoritarian Central Powers. Catholics supported Austria-Hungary as a bastion of the Church. Capitalists favoured neutrality because it offered attractive opportunities to do business with both sides. On the interventionist side there were nationalists who dreamt of glory and conquest, Radicals who found the prospect of war invigorating, and Reformist Socialists who had managed to convince themselves that war was in the best interests of the proletariat. The vast mass of Italians found all this most confusing. A small but resolute minority in favour of war got their way in May 1915. The middle classes supported the decision reluctantly, for the neutralist high ground had been captured by strident socialists who equated neutrality with revolution. Many Italians therefore came to believe that the choice was between war and revolution, and felt that war was the lesser evil. The socialists, for all their fiery rhetoric, did not dare to confront the interventionist mobs which roamed the streets and would not risk calling a general strike.

The Chamber of Deputies voted overwhelmingly but unenthusiastically in favour of war, having been manipulated by the government and cowed by the interventionists. After this unfortunate capitulation parliament was further discredited by the inept conduct of a war for which the country was ill prepared, which was widely unpopular and which brought not national glory but the humiliation of defeat at Caporetto. The government was under constant attack from the socialists who adopted the slogan 'neither support nor sabotage'. The interventionist deputies and their hangers-on formed a 'Union of National Defence' (*Fascio di Difesa Nazionale*), but the majority belonged to neither extreme and were at a loss what to do. In the spring of 1917 the extreme left of the Socialist Party, under the leadership of Amadeo Bordiga, formed an independent socialist party from which the Communist Party was later formed. Widespread discontent with the conduct of the war, shortages of food, war profiteering and revolution in Russia helped win the radical left a considerable following in the industrial centres of the north. In August 1917 there were riots in Turin. They were a spontaneous demonstration of popular anger rather than a conscious revolutionary attempt to overthrow the existing order, but they terrified the authorities who blamed the subsequent disaster at Caporetto on the socialists, strengthened the intransigence of the extreme left, and convinced many moderates that the government needed to take more decisive action against subversives and defeatists. The government took firm steps against the socialists, but this merely drove the socialists further to the left. At their party congress in September 1918 it was agreed that there should be no compromises with the bourgeois state and that the aim of the party should be to establish

the dictatorship of the proletariat. Reconciliation between the socialists and the bourgeois democrats was thus no longer possible, and
the victorious conclusion of the war did nothing to end their
fundamental rejection of the liberal regime.

Victory soon turned sour. Italy was denied the annexations she
had been promised in the Treaty of London, and the nationalists
denounced the peace conference as a fraud which had given Italy a
'mutilated peace'. Extremists on the left and the right denounced the
moderate interventionists who lost most of their remaining
followers. In such an atmosphere the appeals by the Prime Minister,
Francesco Nitti, for moderation, tolerance and aquiesence to the
peace settlement for fear of alienating Italy's wartime allies fell on
deaf ears. The army was determined to resist Nitti's plan for rapid
demobilization and there was much murmuring in the messes about
the desirability of a military coup. On 12 September 1919 Gabriele
D'Annunzio, a fashionable *literato*, adventurer and war hero whose
melodramatic effusions were widely admired, led some 2,000 rebel-
lious troops into Fiume in defiance of the peace settlement.
D'Annunzio stayed in Fiume until the end of 1920 when the government reached an agreement with Yugoslavia and at last felt able to
act. His somewhat comic opera coup was applauded by the nationalists but failed to bring down the Nitti government as he had hoped,
nor did it inspire a military coup on the mainland.

The helplessness of the government in the face of such posturing
was indicative of the degree of political fragmentation in Italy. Nitti
was unable to get any support from the left against D'Annunzio for
they had no desire to help the bourgeois state out of an embarrassing
situation however much they disapproved of his antics in Fiume.
The right supported D'Annunzio and thundered on about the
'mutilated victory' and unrest at home. The political situation was
further destabilized by the introduction of proportional representation which made it no longer possible to control parliament by the
traditional liberal methods of political horse-trading and influence
peddling known as *trasformismo*. Turati and the socialists refused to
co-operate with the bourgeois parties. Don Sturzo and the populists
(PPI) were reluctant and exceptionally difficult partners. Proportional representation tended to exaggerate the antagonisms between
neutralists and interventionists, as well as between north and south,
which plagued the traditional constitutional parties to which almost
half the deputies belonged. Even the aging wizard of Italian politics,
Giovanni Giolitti, who replaced his arch-rival Nitti in June 1920, was
unable to form an effective coalition out of these hostile factions. It

was small wonder therefore that the prospect of an authoritarian regime seemed increasingly attractive.

In the 'two red years' of 1919–20 there was a wave of strikes throughout Italy in both industry and agriculture. The employers, faced with militant unions emboldened by high employment, gave way to many of their demands, and hoped that inflation would diminish the real cost of such concessions. The middle classes were unable to make any similar gains. They found it difficult to adjust to the relative tedium of civilian life, they were hurt by inflation and their average incomes were lower than they had been before the war. They resented the peace settlement which had failed to give Italy Dalmatia, parts of Istria and the hinterland of Trieste. They abhorred the socialists and regarded Giolitti as a discredited 'defeatist'. They were frustrated, bitter and disillusioned and looked for a radical solution to their predicament.

The 'two red years' reached a climax in September with the occupation of the factories in the industrial centres of the north. This was a spontaneous and disorganized outburst which never developed into a revolutionary movement. Its failure demoralized the working class and showed up the bankruptcy of the 'maximalist' line. Bordiga and Gramsci formed the Communist Party (PCI) at the Congress of Livorno in January 1921, convinced that only a revolutionary party on the bolshevik model could realize the aspirations of the working class. Most socialists workers were demoralized by the failure of the occupation of the factories and by rising unemployment as the effects of a depression began to be felt. Thus by 1921 the Italian labour movement was further divided and in no mood to offer united and determined opposition to the growing danger from the extreme right.

In spite of this defeat of the left, the industrialists were badly shaken and blamed the government for failing to take more decisive action against the strikers. The agrarians also loudly denounced the government for failing to come to their assistance against the share-croppers and labourers who had been organized into unions, both socialist and Catholic, and who were striking throughout the Po Valley, Tuscany, Umbria and the Veneto. In the towns the bourgeoisie were horrified when the local elections of late 1920 returned a number of socialist councils posing a direct threat to traditional urban culture and to the privileges of entrenched elites. In such a situation Mussolini and his *squadristi* seemed to offer hope of deliverance from the socialists, the unions and a pusillanimous government.

Mussolini founded his first *fascio di combattimento* on 23 March 1919 as a continuation of the wartime *fasci di combattimento*. The movement was a curious blend of rabid nationalism and revolutionary syndicalism. Its first programme, which was published several months later, reflected these two trends. It called for the annexation of Fiume and Dalmatia as well as an 85 per cent tax on war profits, progressive income tax, workers' participation in management and the confiscation of all remaining Church property. Mussolini hoped to win support from right-wing socialists and trades unionists as well as disaffected members of the centre parties, but in the election in November 1919 the *fasci* did so badly that the whole movement seemed on the verge of collapse. Its only hope of survival was to move dramatically to the right. Those elements of the programme which were tinged with socialism were either dropped or watered down. Mussolini announced that he was in favour of 'free trade', which implied freedom from the unions, freedom from high taxation and freedom from excessive government intervention in the economy.

Erstwhile syndicalists and socialists were prominent in the movement from its inception. They made up the majority of the rank and file, held most of the important positions, and set the tone. The attempt to win over ex-servicemen did not succeed for they remained loyal to government-sponsored ex-servicemen's organizations. But a significant number of officers and members of the elite shock troops (*arditi*) were greatly attracted by the *fasci*, and it was they who gave the movement its distinctly military flavour, its distrust of programmes and platforms, its empty radicalism and its violence. The petite bourgeoisie of shopkeepers and small businessmen looked to the *fasci* to revive their sinking profits and restore their status, and their children were attracted by the excitement, comradeship and sense of purpose which the fascists provided. Mussolini was given substantial financial assistance by the business world of Milan but in his capacity as a brilliant anti-communist journalist rather than as leader of the *fasci*. Such close association with prominent capitalists provided a further reason for the fascist left to distance themselves from Mussolini at a time when they were already annoyed by the rightward shift of the movement.

In early 1919 Mussolini began to organize armed squads made up largely of ex-servicemen, particularly from the *arditi*, who first went into action in April when the building of the socialist newspaper *Avanti* was set on fire. Although some of the *squadristi* dreamed of a putsch the squads did nothing to help D'Annunzio when he was ousted from Fiume, and most of their energies were devoted to terrorising the socialists and the unions. This *squadrismo* was characteristic of the next phase of fascism, giving the deracinated and the confused a sense of belonging to an elite, to the shock troops of a new and greater Italy.

This campaign of violence was enormously successful. They attacked the municipal institutions run by socialist councils. They terrorized the unions. They attacked the agricultural co-operatives and destroyed the socialist peasant leagues. They dominated the countryside of the Po Valley, Emilia and Tuscany. Some fascists felt that this violence was excessive and that the party should become a responsible party of the centre. Radical fascists had no sympathy for such traditional politics and revelled in the use of terror which they felt was part of a truly revolutionary cult of self-sacrifice, heroism and idealism. These two wings of the fascist movement were joined by their common detestation of socialism in all its forms, and it was this anti-socialism which was to win the fascists their mass support.

The Italian bourgeoisie had been badly shaken in 1920. Workers had occupied the factories and had then made impressive gains in the municipal elections. Maximalist socialists revealed their apocalyptic visions of an imminent revolution while doing nothing to prepare for the millenium. The respectable classes therefore looked for protection against the red peril, and the local *fasci* were delighted to oblige, even though they despised the bourgeois as selfish, conventional and cowardly. Most fascists cynically accepted this alliance with the bourgeoisie as a tactical move, but the more idealistic among them felt that the movement was degenerating into a protection racket for the naked class interests of the bourgeoisie. In 1920 fascism was strongest in the countryside where there were similar problems. Large numbers of agricultural workers had joined the *fasci*, attracted by promises that they would be protected against the landowners, but it was precisely these agrarians who dominated and controlled rural fascism, much to the disgust of the urban idealists. This fundamental contradiction could only be overcome by imposing rigid discipline and by the further militarization of the rural *fasci*.

In the elections of May 1921 Mussolini joined the 'National Block' with Giolitti's liberals and the nationalists and his followers won thirty-five seats. Giolitti's government depended on the support of the populists and in July, when he could no longer count on them, he resigned. A new government was formed by the weak right-wing socialist Bonomi who agreed upon a 'Pact of Pacification' with Mussolini, a move which was bitterly resented by the violent rural *fasci*. Mussolini gave way to pressure from the local leaders (*Ras*), extremists like Balbo and Dino Grandi, telling them that they could ignore the pact if they wished, and at the founding congress of the Fascist Party (PNF – *Partito nazionale fascista*) in November he announced: 'We do indeed wish to serve them [the people], to educate them, but we also intend to flog them when they make mistakes.' Italy was plunged into a virtual civil war between fascist blackshirts and socialist redshirts. Bonomi outlawed all armed bands, but there was no way of enforcing this decree and the government was further discredited.

The democrats withdrew their support from Bonomi and his government fell. The populists would not support Giolitti, the socialists would not join in an anti-fascist coalition, nor would they co-operate with the fascists in a 'ministry of concentration'. A weak government was patched together by Facta, but this proved to be only a stop-gap measure which paved the way for the Grand Old Man's return, although Facta was much more than a mere stalking-horse for Giolitti. The fascists stepped up their violence and the government was incapable of maintaining law and order. The social-ists and the populists now announced that they were prepared to support an anti-fascist government in an attempt to put an end to the intolerable violence and lawlessness which was sweeping the country. This constructive move was torpedoed by Giolitti and in desperation the socialists called an anti-fascist general strike in July. This was a fatal mistake, for the strike was broken by the fascists. The bourgeoisie applauded this crushing defeat of the organized and militant working class. Mussolini's one remaining fear was that the eighty-year-old Giolitti might form a government which would absorb the fascists. He therefore supported the radicals in the move-ment who called for a march on Rome to overthrow the government while at the same time he negotiated with the politicians and professed to be ready to compromise. Facta took these discussions to mean that the crisis was waning and mistook his own weakness for a statesmanlike display of flexible patience. Meanwhile Giolitti waited in the wings for the call to unite the nation.

At the end of October Mussolini finally agreed to march on Rome. As a military operation it was singularly ineptly planned and would have been easily stopped had there been any serious oppo-sition. As a piece of political theatre it was superb. Throughout northern Italy the authorities capitulated to the fascists and it seemed that the state was falling apart. Most of the army sympathized with the fascists. The politicans, with the exception of the communists and most socialists, and including Giolitti, Bonomi, Orlando, Salandra and Alcide de Gasperi, were prepared to accept the fascists in the belief that they would respect the law and that the country would have some peace and quiet. The king agreed with this view and, although he was hardly a friend of the fascists, he saw a government headed by Mussolini as the only alternative to bloodshed and anarchy. Mussolini arrived in Rome in a sleeping car from Milan and arrived on the morning of 30 October incongruously but symbolically attired in a black shirt and a bowler hat. His troops held their victory parade through the streets of Rome. They were a sorry sight, for it had been pouring with rain for two days and they had been given little to eat. Even this bedraggled spectacle worked to Mussolini's advantage, for too vivid a demonstration of strength might well have alienated the more fastidious elements of society, and would not have exposed so dramatically the weakness of his opponents.

There were only thirty-two fascist deputies in the Chamber, and Mussolini's cabinet included very few fascists. The prominent fascists were all excluded, much to their disgust, and the government included two populists, three democrats, one nationalist and one liberal. This secured Mussolini a parliamentary majority, but it seemed too conservative an alliance for his more radical followers. Conservatives were alarmed that Mussolini appointed himself Minister for Foreign Affairs, for diplomacy was regarded as a conservative preserve, as well as being Premier and Minister of the Interior. Radical fascists were disgusted by Mussolini's caution and willingness to compromise, and the left were outraged by his hectoring speeches in the Chamber such as his famous tirade on 16 November 1922 in which he said: 'I could have made this grey and dreary hall into a bivouac for my legions'. Mussolini was not yet strong enough to establish a dictatorship and still had to make some concessions to parliamentary democracy.

The first important steps towards creating a permanent dictatorship were taken in December. A Fascist Grand Council was established, ostensibly to facilitate liaison between the party and the government, but it soon became a more important institution than the cabinet. On 30 December Mussolini ordered the arrest of the communist leaders Bordiga and Gramsci along with all the other members of the Communist Party whom he could lay his hands on. The party was driven underground, and although Gramsci escaped arrest until 1926 the final destruction of the left had begun. But the radicals in Mussolini's own party were also brought into line. A militia was formed which controlled and disciplined and absorbed the rowdy *squadristi* and provided a military force which was unquestionably loyal to Mussolini. Fascist radicals also had to accept the absorption of the nationalists into the PNF and complained about their new comrades as conservative moderates with clerical sympathies. Such fears were partly justified, for the nationalists played a role in the fascist movement which was out of proportion to their numbers, and the fusion of the two parties marked a further distancing from the radical activists' position.

In April 1923 the populists were expelled from the government, for a sizeable faction of the party opposed any co-operation with the fascists, and Don Sturzo sympathized with them. Mussolini was determined to weaken the populists, largely because they were strong opponents of his proposals for electoral reform. Under the Acerbo Bill, passed in November, the party which obtained the highest number of seats in an election would automatically obtain two-thirds of the seats in parliament. Sturzo had been obliged as an obedient priest to resign his leadership of the populists when he came under increasing pressure from the Vatican to accommodate with the fascists. Without his leadership the party began to split into two groups: one which was prepared to co-operate with the fascists and another which wanted at all costs to preserve the last remnants of Italian democracy. In the end the party voted by one vote to abstain from the vote on the Acerbo Bill, and this virtually ensured that it would pass. Those who voted for the bill hoped that Mussolini would distance himself from the radicals of the party and act as a more responsible and conventional politician, his government legitimized by the electoral process. The liberals supported the fascists in the elections held under the new law in April 1924 in the hope of getting jobs and patronage under the new government. Intimidation and violence, a massive propaganda campaign sponsored by the government, the support of big business (as Agnelli said, they were 'government supporters by necessity') and outright swindling in counting the ballots and allowing fascists more than one vote, resulted in an overwhelming victory for the National Block. They did best in the south where intimidation and bribery was more widely used, but failed to win a majority in the industrial cities of the north. The working class could not be won away from their traditional allegiances and faced with this solidarity the fascists were less violent and extreme.

With parliament now dominated by the fascists it was obvious that the regime was about to enter a new phase. Liberals hoped that there would be a return to normalcy and a disavowal of violence. Fascists rejoiced that at last it was possible to lay the foundations of a truly fascist state, although there was considerable disagreement as to what this state should be like. When parliament reassembled the reformist socialist leader, Giacomo Matteotti, led a blistering attack on the government and denounced the elections as a fraud. A few days later, on 10 June, Matteotti disappeared. He had been kidnapped in the streets of Rome, bundled into the back of a car and murdered. His body was not discovered until months later. Matteotti's courage, honesty and outstanding qualities were widely respected, and his disappearance caused an uproar. There can be little doubt that his murder, or possibly a severe beating, had been ordered either by Mussolini or someone in his immediate entourage, and Mussolini's attempts to blame his abduction on Jews, freemasons, bankers and assorted enemies of fascism did not impress the deputies. Moderate fascists such as De Stefani, Oviglio, Federzoni and Gentile threatened to resign from the cabinet if Mussolini did not get rid of the extremists. Mussolini was at a loss what to do. After some hesitation he gave way to the moderates. The suave Federzoni was made Minister of the Interior, and the undersecretary of state in the ministry, Finzi, was forced to resign. Mussolini hinted that Finzi, who was Jewish, was somehow implicated in the Matteotti affair. He was to die in 1944 fighting for a partisan unit against the Germans. Alfredo Rocco, a distinguished law professor, was made Minister of Justice. General de Bono, the Director of Public Security, on whom justified suspicion had fallen, was also dismissed.

The opposition was equally confused. A general strike would have terrified the bourgeoisie and would have played into the fascists' hands. Some talked of arresting Mussolini, but there were no suitable candidates to organize such a daring coup. On 12 June the opposition deputies, with the exception of the communists, decided to withdraw from parliament, refusing to return until law and order was restored and the constitution respected. These deputies, soon to be called the 'Aventine Secession' after the plebeian movement in the fifth century BC, did not form an anti-parliament nor even an effective alliance that might have been a credible alternative to the fascists. In part this was due to Pope Pius XI, who not only forbade the populists to co-operate with the socialists, but even ordered the unfortunate Don Sturzo into exile. There was little that the Aventine opposition could do except hope that there would be a massive swing of public opinion away from the fascists, and that the fascist movement would fall apart under the strain of the crisis.

Many radical fascists felt that Mussolini was being far too conciliatory and that the time had come to destroy the opposition and establish an outright dictatorship. They were outraged when the militia was obliged to take an oath of allegiance to the king, a move designed to appease the nationalists and conservatives. A group of Consuls of the militia warned Mussolini that a 'second wave' of violence would errupt if the government did not take decisive action, and demonstrations in some of the major cities were held to the same effect. Mussolini decided to give way to this pressure and to establish a full dictatorship.

Prior to the murder of Matteotti, Mussolini had intended to shore up his authoritarian personal rule by strengthening the ties with the political parties of the right and centre who saw him as the best guarantee against socialism, and with big business who approved of his economic liberalism and his destruction of the labour movement. Some important politicians such as Giolitti, Salandra and Orlando ceased to support Mussolini when freedom of the press was abolished in November. Industrialists were alarmed at the fascist-sponsored strikes, prompted by the high inflation rate and the refusal of the employers to honour their undertaking to increase industrial wages. With his support eroded and faced with the increasingly threatening attitude of the fascist extremists, Mussolini decide to make a bid to establish a 'totalitarian Fascist state'.

On 3 January 1925 Mussolini announced in the chamber that 'I, and I alone, assume the political, moral and historical responsibility for all that has happened', and warned that 'If two irreconcilable elements are struggling with each other, the solution lies in force'. Although he promised that the situation would be cleared up in forty-eight hours, he still moved slowly. He purged his government of non-fascist ministers. In March he appointed the radical Farinacci to head the Fascist Party. The militia was mobilized and countless arrests were made. In January the Aventine opposition lost their parliamentary seats, but it was not until October that the PSU became the first of the political parties to be banned, when one of the deputies from Matteotti's old party attempted to assassinate the *Duce*. In January 1926 the populist deputies who tried to take their seats in parliament were chased away by the fascists. In October there was another attempt on Mussolini's life. A sixteen-year-old who was almost certainly innocent was killed on the spot, torn to pieces and his body hauled around Bologna in a disgusting display of fascist violence. This was taken as an excuse to ban all political parties. The communist leader, Antonio Gramsci, was thrown into jail where he was later to die. Italy was now a one-party state, but there were still powerful interests with which Mussolini had to contend: the Crown, the Church, the Army, big business and even the PNF.

For the party the big question was whether it would be captured by the intransigents or whether it would be subordinated to the state. Federzoni brought matters to a head when he ordered the arrest of some fascist hoodlums in Bologna. Mussolini supported the minister of the interior, but there was much grumbling among the ranks which died down somewhat when Farinacci was made general secretary of the PNF, a move which was applauded by proponents of the 'second wave'. Under Farinacci rigid discipline was imposed on the party and it was submitted to an inflated bureaucracy, but the *ras* still ruled their provincial feifdoms with few restraints from the party directorate. The party managed to secure the dismissal of a large number of state officials who were deemed not to be sufficiently fascist. The violence of the *squadristi* continued, aimed mainly against the freemasons who were denounced as a sinister underground movement which controlled the professional middle class. Mussolini denounced this lawlessness as 'grotesque and criminal', but it proved difficult to curb, for violence was such an integral part of the fascist movement that it was difficult for it to survive without it. Farinacci saw the party faithful as guardians of the sacred flame of fascism and thus superior to the state apparatus which had to be purged of 'moral inertia'. Mussolini, who has hoped that he had co-opted Farinacci, saw in this attitude a challenge to his undisputed leadership. He regretted that revolutionaries remained after the revolution was over, and that although parliament, the civil service and the judiciary was firmly under government control and the opposition had been routed, the party still found it necessary to challenge the officers of the state such as the prefects. On 30 April 1926 Farinacci was relieved of his post and succeeded by Augusto Turati. In order to appease the malcontents in the party Mussolini dismissed Federzoni and once again became minister of the interior. Some of the less popular prefects were removed from office and replaced by party activists. But the rejoicing in the party did not last long. On 5 January 1927 Mussolini issued a circular which affirmed the superiority of the prefect over the local party leader (*federale*). Elections within the party were no longer permitted, the *federali* were appointed by the general secretary, and the party press was brought under tight central control. Intransigents like the unrepentent Farinacci suggested that the party and the state should be merged, so that the militant Fascists could have the instruments of institutionalized violence in their own hands and the state would become truly fascist after some further purging. Mussolini preferred to subordinate the party to the state, and to hold it in reserve to be used when needed.

Under Turati the radical fascists were removed and the 'revisionists' at last came to the fore, but this did not mark an end to the tension between the *Duce* and the PNF. Even the revisionists like Bottai resented the subordination of the party to the state and criticized the interference of the prefects in their affairs. They also resented Mussolini's charismatic personal dictatorship, and preferred to think of him as *primus inter pares* in the party elite. The party tended to become middle-class, respectable, and in many areas frankly apathetic. The more ambitious fascists pursued their careers within the grossly inflated government bureaucracy, a phenomenon called *ventottismo* (28-ism) since it was most prominent in 1928. But the party never completely atrophied. It remained an important source of influence and patronage, the fascist 'sub-government' (*sottogoverno*) playing much the same role as the old liberal pork-barrelling. The radical proponents of the supremacy of the party did not disappear from the scene. In 1930 Farinacci got his revenge on Turati, who had foolishly tried to resist Mussolini's decree that there should be no further elections in the party, charging him with sundry crimes and shortcomings including drug addiction, pederasty and even insanity. Later Farinacci was to become the great advocate of the alliance with Nazi Germany and of Nazi racial policies. These divisions within the party were never overcome, for it was the moderates in the party who overthrew Mussolini in 1943.

The fascists had always loudly trumpeted the harmony of interests between capital and labour. This had been the basis of the Palazzo Chigi agreement in 1923 when Mussolini told the assembled industrialists that the government would keep the labour movement in order, but also warned them that they would have to increase wages to placate the workers. The industrialists did not keep their side of the bargain and working-class militancy could not be easily crushed. The facist union boss, Rossoni, was too radical for the industrialists but far too moderate for those fascists who were still steeped in the syndicalist tradition. It had to be reluctantly admitted that the class struggle still existed. The Palazzo Chigi agreement acknowledged that employers and workers formed two separate and distinct entities and that Rossoni's idea of 'integral syndicalism', whereby workers and employers should be organized in mixed syndicates, was a dead letter. The mounting tensions between capital and labour, which were intensified after the Matteotti crisis, were such that Mussolini was prompted into action and it was announced that these contradictions would be overcome in a higher fascist synthesis.

The first major practical step to achieve this exotic Hegelian ideal was the Palazzo Vidoni pact of 2 October 1925. The Italian Confederation of Industry (Confindustria – CGII) and the fascist trades unions agreed that all labour negotiations should take place between the fascist unions and Confindustria and its affiliates. It was further agreed that the factory councils should be abolished and that the non-fascist unions should no longer be accepted as legitimate representatives of the workers. These negotiations involved concessions on both sides. The industrialists were concerned about government control of labour relations and were appalled at the prospect of binding arbitration which they were determined to resist. The fascist unions rejoiced at the abolition of the factory councils, many of which were still dominated by socialists, but were unable to win acceptance for their proposal for fascist factory representatives (*fiduciari di fabbrica*). The unions also had to give up the right to strike.

The Palazzo Vidoni pact became the basis of the syndical law of 1926 which abolished the right to strike and the factory committees but also obliged the industrialists to accept compulsory arbitration. The industrialists complained that they had been forced to make considerable concessions, but they amounted to very little in practice. A review body was established to examine all labour disputes before they went to the courts. By 1937 only twelve such cases had been settled by a court ruling. Confindustria was recognized as the official representative body of the industrialists and was given a seat on the Fascist Grand Council, in government economic planning agencies and was even allotted a seat in parliament.

Under the new law economic activity was divided under a number of headings such as industry, agriculture, commerce, banking and insurance, transportation on land and inland waterways, and transportation by sea and air. In each group employers and workers were organized separately. A further association was formed for intellectuals, artists and professionals. Confindustria was recognized as the official organization of industrial employers. Although it thus became an official public agency with juridical authority it was still run by and for the industrialists to further their own aims.

The syndical law also created a Ministry of Corporations and a National Council of Corporations, creating the impression that the much vaunted 'corporate state' was about to become a reality. In fact for the next eight years the only corporation which was fully functioning was the corporation for artists and intellectuals which was hardly of great economic significance. The industrialists were opposed to corporatism because they feared that it would give the workers too much influence, and most fascist leaders sympathized with this point of view. Rossoni fought a lonely fight for corporatism but he was isolated from Mussolini who resented his popularity and his power.

On 21 April 1927 the Fascist Grand Council promulgated the Charter of Labour which was heralded as the 'Magna Carta of Fascism'. Although there are some nebulous references to the ways in which capital and labour could co-operate, in essence the charter marked a further step in the domination of labour by capital which was characteristic of the fascist regime. It was solemnly declared that private enterprise was in the true interests of the nation and that the state should only interfere with production when private initiative was seriously deficient or when the political interests of the state were directly involved. The charter affirmed that employers no longer had to worry about trades unions, shop stewards or factory councils. A Labour Board was established which set about reducing wages by 10–20 per cent in support of a revaluation of the lira which in turn caused unemployment to rise as Italian exports became uncompetitively expensive. The fascist Magna Carta thus helped the barons of industry and finance but further restricted the rights of the workers. It marked a further defeat for Rossoni and for fascist syndicalism. Opposed by both the industrialists and by the PNF and denounced for promoting selfish class interests for which there was no place in the fascist state, Rossoni was soon to fall. In 1928 he was forced to resign, an impressive file having been produced with many lurid details of his sex life and dubious financial dealings. With his resignation the National Confederation of Fascist Unions was broken up into six independent confederations to correspond with the six employers' confederations. This was a victory for the employers, but they still had to face the fact that the fascists insisted that Italy was undergoing a revolution and that some of them might be tempted to try to make the corporate system work. It needed skill, patience and cunning to render this lofty experiment innocuous.

Mussolini had managed to reach a satisfactory compromise with the employers with whom he had been on good terms since the

March on Rome. He was also anxious to reach an understanding with the Church which would, he hoped, greatly enhance his prestige and to enlist the Church's support for the corporate state which seemed theoretically similar to the social doctrines of Leo XIII's encyclical *Rerum Novarum* of 1891 which formed the basis of Catholic social teaching. The prospects for such a rapprochement were not promising. Ever since the occupation of Rome by Italian troops in 1870 the popes had refused to recognize the Italian state. Mussolini, whose first pamphlet was entitled 'God Does Not Exist', and who remained resolutely anti-clerical, seemed an unlikely person to heal these long-standing wounds.

There was much in the fascist movement which was attractive to the Church. Fascists were opponents of the liberal state which the Vatican abhorred, and they were the most effective antidote to communism and socialism. Pius XI, whose pontificate began in 1922, was a diehard conservative who was considerably more rigid and inflexible in outlook than his predecessor, Benedict XV. He had little sympathy for Don Sturzo and his politicized Catholics in the Populist Party and had little compunction in dropping him in 1923. For motives of pure expedience Mussolini allowed the crucifix to be exhibited in schools and public places, permitted religious instruction in primary schools and saved the Bank of Rome, the Vatican's bank, from ruin. Pius XI reciprocated by ordering the faithful to remain silent during the Matteotti crisis. But the pope was soon worried that Mussolini's totalitarian aspirations, and the virulent anti-clericalism of many of his followers, might lead to the exclusion of the Church and to an attack on Catholic Action, which he had reorganized and brought under strict clerical control and which was designed to involve the laity in the work of the Church.

Negotiations began in the summer of 1926 and resulted in the signature of the Lateran Pacts of 11 February 1929. Substantial concessions were made to the Church. Catholic Action was permitted to continue its work and was thus by far the largest organization remaining outside fascist control. The Concordat recognized the Church as a fully autonomous and self-regulating institution within the state. It gave the Church full jurisdiction over marriages between Catholics. It made religious instruction compulsory in primary and secondary schools. The Conciliation Treaty, signed at the same time, recognized the full sovereignty of the Vatican City, the independence of the Holy See and recognized the Catholic Apostolic Roman religion as the only state religion. In a third document, the Financial Convention, the Italian state agreed to give the

Holy See 750 million lire in cash and 1 billion lire in state bonds.

At first the fascists gained immeasurably from the Lateran Pacts, for there was a wave of popular Catholic support for the regime. But before long the organizations of Catholic Action became the training ground for an alternative elite to the fascists which was to become the basis of the anti-fascist Christian Democratic movement. Radical fascists launched a concerted attack on Catholic Action in 1931 which resulted in the loss of certain privileges and its independence, particularly in its youth movement. The Church fought back by placing leading fascist thinkers such as Gentile on the Index and the pope made it clear that he could not approve of the idea of the totalitarian state, for rights were given by God not the state, and the Church could never be subordinated to any man-made authority, and he expressed his horror at Mussolini's heretical insistence that without the might of Rome Christianity would have remained an obscure and powerless sect. But relations between the Holy See and the fascist state were correct and frequently cordial until the closer ties with Nazi Germany confronted the Church with racialism and increased violence in the fascist movement. However, the Church was already badly compromised. It applauded the war in Ethiopia as a civilizing mission and even as a crusade. The war in Spain was similarly heralded as a battle against the forces of evil. The corporate state was praised as the closest approximation to the social teachings of the Church and many aspects of the new order were expressly approved in the encyclical *Quadragesimo anno* of 1931. Many clerics and laymen in Catholic Action courageously pointed out the profound incompatability of Christianity and fascism, and the Church was the only institution able to challenge the totalitarian aspirations of the fascist regime. But the many compromises and concessions made to fascism in the name of expedience, or for the future good of the Church, caused much soul-searching among many of the faithful, and are still the cause of bitter controversy.

Lacking any coherent economic policy, the fascists talked bombastically about willpower as the key to economic success and economic life as a battle ground on which the disciplined ranks of the fascists would triumph. Thus there was the 'battle for wheat', the 'battle for the lira' and sundry other battles, campaigns and mobilizations. This language disguised the fundamental contradiction within fascist thought between the ideal of community and the transcending of the class struggle through corporatism, and belief in leadership, obedience, heirarchy and the command economy. This confusion was also found in the rejection of the free market economy as being politically undesirable as well as impractical, while at the same time a planned economy was felt to be unacceptably socialist. A political movement such as fascism which tried to reject politics found itself tied in some curious knots which could not be undone by dewy-eyed references to a 'higher Fascist synthesis'.

Initially fascist economic policy was traditionally liberal and minimized the economic role of the state. De Stefani as minister of finance denationalized the telephone company and insurance, along with other nationalized industries. He reduced the marginal rate of income tax, abolished death duties, lowered business taxes and emphasized indirect taxation, all with a view to encouraging productive investment. He subscribed to the popular view that public works could not solve unemployment, a problem which could only be tackled by rigorous economies, a balanced budget, and by the free play of market forces.

De Stefani was essentially a free trader, a policy which suited the textile manufacturers of his home town of Vicenza but which was opposed by the iron and steel industries, by the armaments manufacturers and by the chemical and electrical concerns. Against his better judgement he intervened to save the Bank of Rome from bankruptcy and invested state funds in the steel combine Ansaldo, a huge corporation run by the brothers Mario and Pio Perrone who were advocates of a command economy which would benefit heavy industry. The bank of Italy granted massive credits to industry through various intermediary agencies, and was thus undermining De Stefani's policies. A declining lira, a bout of unseemly stock exchange speculation, the opposition of the financiers and heavy industrialists, his opposition to protectionism, and the new authoritarian trend of the regime lead to De Stefani's downfall in 1925.

In August 1926 Mussolini gave a speech at Pesaro in which he announced a drastic policy of deflation which included the *quota novanta*, the revaluation of the lira from about 154 to about 90 to the pound sterling. Since Winston Churchill had revalued the pound the previous year to an unrealistically high level, the effects of this policy were dramatic. It seriously hurt all those branches of industry and agriculture which had large export orders, along with the banks which financed them. The cost of deflation was borne by the working class once the employers won their battle with Rossoni and the fascist unions. Businessmen favoured revaluation, but most agreed that the *quota novanta* was set far too high, and there was considerable protest against the measure, especially from the textile industry.

Mussolini's motives for revaluation were mixed. In part it was a matter of prestige, and a dramatic demonstration of fascist will-power triumphing over the international financial plutocracy and their hangers-on among Jews and freemasons. It was designed to head off mounting speculation against the lira on the foreign exchanges, to reduce the price of imports which had risen owing to protectionist policies introduced in 1925, it would give the fascists a new mission which could replace the disorderly violence of the squads, it would depress wages but favour those on fixed incomes, and would hopefully strengthen the state at the expense of the private sector. In one important respect the Pesaro policy had the opposite effect to that which Mussolini intended. He disliked the big banks like the Banca Commerciale with which his new minister of finance, Volpi, was closely connected, and big industrial firms like Fiat which were so powerful that they could resist measures proposed by the state of which they did not approve. In fact the *quota novanta* led to an increase in industrial concentration which could not be overcome by feeble attempts to introduce anti-trust measures, by central planning, or by attempting to increase the importance of the public sector. Smaller firms which were directly hurt by the artificially high rate of exchange tried to weather the storm by mergers, the larger corporations rejoiced as their smaller competitors were eliminated. Big business became concentrated and strengthened and was in an even stronger position to meet the challenge from the fascist unions and to safeguard its interests within the corporate state.

The 'battle for wheat' was designed to make the country self-sufficient in wheat and to make Italians aware of the sterling virtues of 'rurality' and the need to increase the birthrate in a bid for 'demographic power'. The first campaign in the battle was fought in July 1925 when Volpi introduced protective tariffs on wheat in order to stem the flow of imports caused by a poor harvest in 1924 and which was seriously affecting the balance of payments and the exchange rate. The tariffs, which may well have been justified in 1925, were increased in 1928 and 1929 when the emergency had long passed. They served to protect the large and uneconomic producers, for the peasants consumed virtually all they produced. Although agricultural imports declined, so did exports as producers switched to wheat. The effect on the balance of payments was therefore not as impressive as had been hoped. The increased cost of wheat counteracted the deflationary effects of the government's economic policies and thus made the lot of the common man even more wretched. This applied equally to the peasants who were hurt by higher rents and by the rising cost of artificial fertilizers which were controlled by Montecatini, whose monopoly hold over production of fertilizers resulted in increased prices while production quadrupled between 1922 and 1929. Mussolini, unable to force Montecatini to lower prices, reduced the freight rates on the railways and thus put the entire railway system into the red. Animal husbandry was neglected as were specialized crops which had been a lucrative source of export income. The 'battle for wheat' was a success in that Italy did become self-sufficient, but in economic and in social terms it was a disaster which none of the inspiring photographs of the *Duce*, stripped to the waist and transformed into the First Peasant of Italy, helping with the harvest or chatting to enthusiastic rice pickers, could possibly conceal.

In 1928 Volpi was replaced by Antonio Mosconi who set about overcoming the problems of the depression by increasing taxation and by undertaking massive public works projects. Land drainage and reclamation, which was part of the battle for wheat, was another spectacular propaganda success, and the draining of the Pontine marshes was seen both at home and abroad as one of the regime's outstanding achievements. Praiseworthy as these efforts might have been they did not lead to a significant rise in agricultural productivity, they were enormously expensive and they largely profited private land speculators and contractors. The most beneficial side effect of the land reclamation programme was a significant reduction in the incidence of malaria.

Attempts to encourage an increase in the birthrate were largely unsuccessful. That there was a population increase was due in large part to a population increase that predated fascism and to the restriction of emigration to the United States and to South America. It was fortunate for the regime that this programme was a failure, for peasants continued to flock to the towns in search of work, and none of the sentimental glorification of the life of the share-croppers (*Mezzadri*) was sufficient to stop this movement away from the land, and unemployment was a serious problem. The demographic battle, which was lost, and 'ruralism', which was little more than a rhetorical device, were evidence of a lingering anti-modernism and anti-rationalism within fascism which was incompatible with economic growth and preparation for war. Mussolini's slogans like 'empty the cities' in 1926, his praise of a particularly backward province as being not yet 'infected by the pernicious tendencies of contemporary civilization' and his approval of the horrendous birthrate in the slums of Naples and Palermo were not mere propagandistic devices to disguise the harsh lot of the rural poor or an attempt to create an illusion of class harmony, it was an indirect admission that fascism had managed to control labour, but had been far less successful in controlling the nation's economy. For all the paraphenalia of the corporate state, big business, like the Church and the armed forces, ran its own affairs and co-operated with the regime largely because it suited them. Mussolini needed big business if he were to make Italy truly great and pursue his imperial adventures, but there were limits to the extent which he was able to dominate a firmly established economic structure. The economic measures which were introduced to achieve a degree of autarky and to overcome the effects of the depression increased the totalitarian tendencies of the regime, but at the same time they favoured certain sectional interests and made the achievement of a homogenous Fascist society even more remote. Fascism was no more able than was national socialism to overcome this contradiction between modernity and a sentimental, reactionary hankering after the simple life of the past, with its certain values and sturdy culture. Behind the facade of totalitarian dictatorship both states were profoundly unstable. Unable to find the 'higher fascist synthesis' in peace time they eventually imagined it could be found in a victorious war.

The government largely ignored the signs of an impending depression, fondly imagining that it was an essentially American problem and that the steps they had taken towards autarky combined with resolute fascist willpower would be sufficient to deal with the situation. By 1930 the crisis was upon them in full force, exacerbated by the overvaluation of the lira, high levels of government expenditure and structural imbalances within the economy. The effects were predictable. Unemployment increased dramatically, and many workers were only able to find part-time employment. Although industrial wages remained stable, in agriculture and among the lower-paid workers incomes fell significantly. Industrial production fell by 25 per cent between 1929 and 1932. Smaller firms were particularly badly hit, and there was a further increase in the tendency towards concentration as the larger concerns swallowed up their enfeebled competitors. By 1935 industrial production recovered almost to the level of 1929, the rate of recovery of the larger firms far outstripping that of the smaller ones, many of which were still unable to show a profit.

Government expenditure was increased to stimulate the economy and consumer taxes were adjusted in an attempt to meet the cost of these public works projects; but in spite of these measures, which were relatively modest since the level of taxation was already very high, the government deficit grew alarmingly. The government defended the high exchange rate even though sterling was devalued in 1931 and the franc two years later. This further damaged the smaller exporting industries such as textiles and helped heavy industry which paid for imported raw materials with an inflated currency.

In January 1933 the government established a new institution to intervene in banking and industry. The *Istituto per la Ricostruzione Industriale* (IRI) bought up shares in industries which were particularly hard hit by the depression and which were held by the big banks. The banks were thus given an injection of liquid capital which enabled them to operate more effectively. IRI set out to assist enterprises to run their own affairs as they saw best; it was not an attempt by the government to direct the economy. It was run by and for businessmen who were determined to resist any such government intervention. In this they were only partially successful. IRI became a vast public holding company devoted to financing the rearmament programme and encouraging autarky. It did not disappear once the depression began to abate as the businessmen had hoped.

In 1936 IRI ceased to grant credit to industry, a role now performed by the *Istituto Mobiliare Italiano* (IMI). Henceforth the banks were only permitted to extend short-term credit to industry, medium- and long-term credit was now provided by government agencies. Government control of industry was thus greatly increased, although this took the form of financial inducements rather than direct intervention. In some sectors private enterprise bought out IRI's holdings, but in the less profitable industries such as steel, machinery, shipping, electricity and telephones IRI had a controlling interest. This did not amount to outright nationalization because many private firms continued to operate beyond the direct control of IRI and private investors were able to buy IRI stock. Direct government involvement in firms in which IRI had a controlling interest seldom amounted to more than finding comfortable positions on the board of directors for privileged dignitaries sent out to pasture. An attempt by IRI to rationalize and concentrate the steel industry failed and this was only achieved after the fall of fascism. IRI survived to play a vital role in post-war reconstruction and was an important factor in Italy's 'economic miracle'.

The depression forced the government to address the question of corporatism which had been tabled since 1926. A Ministry of

Corporations had been established, but as yet there were no corporations in large part because they were fiercely resisted by the industrialists who feared that the workers would be given a voice in management. These fears seemed amply justified when the fascist philosopher Ugo Spirito gave a much publicized speech in May 1932 in which he proposed that private property should be abolished and 'proprietary corporations' created which would abolish the distinctions between the public and the private, as well as between capital and labour, thus revealing 'the whole political, moral and religious meaning of the fascist revolution'. The industrialists were horrified at this suggestion, and most of the fascist bosses condemned it as 'bolshevism', but an issue had been raised which the fascists were determined to resolve. The business world knew that the fascists clung to the notion that theirs was a continuing revolution and that they would not abandon the idea of corporatism and therefore resolved to get as much out of the system as they could. The goverment was determined to appear to be dealing resolutely with the problems of the depression, and the businessmen were equally determined to ensure that the corporations were not given too much power and that they should work to their advantage.

Faced with the difficulties of the depression businessmen badly needed government assistance, but they did not want government control. In 1932 Mussolini appointed himself minister of corporations. He proclaimed that capitalism was dead and that corporatism was the only way to overcome the deficiencies of economic liberalism, just as fascism had replaced political liberalism. Twenty-two corporations were created, the first in 1934, bringing together employers and workers and including most sectors of production within specific areas of economic activity. The massive bureaucratic structures of the corporations disguised the fact that the big producers decided quotas and the assignment of raw materials. The workers were given equal representation on the boards of the corporations where they wasted their time in futile debate while their colleagues on the shop floor were further subordinated to the employers. Felice Guarneri, a financier and cabinet member, said of the corporations that they 'began their lives as insitutions operating in a void, without any hold on the state organization, of which they were organs, or on those of production of which they were supposed to become instruments of discipline and coordination.' For all the claims that this was a revolutionary new form of economic organization it soon became obvious that the corporations were a sham. By 1937 the National Council of Corporations no longer met, and in 1939 Mussolini handed over the Ministry of Corporations to a nonentity. He had said that corporations were 'the Fascist institution *par excellence*' and that 'the fascist state is corporate or it is nothing', but they never amounted to much more than a smokescreen and he lost interest in them. Perhaps Mussolini was right after all, for the corporations which appeared to control the economy in the public interest did nothing of the sort, and in this they were typically fascist institutions.

In order to give back to fascism some of its dynamism and myth, to identify the masses with the regime and no doubt also to satisfy his peculiar psychological needs, Mussolini paid close attention to the cult of his personality. In this he was ably assisted by Giovanni Starace who was appointed secretary of the Fascist Party in 1931. Starace was stupid, sycophantic and corrupt. He was known to be a rapist and a pederast and dabbled in prostitution and drug peddling, but he was a capable organizer and was so devoted to Mussolini that he is said to have stood rigidly to attention whenever talking to him on the telephone. Starace introduced the 'Roman salute' and the cry *Viva il Duce!* He put on massive parades and demonstrations to the glory of fascism and its martyrs and for the adulation of Mussolini. He encouraged the use of uniforms to such a ludicrous extent that cabinet ministers had up to twenty different outfits for different ceremonial occasions. The result of all his bombast was that Mussolini became even more isolated from the people and was deluded by the flatterers who surrounded him into believing that he could demand anything of them. After 1932 ministers virtually ceased to advise him and were reduced to being mere executants of his will. Success in the war against Ethiopia greatly enhanced his popularity and he became increasingly prey to his own myth to the point of almost becoming a caricature of himself.

When the League of Nations imposed economic sanctions against Italy, Mussolini announced the policy of autarky to defend Italy against its enemies abroad and to set an exhilarating goal that would test the country's mettle. Economic nationalism was common to all countries during the depression, but the attempt to make Italy largely self-sufficient went far beyond this and was bound to fail. Autarky led to an increase in prices which was not offset by higher wages. Privileged firms were granted fixed quotas which guaranteed a steady supply of iron and steel, whereas smaller concerns were severely affected by import restrictions. The economy became frozen in that the powerful firms were favoured, the weak discriminated against. The war in Ethiopia and intervention in the Spanish civil war had a devastating effect on the balance of payments and the efforts to achieve self-sufficiency did little to lessen this serious problem.

Mussolini's expansionist and aggressive foreign policy was yet another attempt to give a sense of direction and dynamism to a society that was beginning to show an increasing lack of cohesion and a widespread sense of resignation and cynicism. As Italy drew closer to Germany Nazi racist policies were implemented to stir up the hatreds and passions of the mob. Italians were ordered to use the pronoun *voi* which Mussolini felt was more noble than *lei*, the whole ridiculous exercise designed to strengthen the Italians' character. In the army the Italian equivalent of the goosestep, the *passo romano*, was introduced for the same purpose. None of this had much effect. Conservatives were unenthusiastic about the prospect of war and became increasingly estranged from the regime. The Church was alienated by the regime's racialism. The king was distressed by Mussolini's pretensions to be regarded as his equal. Landowners complained of excessive taxation and businessmen resented the privileged status of the big corporations. Most Italians still tacitly accepted fascism, and it would be mistaken to suppose that the regime was falling apart. Nor was Mussolini's warlike policy a mere political ploy to overcome the contradictions and conflicts within Italian society; it was an essential ingredient of fascism and Mussolini's famous aphorism that 'war is for men what motherhood is for women' is a typical instance of his constant glorification of war. But under the strains of a war in which the Italians were supposed to prove themselves and be tempered into the new fascist man, all the strains and divisions of the pre-war period were intensified and the situation became so hopeless that Mussolini was overthrown by the Fascist Grand Council and placed under arrest. The imposing dictatorship collapsed like a pack of cards and none of his followers lifted a finger to save their deposed *Duce*. Some fascist leaders fled to the protection of the Germans, others began to ingratiate themselves with the victorious allies, only a handful committed suicide in the Roman manner.

CHAPTER SEVEN
The Weimar Republic

The German revolution of 1918–19 began in the time-honoured Prussian tradition of a 'revolution from above'. Admiral Paul von Hintze, the state secretary for foreign affairs, suggested that as the war was obviously lost and an armistice had to be signed, some modest democratic reforms would have to be made, so as to meet the Allies' insistence that they would only treat with a democratic German government, and also to avoid a 'revolution from below'. On 29 September 1918 General Ludendorff, Hindenburg's second-in-command, but *de facto* head of the High Command, agreed to this proposal. The kaiser concurred, and the ancient and somewhat ineffectual chancellor, Hertling, made way for a moderate liberal, Prince Max of Baden. The new cabinet was made up of middle-of-the-road liberals, Catholic Centre Party members and, most shocking of all, a member of the Social Democratic Party. These reforms turned Germany into a constitutional monarchy, with ministerial responsibility and a government representative of the majority parties in a Reichstag elected by universal suffrage.

Some politicians were dimly aware that these reforms were largely designed to bring down upon the democratic parties the odium of defeat and responsibility for what was likely to be a harsh peace settlement. As Ludendorff put it: 'They have made their bed, now they can lie on it!' Their motives for going along with the 'Hintze Action' were mixed. Even the social democrats, reviled for years as red revolutionaries, were terrified at the prospect of a 'revolution from below'. All the majority parties agreed that the Allies were likely to be more lenient towards a decently democratic Germany. Many were motivated by less exalted concerns. They wanted to exercise political power after years in the political wilder-

ness. They imagined that the reforms of October were enough to
ensure a secure democratic future for the country, and they
discounted the threat from those who were determined that the old
regime should be restored.

It was the new government which hoisted the white flag, not the
soldiers, and in doing so they played directly into the hands of those
who were determined to strangle parliamentary democracy at birth.
They told the press that it was essential to create the impression that
the decision to ask for an armistice was a political decision and that
it did not come from the military. In doing so they were acting
responsibly and patriotically, for they did not want to give the Allies
the impression that the front was about to collapse. This proved to
be a fatal mistake, for the defeated army and the bankrupt politicians
on the right were quick to blame the defeat on the feeble civilians
who betrayed an undefeated army which was, in some exalted
versions, close to bringing a final victory. The 'stab in the back'
legend, which was such a powerful weapon against the republic, was
an essential part of the Hintze Action. Very few realized that they
were being led into a trap, and Scheidemann was almost alone in
warning the social democratic parliamentary party that this was a
bankrupt enterprise' and that the majority parties were being used
as scapegoats. He was reprimanded by his party leader, Ebert, for
forgetting his duty as a patriotic German, and on the next day
he joined Prince Max's government as an imperial secretary of
state.

The revolution from above seemed to be going like clockwork
until it was suddenly sabotaged by the imperial navy. The Admiralty
decided that the fleet should be sent to do battle with the Royal Navy
in the North Sea. It was hoped that this suicide mission would serve
several purposes. It would restore the honour of the fleet which was
somewhat tarnished after two years of inaction. The battle fleet
would then not be ignored in post-war military planning, and would
be seen as an important branch of the armed services with a significant contribution to make to Germany's defences. Lastly, the sortie
would hopefully shatter the illusion that an armistice was necessary.
The sailors were in no mood to risk their lives on this unpromising
mission and they mutinied. Demonstrations were organized in Kiel
in which defiance of the Admiralty was mixed with radical political
demands. Throughout Germany meetings were held which
expressed support for the sailors, and no amount of blaming the
mutiny on outside agitators, British money, or bolshevik cells could
halt the demands for radical reforms which went far beyond those

granted in October, and for an immediate peace. It looked as if the revolution from below had come at last.

Ebert suggested to Groener, who had replaced Ludendorff at the High Command, that the only way of saving the monarchy was to appoint one of the kaiser's sons as regent; but it was already too late. On 7 November Kurt Eisner, an anarchist, seized power in Munich. On 9 November Prince Max resigned, just before the kaiser announced his abdication. In Berlin the troops refused to stop a massive demonstration by factory workers and revolutionary sailors demanding an immediate end to the war. Later in the day the kaiser was sent packing by the generals, to spend the rest of his life in exile in Holland.

In a somewhat bizarre encounter, Prince Max handed over the office of chancellor to Ebert, and although he had no constitutional right to do so, it soothed the consciences of the civil servants and the generals who remained loyal to the kaiser and yet stayed in office. Ebert's government consisted of his own SPD (Social Democratic Party of Germany) and the USPD (the left-wing independent socialists), and called itself the Council of People's Representatives. Philip Scheidemann appeared on the balcony of the Reichstag and called out to the vast crowd below: 'Long live the German republic!' From the balcony of the Royal Palace in Berlin, Karl Liebknecht, the spokesman of the left wing of the labour movement, proclaimed to an equally large and excited throng a 'free, socialist German republic'. Ebert was appalled at these declarations, and told Prince Max that he was 'still trying not to break the organizational link to the past', suggesting that Prince Max should become regent in an attempt to save the monarchy. The prince, not wishing to be in so uncomfortably close an association with socialists, told Ebert that he felt that the affairs of state were in trusted hands, and promptly departed for his estates in Baden.

The left had seized the initiative. The Revolutionary Shop Stewards, militants who had organized the great wartime strikes, met in the Reichstag and called for elections for workers and soldiers councils to be held the following day in all Berlin factories and barracks. Elections were held the following morning, a Sunday, and in the afternoon the councils all met at the Busch Circus in the east end of Berlin. They passed a resolution supporting Ebert's government, which included Scheidemann and Otto Landsberg for the SPD and Hugo Haase, Wilhelm Dittmann and Emil Barth for the USPD; the latter also serving as the representative of the Revolutionary Shop Stewards. Elections were also held for an executive council of the oldiers and workers councils. It was hoped that they would push Ebert's government to the left, but they resulted in the SPD winning a majority of two-thirds. The soldiers and workers councils, which sprang up spontaneously throughout Germany, seemed to the horrified bourgeoisie to be alarmingly revolutionary. But almost all of them were dominated by moderate social democrats, particularly in the soldiers councils, and in the provinces even more so than in Berlin. They were certainly not Soviets on the Leninist model, and they saw their principal task as giving democratic legitimacy to Ebert's cautious cabinet.

The left of the USPD and the Spartacus League, which was to form the nucleus of the German Communist Party, hoped that the council movement would mature into a genuinely revolutionary alternative to bourgeois democracy, and would make it possible to restructure society along socialist lines. The SPD feared that this was a possibility, and was determined that Germany should be a parliamentary democracy. Representatives of a gigantic bureaucratic party apparatus, the Majority Socialists, were deeply suspicious of a movement which, with its belief in direct democracy and constant accountability, was inimical to the notion of party rule. In fact, the vast majority of Germans did not see themselves as being faced with a choice between soviet or bourgeois democracy, and the great debate was over the date of parliamentary elections. The USPD wanted to postpone them so as to have time to organize themselves effectively, and also to make sure that some thoroughgoing democratic changes were made in the economy, the civil service and the army. The SPD wanted the elections to take place as soon as possible, so that the country could get back to normal; exotic socialist experiments could be avoided, and the support of the army and the industrialists would hopefully continue.

The army was even more determined than the SPD that the country should not fall into the hands of the revolutionary left. On 10 November, Groener had telephoned Ebert and promised his support, provided that he would crush bolshevism and the council movement, call a National Assembly and restore 'orderly conditions'. Ebert, a stolid authoritarian who 'hated revolution like sin', eagerly agreed. The industrialists were also prepared to compromise with the new government to protect themselves from the left. On 15 November representatives of the employers and the unions produced the Stinnes–Legien Agreement whereby the employers recognized the unions and their full right to collective bargaining, agreed that all firms employing more than fifty workers should have works' councils and arbitration boards, and accepted the eight-hour working day. In return the unions promised to respect capitalist property relations and oppose any socialist experiments.

Although the government was in the hands of the socialists, and although some important concessions had been made, the old ruling class was still firmly in the saddle. All the senior civil servants remained in office, and the important ministries of War and Justice remained under the control of conservatives who were loyal to the old regime. The leaders of industry and finance had shown enough flexibility to ensure that they were untouched, and were biding their time, waiting to make themselves once again masters in their own houses. Above all, the army was still commanded by the old officer corps, whose authority had only in a few instances been challenged by the soldiers' councils. Although the soldiers' and workers' councils were far from revolutionary, and the vast majority of their members were loyal to the SPD, Ebert was determined that they should be destroyed. He therefore agreed to Groener's plan to send ten divisions from the western front to Berlin. They were due to arrive on 10 December so that the councils could be disbanded before the General Congress of all the councils in Germany could assemble as planned on 16 December.

The army were so eager to destroy the councils that they did not wait until 10 December. On 6 December troops from the Berlin garrison arrested the Berlin council, and others attacked a demonstration by the Spartacus League, leaving sixteen dead, and yet another unit marched to the Chancellory and proclaimed Ebert President. But this curious episode ended as mysteriously as it began. The council was set free and the troops returned to their barracks. Four days later the troops entered Berlin as planned. Ebert met them at the Brandenburg Gate and told them: 'The enemy did not defeat you! The unity of Germany is now in your hands!' The socialist leader thus gave his support to the 'stab in the back' legend, virtually admitted that the armistice was a betrayal, and recognized the army as the principal support of the new regime. No Wilhelmine militarist could have done better.

Unfortunately for Ebert and Groener the 75,000 soldiers who entered Berlin on 10 December had no desire to destroy the councils, and simply wanted to go home for Christmas. Within a few days only 800 of them were still under orders; hardly enough to carry out an effective counter-revolution. The Congress of Councils took place and dutifully voted in favour of early elections for a National Assembly, and thus for their own dissolution. But they did pass one resolution which was highly alarming to the army. They voted for the so-called 'Hamburg Points' for the democratization of the army. Officers were to be elected, there were to be no badges of rank, discipline was to be in the hands of the soldiers councils and the army was to be under strict civilian control.

The army reacted to the Hamburg Points with shrieks of protest and threats of resignation, but they also began to organize the Free Corps: mercenary bands of right-wing extremist adventurers, commanded by generals who were determined to destroy the 'red pack'. It was not only the swastikas on their helmets which made them the precursors of Hitler's armed bands, although the future Führer was at this time an invalided nonentity in a provincial military hospital.

Some soldiers sympathized with the left and were organized into the People's Marine Division which took possession of the royal palace and its adjacent stables. Although these troops were utterly loyal to the regime, Ebert and the civilian commander of Berlin, Otto Wels, were determined that they should leave Berlin and therefore stopped their pay to force them to disband. Negotiations between the two sides continued until 23 December when the division lost patience and occupied the Chancellory for a short time and took Wels hostage. After further negotiations the division set Wels free, retired from their positions in the centre of Berlin and returned to the palace. On the morning of 24 December the army opened fire on the palace. The troops had little stomach for the fight, the people of Berlin demonstrated in favour of the division, and by the end of the day the army retired, leaving the division in control of the city. Ebert made plans to move the government from Berlin, but he need not have worried. The people of Berlin were more interested in celebrating Christmas than they were in starting a revolution. The division had no political programme, were duly paid and agreed to leave the palace. They had enjoyed the support of the working class of Berlin, they had defeated the counter-revolutionary troops of General Lequis, but they made no significant contribution to the German revolution. They made no political capital from the wave of popular support which they enjoyed, and during the Spartacus uprising in January they were passive bystanders.

In protest against the attack on the People's Marine Division the USPD resigned from the Council of People's Representatives much to the delight of Ebert who now called his cabinet the 'Reich Government' to underline its respectability. On the left the Spartacus League reconstituted themselves as the Communist Party of

Germany (KPD) at the end of December, but although the new party had outstanding leaders in Rosa Luxemburg and Karl Liebknecht it was poorly organized and had little support. In early January the police chief of Berlin, Emil Eichhorn, who was a member of the USPD, was dismissed. The USPD, the Revolutionary Shop Stewards and the KPD organized a massive demonstration in support of Eichhorn. Some government buildings and newspaper offices were occupied, but no plans were made for an armed uprising which might very well have been successful if it had been properly organized. Ebert and Noske, who had made the notorious remark that 'someone must be the bloodhound' and who had replaced one of the USPD members of the cabinet, sent the Freecorps and the army against the demonstrators, thus unleashing a white terror. Liebknecht and Luxemburg were brutally murdered along with some 150 others. In the following weeks, according to Noske, who had no reason to exaggerate, 1,200 more were killed. The murderers were never punished, Ebert remained silent, Noske expressed his satisfaction, and the SPD press suggested that Liebknecht and Luxemburg had got their just desserts. The left called it a criminal betrayal of socialism, the right called it law and order. Whatever the case, Ebert and his government had effectively destroyed the radical left which was never to recover from its shattering defeat in January 1919.

Although these events have gone down in the history books as the 'Spartacus Revolt', the KPD played a subsidiary role. Far from being a determined effort by unscrupulous bolsheviks to overthrow the regime, it was an ill-considered and chaotic demonstration by the loosely organized Popular Front against the Ebert government's rightward course. The government had used ultra right-wing troops against people who were in many instances loyal to the SPD, even if they were critical, and they had condoned murder. So great was their culpability that they had as strong a motive as the right to claim that they had resorted to extreme means to save Germany from communism. It was a sordid fiction, but one which has persisted.

While the Free Corps rampaged across Germany crushing the militant left, elections were held on 19 January for the National Assembly. The result was a victory for the moderate republican parties. The SPD got 163 of the 421 seats, the Centre Party 91, and the liberal German Democratic Party (DDP) 75. The KPD refused to take part in the elections, but they would have made little impact. The USPD only won 22 seats.

On 11 August 1919 Ebert, as President of the Republic, signed the new constitution. It was a thoroughly liberal and democratic document, but it was an unfortunate compromise between representative and plebiscitary ideas. The Reichstag was to be elected by universal suffrage, with proportional representation. This gave the splinter parties a far better chance to be represented and, given the political divisions within Germany, it made it virtually impossible for any one party to gain an absolute majority; even the formation of majority governments became increasingly difficult. Proportional representation further increased the tendency for the political parties to become uncompromising interest groups, for there were few floating votes to win. By contrast to the legislature, the president was elected directly by the people, served for seven years, and had far-reaching powers. The government was dependent on the support of the Reichstag, which thus had full legislative authority, but the president alone could appoint and dismiss governments. Legislation could also be initiated by plebiscite. The emergency powers granted by Article 48 of the constitution gave the president virtually dictatorial powers. Given that anti-democratic ideas were ever increasing on the right and on the left, and given the fractionalism and antagonisms within the ranks of the democratic parties, the president was seen more and more as the true representative of the people. As it became increasingly difficult to form a majority government, there was a corresponding tendency to seek an authoritarian solution to constitutional problems by use of presidential decrees, and to avoid the compromises and tolerance needed for a functioning parliamentary democracy. Article 48, which had been designed to deal with dire emergencies, was to become a weapon to destroy a detested parliamentary system and to open the way to dictatorship. Oskar Cohn of the USPD was alone in warning of the dangers inherent in this provision. The Reichstag only had retroactive authority to control the use of paragraph 48, but throughout the Weimar Republic it was eager to further lessen its authority by passing enabling acts which were used for matters as remote from emergency as judicial reform. The courts had no control over the use of Article 48, which was frequently used to deal with economic, fiscal and social problems. In 1924, for example, when the emergency of the previous year was over, it was used as the basis for forty-two decrees. It is hardly a wonder that an anti-democratic politician like Brüning made use of it rather than bother to hammer out the compromises needed to form a majority government. In 1932, sixty laws were passed by decree and only five by normal parliamentary legislation. Hindenburg as president successfully resisted the attempt by the Marx government to limit the emergency powers of the president, and little stood in the way of those who planned to use a presidential regime to undermine parliamentary democracy.

While the Reichstag debated the details of the constitution the sixty-eight 'official' Free Corps units with almost 400,000 men continued their offensive against the councils, even though, as the election returns showed, the vast majority of them were loyal to the SPD. They smashed the Bavarian Soviet Republic, killing some 1,200 people in the reprisals that followed the capture of Munich, among them a number of women (*Spartakistenweiber*) who were tortured and killed. The murder of twenty-one Catholic apprentices who were mistaken for Spartacus supporters caused some upset in respectable circles and the Free Corps felt obliged to stop the summary execution of all whom they considered suspicious.

In March 1920 it became obvious that the real danger to democracy came not from the left, but from the Free Corps whom Ebert had used as the principal support of his regime. The 'Ehrhardt Brigade', otherwise known as 'Noske's Firemen', were well known for their extremism and for their antipathy towards the 'November criminals' in the government. In February, Noske ordered General Lüttwitz, who commanded all the irregular troops in Germany, to disband the brigade. He refused. Rather than fire Lüttwitz on the spot, discussions took place between the General, Ebert and Noske. Lüttwitz demanded the dissolution of the Reichstag, a bourgeois-nationalist government, and the continued existence of the Ehrhardt Brigade. Noske demanded his resignation. Lüttwitz replied by ordering the Ehrhardt Brigade to occupy Berlin, chase the government away and establish an extreme right-wing regime under Wolfgang Kapp. Noske ordered units of the army and the security forces to protect government buildings, but they promptly began negotiations with the rebels. When asked to stand by the government, the Chief of the General Staff, von Seeckt, replied 'troops do not shoot at troops' and said that he had 'no intention of conducting a manoeuvre with live ammunition between Potsdam and Berlin.' Ebert and the government saw no alternative but to flee to Dresden and leave the capital in the hands of the rebels. Having spent the last year warning against the danger of strikes, the SPD now called for a general strike against those who had done their dirty work for them, and whom they now denounced as 'Baltic criminals', conveniently forgetting that they had fought against the bolsheviks in the Baltic with the full support of the government. In Dresden, Ebert and Noske were arrested by one of their own creatures,

General Maercker, having denied that they had signed the call for a strike which bore their names. Shortly afterwards they were able to make an ignominious escape to Stuttgart.

The general strike was a triumphant success, the USPD and KPD deciding that Ebert and Noske, whom they denounced as the murderers of Luxemburg and Liebknecht, were a lesser evil than Kapp and Lüttwitz. With the country paralysed the rebels were helpless and the Kapp putsch collapsed. Lüttwitz and Ehrhardt were allowed to escape abroad, and Kapp went to Sweden where he died a natural death in 1922.

The Kapp putsch convinced many socialists and communists of the dangers of SPD's alliance with the counter-revolutionary forces. In Saxony, Thuringia and the industrial area of Rhineland–Westphalia the strike against the putsch turned into mass demonstrations demanding that the revolution of 1918–19 should be completed so that nothing like this could happen again. Armed bands were formed: in the Ruhr there was a Red Army which was several divisions strong. Faced with this new threat from the left, the Vice Chancellor and Minister of Justice, Eugen Schiffer of the DDP, decided that the real danger came from the 'bolsheviks', not from the extreme right, and began negotiating with Kapp. With the collapse of the putsch Schiffer had to resign from the cabinet, but the alliance between the government, the army and the Free Corps against the forces of the left which he had suggested was achieved under the new chancellor, Hermann Müller of the SPD. The Reichswehr and the Free Corps regarded anyone who had actively defended the republic against Kapp and Lüttwitz as a bolshevik, and considered it their patriotic duty to destroy all such dangerous elements. The Ruhr was subjected to a white terror every bit as horrific as that which Berlin had suffered in 1919, and was only saved from further brutality by the arrival of French troops sent to uphold the Treaty of Versailles and to stop this violation of the demilitarization of the Rhineland.

Putsch and protest were over, but virtually no one was brought to account for treason and murder. All the leaders of the putsch were allowed to go free. Only three putschists were brought to trial; one received a very mild sentence, the other two were set free. No one was seriously punished for the countless brutalities committed by the whites. Many who had loyally defended the republic had been sentenced by courts marshal to lengthy prison terms, hundreds were executed on the spot, others slaughtered in outbursts of blind fury. It is hardly surprising that the election results of 1920 were a crushing defeat for the SPD and the other Weimar parties. Eleven and a half million voters had supported the party in 1919, now it only got 5.6 million votes. The Democrats dropped from 5.7 million to 2.2 million votes; the Centre from 6 million to 3.5 million. On the left the USPD increased its number of supporters from 2.3 million in 1919 to 4.9 million, and the KPD, fighting its first election, got 440,000 votes. On the right the National Liberals (DVP) increased their share of the vote from 1.6 to 3.6 million, the DNVP from 2.9 million to 3.7 million. The election marked the end of the 'black, red and gold' coalition of the Weimar parties under the leadership of the SPD which now lived in fear of the constant threat from the left and the right. The democratic process was paralysed, and only in exceptional circumstances could an uneasy coalition from the SPD to DVP be made, only to fall apart again through pressure from both extremes. The right were the real winners in 1920, for not only did their share of the vote increase the most, but the victors on the left, the USPD, were hopelessly divided among themselves and the party was soon to be disbanded. The success of the left was hollow, it was enough to inspire the powerful propagandists of the 'red peril' to fresh flights of fancy, but it was not enough to encourage a determined effort to achieve unity on the left. Socialists voted for the USPD because they did not wish to vote either for the SPD or for the KPD. The party had little positive to offer.

As a result of these elections a new government was formed under Fehrenbach, a politician from the Centre whose cabinet was made up of men from the DDP and from the party of big capital and monarchists, the DVP. As a minority government it had to rely on the support of the SPD. This was given through fear that new elections would further strengthen the right, or that the country would become ungovernable.

The Fehrenbach government resigned in order to avoid the odium of accepting the Allies' reparations bill which was presented at the London Conference in March 1921. The DVP left the government rather than break with the nationalist right, and the SPD returned to the coalition. The new chancellor was Joseph Wirth of the left wing of the Centre, and the outstanding figure in the cabinet was Walter Rathenau, an industrialist and intellectual who was particularly detested on the right for being a Jew and for the 'fulfilment politics' towards the Allies which he and Wirth pursued. Rathenau was murdered in June 1922 by erstwhile members of the Ehrhardt Brigade. Wirth said at his funeral that 'the enemy is on the right' and did the best he could to defend the republic against such elements. His efforts, however, were doomed to failure because the courts would not enforce the legislation he introduced to protect the state and its servants from right-wing outrages. Wirth's proposal to bring the DVP under Stresemann back into the cabinet were opposed by the SPD. Stresemann supported the attempts to stop right-wing terror and accepted the need to improve relations with the Entente by showing a willingness to meet the terms of the Peace Treaty. Unable to find any solution to the problems of reparations and of rising inflation, faced with a rightward shift within his own party, and unable to stop the excesses of the right, Wirth resigned. Cuno, who did not belong to any party and who was managing director of the Hamburg-America line, formed a new cabinet of 'experts': businessmen who were close to the DVP or the extreme right of the Centre and who claimed to be able to provide the practical knowledge needed to solve the economic crisis which mere politicians so sadly lacked. Instead, they presided over an inflation so spectacular that it became the classic example of an economy gone wild.

The inflation of 1923 had many causes. The enormous cost of the war had been borne by credits, the assumption being that Germany would win the war and the enemy would be made to pay on a scale far greater than that imposed on Germany by the Peace Treaty. Demobilization and the changeover to a peacetime economy necessitated further investments which could not be met without borrowing even more money. The shortage of food and manufactured goods at the end of the war resulted in a sharp rise in prices. Lack of confidence led to the outflow of capital and to widespread speculation against the mark, and gold reserves were depleted by the requirement to pay reparations in gold marks. The president of the Reichsbank, Havenstein, imagined that he could overcome inflation by printing more money. One hundred and fifty printing works struggled to meet this insatiable demand for paper money, but the cure proved far worse than the disease.

The state had a vested interest in inflation, for it seemed to be a cheap way to pay off its debts and to convince the Allies that their demands for reparations were out of all proportion to Germany's ability to pay. Industry also profited substantially by using devalued money to pay off outstanding debts, by granting seemingly generous wage agreements, and making investments that were to be paid off with worthless money. With a state dominated by the 'November criminals' and held to ransom by the rapacious Allied powers, it became almost a patriotic duty to avoid taxes and to speculate against the mark. In 1914 one dollar was worth 4.20 marks; in July 1919,

14 marks; by 1921, 64.90; by January 1922, it was worth 191.80, yet Hugo Stinnes, who profited more than any other industrialist from inflation, proudly announced in 1922 that he had always been firmly opposed to any attempt to stabilize the mark and saw no reason to change his mind. By January, 1923 the dollar was worth 17,972 marks, and by the end of the year it was not worth the paper it was printed on. 4,420,000,000,000 marks were by then needed to buy one US dollar.

In spite of wide variations between different industries and between skilled and unskilled labour, real wages were in almost every instance below the level of 1913, and attempts to prove the contrary do not carry much conviction. Wages fluctuated wildly, collapsed after March 1922 and in 1923 were paid with worthless paper. The working class enjoyed few of the benefits of the industrial expansion and export drive which the government actively encouraged, for this policy increased the deficit, further encouraged inflation and thus devalued wages.

Inflation wiped out the savings of the middle class. Those who had dutifully bought war loans were left with nothing. Civil servants, particularly those at the upper end of the pay scale, suffered a severe reduction in their living standards, and the military clauses of the Treaty of Versailles resulted in a large number of officers being retired and getting pensions which were constantly devalued. But their position was enviable compared to that of the hundreds of thousands of hapless disabled servicemen and war widows for whom pitifully little was done. This expropriation of the middle class was the extraordinary achievement not of a determined group of socialist revolutionaries, but of solid bourgeois politicians who resolutely upheld the principles of private property and free enterprise. They received none of the blame for the inflation from this group of their victims. They attributed it to the machinations of the 'November criminals', to creeping socialism, or to the sinister intrigues of international Jewry. They flocked to the banners of the right-wing parties which were dedicated to overthrowing the democratic republic, and they were later to form the backbone of the Nazi Party.

Although Germany had gained a number of concessions over reparations, among them an agreement in August 1922 that no money payments were required until the economy improved, payments in kind got seriously in arrears. In January 1923 French and Belgian troops entered the Rhineland to ensure that these deliveries were made. The government called for passive resistance. The economy ground to a standstill, thus hurting the Germans far more than the French. Those who did the government's bidding and ceased to work were paid with fistfuls of utterly worthless marks, for work stoppages resulted in hyper-inflation. Passive resistance was an impressive demonstration of national unity and recreated something of the long-lost spirit of August 1914, but it was a complete failure. On 12 August Cuno resigned and Stresemann formed a coalition government ranging from his own DVP to the SPD. He called for an end to passive resistance, set about lessening the burden of reparations and revising the peace settlement; not by confrontation, but by negotiation and by skilfully hiding his long-term aims by professing his devotion to international understanding and the principles of the League of Nations.

There were many who hoped to use the crisis of the 'struggle for the Ruhr' to topple the republic. There was an abortive right-wing coup in Küstrin, and the KPD made a half-baked attempt to seize power in Hamburg in a repeat performance of an equally futile putsch in 1921. In Saxony and Thuringia there was a move to the left and SPD governments were formed in both states which included members of the KPD. Stresemann saw these perfectly constitutional and democratic moves as a serious threat, and promptly sent in the Reichswehr to overthrow both governments.

The government showed none of this determination in dealing with Bavaria. President von Kahr and the commander of the VII Division, von Lossow, openly defied the government in Berlin, claiming that it was under 'marxist influence'. The extreme right throughout Germany looked to Bavaria to overthrow the republic, but Kahr and his government hesitated. A meeting was called in the *Bügerbraükeller* in Munich, at which Kahr was to address businessmen, farmers, churchmen, and representatives of the more moderate right in order to test their reactions. After thirty minutes of amiable banter the proceedings were interrupted by the arrival of Adolf Hitler and his SA fraudulently announcing that the police and the army stood behind him. General Ludendorff appeared on the scene and joined in the attempt to convince Kahr to support the 'national revolution'. The next morning, on the fifth anniversary of the 'revolution' of 9 November 1918, Hitler and Ludendorff paraded through the streets of Munich. Kahr, however, had reconsidered his position and decided to oppose Hitler. His aim was to restore the Bavarian monarchy and secede from the reich, not to support Hitler's idea of a 'march on Berlin' in an attempt to become the German Mussolini. Munich's police force stood by Kahr, opened fire on the procession, and Hitler's coup ended in panic-striken flight. The leaders of the putsch were brought to trial. Ludendorff was set free, and Hitler spent less than a year in a comfortable prison dictating *Mein Kampf* to his devoted friend, Rudolf Hess. In the eyes of the court they were decent, if over-enthusiastic, patriots. Ebert had asked Seeckt to chose between the coup and the republic, but once again the army stayed out of the way. Seeckt announced that the army would not tolerate any 'unauthorized meddling with the affairs of the Reich', but it was the police that acted, not for the sake of Germany and its republican government, but for Bavaria which continued to be a happy hunting ground for every species of right-wing extremist.

Although the republic survived, Stresemann had to go. Nationalists could not forgive him for abandoning the 'struggle for the Ruhr', and the left were disgusted at the contrast between his government's treatment of the left in Saxony and Thuringia and the right in Bavaria. Marx from the Centre formed a new cabinet, with Stresemann as foreign minister. Marx, much to the disappointment of the right, did not use the enabling act to do away with the Reichstag, nor did he invoke the law on the state of seige to establish some form of authoritarian government. Currency reform in November 1923 ended inflation and the new *Rentenmark* remained remarkably stable. Elections in Britain and France returned the leftward leaning governments of Ramsay Macdonald and Herriot, both of which readily accepted the proposals put forward by the American financier, Dawes, to help Germany meet its reparations payments. His plan was published in April 1924.

The end of the 'struggle for the Ruhr', currency reform and the Dawes Plan stabilized the economy and parliamentary democracy seemed to function relatively well. That this was due almost solely to the relative prosperity of the period can be seen from the fact that as soon as the economy took a serious downward turn in 1929, Germany was plunged once again into a serious political crisis. None of the underlying political problems had been solved in this most peaceful period in the history of the Weimar Republic.

This superficial political stability was based on the reluctant co-operation of the two right-wing parties, the DVP and the DNVP, with the parliamentary process. Stresemann's DVP was determined to revise the Versailles settlement, cunningly concealing its more excessive aims, and in domestic politics was prone to indulge in mindless red-baiting, but since 1920 it was a party of *Vernunftrepublikaner* – men who accepted the regime but who had no emotional attachment to it. The DNVP had not entirely abandoned the idea of seizing power by a military coup, but after 1923 they began to think about entering the government by constitutional means. Unable to beat the republic, they decided to join it, but only to get as much as they could out of it. Thus although the DNVP regarded the Dawes Plan as simply a revised version of the *Diktat* of Versailles, they realized that something could be got out of it by way of credits and tariff reform.

The right decided that they had to abandon their position of endless opposition and get some share of political power, if they were to survive as a viable political movement; but the left decided that 1923 had been an object lesson in the virtues of abstinence. This meant that between 1924 and 1928 governments were either in a minority and dependent on the good will of the social democrats, or they were majority governments in a singularly uneasy coalition with the right. Stresemann could count on the left for support for his foreign policy, and skilfully used the howls of protest from the nationalists against the Locarno Pacts and the League of Nations to gain concessions from France and Britain. No such consensus was possible in domestic politics. The SPD represented the interests of organized labour, the DVP those of industry, the DNVP the agrarians, and there was virtually no common ground between them. The DVP wanted to increase the export of German manufactured goods and therefore favoured low tariffs. The DNVP wanted to protect German agriculture and therefore wanted tariffs to be restored to the level set by Bülow in 1902. Both parties opposed the encroachments of organized labour, particularly the agrarians, for agricultural labourers now enjoyed the same rights as any other worker to join a union and to withhold their labour. On the other hand, the DVP were perfectly prepared to seek the support of the SPD against the DNVP, as they did in 1926, but the DNVP could never consider such an alliance.

The big winners in the elections of May 1924 were the DNVP with 95 seats to the SPD's 100. With the support of a handful of right-wing splinter groups they were the largest faction in the Reichstag. Their attempt to secure the appointment of Admiral Tirpitz as chancellor failed, and the right-wing coalition fell apart. Marx formed a new cabinet of the middle-of-the-road parties which was tolerated by the SPD, but this collapsed under the constant and frequently scurrilous attacks of the DNVP. Elections were held on 7 December in which the left and right extremes lost heavily. The Nazis, who won 32 seats in May, now had 14; the KPD dropped from 62 seats to 45. The SPD were the major winners with 131 seats and 26 per cent of the vote. Dr Hans Luther, who belonged to no party, formed a cabinet of 'experts', a euphemism for men who stood solidly in the nationalist camp and who had even less attachment to the republic than the *Vernunftrepublikaner*. The new government planned to undo many of the social achievements of 1918–19, including the eight-hour day, and to drop the scheme for improved unemployment benefits. This caused such a reaction on the left that the unity and determination of the days of the Kapp putsch were almost revived. Then suddenly, on 28 February 1925 Friedrich Ebert died.

The first round of the presidential elections showed that had the left been able to unite with the parties of the middle they could have secured the election of their candidate. But the KPD and SPD were incapable of coming to any such agreement. In the second round the KPD fielded their lack-lustre leader, Thälmann, the parties of the Weimar coalition the ex-chancellor, Marx, and the right picked Hindenburg who won a narrow victory.

Stresemann feared that Hindenburg's election would make his task of reaching an understanding with Britain and France more difficult, but this did not prove to be the case. The Locarno accords of 1925 were accepted by a vote of 291 to 174 in the Reichstag, although the DNVP left the cabinet in protest against what they felt to be a one-sided agreement. Shortly afterwards the government resigned, but Luther formed a new cabinet in January 1926 which excluded both the SPD and the DNVP. He remained in office for less than four months, and was forced to resign when he attempted to order the navy to use the old black, white and red ensign of the imperial merchant navy. Marx, the great co-ordinator, returned to form his third cabinet. The Minister of Labour, Heinrich Brauns of the Centre, did much to overcome the suspicions of the SPD by introducing an unemployment insurance bill which was the last great piece of social legislation by the Weimar Republic. This bourgeois bloc came unstuck when the Centre and the DNVP tried to introduce a bill creating confessional schools for Protestants and Catholics. This was unacceptable to the DVP who withdrew from the coalition.

The elections in May 1928 resulted in losses on the right, the DNVP losing 2 million votes and the Nazis winning only 12 seats. The SPD increased their share of the vote from 26 per cent to 30 per cent, getting 152 seats. A collection of bizarre little parties to the right of centre got over 13 per cent of the vote, and this did much to offset the swing to the left. A new cabinet was formed by Hermann Müller who returned as chancellor after eight years to head the last government of the Weimar Republic to be led by a social democrat Hindenburg was delighted with the appointment and is said to have remarked that Müller was the best chancellor he had had, the only thing wrong with him being that he was a social democrat. The right had yet to recover from the shock of defeat, and there was little opposition voiced against Müller's programme of social legislation, home building, subsidies for agriculture, reduction of interest rates, and getting Britain and France to agree to disarmament, the settlement of the reparations question and the evacuation of the Rhineland.

This was merely a lull before the storm. The right-wing press baron, Hugenberg, decided to take over the leadership of the DNVP and to mount an all-out assault on the republic which looked so alarmingly stable to the nationalists. Hugenberg held a number of trump cards: he had the tacit support of the president, the officer corps, most of the judges and senior civil servants, many bankers and industrialists, leading protestant churchmen and a substantial section of the middle class. He had a vast newspaper and film empire which dominated the whole of Germany with the exception of Berlin. He also had the support of the veterans' association, *Stahlhelm*, with its 500,000 members.

The *Stahlhelm* was led by a soda-water manufacturer of relatively moderate views, Franz Seldte, and by a radical, Theodor Duesterberg, whose extremism was such that his admirers tactfully overlooked his Jewish background. In September 1928 the Berlin–Brandenburg branch of the *Stahlhelm* issued a declaration which attacked the republic and everyone who ruled over it, or who made any compromises with the system. This was designed to distance the DNVP from the moderate right and to make a direct appeal to Hitler's NSDAP to join in a combined effort to overthrow the republic. The declaration could have come directly from a Nazi, for it read in part: 'We hate the present state structure with all our hearts, for it denies us the possibility to free our enslaved Fatherland, to rid the German people of the mendacious war guilt, and to win living space (*Lebensraum*) in the east.'

Hitler replied to this offer by joining Hugenberg and Seldte in a committee to launch a referendum against the Young Plan which had been announced in September 1929, and which allowed Germany to reduce her reparations payments by hundreds of millions of marks. To the extreme right any reparations at all were too much, for they implied an acceptance of the 'war guilt lie'. They demanded that the chancellor, his ministers, and all representatives of the government should be charged with high treason. Dr Josef Goebbels was bitterly disappointed that Hindenburg was not included in this list of criminals. The Young Plan referendum was a failure for the DNVP, for not even all the party members supported it, but it was an important step forward for Hitler. He was now welcomed into the charmed circle of the 'respectable' right and established useful contacts with men of power and influence. He was fêted in the Hugenberg press, and by giving up the attempt to win over the working class to his views and concentrating on the middle classes he was to win steady support, initially at the local level, but shortly in the staggering breakthrough by his party in the elections of September 1930. The nationalists fondly imagined that Hitler would play the 'drummer boy' and would use his extraordinary political skills to win support for a movement that would still be controlled by Hugenberg and his cronies. They were not to be the last to entertain such illusions.

The failure of the Young Plan referendum was in effect a vote of confidence in the Müller government, but it was already beginning to fall apart. On 3 October 1929 Stresemann died suddenly at the age of fifty-one. The commanding figure in the republic since 1923, he played an essential role in bridging the gap between the middle-of-the-road parties and the right, between the black, red and gold of the republic, and the black, white and red of the old reich. But a more serious immediate problem concerned unemployment insurance benefits. With ever rising unemployment since the winter of 1928–29 the kitty was empty. The DNVP demanded that unemployment insurance should be dropped altogether. Employers' groups suggested that the payments should be drastically cut. The SPD proposed that contributions to the fund should be increased from 3 per cent of a worker's income to 3.5 per cent. As half of these costs were born by the employer the bourgeois parties protested vehemently, but on the day that Stresemann died they reluctantly agreed, and the Müller government survived the crisis. Two weeks later came 'Black Friday' on Wall Street. Germany was unable to borrow any more money from the United States and unemployment continued to rise at an even more alarming rate. By January 1930 there were more than 3 million unemployed. The SPD called for a further increase in unemployment contributions by 0.5 per cent of incomes. The bourgeois parties wanted to reduce the contributions, reduce wages and increase taxes on commodities such as tobacco.

At the same time there was a fierce debate among the government parties whether or not to accept the Young Plan now that the economic crisis was so severe that Germany was unlikely to be able to meet even these reduced payments.

The SPD would probably have agreed to drop the demand for the 0.5 per cent increase had it not been for the determined opposition of the trades unions, represented in the cabinet by the Minister of Labour, Rudolf Wissell, who had been on the Council of People's Representatives in December 1918. He knew full well that to give way on this point would encourage the employers to roll back wages and to cut benefits. He convinced the SPD that this was indeed the case. The bourgeois parties would not budge and the coalition fell apart. Hugenberg, the Reichsbank president, Schacht, and their friends in industry and finance had, without realizing it, destroyed democracy in Germany. As the finance minister, Rudolf Hilferding, remarked: 'For 30 pfennigs they have let the German Republic go to the devil.'

The new chancellor was Heinrich Brüning, a virtually unknown and colourless Westphalian from the Centre. General Kurt von Schleicher, the head of the political office of the Reichswehr Ministry, boasted that he had discovered Brüning, and that his appointment was due to his and Groener's advice to Hindenburg. Brüning dubbed his government a 'cabinet of soldiers from the front' and it was strongly conservative and nationalist. In his first address to the Reichstag he warned that this would be the last attempt at parliamentary rule, and that he would use emergency decrees if necessary. As a deliberate provocation to the left he reminded his audience that he had led a machine-gun company against Red mutineers in November 1918.

Brüning's proposals for increased taxes and protective tariffs divided the DNVP. The Nazis opposed the Brüning cabinet regardless of what they proposed. Hugenberg wished to preserve the alliance with the Nazis and therefore mounted a massive press campaign against these changes. Other nationalists supported Brüning, for they had long been agitating for higher tariffs for agricultural products. There was opposition from within his own party to such reactionary moves, particularly from the Christian labour movement, but he was able to gain enough support from the right to sneak through this first trial of strength.

Brüning was unable to get a majority for his sweeping budgetary proposals, for the left rejected them as a reactionary attack on the poor and needy, and the right felt that they were *dirigiste* and smacked of socialism. When the Reichstag voted against cutting the salaries of civil servants he appealed to Hindenburg, who promptly passed all outstanding legislation by means of Article 48. The Reichstag voted overwhelmingly against this move, and Brüning had to rescind it. But he was not to be so easily discouraged. The most important parts of the legislation were again pushed through by use of the emergency powers of the president and the Reichstag was dissolved before they could complain.

Brüning imagined that the elections would give him a majority by increasing the vote for the centre and the moderate right. This was a disastrous miscalculation. The left remained relatively stable, with some shift from the SPD to the KPD. The DDP, which had moved to the right and had amalgamated with the fascistic *Jungdeutschen Orden*, and the Centre only suffered very modest losses. On the right the DVP and DNVP lost half their voters, but the smaller right-wing parties, the *Wirtschaftspartei*, the *Deutsche Landvolkpartei*, and the *Christlich-Soziale Volksdienst*, did remarkably well, winning 69 seats. But the most spectacular success of all was the 107 seats won by the Nazis which made them the second largest party in the Reichstag, the SPD having 143 seats. Hitler had managed to win support away from the two established right-wing parties, but had made no impact on the left or the centre. The policy which he had adopted since the Young Plan referendum was now paying handsome dividends.

Hitler's appeal did not depend on his pathological anti-Semitism, for Germany was no more anti-Semitic than any other European country. Nor did his other abiding obsession, *Lebensraum*, prove a vote-catcher, for the country was in no mood to think of a war of conquest when there were such serious immediate economic problems. Voters flocked to Hitler because of his virulent anti-Marxism and for his constant reiteration of the theme of national renewal. Anti-Marxism was directed principally against the SPD, but also by implication against the entire Weimar Republic and against the principles of parliamentary government. It was all too obvious that the system was not working, and Hitler offered what seemed to be a workable alternative. His party was young, vigorous, on the move, idealistic and deserved to be given a chance. The Nazis appeared to be both radically new yet reassuringly traditional, impeccably philistine but excitingly bohemian and even avant garde. Youth was irresistibly attracted to the party, for they were against the stuffy old monarchists and old-style imperialists on the traditional right, and loathed the republic which seemed to have nothing to give them, not even a job. The Nazis offered deliverance from the psychological burden of Versailles, which was so much greater than the material imposition, and they knew that the stab in the back legend, which they shouted from the roof tops, made the defeat and the Peace Treaty a domestic political problem, not one of foreign policy. The further implication was that once the 'November criminals' were chased out of their piggery, Germany would be in a position to undo the decision of 1914–18. It is for this reason that the demonstrations welcoming Hitler's appointment as chancellor in 1933 looked more like a victory parade after a glorious foreign war, rather than a celebration of yet another change of government.

There were two main reasons why the Nazis were so successful in this and subsequent elections. After the Young Plan referendum a number of local worthies had begun openly to support the party and had thus made it appear respectable and patriotic to be a fascist. Secondly, the Nazis struck a powerful chord in the German middle classes with their revamped version of the traditional imperialist ideology which they had imbued in the *Kaiserreich* and which was irreconcilable with democratic republican ideals. Hitler was not a pied piper who led the people astray, as apologists would have it. His followers were ready and waiting, eager to join a movement which offered salvation from organized labour, from powerful business interests and from the corrupt and futile republic.

Brüning's only hope of getting a parliamentary majority was to work with the SPD, but this he would not consider even though his party co-operated with the social democrats in the Prussian government. He stuck to his policy of increasing taxes, cutting expenditure, maintaining prices in spite of shrinking incomes and increasing the price of foodstuffs by higher tariffs. The SPD would not dare to challenge the use of Article 48 to push through this anti-social legislation for fear either of another election and a further victory by the NSDAP, or possibly a military dictatorship. They adopted the passive policy of the lesser evil, and awaited the end of the republic with increasingly grim fatalism.

The right was determined to seize the initiative. In October 1930 representatives of the DNVP, the Stahlhelm, the Free Corps, the army, banking and industry met at Bad Harzburg. All the parties to the right of the centre were invited and Hitler arrived with his paladins. Hugenberg proclaimed a 'National Front', others held equally bombastic speeches, but there was no doubt that Hitler was now the leading figure on the right, and he skilfully avoided any compromises that might affect his freedom of manoeuvre. His main difficulty was that he was still seen by many as too radical. Respectable citizens were horrified by the brutality of his rowdies in the SA, and businessmen were alarmed by the apparently socialist content of the party programme with its attacks on big business, the cartels and 'interest slavery'. Hitler devoted much of his energy in the following months to convincing industrialists and bankers, generals and civil servants, churchmen and politicians that he was no radical, that he did not approve of the excesses of the SA, which he attributed to communist provocation, and that the party programme was simply designed to keep his followers happy and should not be taken seriously. Modest sums of money began to trickle into the party coffers from the Rhine and the Ruhr; from Thyssen, Hermann Reusch, Emil Kirdorf; Schnitzler of IG Farben, Finck of Allianz Insurance, the banker Schröoder, the ex-Chancellor Cuno of HAPAG and Dr Schacht of the Reichsbank. They gave the money to encourage Hitler in his efforts to restrain his radical followers, and to tame him so that he might be of use to them at some later date. Hitler did not need the money, for the party was adequately funded from members' subscriptions and from small businessmen, sometimes admittedly in the form of protection money. But he badly needed their support if he were to present himself as a respectable politician, and as a serious contender for the highest political office.

In 1932 Hindenburg decided to stand for election as president once again. The Harzburg Front wanted either the industrialist Albert Vögler or Prince Oskar of Prussia as their candidate, but Hitler decided to stand. The nationalists were furious and decided to field Duesterberg as their candidate. The SPD supported Hindenburg rather than run the risk of Hitler winning the election. The KPD once again put forward Thälmann. It was an ugly campaign. Goebbels said that a vote for Hindenburg was a vote for deserters and traitors, and a number of generals, landowners and even the Crown Prince voted for Hitler rather than Hindenburg. Hindenburg almost got the necessary 50 per cent in the first round of the election, and in the second round he won comfortably, but Hitler got an impressive 36.8 per cent of the vote. The Nazis had been beaten back and the republic saved, but its fate was in the hands of an ancient reactionary monarchist field marshal. The republican forces were demoralized and purely defensive. The economic situation was catastrophic. There was no possibility of forming a majority government. Hitler had been defeated, but German democracy had only been given a breathing space.

As soon as Hindenburg was re-elected, Brüning outlawed the SA and the SS at the prompting of Groener who had been given evidence of a coup planned by the SA if Hitler had been elected president. Hindenburg was unhappy about this move, for although he considered the SS and SA to be misguided, he thought of them as useful reserves for the armed forces. Brüning's next move brought about his downfall. He had appointed a commissioner for the eastern provinces, Hans Schlange-Schöningen, who proposed to settle a large number of the unemployed in subsidized farms in the east. Hindenburg and his Junker cronies regarded this proposal as 'agrarian bolshevism'. Schleicher had now decided to overthrow Brüning, oust his old friend and supporter, Groener, co-operate with the moderate Nazis, integrate the SA into the Reichswehr and create an interim cabinet pending his own appointment as chancellor. Hitler went along with these schemes, for he realized that he stood a good chance of using the interim cabinet to secure his own ascent to the throne. Through Hindenburg's son Oscar and through his own manipulations in the Reichswehr, Schleicher secured the resignation of Groener. It was a shabby betrayal, for Schleicher owed his career to Groener's support and encouragement.

At the end of May 1932 Hindenburg returned to Berlin after a holiday on his estates. He told Brüning to drop Schlange-Schöningen and his settlement scheme. Brüning refused and offered his own resignation which was promptly accepted. The chancellor, imagining that he had just about solved the economic crisis and was about to score some major successes in foreign affairs, had announced that he was 'one hundred metres from the finishing line'. This was partly true, for the Lausanne Conference cancelled reparations, and the Geneva Disarmament Conference gave Germany military equality with the other powers. But neither of these successes helped to ease the domestic political crisis, and at the last moment he was tripped up by an eighty-five-year-old president who had just been elected by the same forces which supported the chancellor.

The new chancellor was Major von Papen, a wealthy, well-connected, suave, reactionary centre deputy in the Prussian parliament (*Landtag*). He was a second-rate intrigant, certainly not a politician of any stature, who was blinded by his vanity and ambition, and his appointment was greeted with incredulity or mirth. His 'cabinet of the Barons' was made up largely of landowners (including the rocket specialist Werner von Braun's father who was minister of agriculture) and Schleicher took over Groener's post as reichswehr minister. Papen promptly lifted the ban on the

SA and the SS, announced that 'the state should not be a kind of charitable institution', declared a state of emergency in Prussia, overthrowing the government and ruling Germany's largest state by means of Article 48, and awaited the result of new elections which in his folly he imagined would give him a workable parliamentary majority. The SPD and its paramilitary force, the Iron Front, stood helplessly by as the Prussian government was destroyed by this *coup d'état*. Goebbels was delighted and confided in his diary: 'The Reds have missed their big chance. It will never come again.'

Hitler conducted a masterly campaign, making the wildest promises in all directions. During a speech in Berlin he even gave his word that 'In the Third Reich every German girl will find a husband!' But the promises were combined with sinister threats. The SA ran amok throughout Germany. Hundreds of dead and wounded were left in their wake. The country seemed to be on the brink of a civil war. The middle classes called for law and order, and imagined that they would get it from the party which was the cause of the bloodshed: the NSDAP.

The election of July 1932 was the Nazis' greatest success. They more than doubled their vote to win 230 seats. Once again the KPD gained at the expense of the SPD, for many on the left were disgusted with the SPD's supine attitude towards the coup in Prussia and its refusal to co-operate with the KPD against the mortal threat to the last remnants of a parliamentary regime. The small parties on the right virtually disappeared, and many who had voted for the DNVP in 1930 now voted for the NSDAP. The centre won a few extra seats as did the DVP. For Papen the result was a disaster. The 'cabinet of the Barons' now had 90 per cent of the Reichstag against them.

For all on the right the only way out of the crisis was to bring Hitler into the cabinet, but neither Hindenburg nor the Reichswehr nor the DNVP nor the Centre would accept his terms. He wanted to be made chancellor, he demanded the Ministries of the Interior, Justice and Economics for his party, and in addition insisted on having direct control over Prussia, plus two new Ministries of Aviation and Propaganda for Goering and Goebbels. With Hermann Goering in the speaker's chair and a vote of 512 to 42 against him, Papen saw no alternative but to call new elections. These were held on 6 November 1932. Again the SPD lost to the communists, but the Nazis won 34 fewer seats than in July, dropping almost 2 million votes. The NSDAP was losing steam, it could not keep up voter enthusiasm over a series of elections and it was running desperately short of money. Although Hitler's position was greatly weakened, Papen was no better off than he had been before the election.

Hindenburg received Papen and Schleicher and asked them what they intended to do. Papen suggested governing without the Reichstag, suppressing all parties and political organizations, and calling a referendum to test popular support for this policy. Schleicher claimed that if he were made chancellor he could split the Nazi party, bringing the 'left' under Gregor Strasser into a broad coalition that would include the SPD. Hindenburg favoured Papen's plan, but Papen found to his amazement that the majority of his cabinet supported Schleicher's suggestions in the hope of creating a workable parliamentary majority. Schleicher produced a study by Colonel Ott which purported to show that the army would be unable to maintain the peace in the event of an armed uprising by the left and the right. In other words, the General Staff insisted that Papen's plan was unworkable. Hindenburg therefore saw no alternative but to accept Papen's resignation, giving him his photograph with the touching inscription "*Ich hatt' einen Kameraden*' (I had a comrade), muttering 'so, in God's name, we have got to let Herrn von Schleicher try his luck.'

Schleicher was not without support. Krupp, and a number of like-minded industrialists, did not trust Hitler, liked the idea of a state controlled programme to reduce unemployment as suggested by Gereke, one of the new chancellor's closest advisers, and they also favoured an authoritarian regime under a general. They were, after all, used to dealing with the army, who did not treat them to the anti-capitalist fulminations of the Nazi radicals. Others, particularly in the army, hoped that Schleicher's plan to split the Nazi party would work after the set-back suffered by the party in the November elections, for most officers disliked the Nazis as a vulgar rabble and resented the SA's claims to be the prototype of a new National Socialist Army. Schleicher intended to give prominent Nazis cabinet posts, the rest would be arrested. But he was without support in the Reichstag or in the country at large. Hitler countered his plan to split his party by expelling Strasser and his sympathizers and taking over the organization of the Nazi party himself. The chancellor's radio speech, in which he stated that wages had been allowed to sink too low, that industry enjoyed too many privileges and needed to come under some form of state control when working on government contracts, sounded to the Ruhr barons like pure socialism. The agrarians were outraged when he suggested that about 650,000 acres in the east should be given to small farmers.

'Agrarian bolshevism' was once again on the agenda. He also alienated the landed interests by failing to hush up a series of scandals over the *Osthilfe* by means of which vast sums of money had been given to help the Junkers get out of debt, debts which were often caused by their predilections for wine, women and the gaming table, as in the spectacular case of von Quast-Radensleben.

While Papen professed to be Schleicher's friend and supporter, he intrigued behind his back to secure his dismissal and thus get his revenge. On 4 January 1933 he organized a meeting at the house of the banker Schröder in Cologne, which was attended by Hitler, Himmler and Hess and by Wilhelm Keppler who had extensive contacts in the world of banking and industry. Hitler and Papen discussed the formation of a new government in private. Hitler got Papen to agree to be his vice chancellor and to support his efforts to get rid of all social democrats, communists and Jews from important positions. Hitler agreed to form a 'national' government with only a few ministers from the NSDAP. Industry began to finance Hitler on a more generous scale to make sure that he stuck to this compromise and because they began to feel that they had at last picked a winner. Goebbels noted in his diary that the financial situation of the party, which had been desperate, had improved 'suddenly overnight'.

A slight improvement in the performance of the NSDAP in the local elections in Germany's smallest state, Lippe-Detmold, was enough to stop Strasser from joining Schleicher's cabinet, for he knew that the SA chief and leading radical Nazi, Röhm, along with Frick and Feder would not break ranks with Hitler and join him in the cabinet. Hugenberg also decided not to enter the government. Hindenburg's advisers now felt that the alternatives were either to have a military dictatorship under Schleicher, or to appoint Hitler chancellor. The first was impossible if Colonel Ott's study was correct. Schleicher asked Hindenburg for permission to dissolve the Reichstag, but the president ordered him to create a parliamentary majority. This was clearly impossible, and Schleicher now found himself in exactly the same position as Papen had been a few weeks before. Hindenburg was advised from all quarters to appoint Hitler chancellor, but he hesitated, for snobbish rather than political reasons. He did not like this vulgar, low-born, loud-mouthed Bohemian corporal. In the end he felt he had no choice. A right-wing parliamentary solution was not possible without the NSDAP, which was still the largest faction in the Reichstag. On dismissing Schleicher the president said: 'I have one foot in the grave and I do not really know whether I shall regret this decision later on in heaven.' On 30 January 1933 Adolf Hitler was at last appointed chancellor.

CHAPTER EIGHT

Britain

The popping of the champagne corks and the dancing in the streets in celebration of victory soon ended and Britain awoke with a severe hangover. Three days after the armistice the government announced that there would be a general election on 14 December. Lloyd George had led the country to victory and was enormously popular. The Conservative leader, Bonar Law, assumed that it would be disastrous for his party to withdraw from the coalition. The Welsh Wizard knew better. He realized that if a deal was not made with the Conservatives his Liberals would go down to certain defeat, just as was to happen to Churchill's Conservatives in 1945. As a result it was agreed that 159 Liberal candidates should be unopposed by Conservative candidates, and that Lloyd George's Liberals would not vote against approved Conservatives. These selected candidates were given a letter of endorsement by Lloyd George and Bonar Law which the opposition Liberal leader, Asquith, called the 'coupon'.

In opposition to the 'coupon' candidates were the Asquith Liberals, the 'Squiffites', whose leader had refused the offer of the Lord Chancellorship in a new coalition government. The Labour Party resolved to break with Lloyd George in the hope of becoming the main opposition party. Lloyd George had no desire to purge his party, and even gave the coupon to candidates who had voted against him in the Maurice debate of May 1918 when the Liberals split on the issue of whether or not the prime minister had lied to the House of Commons. His sole concern was to get as many Liberals elected as possible, for he knew that in spite of his enormous popularity without the coupon his party would be soundly defeated.

Although often called the 'khaki election', arrangements were so hurried that only about a quarter of the soldiers were able to vote. Some 8.5 million women over thirty who met a modest property qualification were allowed to vote for the first time, and all males over the age of twenty-one, except peers, lunatics and convicted felons, were given the vote. By these means the electorate doubled. This increased the uncertainties about the outcome of the election, even though it was a foregone conclusion that Lloyd George would return as prime minister and that the Conservatives would be the big winners.

Of the 474 members of the new House of Commons there were 338 Conservatives and 136 Liberals. The Labour Party, although Ramsay MacDonald, Snowden and Henderson lost their seats because of their opposition to the war, became the official opposition with fifty-nine members led by a lacklustre Scottish miner, William Adamson. Beatrice Webb was scornful of this achievement, calling the Parliamentary Labour Party 'a very sham lion' and their leader 'dull-witted'. There were twenty-six Squiffites, but their leader was not elected until 1920. The seventy-three Sinn Feiners, including the first woman elected to the House of Commons, Countess Markiewicz, refused to take their seats.

The new cabinet was full of men of considerable talent. Both Balfour and Curzon, who succeeded him as foreign secretary, were exceptionally able. The lord chancellor, F. E. Smith, later Lord Birkenhead, was a brilliant man of sparkling if somewhat unruly wit. Austen Chamberlain was an honest and dedicated chancellor of the exchequer. Churchill was minister of war and the most energetic and influential of all the Liberal ministers. Lesser posts were held by men of above average gifts, including Milner at the Colonial Office, the historian H. A. L. Fisher at Education, and Christopher Addison became the first minister of health. Bonar Law was conscientious, loyal and moderate. He provided a necessary contrast to Lloyd George's mercurial and frequently dictatorial temperament.

This remarkable government, led by a politician of genius and with an overwhelming parliamantary majority, soon began to flounder. Lloyd George, in Paris to negotiate the peace treaties, continued to use his small war cabinet and did not convene a full peace-time cabinet until October 1919. Even then he treated his distinguished colleagues as inferiors and preferred to run the affairs of state through his private staff. They were housed in the garden of No. 10 Downing Street, soon to be christened the 'garden suburb'. In part this was the consequence of the prime minister's imperious temperament, but it was also because the Conservatives had a majority and could perfectly well govern without him. Only a series of personal triumphs and the loyalty of Bonar Law could keep him in office.

In Paris, Lloyd George cemented his reputation as a statesman of world stature and returned to England in triumph, even though most Conservatives complained that he had been far too lenient towards Germany and failed to recognize the mortal dangers of bolshevism. This success was short-lived, for the concensus over the peace was soon to collapse. Similarly, intervention in Russia was too feeble for the right and was denounced by the Labour Party who still imagined that the Soviet Union was a workers' state which was struggling against common enemies – capitalism and Lloyd George.

At home, demobilization caused the greatest difficulties. The ministry of reconstruction required that those who were most needed in industry should be released first. As these men were usually among the last to have been called up, this caused widespread discontent in the armed forces. After a number of protest demonstrations, riots and mutinous outbreaks, Churchill announced the principle of 'first in, first out' which most servicemen found reasonable.

The Conservatives had no desire to placate the trade unions which had doubled in membership during the war and which had become increasingly militant. In Glasgow there was a violent strike for a forty-hour week, the red flag was hoisted on the town hall, and the revolutionary flames were fanned by William Gallacher, soon to be a communist MP, and by two future Labour peers – Emmanuel Shinwell and David Kirkwood. The troops were called in, Gallacher and Shinwell sent to jail and the revolution was postponed. Meanwhile the miners demanded the nationalization of the mines under workers' control, a six-hour day and a 30 per cent wage increase.

Lloyd George threatened to use force if the miners went on strike, but he also proposed that they should co-operate with a commission headed by Sir John Sankey, who was to sit on the woolsack in the second Labour administration. The miners agreed, provided that the commission included Sir Leo Chiozza Money, a wealthy and aggressive Labour sympathizer whose political career was to be compromised by two charges of indecent assault on young women, and the infinitely more respectable Sidney Webb and R. H. Tawney. The prime minister agreed. In doing so he made a serious tactical error, for the Sankey Commission's interim report denounced the 'present system of ownership and working' in the mines, called for a degree of workers' control, a reduction of working hours and a significant improvement of the miners' working conditions. It appeared that private enterprise had been weighed in the balance and had been found wanting. The government used the excuse that the commission was unable to agree on a final report in order to do nothing. Strikes broke out in the Yorkshire mines and Lloyd George took these as a pretext to reject even a modest degree of reform. The miners admitted defeat, and a seven-hour work day was legislated in the Coal Mines Act.

Immediately after the war the miners, the railwaymen and the transport workers had renewed their 'triple alliance' which had been planning a general strike in 1914. In September 1919 the railwaymen went on strike when the government 'standardized' wages in the industry, a euphemistic practice which resulted in substantial reductions for most workers. The government reacted with the predictable argument that the railwaymen were holding the country to ransom. They called out the troops and threatened to form bands of 'Citizens Guards'. Under the skilful and moderate leadership of J. H. Thomas, a man later to be excoriated as a traitor to socialism for his support of the national government, the railwaymen fought back and the government felt obliged to maintain their wage rates.

The railway strike was a defeat for the government, but it was also a defeat for the extremist elements within the labour movement who posed an extra-parliamentary challenge to the bourgeois state. These revolutionaries were hopelessly divided and devoted much of their energies to interminable and bitter internecine squabbles. During the post-war boom their fiery rhetoric met with little response. Their wrangling continued until a stalwart residue formed the Communist Party of Great Britain, but in 1921 the party was a small sect of some 5,000 members which was no more a threat to the established order than were the Jehovah's Witnesses to the established church or the Mormons to the institution of marriage.

All this was not quite so obvious at the time. The example of the bolshevik revolution was further inspiration to those who felt that capitalism was on its last legs, and otherwise intelligent observers of the contemporary scene managed to persuade themselves that the Soviet Union had much to teach the world about economic planning. The government determined to end wartime controls and was unsympathetic to any schemes for industrial reorganization. Factories were sold off, large profits were made in war surplus goods, and only the dreary nationalized pubs remained under government control to the lasting misery of tipplers in Carlyle and Gretna. This

187

'business as usual' policy triggered off a speculative fever which diagnosticians on the left enthusiastically pronounced to be terminal, and capital which was badly needed for the modernization of industry was absorbed in the pursuits of bargains in the cotton industry, in ship building and engineering. The boom was soon over and was followed by steep inflation. This also obliged trade unionists to concentrate on securing higher wages, rather than pressing for nationalization or shorter hours.

Reactions to the Russo–Polish war also made the labour movement seem more radical than it was in fact. The Dockers' Union, led by Ernest Bevin who as foreign secretary in 1945 was to be unflinching in his opposition to Soviet ambitions, refused to load any weapons which might have been used against the bolsheviks. When Warsaw was threatened, the Trades Union Congress and the Labour Party told the government that they would call a general strike if they intervened. Councils of Action were formed to organize the strike and Lenin, who was singularly inept in his judgements on British affairs, announced that they were true soviets. They were nothing of the sort. In spite of much excitement and exaggerated talk, the vast majority of the British left had no desire to follow in Lenin's footsteps. They were simply against intervention. They did not want to copy the Soviet Union, they wished to leave it alone. As it turned out, the Poles did very well without the assistance of the British government.

In October 1920 the miners went on strike again, more out of accumulated frustration at the government's refusal to tackle the structural problems of the industry than for the immediate demand for higher wages. The government passed the Emergency Powers Act but also agreed to a modest interim increase in wages. The miners, knowing that they could not count on the support of J. H. Thomas and the National Union of Railwaymen, accepted the offer. Before the five-month interim period was over the mine owners announced that they would roll back wages, in some areas by as much as 45 per cent. The miners were locked out on 1 April 1920. The Emergency Powers Act was swiftly passed and troops were moved into the mining areas. The triple alliance met and agreed on a general strike in support of the miners. The government reopened negotiations and the strike was postponed. The negotiations broke down and the miners renewed their call for a general strike. On 'Black Friday' the triple alliance refused to act. In the history of the labour movement this went down as a day of infamous betrayal with the miner's secretary, Frank Hodges, cast as Judas, Thomas and

Bevin as reactionary toadies. All this is somewhat overdramatized. The miner's president, Herbert Smith, was a stubborn and inflexible Yorkshireman of the most tiresomely familiar sort. The villains of the piece were eager to negotiate, as was Lloyd George. On the one side were the apostles of class warfare whatever the cost, on the other the advocates of compromise and negotiation. It was a division within the labour movement that was never to be completely overcome.

It would be a mistake to believe that the first years of peace were characterized solely by a return to rampant *laissez-faire* capitalism and by increasingly damaging class warfare. Two important welfare measures were passed by the administration which were to have far-reaching effects. The Housing and Town Planning Act of 1919, the work of Dr Christopher Addison, provided subsidies for local authorities to provide the much vaunted 'homes fit for heroes' and compulsory powers to make sure that they were built. Government-assisted house building became the most important collective endeavour in the inter-war period. In spite of enormous difficulties almost a quarter of a million houses were built under the Addison Act. This was not nearly enough, but Addison had established the principle that the people had a right to decent housing and that governments had a duty to provide it for them. The programme was stopped in 1923 and there was much talk of a housing scandal involving the frivolous waste of public funds, but government subsidies for housing continued in different forms.

The Unemployment Insurance Act of 1920 was the administration's greatest achievement in the field of social welfare. The National Insurance Act of 1911 had provided unemployment benefits for workers in building, engineering, and shipbuilding where seasonal unemployment was a chronic problem. During the war this had been extended to munitions workers. Ex-servicemen were given benefits for up to fifty weeks if they were unable to find work. When this scheme ran out it was replaced by a contributory plan which covered virtually all workers except domestic servants, agricultural labourers and civil servants. The scheme was based on the actuarial assumption of a low rate of unemployment. This soon proved to be false and what had been intended to be an insurance scheme became, by the payment of 'uncovenanted benefits' and allowances for dependents, a new system of poor relief or 'dole'. Because the Act was passed at a time when there was a sudden rise in unemployment, the right to maintenance was firmly established. At the same time far too much energy was devoted to endless discussions of appropriate levels of support for the unemployed, and not nearly enough on a determined attempt to tackle the root causes of unemployment.

It was assumed that unemployment benefits would be covered by contributions and that housing subsidies would be modest. The majority of MPs felt that since government programmes cost money there should be as few as possible. When the cost of these programmes rose sharply with the general inflation Sir Eric Geddes wielded the 'Geddes Axe' against 'squandermania'. He demanded drastic cuts in expenditure on the armed forces, education, child welfare and the dole. Fortunately the axe was blunted somewhat, but the government failed miserably to tackle the serious problems of economic and social reconstruction. The rich began to recite their nauseatingly unconvincing litany of poverty with such regularity that it was widely believed. Fortunately for them just enough crumbs fell from their lavish tables to prevent a serious threat to their wealth and privilege.

Lloyd George was a politician without a party. He had power, he had patronage which he doled out unscrupulously, and he was the outstanding politician of the time, but most Conservatives loathed him both for his personality and for his policies. As long as Bonar Law was in the government the Tory backbenchers would support him, but in March 1921 the Conservative leader resigned because of ill-health. In 1922 the Chanak crisis brought Britain to the verge of an unpopular war with Turkey and Curzon resigned as foreign secretary. The Irish settlement effectively destroyed the Unionist cause. Then in October 1922 Lloyd George announced that he would go to the country to renew the mandate for the coalition.

The prime minister's Conservative opponents met in the Carlton Club, convinced that he was out to destroy their party just as he had divided his own party. Bonar Law, prodded by his fellow-Canadian, Beaverbrook, attended the meeting. It was resolved to end the coalition. Lloyd George promptly resigned, never to return to office, and Bonar Law's administration went to the country in November 1922, winning a decisive victory under the banner of 'tranquillity and freedom from adventures and commitments both at home and abroad'.

The stars of the previous administration – Balfour, Birkenhead and Austen Chamberlain – opposed the decision of the Carlton Club meeting. Only Curzon joined Bonar Law's government for he had no good reason to be loyal to Lloyd George and was always one of the first to swim vigorously away from any ship that sank under him. Bonar Law was soon found to be terminally stricken with cancer of the throat and promptly resigned. It was generally assumed that Curzon would become prime minister, a prospect which filled most politicians with horror for 'dear George' was almost universally detested for his overbearing arrogance, his treachery and his fundamental weakness. Even his coachman called him the 'damnedest cad in England'. Baldwin, whom Curzon characteristically called 'a man of the utmost insignificance', was called to the palace, his strongest recommendation for the premiership being that he was neither Curzon nor Austen Chamberlain. The latter had little support in the party after the Carlton Club affair and lacked political skill.

The man who gave his name to the 'Baldwin Age' was a decent and scrupulously honest man who, with his heavy watch-chain, wing collar, bowler hat and pipe, and his well-known interest in pig breeding, seemed boringly ordinary and bourgeois. To the bright young things and the flappers he was the epitome of the philistine, to Churchill he was one of the 'pedlars of Brummajam'; but behind this stolid façade lurked an exceptionally astute politician, a good judge of men and an often cunning tactician. Austen Chamberlain's brother, Neville, who had been appointed minister of health just before Baldwin became prime minister, became his closest political associate and eventually his unhappy successor.

Chamberlain's Housing Act was the only solid achievement of Baldwin's first administration. It provided modest subsidies for low-cost housing to be built largely by the private sector. The result was that more than 400,000 small and ugly dwellings were built for the lower middle class by 1929, most of which continue to blight the British landscape. At least they provided acceptable accommodation, but although they were inexpensive they were well beyond the means of the working class.

Baldwin decided that protection would relieve unemployment, 'dish the Goat' by forcing Lloyd George to come out in favour of free trade, and unite the Conservatives in principalled opposition to the Liberals. In December, elections were fought on the single issue of protection. Baldwin's critics pointed to the catastrophic fall in the number of Conservative seats from 346 to 258 and were full of the self-righteousness of the ignored prophet. His supporters could justly claim that Baldwin had indeed united the party which was now in opposition to a weak minority government. Conservatives braced themselves for the unimaginable horrors of a Labour government, the king wondered that his grandmama would have thought of it all, but the more valiant Conservatives were convinced that it would not be long before they would be back in office and natural right would be restored.

That Labour was asked to form the government was largely the result of the peculiarities of the electoral system. Labour's share of the vote only went up from 29.5 per cent to 30.5 per cent, but this translated into forty-nine more seats, making Labour the second largest party in the House. King George V acted correctly in asking the leader of the next largest party to Baldwin's Conservatives to form a government. MacDonald, although later reviled either as an empty windbag or as a traitor to the cause of socialism, was the outstanding figure in a party made up of dreary trade unionists, wide-eyed idealists of every imaginable hue and even a sprinkling of self-professed revolutionaries who, like the Clydesider David Kirkwood, were given to making unfortunate remarks such as: 'Bishops, financiers, lawyers, and all the polite spongers upon the working classes know that this is the beginning of the end'. MacDonald was a very capable administrator. Lacking any political convictions, he stood above the petty factional strife which has always rent the Labour Party, and in a mellifluous Scots accent he delivered speeches of almost intoxicating effect. It was only later that his entranced audiences realized that he had said nothing at all. 'Gentleman Mac' was handsome, an appalling snob and, in spite of his board-school education, totally lacked the common touch.

If MacDonald was built of prime ministerial timber, his party was hardly ready for office. Labour had not yet become a truly national party. Its complex constitution barely papered over the divisions between the endless number of sects and working-class groups from which the party had sprung. The trade unions had a disproportionate influence over the party which therefore appeared to be a class rather than a national party. Furthermore, it seemed to be a party which was largely concerned with the immediate and selfish interests of the organized sector of that class. There was inadequate liaison between the cabinet and the parliamentary party, and between Labour MPs and the national party. The government and the trade union movement were soon at loggerheads. Instead of working out a comprehensive political strategy with the Labour Party the unions, particularly Ernest Bevin's Transport and General Worker's Union, began a series of strikes much to the embarrassment of the government who even considered using the hated Emergency Powers Act against their own supporters.

MacDonald could only govern with the consent of the Liberals and this meant that exotic socialist schemes had to be shelved and patience had to be demanded of the revolutionary chiliasts. This suited the prime minister's temperament and he announced that one step was enough for him, adding with a characteristic flourish that it would of course have to lead to another step.

The outstanding achievement of the first Labour government was the work of John Wheatley. A successful businessman, a Catholic and chronically myopic, he was the most brilliant, forceful and militantly socialist of all MacDonald's colleagues. His Housing Act accepted the fact that housing was a long-term problem and that housing should be built for rent and not for purchase. He increased the subsidies and called for 2.5 million houses to be built by 1939. Although the programme was stopped in 1932 because of financial problems, and although it did nothing to help slum dwellers, it was a singular achievement which ended the housing shortage for the better-paid workers.

Although unemployment had declined since 1921 it still remained unacceptably high. Labour had no idea how to tackle the problem. It was part of their eschatology that unemployment would disappear under socialism, but socialism had been removed from the agenda. Unemployment benefits were increased, but Philip Snowden at the exchequer refused to loosen the purse strings for more public works. Keynes had not yet formulated his theories and careful housekeeping was as much an orthodoxy of the left as it was of the right.

The government fell as a result of a relatively trivial incident. J. R. Campbell, a communist, was charged under the Incitement to Mutiny Act of 1797 for publishing a 'Don't Shoot' appeal to soldiers in the *Workers Weekly*. Realizing that many Labour MPs had made similar routinely seditious remarks, MacDonald asked the attorney general to drop the charges. The Conservatives immediately denounced this bungled affair as a shocking example of political interference in the course of justice. The Liberals supported a Conservative vote of censure and the government fell.

Just before the poll the *Daily Mail* published a letter purporting to be from Zinoviev, President of the Comintern and one of the Soviet Union's ruling triumvirate, which called upon the Communist Party of Great Britain to engage in all manner of seditious activities. The Foreign Office, without consulting their political superiors, protested to the Soviet authorities and the letter was published in the press. The public therefore had every reason to believe that the letter was genuine. Although the letter was sharply critical of the Labour government it was used by the right as evidence of how misguided was the treaty with Russia and MacDonald's failure to protest about the letter was taken as indication that he had a lot to hide. Labour insisted, quite correctly, that the letter was a forgery but went down to defeat at the polls.

The main reason for the Conservative victory was that the Liberals, determined not to split the anti-Labour vote, fielded 115 fewer candidates than in 1923. Baldwin, having used protectionism to divide the Liberals, now dropped it in order to win them over to his side. He promised 'sane, commonsense government' and seemed to be reassuringly sane and commonsensical. Hesitant voters, anxious about the implications of the Zinoviev letter, saw Baldwin as the safest bet. The election was therefore an even greater disaster for the Liberals than for Labour. The Liberals lost all but 41 of their 159 seats. Asquith was defeated at Paisley by the Labour candidate. Labour increased its share of the poll but had a net loss of 40 seats. A lone communist, S. Saklatvala, regained the seat in North Battersea which he had lost in 1923. The Conservatives with 419 seats had a commanding majority.

Baldwin's government was not without men of distinction, although most of them were beginning to get rather long in the tooth. Churchill, who had returned to the Conservative fold, was appointed chancellor of the exchequer, not because he had any talent for the post but to stop him sniping from the back-benches. The prime minister prided himself on having no policy and was given to intoning 'Give peace in our time, O Lord!' and denouncing 'internationalism'. The representative figure in the cabinet was the preposterous home secretary, Sir William Joynson Hicks. Armed with DORA, the wartime Defence of the Realm Act, 'Jix' set out to save England from saxophones, cocktails, Jews, undesirable foreigners, communists, pornography, night clubs, homosexuality, kissing in the park, and any changes to the Book of Common Prayer which hinted at Popery. He locked away Mrs Kate Meyrick, the night club queen, in Holloway prison whence she returned as a national heroine, marrying two daughters off into the peerage. In an unguarded moment he promised the vote to women at the age of twenty-one. It was said, incorrectly, that the 'flapper vote' brought back the Labour government in 1929.

Churchill and his Treasury advisers believed that the best cure for unemployment was a good stiff dose of deflation. In 1925 Britain returned to the gold standard at the 1914 parity with the dollar. It was hoped that with an over-valued pound the City would once again be the financial capital of the world and that the higher price of exports would be offset by lower wages, greater efficiency and the consequent reduction of unit costs. Churchill has been somewhat unfairly blamed for this unfortunate measure, for among economists only Keynes pointed out that the pound was overvalued, but only by 10 per cent, and he also believed that wages would have be reduced if exports were to remain competitive.

On taking office Baldwin had been admonished by George V to 'combat the idea of anything like a class war'. Baldwin tried to remain as faithful as possible to this undertaking. When some of his back benchers tried to legislate the abolition of the political levy on trade unions he made sure that the measure was dropped. Neville Chamberlain as minister of health was responsible for most of the progressive legislation of the administration. While he complained of his leader's imperturbable indolence, Chamberlain brought in twenty-one bills of social reform. Working closely with Churchill he introduced the Pensions Act in 1925, a contributory scheme which provided pensions for widows, orphans and dependent children. The act brought great relief to the elderly poor and was one of the major pieces of social legislation in this century. Chamberlain's Local Government Act of 1929 abolished the boards of guardians who had administered the poor law. Public assistance committees were established in the counties and county boroughs which were subsidized by block grants from the Treasury. This ended the system whereby the guardians were obliged to levy their own poor rates, so that areas where the need was greatest were inevitably the areas least able to pay. This had led to 'Poplarism': hard pressed boards following the example of Poplar by borrowing funds to subsidize relief payments. The Labour Party defended Poplarism because it gave more generous relief. They attacked Chamberlain's reforms for perpetrating the system whereby the destitute were seen as a class apart and for deliberately keeping relief at a minimum so as to discourage indolence. Yet for all the shortcomings of such measures introduced by Chamberlain, they were a foreshadowing of the Welfare State. The Man of Munich also deserves to be remembered, along with Lloyd George and Beveridge, as one of the great architects of state-administered social security.

The British Broadcasting Corporation and the Central Electricity Board, both established in 1926, were run by government appointees, but were relatively free from government interference. Both were thus examples of public corporations without a hint of socialism, yet acceptable to socialists because they were not private enterprises. They were to become the model for the nationalized industries once the Labour Party rejected socialist schemes for workers' control.

Baldwin proved unable to preserve industrial peace in spite of his government's creditable reforming record. By 1925 British industry was producing slightly more than in 1913, but exports had declined drastically and there were still 1 million unemployed. Staple industries like iron, steel, shipbuilding and cotton were all producing at well below capacity. British businessmen lacked the drive and initiative to re-equip and to divert money and manpower into newer branches of industry. All these problems were clearly apparent in the coal industry. Exports had declined drastically, in part because of increased German exports, much of which was in the form of reparations, but also because of the price increase caused by the return to the gold standard. Domestic demand had declined significantly. The industry was outmoded, unproductive and badly in needed of drastic reorganization. Baldwin's answer was to call for wage cuts to make prices more competitive, but this would have decreased domestic demand and made unemployment even worse.

On 30 June 1925 the mine owners announced that they would end the national wages agreement of 1924, cut wages between 13 per cent and 48 per cent and maintain the rate of profit. The miners' president, Herbert Smith, replied with a characteristic 'nowt to give' and his secretary, A. J. Cook, a former Baptist preacher, whipped up the miners' enthusiasm for a showdown in a series of spellbinding and inflammatory speeches. Birkenhead remarked that if he had not had frequent occasion to meet the mine owners he would have thought that the miners' leaders were the stupidest men in England.

The TUC agreed to support the miners; Baldwin told the owners that wages had to be reduced. The 'Cripple Alliance' was determined to undo the shame of 'Black Friday' in 1921 and the NUR and the TGWU announced that they would not move any coal. Faced with this determination and without any idea what to do, Baldwin decided to give way. On 'Red Friday', 31 July 1925, he agreed to give the coal industry a subsidy until 1 May the following year so that wages and profits could be maintained. He then appointed a Royal Commission under Sir Herbert Samuel to investigate the problems of the industry. At the same time Sir John Anderson, the permanent under-secretary at the Home Office, set up the 'Organization for the Maintenance of Supplies' (OMS) to combat any future general strike.

The Samuel Commission, none of whose members had the slightest idea about the coal industry, published their report in March

1926. Its long-term proposals included the nationalization of royalties, improved working conditions, and amalgamation of the smaller pits. None of this counted because the immediate proposals were for wage reductions and an end to the government subsidy. Herbert Smith immediately started muttering 'nowt to give', while A. J. Cook coined the slogan: 'Not a penny off the pay, not a minute on the day!'. When the subsidy ran out on 1 May the owners, anxious to have it out with the miners, locked the men out.

Both the TUC and Baldwin hoped that both sides would make concessions, but negotiations for a compromise formula were broken off by the prime minister when the printers of the *Daily Mail* refused to print a leading article condemning a general strike as intolerably unpatriotic and revolutionary. The secretary of their union, NATSOPA, urged them to print it and Baldwin thus used a very trivial incident to precipitate the strike. He did so because the hardliners such as Churchill, Neville Chamberlain, Birkenhead and Joynson Hicks were breathing down his neck and he feared that if he did not take on the miners he might well lose his job. He did not, however, intend to lose a night's sleep and went promptly to bed. When the TUC delegation returned to Downing Street they found the lights out and the door locked.

The strike, which was never general, began at midnight on 3 May. The Triple Alliance went out, as did workers in heavy industry, the gas and electrical workers, the dockers, builders and printers. Other workers were held back in reserve. The response to the strike call was overwhelming. In spite of the government's ludicrous arguments that the strike was unconstitutional, the strikers acted unselfishly to support the miners' claim to a living wage. They thus rejected the government's claim to stand above class interests and to represent the good of all. Although there was considerable sympathy for the miners, public opinion did not support the strike. Some 130,000 men joined Jix's special constabulary to protect the British Way of Life from the revolutionary hordes. Churchill thundered on in the pages of *The British Gazette*, a paper sponsored by the government, about the workers as 'the enemy' from whom he demanded 'unconditional surrender', as if they were Huns rather than his own countrymen.

There were some voices calling for moderation, among them the King, the Archbishop of Canterbury and Lloyd George. Sir Herbert Samuel also tried to mediate, proposing that the wage reductions outlined in his report should only come into effect after the reorganization of the coal industry. The TUC general council did not feel that they were 'justified in permitting the unions to continue the sacrifice for another day' and agreed to these terms. They called off the strike after a meeting with Baldwin on 12 May, even though the prime minister refused to commit himself to the terms outlined by Samuel.

Throughout the country the strike continued without the timid TUC. This time it was much more dangerous, for it was led by local firebrands and the strikers felt angry and betrayed. Baldwin successfully defused this dangerous situation by being extremely conciliatory, but both the miners and the owners refused to budge. It was not until December that the miners were driven back by sheer necessity to work for longer hours and for less pay. In May 1927 the government twisted the knife by passing the Trade Disputes Act. It made sympathetic strikes illegal and banned the political levy unless the individual contracted in. The civil servants' unions were forbidden to join the TUC. Militant trade unionists swore revenge which eventually they got when the mines were nationalized, the act was overthrown and a Conservative government was toppled by a miners' strike.

The Trade Disputes Act was both thoroughly vindictive and utterly useless. The clause against sympathetic strikes was never invoked. Baldwin undid much of the damage it did to his reputation as a 'plain, straightforward Englishman' by doing virtually nothing for the next two years but deliver a series of vacuous speeches to selected and admiring audiences. By going into neutral, Baldwin disassociated himself from the die-hards in the party, and with his only likely successor the prim and lack-lustre Neville Chamberlain, there was no serious challenge to his leadership. Younger Conservatives such as Harold Macmillan, Robert Boothby and Oliver Stanley became increasingly concerned about the fate of the poor, the rights of the working man and the need for economic planning. The influence of this 'YMCA' grew enormously during the depression, but was not to have a profound and beneficial effect on British politics until the war.

The Conservative Party thus went into the election of 1929 divided and directionless. Baldwin's election slogan of 'Safety First' was hardly inspiring. Unlike the Conservatives, Lloyd George's Liberals had an imaginative and progressive electoral programme which was very similar to Labour's. It was all to no avail. Lloyd George seemed untrustworthy, his programme opportunistic, and his party was accused of splitting the vote between Labour and Conservatives. Labour announced to a perplexed public that 'morality is in the nature of things' and MacDonald, who insisted that 'there must be no monkeying', had no more of a clue of what he intended to do if returned to office than did Baldwin. Labour adopted much of Lloyd George's programme and announced that they were better suited to carry it out. It was a boring campaign in which the main issue was whether Baldwin or MacDonald was better fitted to be prime minister. Even the outcome was uncertain. The Conservatives polled almost 300,000 more votes that Labour, but because of the peculiarities of the electoral system Labour returned as the largest party with 288 seats. The Conservatives had 260 and the Liberals 59, an increase of 18 seats, most of which were held by Squiffites who detested Lloyd George. Baldwin, anxious not to seem 'unsporting', resigned and MacDonald somewhat reluctantly became prime minister.

The new government's only distinction was that Margaret Bond-field, the minister of labour, was the first woman appointed to a cabinet post and to become a privy councillor. Those who were alarmed at this innovation were relieved to find that she was a very ordinary and conservative lady. MacDonald avoided all the 'easy-oozey asses' from the Independent Labour Party (ILP) and the unions and favoured ex-Liberals like Sankey, Wedgwood Benn, Addison, Jowett and Trevelyan. Sir Oswald Mosley was a promising recruit from the Conservatives. Rather ridiculously he was made assistant to the only left-wing member of his government, George Lansbury, who became first commissioner of works. Lansbury was the most thoroughly decent man ever to serve the people as a member of parliament. He was responsible for the government's only lasting achievement, the building of 'Lansbury's Lido' on the Serpentine where Londoners of both sexes could bathe in the open air. *The Times* denounced mixed bathing as 'grotesque and horrible' and was outraged when Lansbury announced that men and women should be allowed to bathe together in the nude if they so wished.

Most of the Labour Party had long abandoned their socialism. They no longer felt that capitalism was an evil system that had to be destroyed, but rather that it should be regulated and controlled so that its benefits could be somewhat more equitably distributed. Thus the Coal Mines Act of 1931 established a central council for the industry which set production quotas while district boards fixed prices. To placate the miners thirty minutes was knocked off the working day. Similar arrangements were introduced in agriculture with Addison's Agricultural Marketing Act. Herbert Morrison proposed a public corporation to run public transport in London so that the profits from the buses could be used to subsidize the underground. Arthur Greenwood began seriously to tackle the job of slum clearance. Bills to raise the school leaving age to fifteen, to reform the electoral system and to repeal the Trades Disputes Act of 1927 all failed to reach the statute book.

Such a cautious government was incapable of tackling the chronic misery of mounting unemployment. MacDonald tried to avoid the issue by announcing that he was not responsible for unemployment and that it was all the fault of the capitalist system. Then he called upon J. H. Thomas to draw up a plan of action. Tom Johnston, George Lansbury and Sir Oswald Mosley were appointed as his assistants. Mosley was the only one of the group to show any political intelligence and initiative, but his radical proposals were rejected out of hand by the tight-fisted chancellor of the exchequer, Philip Snowden. His dedication to thrift and economic orthodoxy was to make the parsimonious Neville Chamberlain seem a radical and a spendthrift. Mosley resigned, was expelled from the Labour Party, formed his own radical New Party and then put on a black shirt and founded the British Union of Fascists. Clement Attlee was appointed chancellor of the Duchy of Lancaster. Britain was singularly blessed that Mosley disappeared from the scene, after a brief spell in the limelight, and that such a conscientious and humane man took his place. Mosley, whatever the merits of his proposals, had ruined his much-favoured chances of ever becoming prime minister, but no one imagined that Attlee would be the outstanding leader of Labour's first majority administration.

In March 1931 Snowden, who agreed with the Conservatives that the way out of the depression lay through rigorous economies, adopted a Liberal suggestion and appointed a committee chaired by Sir George May, late of the Prudential Insurance Company, to investigate government expenditure. The committee's report predicted a deficit of £132 million and called for drastic wage reductions for civil servants, the armed forces, the police, judges and even ministers of the crown. Unemployment benefits were to be reduced by 20 per cent. It was a foolish and unfair document which greatly exaggerated the country's plight and the two Labour members of the committee refused to endorse it. Foreigners reacted predictably by selling their sterling, thus precipitating a serious run on the pound.

The financial crisis split the Labour Party. The TUC, with Bevin as their most persuasive spokesman, argued that the proposed cuts were unfair. They suggested that there should be a graduated levy on the profits, income and earnings of all classes. May's proposals would hurt the low paid and the unemployed and protected the middle class. Following Keynes' lead, the TUC heretically argued that there was nothing sacrosanct about either the gold standard or balanced budgets. A number of Labour ministers agreed with this analysis. Nine of them threatened to resign if the government cut unemployment benefits, prompting that stalwart socialist Sydney Webb to call the TUC 'pigs'.

Snowden would not budge, the bankers insisted on the cuts, and MacDonald felt compelled to resign. The king called the oppposition leaders, Baldwin and Samuel (Lloyd George was recovering from an operation), to discuss the crisis. Samuel suggested a national government under MacDonald, and Baldwin agreed. The TUC General Council, the National Executive of the Labour Party and the Consultative Committee of the Parliamentary Labour Party assumed that the new government would be a Conservative–Liberal coalition and were horrified when they heard that MacDonald had agreed to stay at Number 10. In the House of Commons 242 Labour members voted against the 'Government of the unburied dead'. Only 12 voted in favour.

The national government failed to save the pound and Britain went off the gold standard on 21 September. The Conservatives were eager for an election in the hope of winning a majority by making rousing appeals to the national spirit. MacDonald managed to convince himself that the country needed him to continue the national government and believed that an election would make it stronger. The Liberals were as badly divided as ever and were at a loss to know what to do for the best. Neville Chamberlain eventually found a solution to all these problems. The national government would appeal to the country for a 'doctor's mandate', but each party would issue a separate programme. Samuel's Liberals appealed for the preservation free trade. Simon supported the government. The Conservatives preached protectionism. MacDonald called for an open mind. Labour entered the fray with a programme calling for the nationalization of key industries and rigorous economic planning, expelled MacDonald from the party for his treachery and denounced the election as a 'bankers' ramp'. Snowden, who retired from active politics, traduced his old party's programme as 'bolshevism run mad' and Runciman warned an already alarmed electorate that Labour would steal the money from their Post Office savings' account and give it to the unemployed. Lloyd George poured scorn on the national government and claimed that he alone could preserve free trade.

The election, held on 27 October 1931, was a triumph for the Conservatives who returned with 473 seats. Simon's National Liberals got 35 seats, Samuel's Liberals 33. Lloyd George's political career was over, his faction consisting only of his son, daughter and son-in-law. MacDonald's National Labour supporters obtained 13 seats. Labour went into the election with 287 seats and returned with 46. Finding no rational explanation for this catastrophe, the blame was placed on MacDonald, Snowden and Thomas for betraying socialism and for conspiring with the class enemy.

The national government was Conservative in all but name. MacDonald was virtually a prisoner at Number 10, his health was ruined and his speeches became even more arcane. Lloyd George was becoming an increasingly absurd figure. Churchill was again in the wilderness, ranting about the British Raj. Baldwin assiduously set about enhancing his reputation for trustworthiness. The strong man in the government was the new chancellor of the exchequer, Neville Chamberlain. With his unattractive grating voice, his aloofness and apparant lack of charity he was said by a Labour member to have been 'weaned on a pickle'. Such a man was hardly a threat to Baldwin's skilfully cultivated John Bull image.

MacDonald, Baldwin and company's first moves were protectionist. Walter Runciman, formerly a Squiffite free trader, as President of the Board of Trade introduced the Abnormal Importations Bill which allowed for duties up to 100 per cent *ad valorem* on manufactured goods entering the country in unusually large quantities. Samuel's Liberals swallowed this bitter pill and supported the government. A similar bill was brought in to protect agricultural produce. In February 1932 Neville Chamberlain brought in the Import Duties Bill which slapped a 10 per cent duty on all goods which had been previously exempt, but excluded imports from the empire. Samuel, Maclean, Sinclair and Snowden opposed the measure, even though they were all ministers. Chamberlain proposed an 'agreement to differ' which was a serious breach of constitutional practice, and made a nonsense of the principle of collective cabinet responsibility. The free-trading Liberals voted against the bill, but it was still carried by an overwhelming majority. After the Ottawa agreements in the summer of 1932, which established empire free trade and imposed tariffs against countries outside the commonwealth, Snowden, Samuel and Sinclair could no longer agree to differ and left the government. MacDonald was now even more isolated, with only two party colleagues and Simon's small band of faithful Liberals to uphold the pretence of a national government.

In spite of the 'doctor's mandate' the effects of the depression grew steadily worse. Unemployment reached its peak of almost 3 million in January 1933. Between 6 and 7 million people were dependent on the dole. The government refused to consider capital expenditure as a means of overcoming unemployment. They believed that the crash of 1929 was a cyclical problem that would eventually reverse itself naturally. They also felt that unemployment would remain high because Britain could no longer count on her export staples. When the world economy improved dramatically in the mid-1930s this pessimism remained. It was believed that the trade cycle would swing down again, and structural unemployment would remain high. Given these assumptions all that could be done was to protect British industry, reduce interest rates, stay off the gold standard and wait for times to change. The Labour opposition was hardly more imaginative. They claimed that the entire problem was the result of capitalism and thus agreed with the Conservatives that unemployment was perfectly natural. Little could be done except treat the unemployed humanely and await the golden age of the socialist planned economy. At the same time many socialists, like Mrs Webb, were most concerned that the unemployed should not abuse the privileges of the benefits which came their way, should not clamour for too much more and should be duly grateful for the Labour Party's efforts on their behalf.

In 1931 the government cut unemployment benefits and introduced the hated means test. It was pointed out that since expenditure on these benefits was £125 million per annum and income from contributions only £44 million, cuts were essential. They were also felt to be justified because prices were falling.

Improvements were made in the Unemployment Assistance Board Acts of 1934–35 which helped those unemployed who were not covered by unemployment insurance and the 800,000 who were receiving transitional payments. These acts mark the virtual end of the old poor law and were another important step towards the formation of a welfare state. They ended the renewed Poplarism of those Public Assistance Committees controlled by Labour councils which had often paid higher rates. The government responded to the public outcry at the reduction of rates by passing the Standstill Act of 1935 which kept the most favourable rates. Many Conservatives were so concerned about the electoral consequences of appearing to be lacking in compassion that the government eventually gave way over such unpopular measures as the means test of 1931 and the UAB scales of 1934.

Many politicians came up with schemes for reducing unemployment. Harold Macmillan's *Peace and Reconstruction* of 1935, co-authored by Athur Slater and Geoffrey Crowther, proposed government expenditure on housing, electrification and local government projects. Lloyd George had similar ideas, so did Ernest Bevin. Across the Atlantic, Roosevelt tried them out in his New Deal. In 1936 Keynes published *The General Theory of Employment, Interest and Money* in which he explained why these schemes were going to work. The national government listened to more orthodox advice and rejected such notions for the simple reason that they cost money. They have been blamed ever since for their stupidity, but Roosevelt's grandiose experiments did not solve the problem of unemployment and Keynesian economics would not have ended the fundamental structural weaknesses of British industry.

George V's Silver Jubilee in June 1935 was felt to be a suitable occasion for MacDonald to end his prime ministership and Baldwin moved to Number 10. In October he dissolved parliament. The last peacetime election campaign was a dull affair. The Conservatives claimed to stand for the League, sanctions, and disarmament, although Baldwin also promised 'to remedy the deficiencies which have occurred in our defences'. They pointed to their achievements in housing and the reduction of unemployment and they promised to improve welfare benefits and grants to the distressed areas. Labour was in disarray after an acrimonious party conference in which Bevin had attacked Lansbury's Christian pacifism and Stafford Cripps' refusal to accept sanctions on the grounds that the League was a capitalist conspiracy. They could do little but denounce the Conservatives as insincere in their new-found enthusiasm for the League and disarmament while claiming that they were war-mongers who intended to arm to the teeth. The Samuelite Liberals tied themselves to the Conservative's coat tails and no one listened to Lloyd George's plans for government spending and economic planning.

The Conservatives had 454 seats on dissolution and returned with 387. Labour were fortunate in the distribution of votes and with their 154 seats won back most of what they had lost in 1931. The Liberals only had 21 seats, but 4 of those were held by the Lloyd George family. MacDonald was defeated by Emmanuel Shinwell, but returned to office as soon as a conveniently safe seat could be found for him.

The Hoare–Laval Pact in December showed that the government's avowals of support for collective security were a sham. There was such an outcry in political circles that Hoare was obliged to resign. His place as foreign secretary was taken by Anthony Eden who enjoyed an undeserved reputation for being a strong man determined to face the dictators. In March 1936 Hitler re-occupied the Rhineland. Baldwin responded by appointing Sir Thomas Inskip minister for the co-ordination of defence. He was best known for his denunciation of the papistical practice of reserving the sacrament during the richly comical debate on the revision of the Prayer Book in 1928. Politicians in their anecdotage described this as the most extraordinary political appointment since Caligula made his horse consul. Churchill was the only man for the job, but such an appointment would have been too provocative to the thrifty and to those who felt that the best way to deal with the dictators was to set a good example and disarm.

Abyssinia, the Rhineland and Geneva mattered little in a country that was entirely preoccupied with royal romance. On 20 January 1936 King George V enquired 'How is the Empire?' and expired. The Prince of Wales, now Edward VIII, was fashionable, flippant, 41 and unmarried. In 1930 he had met Wallis Warfield Simpson who was married to an admirable man and who had a former husband still alive. She was a somewhat brash American of a type the English mysteriously find refreshingly original and even intelligent. Within a couple of years the Prince of Wales and Mrs Simpson were very close.

Shortly after Edward became king, Mrs Simpson filed for divorce. The king imagined that he could still continue to lead a private life and assumed that he would be able to marry Mrs Simpson. Baldwin told Edward that his wife would automatically be queen and that the country would not tolerate a twice divorced American commoner as his consort. The king replied that he was going to marry the woman he loved and that he was prepared to abdicate. The prime minister would not consider introducing the necessary legislation to permit a morganatic marriage. On 11 December the king abdicated and left England to stay with Baron Eugene de Rothschild in Austria. His brother, the Duke of York, a tense, somewhat incoherent, but conscientious man of modest ability, succeeded to the throne. Ably assisted by his splendid and deservedly popular wife, he became, much to his own surprise, an effective and much loved king. For the British monarchy the abdication was a great blessing. Edward VIII had little appreciation of his responsibilities, was politically inept, particularly in his dealing with the Nazis, superficial and weak. George VI did the job very well and scrupulously took the advice of his ministers.

The abdication crisis greatly enhanced Baldwin's prestige. The king had been dabbling in politics by broadcasting his strong pro-German and anti-Soviet views and by suggesting that parliamentary democracy had its shortcomings. Many feared that Churchill's spirited support for the king was part of an attempt to unseat Baldwin, split the Conservative Party and rule with a firm hand. Instead the prime minister trounced Churchill in the House of Commons. Churchill had assumed that the king was generally popular when he was widely felt to be irresponsible, frivolous and even immoral. The only demonstrations in his favour were mounted by the communists and the fascists. Most politicians insisted that the king had to take the advice of his ministers and since Edward refused to do so he would have to go. The king's supporters were a dubious lot which included the press barons Beaverbrook and Rothermere. Very few MPs were prepared to support them, for they knew how strong public opinion was against the king. Churchill seriously misjudged the situation. His political life seemed to be at an end, and but for Adolf Hitler it would have been.

The Coronation in May 1937 was a splendid affair. Shortly afterwards Baldwin resigned and took the title of Earl Baldwin of Bewley. His considerable reputation quickly vanished. He was soon seen as the man who had left the country defenceless against Hitler and who had failed to provide the leadership and drive needed in the troubled 1930s. Perhaps worst of all, he left as his undisputed successor Neville Chamberlain.

Chamberlain might have been an effective, although certainly not a popular, prime minister if his administration had concentrated on domestic affairs. It was his personal and his country's tragedy that foreign policy was to be his prime concern. He was single minded and supremely confident in his own judgement. His cabinet was made up of men much like himself: people whose strength was administration and the mastery of the details of domestic government. An exception was Anthony Eden at the Foreign Office, but he was never as strong as he appeared to be in contrast to his colleagues, and was to resign in February 1938, taking with him his under-secretary of state, Lord Cranborne. He was replaced by Halifax, who supported Chamberlain's appeasement policy. Chamberlain seldom took his colleagues' advice, neither did he listen to public opinion, nor the suggestions of his experts, particularly not those at the Foreign

Office whom he despised. He believed, all advice and evidence to the contrary, that he could bring peace and practical common sense to the world.

Appeasement was not a total failure. It worked in Ireland. Chamberlain stood firm on partition but ended the trade war and Ireland, now known to Churchill's fury as Eire, became economically a member of the commonwealth. More dramatically, Chamberlain gave up the three treaty ports still held by Britain, and accepted a lump sum payment of £10 million for the £100 million claimed as compensation for land annuities and other payments. Churchill denounced the agreements as seriously weakening Britain's naval defences. Chamberlain argued that the best defence was a friendly Ireland. In the short run he was right, but he was wrong in assuming he had solved the Irish question. De Valera saw the agreements simply as a step towards unification; the Unionists were determined that this should never happen.

Perhaps his success in Ireland encouraged him in his appeasement of Hitler. Like De Valera, the Führer had his grievances. They could be discussed, settled and all would be well. Munich seemed to be a great triumph. There was 'peace with honour', Germany had no more territorial ambitions, and Chamberlain was a favourite for the Nobel prize. The *New York Daily News* even described him as 'Christlike'. There was an almost hysterical hope that Chamberlain was right and that peace was secure. Duff Cooper was the only minister to resign over Munich and he told the House of Commons: 'The Prime Minister may be right. I hope and pray that he is right; but I cannot believe what he believes; I wish I could.'

Within a few weeks it was clear that appeasement had failed. Chamberlain was at first incredulous, then sulky. Finally he became angry. But he still felt his policy had been correct. In his broadcast to the nation on the declaration of war on Germany he said: 'You can imagine what a bitter blow it is to me that all my long struggle to win peace has failed. Yet I cannot believe that there is anything more or anything different that I could have done that would have been more successful.' Chamberlain created a small war cabinet in which the outstanding figure was his great rival, Winston Churchill. He clung tenaciously to office until forced to resign in May 1940. Shortly afterwards on 9 November he died of cancer. It was only then that Churchill became leader of the Conservative Party.

Chamberlain behaved unimpeachably between May and November 1940. Although defeated and mortally ill, he had the courage and magnanimity to support Churchill, thus saving his party from a split such as had destroyed the Liberals in 1916 and giving the country the unity it so desperately needed.

CHAPTER NINE
France

In his speech to the Chamber of Deputies announcing that Germany had agreed to an armistice, Clemenceau warned that the peace might be even more difficult to win than the war. Jules Cambon gloomily proclaimed that 'France victorious must grow accustomed to being a lesser power than France vanquished.' Such statements were no empty rhetoric. France had lost 1.5 million men in the Great War, and 3.5 million had been wounded. Among the civilian population the death-rate had increased substantially during the war, due to acute shortages of food and medical supplies, and the birthrate had declined. The workforce was thus reduced, and would never be fully replaced since the population continued to decline.

The war had had a catastrophic effect on industrial production, in spite of the needs of an almost total war. Steel production was down from 4.6 million tonnes in 1913 to 2 million in 1918. Agriculture also suffered. Wheat production was 73 per cent of the pre-war level and there were 18 per cent less cattle. 9,300 factories had been damaged and destroyed, and 2 million hectares had been ruined. The war had left France owing over 110 billion gold francs. The franc fell by more than 50 per cent in the first year of peace and continued its downward trend. In order to pay off bond holders, the government borrowed more money at even higher rates of interest thus greatly increasing the already horrendous deficit.

None of these economic problems were insurmountable, and in many sectors of the economy France did extremely well in the 1920s. But the political will was lacking to tackle the difficult problems of adjustment, and there was no real willingness to adopt new attitudes commensurable with significant economic and social changes. The politicians of the Third Republic were as solidly and unimaginatively bourgeois as they had been in 1870. They believed that the crisis would be overcome by extolling the virtues of private property and low taxation, and by making the Germans pay for the restoration of the economy.

This complacent bourgeois society was under severe attack. Throughout Europe the left had grown in militancy under the impact of the deprivations of an increasingly unpopular war, widening social inequality, and the repercussions of the exciting and promising revolution in Russia. By 1917 the majority of socialists were opposed to the war and supported the idea of a compromise peace. The wartime political truce, the *union sacrée*, had fallen apart. The socialists were no longer prepared to co-operate with the bourgeois parties, and increasingly looked for some alternative political system to the bourgeois republic. This militancy was fuelled by returning soldiers who felt that the country owed them a substantially better life, and was encouraged by concessions such as the eight-hour working day guaranteed by Clemenceau before the 1919 elections. The socialist leadership, for all their praises of the bolshevik revolution, made it clear that they did not wish to see anything similar happen in France. The working class was impatient, dissatisfied and unsympathetic towards the reformist practices of the leadership. There were a number of strikes and demonstrations which resulted in violence, the most notable being the May Day demonstration in 1919, which ended in a pitched battle between workers and the Republican Guard.

Clemenceau, Poincaré and indeed all of France's rulers were determined to crush the militant left, and this did not prove very difficult. A threat to call in the troops in July 1919 to stop a demonstration by the trades unions (CGT) was enough to ensure that it was called off. Government propaganda that the militant left were in the pay of the Germans, and the bourgeois fear of the revolutionary socialists was out of all proportion to their actual strength. This imaginary 'Red Peril', although it seemed very real when workers attacked the Republican Guards with iron bars, strengthened the appeal of the right-wing parties, for most Frenchmen devoutly desired to return to the peaceful, normal and, above all, bourgeois world of the Third Republic.

Political struggles, of which the most dramatic seemed to be the challenge from the extreme left, were exacerbated by the increased inequalities caused by inflation. The petite bourgeoisie of smallholders, *rentiers*, modest professionals and minor civil servants, who lived largely on fixed incomes, were seriously affected by this process. Some of these professionals and civil servants were attracted by the idea of socialist planning, but the vast majority of them looked to the extreme right for protection. Under the banner of the protection of private property the petite bourgeoisie joined forces with the establishment to meet the challenge from the left: a challenge which was strong enough to bring these forces together, but never strong enough to pose a really serious threat.

The French bourgeoisie and their supporters wanted a return to normality, traditional republican virtues, law and order. Clearly, the virtual dictatorship of Clemenceau would have to end, and elections would have to be held. The results of the elections in November 1919 were somewhat surprising. The political leadership during the war had come largely from the centre-left: the republicans, radicals and socialists had held most of the important posts during the war years. They had always been ready to co-operate with the moderate right, but they had never liked Clemenceau, who was far too authoritarian and independent for their taste. But these middle-of-the-road republicans were swept aside by the *Bloc National*, a coalition of royalists, right-wing republicans, and those radicals who articulated the fears of the threatened petite bourgeoisie. The *Bloc* stood for the continuation of the *Union Sacrée*, the rigorous enforcement of the peace treaties and reverence for the sanctity of private property. Their most powerful appeal was to anti-bolshevism, best shown in their poster provided by the employers' association, the *Union des Intérêts Economiques*, which showed it in the form of a hideous blood-stained head with a dagger between its teeth.

The socialists were incapable of providing any effective opposition to the *Bloc National*. With their mixed feelings about the Russian revolution, they found it very difficult to defend themselves against the accusation from the right that they were all bolsheviks; the more so as many within their ranks proudly annouced that they were. Their sympathy for Woodrow Wilson and the idea of the League of Nations was further evidence to the right that they were out to cheat France of the fruits of victory. Socialists were also seriously divided among themselves: between moderates and enthusiasts for Lenin, between those who scrupulously upheld republican legality and those who preached the violent overthrow of the state, and between moderates who were prepared to ally with the bourgeois parties and militants who felt that any alliance with capitalist forces was a betrayal of socialism. Many of those who traditionally sympathized with the socialists, particularly among the radicals, were concerned that the movement was far too sympathetic to communism. This was particularly unfortunate, given the peculiar electoral system which was adopted in 1919, which used a curious form of proportional representation which set a high premium on organization and the formation of electoral alliances. Since each constituency elected a number of deputies, and since any combination of parties which gained a majority in that constituency took all the seats, the socialists' refusal to enter into electoral alliances was particularly disastrous. In spite of these divisions among the socialists the parties of the left increased their share of the popular vote compared with their performance in 1914, and went on to win every election for the next twenty years, with the exception of 1928.

Although the socialists got 25 per cent of the votes they only returned 68 of the 610 deputies. With 86 radical socialists and 26 republican socialists (among them Painlevé and Briand) the left was hopelessly outnumbered by the 433 deputies from the *Bloc National*. Since the radicals and the republicans frequently voted for the government, the *Bloc* was in an overwhelmingly powerful position. In 1920 only 68 votes were cast against the budget. This *Chambre horizon bleu* (so called because of the large number of ex-servicemen) was the most reactionary Chamber since 1876. It was opposed to all change, was determined that Germany should be made to foot France's bills, and was united in its resistance to the aspirations and needs of the working class.

Two months after the elections, Poincaré's term of office as president expired. The public called for Clemenceau to take his place, but Poincaré and Briand, both of whom detested him, started a vigorous campaign among the right-wing deputies against the 'Tiger'. For the first time in the history of the Third Republic the majority of the Chamber were practising Catholics, and they were greatly distressed by the suggestion that if Clemenceau died in office there would be a secular funeral. It was also generally agreed on the right that Clemenceau had been far too lenient to the Germans. Paul Deschanel, a pleasant nobody, was elected president. Clemenceau prompty resigned as prime minister, to be succeeded by an ex-socialist, Alexandre Millerand. As a final insult, the unfortunate president had to retire to a psychiatric hospital after a few months. Millerand was elected as his replacement, the general feeling being that France needed a strong man as president. The new president had little patience with parliamentary bickering and sought to strengthen the executive powers of the presidency.

Millerand's successor as prime minister was one of his creatures,

Leygues. The Chamber promptly decided that they did not want to have a strong president after all, and did not wish to lose their power to the executive by adopting something approaching the American system of government. In January 1921 Leygues government was overthrown and he was succeeded by Briand. Briand, whose best known remark was that 'life is made of rubber', was viewed by the *Bloc National* with mixed feelings. He had been a Boulangist, an anarchist, and a socialist before deciding that convictions and principles were a hindrance to a political career, and that charm, connections and oratorical skill were the best guarantees of success. Briand inherited a difficult situation. The *Bloc* had followed traditional conservative policies of keeping taxes to a minimum, balancing the budget, by borrowing the money if necessary, and avoiding any innovation. The result had been a series of strikes in 1920 in which the communists played an important role, but the government had taken strong action and demoralized workers had left the trades union movement in droves. The effects of the fall of prices on the world market and a depreciation of the franc could not be offset by manipulating the budget, but the *Bloc* would not increase direct taxes, as the left demanded, preferring to continue borrowing money, hoping that the Germans would eventually pay.

Much to the alarm of the right, Briand proposed a rapprochement with the Germans. This was intolerable to the majority of Frenchmen who saw no reason why the Germans should not be made to pay in full for the cost of veterans' and widows pensions, and for the reconstruction of the devastated areas. As it was, reparations were not even enough to cover the cost of the French troops stationed in Germany. Briand clearly had to go, and in January 1922 Poincaré, whom none could accuse of being soft on the Germans, was appointed in his stead.

Poincaré was almost the exact opposite to Briand, for he was inflexible, almost painfully honest, and rigidly principled. He was totally committed to the idea that Germany should be made to pay, so much so that the slogans on the left were 'Poincaré Means War' and 'Poincaré: The Man Who Laughs in Graveyards.' He had no reason to be particularly concerned about these jibes since the socialists were in a state of disarray. In December 1920 the Socialist Congress at Tours resulted in the majority voting in favour of joining the Communist International, and a minority under Léon Blum forming a new party on social democratic lines. Poincaré's greatest difficulties were financial. The United States and Britain tried to discourage France from asking too much of the Germans, but at the same time demanded that their own debts should be promptly paid. Only drastic fiscal measures at home would save the situation, but these were unacceptable to the *Bloc*, and Poincaré was temperamentally opposed to any moves that smacked of socialism. There was widespread criticism of the policy of endlessly borrowing money, but any attempt to raise taxes or to inquire into tax evasion was promptly denounced as inquisitorial and sadistic. Only some ingenious deals on the stock exchange, largely with funds borrowed from the Morgan Bank, saved the franc from collapsing. Poincaré decided not to give an inch, and when the Germans asked for a moratorium on reparations payments, he responded by sending 40,000 troops into the Ruhr, in spite of the warnings of Briand and Clemenceau.

The occupation of the Ruhr in 1923 was a gesture of frustration which brought France no benefits. She had no backing from her allies, the operation was very costly, it further poisoned relations with Germany and it put the franc under very serious pressure. The failure of the occupation of the Ruhr left the *Bloc National's* policies in ruins. Germany had not been made to pay, and demonstrably could not be made to do so. Leaving well alone was hardly a viable policy at a time of serious economic crisis. In the elections of 11 May 1924 the *Bloc National* was replaced by the *Cartel des Gauches*, an alliance of radicals and socialists. This was not the result of an enormous swing in public opinion, but because the *Bloc National* was beginning to fall apart. Rifts began to appear between Catholics and anti-clericals, and the failure of the Ruhr occupation and the government's attempt to overcome the economic crisis inevitably led to serious differences of opinion. The *Cartel*, by contrast, were able to form a workable alliance, in spite of certain misgivings on the left, and the communists were not yet strong enough to undermine this alliance of the left and centre-left.

The *Cartel* refused to form a government until Millerand resigned. An insipid moderate, Doumergue, was elected in his place and a new government formed under the radical leader, Herriot, a man best known for his pipe and his impressive appetite, but who had proved himself to be a brilliant administrator while mayor of Lyon. He was a capable if somewhat flowery orator, an intellectual, and a man of flexibility and compromise. Herriot was shrewd yet decent, but the alliance over which he presided was only good for winning elections and was hopeless as a governing coalition. Radicals and socialists could only agree on one thing – that the Catholic Church was the most sinister of the republic's enemies. There was no agreement about how to treat Germany, and even less on economic policy. Socialists, who espoused the ideas of nationalization, greatly increased taxation and state planning, could hardly agree with petit bourgeois radicals, shopkeepers and artisans who worried about inflation and high taxes, or civil servants and school teachers who wanted job security and a decent pension, all of whom flocked to the banner of the 'League of the Republic' which was financed by the brandy baron Hennessy.

Herriot''s greatest problem was how to deal with the economic crisis. Drastic increases in taxation were unacceptable to the radicals, deflation would not be tolerated by the socialists. Rightist bankers would not support loans to a government which included socialists. Meanwhile, the franc continued its fall, small investors saw their life savings vanish, and workers were hurt by the fall in real wages Herriot saw no way out of these difficulties and his government fell, destroyed, he said, by a 'wall of money'.

Clearly there was a need for a strong man, and the only strong man available was Poincaré. Here was the right incarnate, calling for restraint, a balanced budget and an increase in indirect rather than direct taxation. His coalition government included many of the leading political figures of the day, among them Briand, Painlevé, and Herriot, somewhat to the alarm of those who were safe behind the 'wall of money'. He was granted the exceptional right to govern by means of decree-laws. His obvious determination to do something after the indecision of the *Cartel* did much to restore confidence in the franc which quickly doubled in value on foreign exchanges. Now the franc was grossly over-valued, creating a new crisis which was severe enough for Poincaré to come forward with a solution which would have been unacceptable from anyone else. Devaluation was sacrilege to the financial establishment, but he had sufficient popularity to be able to choose devaluation rather than deflation and to favour increased production over an over-valued currency. Thus in 1928 the franc was fixed at one-fifth of its value. The results were spectacular. Capital flowed back to France, loans were easily obtained at home and abroad, and industrial production increased significantly. But there were new problems created by this success. The 'Poincaré franc' became virtually sacrosanct, to be defended at all costs. During the depression this proved to be a disastrous obsession. Poincaré had also created the myth that there were magic solutions to economic problems, and there was no understanding of the complex psychological mechanisms of confidence.

It was hardly surprising that the centre coalition won a resounding victory at the elections of 1928. In spite of some misgivings over foreign policy, the right decided to support Poincaré in the hope of getting some credit for his economic success. The alliance of the right, renamed *Union Nationale* so that people might forget the failures of the *Bloc National*, included some fascist elements like Taittinger's *Jeunesses Patriotes*, but the most active and virulent of the ultra organizations, the *Action Francaise*, was still recovering from the Vatican's condemnation. On the left the *Cartel des Gauches* was revived, but as the socialists announced that they would never take part in a bourgeois government, even one dominated by their radical partners, and as the socialists and communists were incapable of working together, this effectively excluded their supporters from active political participation, and was hardly an inspiring platform. The communists' refusal to enter into any electoral pacts cost the left over a million votes, and gave the right more than sixty additional seats. In any case the left had little chance of beating Poincaré, of whom it was said that he was the most popular monarch since Saint Louis.

Poincaré represented the stability of the republic, a sense of continuity with the republic of Ferry and Waldeck-Rousseau, a republic which had the confident support of the business world, and also of the small investor. It was a republic of laymen, but with no trace of anti-clerical fanaticism. It was a republic which was intensely patriotic, but which stood for collective security, as well as an understanding with Germany. By this time Poincaré, the strongest voice for a harsh peace, agreed with Briand's view that reconciliation was the key to future security. Briand's long tenure of office as minister of foreign affairs was another major factor in this sense of stability, as was Berthelot's at the head of the Foreign Office.

Although between 1920 and 1940 the average government only lasted for seven months, Poincaré was prime minister from 1922 to 1924 and 1926 to 1929. Many of the leading political figures held office for long periods throughout this decennium and the administration remained similarly stable. Even in electoral terms there were no dramatic swings. Discounting the rather curious elections of 1919, only 200,000 votes decided between left and right. The two blocs were thus approximately equal. They alternated regularly, but they were uneasy alliances which usually slipped into power because of the weakness of the opposing bloc, not because of the attractiveness of their programmes to the electorate. It was certainly not two-party system as in Britain or the United States.

There seemed to be little danger to the republic either from th left or the right. Victory in 1918 and the success of the *Bloc National* in the elections of 1919 did much to reconcile the extreme right to the republic, and it was not until the beginning of the 1930s that fascism began to have a significant impact on French political life. On the left the communists had formed an intransigent bolshevik party by 1925, utterly subservient to Moscow and militantly opposed to any compromise with the bourgeois republic. But the party was hardly significant. Although it had 110,000 members in 1921 this number had declined to about 35,000 by 1930.

In July 1929 Poincaré, who was ill, retired from politics and his place was taken by Briand who spent much of his time talking of international peace and planning a United States of Europe. But Briand was also ill and was obliged to hand over the office of president of the council of state to André Tardieu. The latter came from a wealthy Parisian background, had been a brilliant student of political science, a successful journalist on the *Temps*, and was one of the outstanding statesmen of his day. Far too rich to be venal, too fastidious to be ambitious, he was justly suspicious of others, for he had many enemies. He attempted to deal with the problems of the depression, which were initially far less severe in France than in the other capitalist countries, by an extensive programme of public works and investment in agriculture and industry. This scheme, proposed by his wily minister of finance, Chéron, was far from successful. On the right it was regarded as unorthodox and profligate, on the left as an attempt to bolster up a crumbling capitalist system without tackling the root causes of the problem. But it was the Oustric affair, which involved the bankruptcy of a bank and some highly irregular behaviour by a number of deputies, which led to the downfall of the Tardieu government.

After a brief interval, Laval formed a new government in January 1931. Of very modest origins, Laval had been a rampant socialist, a pacifist and an anarchist, eventually to become an exceptionally shrewd and manipulative moderate. Unlike Tardieu, he was a political *parvenu*, always ready to appeal to man's basest instincts. The election of Doumer as president, who was preferred to Briand, further strengthened the centrist position, for it was felt that Briand relied too much on the support of Blum and the socialists. Laval's government, however, did not last, and he was replaced by Tardieu, the government remaining virtually unchanged.

This was all a sign that the republic was running out of steam. Political expediency and economic eclecticism was not enough to avert a crisis. To many, particularly among the young, the spectacle of an unimaginative ruling class incapable of handling an unprecedented crisis, along with the financial scandals and political dealings, was clear evidence that a world was collapsing and that a new one would take its place. Some saw the solution in communism, for the Soviet Union's socialist economy appeared to withstand the worldwide crisis and to maintain its extraordinary rate of growth. Others were attracted by fascism, and saw in Mussolini the harbinger of a new culture. This 'spirit of the thirties' (*esprit des années 30*) was a widespread expression of disillusionment with republican principles, practices and aspirations.

At first only disaffected literati were affected by the new spirit: men like Déat and Marquet who left the socialists to form their own fascist party. But the leagues were steadily gaining members. The *Croix-de-Feu*, which had started out as a veterans' association, became an important political movement, richly financed by the likes of the perfume manufacturer François Coty. Many peasants joined the Greenshirts who theatened to 'clean up Paris with their bare arms and clean hands.' As yet these were still essentially fringe movements, but they were growing in numbers and audacity, and circumstances were favourable to them.

As agricultural prices began to drop because of a successful harvest, the domestic market contracted and industrial production fell off. Increased tariffs did not offset the fall in world prices and there was a steady fall in French exports. By 1932 exports had fallen to 40 per cent of the level of 1929. Since the government was unwilling to increase taxation, the revenues of the state diminished. In such circumstances very little was done to relieve the burden of the unemployed and those who suffered from the increasing effects of the depression.

In May 1932 elections were held which returned a radical government under Herriot, supported by the socialists. The *Bloc* had little to offer but appeals to patriotism, promises to defend property and privilege, and appeals to the workers to make further sacrifices for the national good. But the radicals' programme was hardly more inspiring. They made vague promises of decent government, tolerance, honesty and economy. The socialists warned of the dangers from the right from anti-democratic extremists. They called for a forty-hour week and the introduction of certain social services such as unemployment insurance, close state control of the banks and the nationalization of key industries. The communists once again would not consider any electoral alliances and spent most of their time excoriating the socialists, calling for closer ties with the Soviet

Union, denouncing the entire Versailles system, demanding that the retirement age should be reduced to fifty-five and calling for revolution in Indo-China. The electorate had little patience for such stuff, and the communists lost 250,000 votes to win a mere ten seats. The radicals and socialists, along with their supporters, got 334 seats while the right won 257.

Herriot attempted to balance his budget by increasing taxation and cutting back expenditure. The right was outraged by the suggestion that taxes should be raised, but the socialists, who refused to participate in the government, did not want to be associated with such unpopular measures which directly threatened the interests of those who had voted for the radicals only a few months previously. Herriot, unable to get his budget accepted by the Chamber, clung on to office, but had to resign in December 1932, when his proposal to pay the debt owing to the United States was rejected by a majority of the deputies. Indeed, the proposal was so obviously bound to fail, given the strongly anti-American mood of the country, that it was suggested that he made it simply to find an excuse to resign.

Paul Boncour, an independent socialist, formed a new government, but it only lasted for forty days. Daladier, a feeble radical who enjoyed the reputation of being a strong man, largely because of his laconic and taciturn nature, was his successor and remained in office for all of nine months. For months he did nothing, then he introduced a budget similar to that of Herriot. The socialists voted against it and Daladier resigned. Another radical, Sarraut, tried his hand but was even less successful, falling from grace three weeks later. Camille Chautemps, also a radical, at last succeeded in getting a budget passed which was very similar to Herriot's original proposals. This time the socialists cravenly absented themselves from the Chamber, thus avoiding the odium of bringing down yet another government, hoping not to be seen as responsible for a budget which was likely to be widely unpopular.

This seemingly endless series of ineffectual and unpopular governments, incapable of grappling with increasingly serious problems, were all grist to the mills of the extreme right and of the communists. Then, late in 1933, a fresh and spectacular scandal hit France. A crooked financier, Stavisky, who made up for what he lacked in financial cunning by creating a network of influential figures from the worlds of politics and high society, came unstuck. He was discovered to have swindled tens of millions of francs in bonds issued by the Municipal Credit Bank of Bayonne of which he was a director. Stavisky fled from the law, and in January, 1934 committed suicide in Chamonix.

The radical right used the Stavisky scandal to pour scorn on the entire parliamentary system, and Charles Maurras had a field-day in his scurrilous but brilliant journal, *Action Française*, lambasting the 'thieves' in the Chamber of Deputies, and suggesting that Chautemps had ordered the police to 'suicide' Stavisky to avoid embarrassing revelations. Stavisky, who was by origin a central European Jew, was an ideal target for anti-Semites and nationalists, and his friends in high places were one by one knocked from their perches much to the satisfaction of the ultras. Chautemps, who was hardly lily-white, was obliged to resign and Daladier returned to office, President Lebrun having first offered the appointment to Doumergue, a profoundly silly antiquity who had the good sense to refuse the offer. Daladier began by dismissing Jean Chiappe, the Corsican Prefect of Paris whose son had been Stavisky's lawyer. Chiappe had connections with the radical right, but also with many leading radicals. This created a somewhat awkward situation which Daladier attempted to avoid by appointing him Governor General of Morocco, a post which Chiappe refused out of hand. In a farcical repeat of this axing, Daladier fired the director of the *Comédie Française* who had dared to put on a performance of *Coriolanus*, a play with a profoundly anti-democratic bias which was seen to be a direct incitement to the fascist leagues to take to the streets.

The extreme right reacted to the dismissal of Chiappe by claiming that the government was giving way to communist pressure, at the same time insisting that the defence of the prefect was also the defence of the municipal freedom of the capital. They therefore called for a demonstration in front of the Chamber of Deputies, to take place on 6 February, the day when the Chamber returned from its recess. Whether or not the demonstration took place at the instigation of Chiappe is open to question. Some 100,000 people from the *Croix-de-feu*, the *Action Française*, the *Jeunesses patriotes*, veterans' organizations and other fascistic groups assembled on the evening of 6 February in the Place de la Concorde. It was a mob without any common purpose or platform, a collection of aspiring intellectuals, small shopkeepers, artisans, professionals and students, whipped up by demagogic journalists and held together by a common anti-parliamentarianism and anti-Semitism. Among them were communist ex-servicemen ordered out by their leader, André Marty, their desire to destroy the bourgeois state being greater than their aversion to fascists. Clearly they hoped to seize the Palais

Bourbon, but the demonstration was so poorly planned that it could never have resulted in a successful *coup*. Six volumes of the official report on this *journée* failed to give any adequate explanation what it was all about, largely because each of the groups involved had their own programmes and their own grudges which they wished to see redressed. The police were waiting for them and in the fighting that ensued 14 people were killed and 2,500 wounded, of whom 200 were sufficiently seriously hurt to be sent to hospital. One policeman was killed, and about 100 injured.

Daladier, ferociously attacked from both the left and the right, no longer enjoying the confidence of the President of the Republic and threatened by Marshal Lyautey, who announced that he would unleash the *Jeunesses patriotes* against the Chamber if he did not go, resigned, to be replaced by Doumergue, a radical who was acceptable to the right. He formed a government which combined elements of the right with the radicals in a sudden revamping of Poincaré's *Union nationale*. Supported on the right by Tardieu and on the left by Herriot, his cabinet included the hero of Verdun, Marshal Pétain.

On 7 February the socialist trades union federation (CGT) called for a twenty-four-hour general strike to take place on the 12th. The communists reacted by staging their own demonstration on 9 February at the Place de la République. Justly ashamed of the sinister role they had played on 6 February, the communists now attempted to place themselves at the head of the anti-fascist movement, while at the same time sticking to the absurd notion that the most effective way of attacking fascism was to attack social democracy. A series of bloody scuffles took place between communists and the police, and on 9 February barricades went up around the Place de la République. More lives were lost in these pointless demonstrations. On the following day the communists had a sudden change of heart and announced that they would join in the general strike, thus opening the way for a united front which the socialists enthusiastically welcomed.

Doumergue was hardly the man to head an effective government of national unity. He was well liked, largely because of his broad grin which he had habitually worn on official occasions as president, but he was thoroughly second rate and hopelessly vain. He attempted to rule by using decree laws which created the impression of determined government while at the same time absolving the deputies from taking any responsibility for the government's unpopular measures. He attempted to increase revenues and reduce expenditure, but this was hardly possible when his foreign minister was pursuing collective security against Germany, which in turn necessitated an increase in military expenditure. His attempts to increase the powers of the premier became increasingly worrying to the radicals, the more so as he called for the union of all Frenchmen other than the socialists and communists, which by implication included the fascists. Some leading ultras, chief among them Jean Goy, a leader of the ex-servicemen and an enthusiast for Adolf Hitler, warned radical deputies that if they overthrew the Doumergue government there would be another 6 February. The radicals ignored these threats and on 8 November withdrew their support from the government. Doumergue left office with singular lack of grace, hinting that the extreme right would fight to restore him to office. They did not oblige him.

Doumergue's successor was Pierre Etienne Flandin, a six-foot-four *grand bourgeois*, a man of the right although he had distanced himself somewhat from Tardieu since 1932, and who, as legal adviser to Aéropostale, was implicated in the scandal surrounding that company's bankruptcy. The Chamber welcomed his government, not so much out of any great enthusiasm for Flandin, who was a somewhat colourless man, but from a sense of relief that Doumergue had gone. Flandin announced that this financial policy would involve neither deflation nor devaluation, insisting that the world economy had turned the corner and that prices were beginning to rise once again. In order to encourage industrial production, Flandin wanted to see interest rates come down, but he soon found himself locked in conflict with the Bank of France, whose Regency Council clung to financial orthodoxy and demanded a deflationary policy. Flandin needed the help of the bank to pay off large numbers of government bonds which matured on 15 June, and therefore agreed to the bank's terms. The Chamber would not give Flandin the plenary financial powers he needed to carry out this deflationary programme, and on 30 May his government fell.

After the brief interlude of the Bouisson government, which only lasted one day, largely because his finance minister, Caillaux, promised drastic deflation which was unacceptable to the radicals, Pierre Laval formed a government. Laval had succeeded Barthou as foreign minister when the latter was assassinated by a Croat terrorist along with King Alexander of Yugoslavia. His foreign policy was distinctly ambiguous, and a Soviet diplomatist described him as 'a dustbin of conflicting desires'. He had little enthusiasm for Barthou's schemes for collective security against Germany, yet he had signed the Franco-Soviet Pact on 2 May, prudently not bringing it to the Chamber for ratification. At the same time, Laval had worked to achieve the closest possible relations with Mussolini. He showed his solidarity with fascist Italy in the Stresa Front of 1935 and by appeasing Mussolini's imperialist expansion into Ethiopia in the notorious Hoare–Laval Pact, which in turn put a further strain on Anglo-French relations. This pro-Italian policy won him the support of the leagues and the right, just as his negotiations with the Soviets had won him some grudging support on the left. But Laval was hardly an economist, and for all his cunning as a political intriguer it was difficult to see how he would be able to master the crisis. His economic policy was rigorously deflationary, and he used decree laws to reduce public expenditure and to cut civil servants' salaries by 10 per cent: measures which the left denounced as causing unnecessary hardship. Taxes were not increased and military expenditure continued to climb. The budget deficit reached 10 billion francs. Gold poured out of the country, showing that investors had no confidence in Laval's ability to restore the economy. It was widely felt that he was far too tolerant of the leagues, who were becoming increasingly belligerent, and that his foreign policy lacked any clear purpose. It seemed that he was either trying to play the dangerous game of playing off Stalin against Mussolini or that he was floundering around, uncertain whether the bolsheviks or the fascists were the greater menace. On 24 January 1936, Laval resigned, the radicals having withdrawn support from his government. He blamed his fall on the failure of the duce to respond to the Hoare–Laval scheme, and as he left the Quai d'Orsay he was heard to mutter: 'Mussolini – what a bastard!'

Sarraut formed a caretaker government pending the elections which were to take place within a few weeks. Its major piece of business was to ratify the Franco-Soviet Pact. The pact was viciously attacked by the right. Although many on the left had misgivings, they finally voted for it in order to maintain the unity of the left parties which was essential for the conduct of a successful election campaign. In March, Hitler sent his army into the Rhineland, claiming that the ratification of the Franco-Soviet Pact was a violation of Locarno, a pact which he now formally repudiated. The French, divided at home and unable to count on any support from the British, were unable to do anything but accept another humiliation.

The first ballot of the election was held on 26 April and indicated that the Popular Front would emerge victorious in the final ballot.

The communists made spectacular gains – over 700,000 more votes than in 1932 – whereas the radicals lost more than 400,000 supporters. The socialists gained very few votes, and the right lost even less. The decisive factor was that the Popular Front stuck together in the second ballot to ensure that their candidates were elected. The results gave the Popular Front what seemed to be a decisive victory: about 386 deputies against about 222 on the right, but it depended on the votes of the radicals with their 115 seats to maintain a majority. Furthermore, the communists with their 72 deputies were uncertain allies, and many Radicals were still deeply suspicious of them.

The election of 1936 indicated that the majority of Frenchmen thought that communism was a lesser evil than fascism. The total destruction of Austrian democracy in February 1934, the brutality of Hitler's Germany, dramatically illustrated in the 'Roehm putsch', the invasion of Ethiopia, the occupation of the Rhineland and the beginning of the Spanish civil war in July 1936, all indicated that fascism was not merely a passing phase of a decadent capitalism, as many communists believed, but a powerful, entrenched and extremely dangerous force. Partly due to pressure from below, and partly through the realization of their past follies, the Communist International finally woke up to the real dangers of fascism, abandoning the absurd notion that there was no 'objective' difference between fascism and bourgeois democracy, and that the real enemy was not fascism but social democracy, ridiculously christened 'social fascism'.

The Popular Front in France was part of this international movement towards the unity of the left in the face of the danger of fascism, but it was also a specifically French phenomenon. The Popular Front government was a classic government of republican defence at a time when the continued existence of the republic was open to question, and both the right and the communists were challenging the entire system on which it was based.

The foundations of the Popular Front had been laid on 12 February when 150,000 socialists and communists met at the Place de la Nation, the communist leaders Cachin and Duclos sharing the platform with Léon Blum. But it was not until the eve of the elections, in January 1936, that the communists and socialists were able to agree on a common programme. For months the communists continued to attack the 'bourgeois' leadership of the socialists who, they insisted, had voted for the credits which had bought the bullets which had killed militant workers in February. The socialists were equally hesitant about becoming too closely involved with the communists, and could not easily forget the fifteen years of bitter rivalry since the Conference of Tours in 1920. But there were powerful forces pushing the two sides together. Rank and file workers in both parties were growing impatient with endless doctrinal squabbles, and demanded a common front against a common danger as their heroic comrades in Austria had made in February 1934. Hitler's appointment as chancellor in 1933 had drastically altered the balance of power in Europe and gave further encouragement to the extreme right at home. A series of governments seemed to be incapable of dealing with France's economic problems or with the increasingly important issue of national security. For the socialists the problem remained whether to trust the communists' avowals that they were prepared to defend the bourgeois republic against its enemies on the right, or whether, as Blum phrased it, 'the current towards unity might be transformed into a current towards communism'.

In July 1934, after much heart-searching, the socialists agreed to the communists' proposals for a programme of action. They had for so long been the object of vicious attacks from the communists, particularly the constant accusation that they were 'social fascists', that they were not unnaturally suspicious of the communists' motives. Nevertheless they agreed to work together to get the leagues outlawed, to see that the Chamber was dissolved and that the electoral system was reformed, to oppose the use of decree laws and to work for peace. An agreement on mutual consultations and joint protection against the fascists was reached. The parties agreed not to attack one another, not to argue over matters of socialist doctrine or practice, and to respect each other's autonomy.

The first test of this pact was in the cantonal elections of October 1934. The results were not very spectacular, largely because local issues were uppermost in the minds of the electorate, but the two parties worked well together and supported each other's candidates. The elections showed a slight swing to the right, but it was the communists rather than the socialists who had the largest gains. As always happened when the Communist Party moved to the right, it immediately gained support. The fall of the Doumergue government shortly after these elections was hailed, somewhat implausibly, as a triumph of the joint efforts of the socialists and communists.

The pact held, but there were still major differences between the attitudes of the two parties. The socialists wanted to work out the details of a common programme before moving any closer towards unity, whereas the communists felt that organic unity should come first, thus making a dramatic gesture and at the same time creating a situation in which they stood a better chance of controlling the direction of the United Front.

In the municipal elections of 1935 the socialists and communists co-operated to great effect, once again the swing benefitting the communists more than the socialists. The communists were delighted at the success of the United Front policy, and became its most enthusiastic supporters. Even the radicals, mindful of the effectiveness of the United Front, began to ask themselves whether they should not consider joining.

There was still a wide gulf between the socialists and the radicals. The radicals were resentful of the socialists' consistent refusal to participate in the governments which they supported, and the socialists demanded that the radicals, like the communists, should agree to a common programme before there could be any serious discussion of a real alliance. Ideological differences were far too great for this to be possible. Blum acidly remarked that the radicals seemed to find it easier to agree with the communists than with the socialists, for the communists with their new-found enthusiasm for the anti-fascist bourgeoisie professed not to be interested in tedious doctrinal issues. With the signing of the Franco-Soviet alliance in May 1935 the Communists had further reason to support the bourgeois republic, and Stalin expressed his approval of French defence expenditures, forcing his followers in France to make yet another political *volte face*.

On 14 July 1935 the communists organized a massive demonstration in Paris which was attended by numerous anti-fascist groups, including the Amsterdam–Pleyel, an international committee headed by Romain Rolland and Henri Barbusse, and which was also attended by representatives of the socialist and radical parties. Many of those attending swore a solemn oath 'to remain united to disarm and dissolve the factious leagues, to defend the democratic liberties won by the people of France, and to give the world a great human peace.' The radicals were beginning to think of themselves once again as a party of the left, and Daladier proudly announced that he was *petit bourgeois* and belonged to a class which had a natural affinity to the proletariat. The socialists, pushed by their rank and file, became somewhat less suspicious of communist motives, and began to consider questions of unity in a rather more serious manner.

The work of formulating a common programme was left to the committee which had organized the demonstration on 14 July. The socialists resisted the communists' attempts to unite the two parties,

and were far more inflexible than the communists in making concessions to the radicals. The communists benefitted from their intransigence, for they appeared to be sensible pragmatists while the
socialists were seen as inflexible ideologues.

Finally, on 11 January 1936, the programme of the Popular Front
was published. It was divided into three sections dealing with general
domestic political demands, foreign policy and economics. Under
the first, headed 'Defence of Liberty', it called for the dissolution of
the fascist leagues, a campaign against corruption in public life, total
freedom for the trades unions, liberty of conscience in schools where
the leaving age was to be raised to fourteen, and a parliamentary
commission of enquiry into conditions in the colonies. The second,
'Defence of Peace', upheld the League of Nations, called for disarmament and the ending of secret diplomacy and supported collective
security based on an extension of the Franco-Soviet Pact. The third,
'Economic Demands', was the most radical of all. It included a
reduction in the working week without a reduction in wages, a
massive programme of public works, and called for better pensions
and unemployment benefits. Central marketing agencies were to be
created in order to strengthen agricultural prices. The Bank of France
was to be reorganized to end the hold of the 'two hundred families',
represented on its Board of Regents, over the economic life of
France. There was also to be a tax reform which would include a
graduated income tax.

The adoption of this programme would mean that the electorate
would be presented with a socialist alternative and with a genuine
choice between left and right. Obviously, the radicals had the most
difficulty in accepting it. The party chairman, Herriot, resigned
rather than enter a pact with the communists, his place taken by
Daladier, who was convinced that the Popular Front would win the
next election. When his party decided to accept the programme,
Herriot felt obliged to resign from the Laval government, thus
hastening its fall. The communists continued to agonize about
whether they should participate in a Popular Front government,
while the socialists debated whether the two party organizations
should be merged, as the socialist and communist trades unions had
done. Neither party had any qualms about accepting the
programme.

The victory of the Popular Front was a triumph for the Communists, a success for the socialists and a severe setback to the radicals.
The communists decided to take on none of the responsibilities of
office, so that Léon Blum's cabinet consisted only of socialists and

radicals. The new government took office on 3 June 1936 in an atmosphere of excited anticipation, mounting industrial unrest from a frustrated and impatient working class, and a degree of self-doubt whether this worthy government would be equal to the enormous task it had set itself.

A wave of strikes, starting in Le Havre and spreading throughout France, greeted the new government. It would seem that these were almost entirely spontaneous outbursts, partly a celebration that France had its first socialist premier, and partly a warning to the Popular Front that they should immediately start to implement their programme. The right detested Blum for his socialism, his exceptional intelligence and for being a Jew. Not since Dreyfus had the right been so united in loathing one individual, and they saw the strikes as the beginning of anarchy, directed from Moscow, for the workers were not content simply to withdraw their labour, they also seized the factories.

Having failed to persuade the strikers to go back to work, Blum invited representatives of the employers and the unions to a conference at his official residence, the Hôtel Matignon. The resulting agreement envisaged an average wage increase of 12 per cent, the nationalization of armaments works, direct government control over the Bank of France, a forty-hour week and holidays with pay. The employers recognized the trades unions as the official representatives of the workers and agreed to begin discussions over collective agreements.

The employers were relieved that the workers had agreed to respect the law and to go back to work, but they were furious at the concessions they had been asked to make. Lacking any confidence in the government's economic policies, gold continued to leave the country in vast quantities, and Blum's assurances that he would not devalue the franc did nothing to stem the flow. Blum and his minister of finance, Vincent Auriol, hoped that the increased wages would provide the necessary stimulus to growth and that a deflationary policy, which would have been politically suicidal, could thus be avoided. Unfortunately this proved to be an illusion. The financial community detested the Popular Front government, and was determined to do nothing to prolong its life. Increases in wages, which were still very low, were spent mainly on extra food rather than industrial goods. Employers offset the costs of the Matignon agreements by raising prices. The government's welfare measures further increased the deficit, the franc remained seriously over-valued, and the gold reserves were depleted. The government resorted to the traditional expedient of more borrowing, thus further fuelling inflation. Speculation against the franc continued, for men of property had no confidence in a government which they were convinced were the dupes of the communists. On 1 October 1936 Blum bowed to the inevitable and devalued the franc.

It was hoped that a cheaper franc would stimulate industrial production, but continued strikes, the forty-hour week, and a further down-turn in the world economy resulted in continued stagnation, and money continued to leave the country in anticipation of further devaluation. Blum hoped to restore confidence by announcing in March 1937 a 'pause' in the reforms proposed by the Popular Front, a pause which had really taken effect months before. The right took this as an admission of weakness, the left as a betrayal of the ideals of the Popular Front. Blum was uncertain what use to make of the pause. Would he use exchange controls to strengthen the franc, thus breaking the tripartite agreement he had made with the United States and Britain; or would he pursue a more liberal financial policy to appease the orthodox bankers? A stern warning from the British treasury prompted him to abandon the idea of exchange controls and the financial community breathed a sigh of relief. Stock prices shot up, and the banks eagerly bought 8.5 billion francs worth of the defence loan which, with its guaranteed exchange rate, was indication that a further devaluation was being considered.

The unions were disgusted at the pause, and on 16 March Blum's enjoyment of a concert by Sir Thomas Beecham was ruined by news of rioting in the Parisian suburb of Clichy directed against the *Croix-de-Feu*. The police had intervened and many workers were seriously injured. The communist leader, Thorez, denounced the government for pursuing a right-wing policy, and the anarchists compared Blum to 'bloody Noske'. The trades unions called for a six-hour general strike to protest against the actions of the police.

At the beginning of June the Bourse collapsed and there was a renewed flight from the franc. The banks were openly critical of government policy, and Blum was at a loss to know where to borrow the money needed to meet the deficit. Finally, Rist and Baudouin, two orthodox financiers who were very close to the banks and whom Blum had appointed to run the Exchange Equalization Fund, resigned, announcing that they could no longer defend the franc as Blum refused to listen to their proposals. Blum felt that he had no alternative but to ask Parliament for plenary powers to get the 30 billion francs needed to pay off the government's debts. The Chamber agreed, after much heart-searching, for socialists and radicals had been traditionally strongly opposed to decree laws. Finally the parties felt that the concession would have to be made to preserve their Popular Front. In the Senate the situation was quite different. The senators hated the Popular Front and Caillaux had a marvellous time ridiculing the government which he compared to a drunken woman (then offering a proforma apology for this unfortunate phrase). It was one of the last and most fitting performances by this deplorable politician. When the vote came the government was defeated. Blum resigned without asking for a vote of confidence, thus avoiding a constitutional crisis which would have been almost inevitable had he survived.

The radicals kept the Popular Front going, but its spirit was broken. The two Chautemps governments which followed Blum's virtually excluded the socialists and sought an opening to the right, but they both failed to master the crisis. On the left the workers continued to strike and demonstrate, on the extreme right the leagues became ever more violent and menacing. The 'wall of money' and the Senate refused to be appeased. Blum tried again to form a government in the spring of 1938, but the experiment only lasted for three weeks. Once again he went to the senate asking for plenary powers, and resigned when the proposals were overwhelmingly rejected.

Indubitably the Popular Front government made a number of serious mistakes which contributed to its collapse. The devaluation of the franc was long overdue and it was devalued too much in relation to sterling and the dollar. But Blum was faced with the combined opposition of the radicals and the communists to devaluation, and the British Treasury was openly hostile to the move. Hesitations over convertibility undermined business confidence and indicated that further devaluation was probable. The government lacked the determination to tackle the serious economic problems that beset France: the low level of industrial production, huge budgetary deficits, and a serious balance of payments deficit. The sclerotic economy, dominated by small and medium businesses which were unable to bear the costs of a French New Deal, needed to be transformed if France were ever to recover. The bourgeoisie quickly recovered from the shock of defeat and mounted scurrillous attacks on the government in the press and in Parliament, and rallied to the calls of 'bosses be bosses' and for a 'bosses' battle of the Marne'. Flandin inadvertently expressed their view of the political process when he said in the Chamber: 'You are not here to execute the actual desires of the masses with all the sordid materialism which that involves'. They effectively sabotaged the economic and social policies of the Popular Front.

The government was also beset by internal strife. The radicals were appalled by the strikes and maintained their distance from the communists. Some of the radical deputies encouraged their colleagues in the Senate to overthrow Blum and worked for a centre coalition that would exclude the socialists.

Blum talked of the 'conquest' of power as revolutionary, the 'exercise' of power as contractual, and the 'possession' of power as defensive, thus showing his scrupulous belief in legality, his lack of dynamism and of revolutionary vision. But whatever his personal limitations, he was constrained by the political and social situation in which he was placed, thus incorporating the strengths and weaknesses of the Popular Front.

It would be mistaken to see the Popular Front solely in terms of its weaknesses and failures. It had many achievements to its credit. The Matignon agreements were significant steps forward. The Wheat Office did much to help agriculture. Most important of all, in a Europe of dictators and appeasers, the Popular Front was a genuine expression of republican democracy which allowed for an extraordinary degree of public participation. It did not fulfil the expectations of its supporters, but the democratic and humane vision it inspired lived on, to be revived in better times.

Blum having failed in his attempt to revive the Popular Front, Daladier tried to form a national government. He hoped to count on the support of the left as well as part of the right. The right saw him as the 'Lion of the Vaucluse' who had been minister of war for two years and they assumed that his government would mark the end of the Popular Front. The radicals also welcomed this move to the right. Blum wanted the socialists to participate in the government, but the rank and file of the party were so disgusted that the Senate had destroyed the last Popular Front government that they would not consider it.

The formation of the Daladier government was welcomed by the business world and there was a brief boom on the stock exchange. Within a few days this collapsed, and in May the franc was devalued for the third time since September 1936. In August 1938 Daladier broadcast to the nation, attacking the forty-hour week and thus distancing himself from the parties of the Popular Front. Two members of the Socialist Union (a small party between the radicals and the socialists) resigned from his cabinet in protest, and were replaced by two members of the same party who were far less sympathetic to labour. The announcement that there was to be a significant increase in arms production would almost certainly have served to unite the left against the government, were it not for the Munich agreement, which was initially extremely popular. Once the significance of Munich began to sink in there was a new alignment of parties. The *Munichois* consisted of pacifists, a few socialists like Paul Faure, radicals who were concerned about the lack of military preparation in France, or who admired Mussolini, or even Hitler in some instances, but above all because of a deep-rooted anti-communism. Almost all the right-wing parties were firmly in the pro-Munich camp. The *Antimunichois* included moderates who were attached to alliance with Britain, chief among them Paul Reynaud, the outstanding man in the Daladier government, the vast majority of the socialists who clearly perceived the danger from Germany and the need for collective security, and the communists who constantly attacked this craven submission to Hitler and the exclusion of the Soviet Union from European affairs. The division between the two camps was profound, and often cut through party lines.

Reynaud, who had been minister of justice, was appointed minister of finance, a position better suited to his talents, but which had been denied to him for fear that his proposed austerity measures would be unacceptable to the left whose support was still needed by Daladier. In November he proposed a modification of the forty-hour week, increased taxes, cuts in government expenditure without reducing the defence budget, and yet another devaluation of the franc. The CGT organized a general strike in protest, but it was a feeble affair. The strikers were divided as to whether the real menace was the 'poverty decrees' or the humiliation of Munich, or whether they were attempting to regain the ground lost since 1936. Enthusiasm for the Popular Front had dissipated, and most workers were principally concerned with keeping their jobs.

Wildcat strikes broke out before the general strike which was due to take place on 30 November. The government acted promptly, sending 10,000 *gardes mobiles* to throw the strikers out of the Renault works. The CGT, faced with such determined opposition, and with serious divisions within their own ranks, desperately looked for some way of calling off the strike without losing too much face, but Daladier was determined to win what he saw as a trial of strength. Jouhaux, the reformist secretary-general of the CGT, wanted to call off the strike, but the communists would not agree. The strike was a sorry failure. Many refused to answer the call to strike, the communist rank and file being even less enthusiatic for the strike than the socialists. The Communist Party and the CGT were discredited, both losing a large number of members. Employers reacted with dismissals and reprisals, directed principally against the ringleaders. Daladier was ecstatic. For all the criticisms of his Munich policy he had shown himself to be truly a strong man.

The government's economic policy was initially a success. Its credit was restored, gold began to pour back into the country, and industrial production increased. But this modest recovery lulled the country into a false feeling of security. The German occupation of Czechoslovakia and the reaffirmation of the Franco-Polish Treaty of 1921 resulted in a rather dilatory approach to the Soviet Union, a policy which caused further divisions on the right The Molotov–Ribbentrop Pact in August restored a degree of unanimity, for Hitler could no longer be seen as the great anti-bolshevik, and the left saw the Soviet Union as traitors to the sacred cause of anti-fascism. There were those, like the foreign minister, Bonnet, who hoped that it would still be possible to negotiate and that Poland might be made to cede to Germany's demands. But Daladier represented the spirit of France in his weary acceptance of the inevitability of war. When France declared war on Germany on 3 September she had well equipped armed forces, but politically and psychologically she was singularly ill-prepared to withstand the supreme test of a nation's fundamental unity and determined sense of common purpose.

CHAPTER TEN

The Spanish Civil War

Spain's defeat in the American War of 1898 and subsequent disasters in North Africa did much to call into question both monarchical leadership and military privilege. The monarchy and the military became isolated from the people and the military became increasingly politicized. But for Spain the First World War was a period of relative prosperity. Substantial profits were made in exports, particularly of textiles and coal to France, the trade deficit was eliminated, the national debt repatriated and there was an impressive growth of banking capital. Although wages rose considerably in some sectors of industry, only in few instances did they keep up with the steep rate of inflation. Regional and sectoral wage differentials were increasing at a time when the employers were assumed to be sharing the boom profits of a neutral country which was able to trade under exceptionally favourable conditions. Inevitably this led to an increased militancy among organized labour and in 1916 the socialist trades union organization UGT (*Unión General de Trabajadores*) threatened a general strike for higher wages and talked somewhat vaguely of revolution. The socialists were then drawn into a rather curious alliance with moderate republicans, disaffected and ineffectual junior army officers organized in their *Juntas de defensa* and Catalan regionalists, all of whom pressed for the convocation of a constituent assembly to work out the details of a scheme for 'national regeneration'.

The alliance had little to hold it together, for the right feared the social revolution which the left was demanding, much to the alarm of the socialist leadership. Strikes broke out in August 1917 which were politically motivated, exceedingly violent, sporadic and ultimately ineffectual. In the Cortes the reform movement fell apart to give

Spain one of its most seriously divided parliaments. With the end of the war the boom was over. Unemployment and falling wages strengthened the unions' determination to fight back, but lower profits and shrinking markets made the employers determined not to give way. This escalation of the class war was furthered by the revolutionary tactics of the anarchist unionists organized in the CNT (*Confederatiön Nacional del Trabajo*). In 1919 there was a general strike in Barcelona which resulted in the declaration of a state of war and an extensive and successful lock-out. Frustrated in this attempt at a revolutionary strike, the anarchists resorted increasingly to terrorism and murder. But these were gestures of sheer frustration as the workers' enthusiasm for strike action had declined markedly. Much of the blame for the failure of the strikes between 1919 and 1923 was placed by the anarchists on the 'yellow' UGT against whom ludicrous charges were levelled and considerable violence perpetrated. The dictatorship of Primo de Rivera did not save Spain from these anarchist revolutionaries, as the mythology of the right would have it, for they had already destroyed themselves in four years of often open warfare with the socialists.

In July 1921 the Spanish army in Morocco suffered an utterly humiliating defeat at Annual. Within a few days some 17,000 soldiers, most of them conscripts, were killed. Subsequent investigations into the disaster revealed an astonishing degree of incompetence and corruption in the army, the left insisted that the conservative politicians were to blame, and there were suggestions that the king had urged General Silvestre to make his ill-considered campaign against the tribesmen. In short, the defeat was held to be due to the conservative system of government. A liberal government was appointed which tried to assert civilian control over the army and threatened to establish a commission to inquire into the causes of the defeat. On 23 September 1923 General Primo de Rivera, the Captain-General of Catalonia and an advocate of withdrawal from Morocco, made a *pronunciamiento* in Barcelona. The king and the army accepted his dictatorship rather than face the humiliation of an inquiry into the Moroccan fiasco, and the middle classes convinced themselves that even a military dictatorship would be better than the unrest and uncertainties of recent years.

Primo de Rivera was an intensely patriotic, intermittently devout, scrupulously honest, brave, hard-drinking, whoremongering Andalusian whose political naivety was presented as pragmatic common sense and whose haphazard working methods were dignified with the impressive neologism 'intuitionism'. He lacked the mass support, the expansionist foreign ambitions, and the systematic and repressive cruelty of the fascist leaders. Political parties were banned, and many of his opponents were gaoled or exiled, but none was executed. He had no objections to organized labour as long as the unions kept out of politics. The UGT leader, Largo Caballero, wept very few tears for the parliamentary system and negotiated with the new regime, prompting fresh rounds of denunciation from the CNT and from the small Communist Party. Repression and internal dissent led to the virtual disappearance of the anarchist movement for several years, and the Communist Party was still a minute clique of dissidents who had broken with the Socialist Party (PSOE) in 1921. Primo de Rivera gave the workers cheap housing, medical services and the labour arbitration of the *comités paritarios*, and the UGT appeared to be more favoured by the regime than the National Confederation of Catholic Workers, a constant cause of complaint by the employers.

In 1925 Primo de Rivera launched a successful campaign in Morocco, in close co-operation with the French, thus revenging the humiliation of 1921 and reaching the height of his popularity. He now distanced himself from the army and established a civilian government of young specialists who set about reforming and planning the economy. An ambitious programme of public works was begun, but the attempt to finance these efforts by introducing an effective income tax was halted by a massive campaign by the bankers against such fiscal infantilism. The money was raised by borrowing extensively in the hope that the ordinary revenues of an expanding economy would be sufficient to pay the interest. A petroleum monopoly was established in a further attempt to obtain additional revenue, but this resulted in a dramatic fall in the rate of foreign investment in Spain as companies feared that they too might not be safe from the ravages of economic nationalism. Yet in spite of such difficulties, and the growing opposition of businessmen to the interventionist state, the achievements of the regime were considerable. Miles of new roads were built, the railways modernized, electrification of the countryside and vast irrigation schemes had a tremendous impact, heavy industry grew at a steady rate and foreign trade boomed. Primo de Rivera had no clear understanding of economics, and his task was undoubtedly made easier by a general improvement in the world economy, but his regime deserves credit for its positive contributions to what was soon to be regarded as a golden age of the Spanish economy.

Yet in spite of these achievements opposition to Primo de Rivera was growing. The intellectuals, most of whom were no great friends of parliamentary democracy, resented his tamperings with the judicial system, and when Unamuno, the distinguished philosopher, was dismissed from his chair and gaoled virtually all Spanish intellectuals became opponents of the regime, and university students registered their dislike of the dictatorship with a plethora of graffiti, leaflets and demonstrations. The parliamentarians, who were constantly abused by the dictator as unpatriotic, incompetent and corrupt, discreetly fuelled this mounting unrest, but it was the attitude of the army which was decisive in bringing about his downfall. Some officers resented what they considered to be civilian interference with exclusively military matters; others felt that the army should never have become involved in politics by supporting a *coup d'état*; but Primo de Rivera's suspension of the entire officer corps of the artillery for refusing to accept promotions on merit rather than by seniority united the army against him. They were joined by landowners alarmed by his modest efforts at land reform, businessmen who thought that his version of the corporate state smacked of socialism, and clerics who feared that he wished to assert royal supremacy over the Catholic Church. Primo had offered prosperity in place of politics, but by 1929 this was no longer possible. The peseta began to collapse in 1928 and the downward slide of the exchange rate could not be halted. The dictator asked the army which had made him whether they still supported him. The first replies were equivocal. On 28 January 1930 he resigned, retiring to Paris where he died a few months later, his life characteristically ending in frantic trips between prostitutes and confessors.

There followed two caretaker governments, the first of the aging and valetudinarian General Berenguer, the second of a political novice with a passion for reading novels, Admiral Aznar. They set themselves the task of returning to normality, but found themselves desperately trying to save the monarchy. In both they failed. Republican sentiment was increasing and the king could no longer rely on the support of the army. In December 1930 there was a badly bungled military rebellion. This was fortunate, for a republic that resulted from the actions of a group of ambitious and irresponsible officers would have been a disaster for the democrats, socialists and intellectuals who formed the core of the republican movement. The municipal elections the following April resulted in an overwhelming republican victory in the larger urban centres. General Sanjurjo, who commanded the Civil Guard, announced that he would not defend the monarchy against such a clear demonstration of public opinion.

Alfonso's advisers knew that only a civil war could have saved the monarchy and that they were unlikely to triumph in such an uneven conflict. They therefore advised the king to abdicate. With the crowds demonstrating outside the palace the king climbed into his car and drove off at characteristically high speed to Cartagena and to exile in France. Hoping one day to return, he did not abdicate.

The provisional government of the new republic was a hopelessly heterogeneous affair, held together by the conviction that the monarchy had to go but lacking in any constructive policies. The Constituent Cortes, elected in June 1931, produced a constitution which was mildly and ambiguously socialist in tone but which separated the Church and state, forbade the religious orders from teaching and removed the crucifix from public schools. The Church had taken an intransigently anti-republican stand during the election campaign, and the anti-clericals had responded in the traditional Spanish manner by burning down a number of churches. Against the moderate republican majority government of Azaña the right rallied in defence of the Church as the 'Mother of Spain'. Catalonia was granted autonomy, somewhat to the distress of many socialists who viewed the Catalan leadership as an anachronistic and reactionary clique, but it meant that Catalonia remained a stronghold of republicanism. Progressive labour legislation was introduced by Largo Caballero which resulted in a further weakening of the CNT which refused to compromise itself by co-operating with any state-sponsored schemes however beneficial they might be to the working class. The government's attempt at agrarian reform was far less successful. Too modest for the left and too excessive for the right, it ground to a halt through lack of funds, the opposition of the landed interests and a lack of understanding of the economic and social ramifications of the programme.

In August 1932 General Sanjurjo, the 'Lion of the Rif', made an abortive *pronunciamiento* in Seville. It was a poorly organized uprising of disgruntled aristocrats against republican 'tyranny' which failed to win the support of the majority of the army. A greater threat to the government was the *Acción popular* of Gil Robles, a Catholic social reformer who set out to lure the youth of Spain away from godless socialism and back into the fold of the Church with the social Catholicism of Leo XIII's encyclicals. Gil Robles did not aim to overthrow the republic, but was determined to reverse its anti-clerical legislation. But it was the anarchists in the CNT who were the most determined and violent opponents of the republic. Increasingly under the influence of the FAI (*Federación Anarquista Ibérica*), an extremist anarchist organization, the CNT organized a series of political strikes and acts of mindless violence. The extreme left denounced the repression of these outbursts as examples of the republic's hostility to the legitimate aspirations of the working class, the right saw it as further evidence of the Azaña government's inability to maintain law and order. In the elections of 1933 the Azaña coalition was defeated and the Cortes was now dominated by the radicals under Lerroux, an ageing and corrupt mob orator who had started his career as the 'Emperor of the Paralelo' (the tenderloin district of Barcelona) but had becoming increasingly conservative in outlook and tone, and by Gil Robles' CEDA (*Confederación Española de Derechas Autónomas*), a coalition of conservative Catholic groups committed to certain vague notions of a corporate state.

The left had little sympathy for Lerroux's middle-class republicans of whose sincerity they remained resolutely dubious, but they were even more strongly opposed to Gil Robles whom they denounced as at worst a fascist, and at best as the 'Spanish Dollfuss'. The PSOE moved increasingly to the left, and Largo Caballero ceased to be the Spanish Ernest Bevin and became prey to delusions that he was the Spanish Lenin. Jejune slogans such as 'either socialism or fascism' and calls for an armed revolution now became standard fare in socialist circles as the party succumbed to a madness which had previously only affected the anarchists.

The 'October Revolution' of 1934 hardly lived up to its impressive appellation. It was, as one intellectual remarked, a 'platonic' revolution, and only in Catalonia and Asturias was there any real action. Catalonian nationalists felt that the inclusion of three CEDA ministers in the cabinet was a direct threat to Catalan autonomy, but they were not supported by the CNT. Only in Asturias did the UGT, the communists and the CNT combine in a dress rehearsal of the Popular Front. The workers' committees survived for two weeks to be brutally crushed by the Foreign Legion and native troops in a conflict which resulted in 4,000 casualties. When it was all over the split between left and right was greater than ever. The right denounced the alleged atrocities perpetrated by ruthless revolutionaries and the left, intoxicated by this first real taste of proletarian brotherhood, swore to avenge the proletarian martyrs and to complete the task of building socialism in Spain.

President Alcalá Zamora resolutely refused to appoint Gil Robles prime minister for he distrusted his anti-republican and monarchist supporters. These in turn began to sympathize with extremists who demanded that Gil Robles should declare for a dictatorship supported by the army to crush the militant left. His social Catholicism had little chance of success after October, and his schemes for land reform were bitterly opposed by the right wing of CEDA. Lerroux became discredited by a series of financial scandals, the result of incompetence rather than venality, and since no majority could be found without including CEDA a general election was called for February 1936.

The left managed to combine in a Popular Front for the elections. The name, but little else, came from the communists who had abandoned their absurd denunciations of social democrats as 'social fascists' at the VIIth Congress of the Communist International in 1935, but the unity of the left was due in large part to the efforts of Azaña. The anarchists were reluctant to join in any electoral pact, but they could hardly denounce the demand for the amnesty of the 1934 rebels, nor could they avoid paying lip service to the ideal of proletarian unity. Many anarchists simply ignored the CNT's plea '*no votad*' (don't vote) and gave their support to the Popular Front. Caballero found it hard to abandon his new-found enthusiasm for ultra-left positions, but finally succumbed to the call for unity by agreeing to work with Azaña's Republican Left and Barrio's Republican Union but refused to enter any future government for fear of compromising his socialist virtue.

Whereas the left came together, the right fell apart. Stern reactionaries denounced Gil Robles' refusal to make himself a *caudillo*, and turned to the monarchist *Renovación Española* under Sotelo who had been Primo de Rivera's minister of finance. Ultra-orthodox Catholics felt that his social policies smacked of 'positivism'. Nothing could be gained from an alliance with Lerroux's radicals who had little support after their financial misdemeanours had been exposed to view; 4,838,449 Spaniards voted for the Popular Front, 3,996,931 for the right. The centre had vanished, leaving the country badly polarized. The socialists had contributed the most to the Popular Front victory but still chose to remain aloof.

Azaña was appointed prime minister then president, his place being taken by Casares Quiroga, an ailing political boss from Galicia. This republican government was trapped between the socialists, who continued with their maximalist demands and their denunciations of the bourgeois state and of Azaña as the Spanish Kerensky, and the right, which was smarting under their electoral defeat, believed that the government was incapable of stopping the inexorable move to the left and would therefore have to be overthrown by force, Gil Robles' legalist policies having failed miserably.

Monarchists, whether Carlist or Alfonsine, were increasingly attracted to the militant counter-revolutionary and fascistic *Renovación Española*. More distinctly fascist in tone was the Falange, which was founded in 1933 by José Antonio Primo de Rivera, the dictator's handsome, charming and highly intelligent son. He set out to create a new and revolutionary right to replace the outmoded Traditionalists and which would, he hoped, attract the working class with his vision of a classless and nationalistic corporatism. The working class was unimpressed, the old right was horrified, and José Antonio's main support came from university students who were deeply moved by his romantic rhetoric. By the summer of 1936 the Falange was still a relatively small organization, but by constantly fighting in the streets with socialists, anarchists and communists, who were also busy fighting one another, they did much to create a state of violence and anarchy which the generals, with their obsession with order, were determined to stop.

Goded, Mola and Franco, all of whom were commanding generals, deeply resented the government's programme of army reform, were appalled at the violence and anarchy into which the country was descending, and called for a rigidly authoritarian regime. Mola in Pamplona organized the revolt, but it was obvious that Franco held the key to its success. The English Catholic publisher, Douglas Jarrold, organized Franco's flight from the Canaries to Morocco, where he was to lead the African army against the republic. There were rumours of an impending coup, but Azaña was convinced that a military revolt was bound to fail, and Caballero managed to convince himself that only the proletariat was capable of true violence. Thus, when Franco flew to Morocco on 9 July and the army 'pronounced' eight days later, the government was caught by surprise.

When Casares Quiroga heard of the generals' revolt he broke down and resigned. His successor, the left-wing radical Martinez Barrio, hoped to negotiate with the army, and like Quiroga refused to arm the workers in defence of the republic. The workers took no notice of this ban and armed militia units sprang up all over republican Spain. Martinez Barrio, unable to resist this pressure from below, resigned and a new government was formed by José Giral, a close friend of Azaña, who had to accept the fact that the workers had taken the defence of the republic into their own hands.

In the first days of the coup neither side acted decisively. Had the workers been armed and loyal troops been mobilized the generals could well have been defeated. The rebels also failed to act swiftly and decisively. Most of the senior army officers and the Republican Assault Guards in Madrid were loyal to the republic, and it was they rather than the workers who stopped the rebels in the Montaña barracks in Madrid. In Barcelona the commanding general and the Civil Guards were also loyal to the republic, and it was the Civil Guards who intervened decisively against the rebels. General Goded arrived late, his hydroplane having broken down, was captured and shot. The CNT claimed they had won a glorious victory, but although the myth persisted, it was the Civil Guards who had saved the city for the republic. Seville, Spain's third largest city, fell to rebels due to the forceful conduct of General Queipo de Llano who single-handedly arrested those officers who were loyal to the republic and then terrorized the citizenry into submission.

In most places where the Civil Guards and the Assault Guards were loyal to the republic, or to their prospects for a pension, the rebels failed; elsewhere they had little difficulty. Once they were in command of an area there was little that the workers could do. Galicia, which had a large organized working class, was quickly overrun by the rebels, as were other strongholds of the left such as Saragossa, Oviedo and Valladolid. Strikes against the revolt were futile, for the strikers were promptly shot. In towns such as Valencia and Malaga, where the vast majority of the population was passionately committed to the defence of the republic, the rebels had little chance of success. Only in Navarra, particularly in Pamplona, was there widespread popular support for the rebels.

After a few days of confused and sporadic fighting Spain was clearly divided. The nationalists controlled a broad strip from the Atlantic coast to the French border, although the northern coast was republican. Southern Spain, from Barcelona to Malaga was republican, and the area around Madrid formed a large salient pushing into enemy territory. Oviedo, Seville and Cordoba were nationalist strongholds deep in republican territory. These divisions did not necessarily correspond to traditional political alignments. Republicans caught in Galicia, Estremadura or Andalusia kept their mouths shut, conformed or were shot. Monarchists and Falangists in Santander prudently did the same. There was no question that the working class remained republican, although there was no agreement on precisely what that involved. The aristocracy and the upper middle class were nationalist in their sympathies. But it was uncertain which way the professionals, civil servants and even the army officers would turn. They had little sympathy for the left and the militant proletarian rigamarole of the militant Popular Front, but for many the nationalists were also too extreme in their mystical nationalism, their anti-intellectualism and their authoritarianism. The peasantry was also divided. The peasants of Castille, Navarre and Galicia were nationalists and provided the mass of Franco's army. The Catalan peasants were fervently republican, and in the south-west the peasants enthusiastically murdered their landlords and experimented with communes under the aegis of FAI or the socialist FTT, but once the region fell to the nationalists they were lost to the cause.

In most of republican Spain the state apparatus collapsed and local revolutionary committees sprang up which were dominated by the anarchists and the socialists. The local militias owed their allegiance to these juntas. The split between anarchists and socialists was still bitter, and both distrusted the bourgeois republicans. In many areas there were indiscriminate and brutal murders committed in a wave of revolutionary mindlessness. Churches were destroyed, priests killed and elaborate public acts of blasphemy staged. All this was grist to the nationalist propaganda mill and horrified the respectable readers of the world press. For the republicans the problem was to channel this energy and enthusiasm into the effective defence of the government, but there was great uncertainty about how this was to be done. In the republican camp there was considerable confusion about whether they were simply involved in a struggle to defend the democratic republic against the rebels, or whether they were in the midst of a revolution. If the latter, then the juntas, the militia, collectivization and even revolutionary violence were all an integral part of the struggle against the counter-revolutionary rebels. If the former, then all revolutionary experiments which were liable to alienate the middle class, loyal army officers and sympathizers abroad would have to be stopped immediately. In Catalonia this confusion was clearly apparent, for there were two 'parallel govern-ments': the *Generalidad* presided over by the left republican nationalist Louis Companys, and the Anti-Fascist Militia Committee dominated by the CNT.

In those parts of Spain such as Catalonia and Asturias which were dominated by the anarchists there was widespread collectivization of the land, industry and even the retail trade. Much fervour went into this transformation of society, but it would seem that it had a deleterious effect on industrial production and horrified the middle class whose support was badly needed. At the same time the anarch-ists refused to seize state power and dreamed of a new state, based on a loose federation of co-operatives.

The communists consistently and vehemently denounced these anarchist experiments for disrupting production and distribution, for alienating the bourgeoisie, and for their failure to realize that some form of planned economy was essential in wartime. The communists insisted that Spain was experiencing a 'bourgeois democratic' revolution, and was not about to be transformed into a socialist state. To the anarchists this was further evidence that the communists were conservatives at heart, but the communists pointed out that there were more important tasks to be performed than absurd anarchist measures such as forcing the unwilling barbers of Alicante into one vast co-operative, and announced that the most revolutionary action of all was to win the war.

This was no empty rhetoric, for the first great victory of the republic, at Guadalajara, was due in large part to the disciplined communist troops, to Soviet tanks and to the advice of Soviet experts. Similarly, the communist 'Fifth Regiment' played a critical role in the defence of Madrid and the International Brigades, which were organized by the communists, arrived at the Madrid front in November 1936 and were admired both for their military prowess and as a clear demonstration of effective international support for the republic. The military efficiency of the communists won them the admiration of those soldiers who remained loyal to the republic, and their spirited defence of the property rights of the peasant farmer, the small shopkeeper and the modest entrepreneur made them the hope of those who wished to save Spain revolution and to undo the work of the anarchists. The communists thus became the party of moderation, normalcy, efficiency and of a broad-based centre-left coalition. The success of this line was spectacular. In July 1936 the party had about 40,000 members, but by March of the following year it had increased to about 250,000, many of the new recruits coming from the middle class and even from the aristocracy.

The moderate republicans lost their will to govern, dramatically symbolized by Azaña who went on a retreat to the monastery at Montserrat. The anarchists distrusted state power, and the socialists were uncertain whether to turn left or right. The communists, with their iron discipline, their consistent political line and their supplies of Soviet arms, thus became the leading political force in republican Spain, but they used their power and influence with such ruthlessness that they gradually lost the vast fund of sympathy they had accumulated in the early months of the civil war. In September 1936 a section of the OGPU was formed in Spain which promptly set about the destruction of POUM, a party denounced as 'Trotskyite' although disowned by Trotsky, which had openly denounced the vicious practices of Stalin's Russia and also condemned the policy of the Popular Front as reactionary and counter-revolutionary while also attacking the anarchists for their refusal to understand the need for seizing state power. The communists' determination to create an effective people's army led to the appointment of political commissars and a degree of control over the armed forces of the republic that was resented by many non-party soldiers, resulting in an opposition group within the army which was to seriously damage its effectiveness.

Clearly no republican government could be fully effective as long as the anarchists refused to join in the common endeavour. In September the CNT underwent a miraculous conversion and decided to enter the government of Catalonia. In November they joined the government in Madrid. All the factions in Spain, apart from some extreme anarchists and POUM, were now represented in Largo Caballero's government. He was probably the only politician in Spain who had the popular support to head such a coalition, but having played the maximalist for years he doubtless felt uncomfortable in his new role as prime minister of a government devoted to curbing any revolutionary enthusiasms.

The CNT had no other choice but to join the government. They knew that if they were to pursue their own vision of a libertarian Spain the republican forces would remain hopelessly divided and victory for the rebels would be inevitable. They knew that their vision of a new society could only be realized by a dictatorship which in itself would be a denial of their fundamental principles. They also realized that the power of the Popular Front government was growing and that their only chance of influencing events was from within that government. This reasoning was unacceptable to most anarchist militants. They insisted that the CNT leadership had thrown away their principles, had allowed the anarchist militia to be absorbed into the republican army, had agreed to the centralization of the committees and had got nothing in return but four minor ministries. Such criticisms were largely justified, for the anarchists henceforth played a secondary role, the leadership lost touch with the rank-and-file and the movement became hopelessly split. Yet it is difficult to see what else they could have done under the circumstances. A wartime alliance was essential if the nationalists were to be defeated, but anarchist philosophy made no allowances for such tactical moves.

Thus Largo Cabellero's government was divided and confused

and the addition of the anarchists did nothing to improve the situation. Nor did they have effective control over the rest of republican Spain. The Basque provinces and Catalonia behaved increasingly like autonomous states and from Madrid it looked as if these provinces were not doing their full share in prosecuting the war. In Catalonia the CNT hoped to realize their dreams of an anarchist revolution and therefore supported the Catalan separatists in their struggle against the government in Madrid. Santander also had its own regional council, but the great anarchist stronghold was Aragon. In anarchist eyes the Council of Aragon presided over a utopia the likes of which the world had not seen before and which combined efficiency with true libertarianism. To the communists it was a mare's nest of venal and incompetent revolutionary infantilists which had to be destroyed. Whatever the rights and wrongs of the case, the squabbles over Aragon, like those over Catalonia, were indicative of the fundamental rift within the republican camp which seriously prejudiced their chances of defeating the nationalists.

The nationalists were beset by no such difficulties. There were different monarchist factions, Falangists and assorted right-wing groups, but when Franco was proclaimed Head of State on 29 September 1936 there was no one to challenge his authority. The army realized the need for a unified command and there was little doubt that Franco was the outstanding candidate for the post of commander-in-chief. Of the leading generals Sanjurjo and Goded had been killed and Mola was soon to be. His army was the most effective force in the nationalist army and he was a thoroughly professional soldier renowned for his cool-headedness, bravery and excellent staff work. The other generals accepted him as their leader by electing him commander-in-chief on 21 September. There was no civilian of comparable stature, for José Antonio Primo de Rivera was in jail and later to be executed, Calvo Sotelo murdered, and Gil Robles had fled the country. Franco was determined not only to command the army but also to wield absolute political power, an ambition which alarmed some nationalists, but such critics were soon silenced by his wily, pragmatic and ruthless exercise of his authority and by the belief that he would soon restore the monarchy. No one foresaw that he would cling on to virtually absolute power until his death thirty-nine years later.

The republican army was intoxicated by the belief that spontaneity, enthusiasm and proletarian spirit was enough to crush the professional and disciplined nationalists. The militia units were beset by party fractionalism, their command structure was haphazard, they were chronically short of essential supplies, lack of discipline was often seen as a positive virtue, training was rudimentary and their courage frequently failed them on the battlefield. Obviously this rag-tag army had to be properly trained and disciplined and converted into a regular army. This process began in October 1936, against the staunch opposition of those who still clung – all evidence to the contrary – to their fond belief that a 'revolutionary' war had to be fought by 'revolutionary' means. Gradually most republicans came round to agree with an anarchist intellectual who wrote: 'There is no such thing as an Anarchist war; there is only one war and we must win it.'

The first step was to create the Mixed Brigades of the Popular Army which ended the identification of military units with specific parties. This process was incomplete, so that the communist fifth regiment was still dominated by the communists, and anarchist units were still led by the CNT. Officers were no longer elected by their men, saluting was enforced, and political commissars were appointed, in theory to handle the difficult relations with the parties, but in practice often to push the party line. Since the communists dominated the corps of commissars this greatly strengthened the hold of the party over the army, but many of the commissars conscientiously supported their officers and encouraged the men in the interests of the common cause.

The Popular Army was in large part the creation of the communists who were the most insistent of the parties on the need for discipline and professionalism. They were supported in this endeavour by regular officers and NCOs who were loyal to the republic and whose contribution would have been even greater were it not for the widespread suspicion that all regular soldiers were potential traitors or 'fifth columnists' (a phrase which dates from the Spanish Civil War). Many of these officers joined the Communist Party in the conviction that they alone understood the imperatives of warfare. Their work was impressive and there can be no doubt that the Popular Army was far more effective than the militias and those, like George Orwell, who argued otherwise were allowing political predilections to override military facts. But the Popular Army still had serious deficiencies. It was chronically short of arms and ammunition. Many of the commanding officers were outstanding, but junior officers were inadequately trained, so that the army performed poorly at the tactical level. Perhaps most serious of all were the persistent political jealousies, rivalries and even hatreds, mainly between the CNT and the communists, which undermined its morale and effectiveness.

The nationalist army suffered from similar weaknesses. Madrid, with the War Ministry and the General Staff, were in republican hands and the command structure of the regular army had been destroyed by the division of Spain. In the first weeks of the war the nationalists also fought in isolated columns with no overall strategic concept. Like the republicans, they suffered from a shortage of officers, but not to the same extent. The nationalists had outstanding troops in the Foreign Legion, which in spite of its name was comprised mainly of Spaniards, and the ferocious and brutal *Regulares*, the native troops from North Africa. As Muslims they made curious allies in Franco's Christian crusade against godless communism and materialism, as the republicans were not slow to point out.

Although Hitler and Mussolini were prompt in sending help to the rebels, an international fascist plot to overthrow the republic existed only in the febrile imagination of republican propagandists. On the other hand, without such help the nationalists might well have been defeated. The Spanish navy had resisted the *golpistas* and still controlled the Straits of Gibralter. The bulk of the army was still stranded in Morocco, the early engagements had not been successful, and General Mola even contemplated suicide. While he was still in North Africa, Franco sent two Germans with excellent connections with the Nazi Foreign Organization (*Ausland-Organisation-AO*) to Berlin. Through the intermediary of the head of the AO, Bohle, and Rudolf Hess the two men were introduced to Hitler, who was in good spirits after attending a performance of *Siegfried* at Bayreuth. He immediately ordered twenty Junkers 52 transport aircraft to be sent to North Africa. This decision, which was taken on the spur of the moment in the hopes of securing a friendly government in Madrid and tipping the balance against the Franco-Soviet alliance, made Franco the most powerful of the generals and did much to secure his emergence as undisputed *Caudillo*.

Mussolini had been involved in Spanish affairs before the revolt and had helped to train Carlist troops and had financed the Falange, but he knew nothing of the generals' plans. He supported the rebels against the advice of his military entourage, prompted by his foreign minister and son-in-law, Ciano. Twelve Savoia bombers were sent to North Africa, to be followed by large numbers of troops. There were almost 50,000 Italian soldiers fighting in Spain at the height of their involvement. Hundreds of aeroplanes were sent to the nationalists, along with large numbers of tanks and artillery.

The Germans were far less generous in their support and extracted far more in economic concessions. They sent the famous Condor Legion of about 100 planes, and also supplied tanks and artillery. Probably more important were the specialist instructors and technicians which were to provide Franco's army with superior communications and helped to ensure more effective deployment of tanks, artillery and aircraft.

The republicans could not count on such prompt support from their supposed friends. The French Popular Front government was naturally sympathetic to the republic, but Blum's freedom of action was circumscribed. Conservatives in the Senate were vehemently opposed to intervention in Spain. The radicals, among them his foreign minister and minister of war, did not want to get involved. On the left there were very strong pacifist sentiments and a widespread fear that the Spanish Civil War might spill over into France where political passions were running dangerously high. But probably most important of all was the attitude of Britain, for the French had no desire to find themselves isolated and in conflict with Germany and Italy. For the British Foreign Office the real danger was the spread of communism not of fascism; many Conservatives within Baldwin's National Government sympathized strongly with the nationalists and admired Mussolini, some even going as far as to extend such cordial feelings to Hitler. There were substantial British investments in Spain and it was feared that these might well be seized by the republicans. The British made no assessment of the strategic implications of a nationalist victory for Gibraltar and the Mediterranean, in spite of Liddell Hart's promptings, and urged the French not to get involved. This attitude, later enshrined in the Non-Intervention Agreement, amounted to tacit but effective support to Franco by ignoring the support given by the dictators to the nationalists, while at the same time denying the republic the right to buy arms abroad to defend itself against the rebels.

The result of this policy was to push the republic into the arms of the Soviet Union, thus directly contributing to the spread of communist influence which the British wished to avoid. Stalin probably decided to help Spain in September. He hoped to strengthen the Soviet Union's position against Nazi Germany, to pose as the upholder of legitimacy and the status quo and also to divert attention away from the Moscow show trials then at their peak. Soviet tanks began to arrive in Spain in October and were superior to the German

Mark IIs, similarly the 1.15 and 1.16 fighters were far more effective than anything on the nationalist side until the Germans sent the Messerschmitt Bf 109, a plane which had its test flights in September 1935 and which was at that time the finest fighter in the world. Soviet equipment gave the republic an initial technical superiority, but this was never properly exploited and was lost by mid-1937. Russian assistance was substantial, although the republic paid for it dearly both in gold and raw materials. It was enough to stave off immediate defeat and to prolong the war, but it was not enough for a republican victory. Although much of Spain's industrial region was in republican hands, it was unable to supply large armies, and supplies from abroad were absolutely critical. The republic only survived in 1938 because the French border was opened, and its defeat later that year was due in part to the closing of the frontier at British insistence, and because the Soviet Union was becoming increasingly concerned about the Japanese threat in the east and after Munich was beginning to abandon collective security and to consider the possibility of reaching an understanding with Hitler.

The most widely publicized example of such foreign aid was the International Brigades. Organized and controlled by the communists, they were manned chiefly by workers who volunteered for a variety of reasons. Boredom, disillusionment and the desire for adventure, all of them fuelled by the depression, were at least as important as political idealism. The intellectuals got most of the glory, but also did their fair share of the dying, soon to become martyrs of the anti-fascist struggle. These included John Cornford, great-grandson of Darwin, a brilliant young historian and promising poet, who was too romantic a soul to be totally bound by the communist orthodoxy he espoused. Then there was the Rev. R. M. Hilliard 'the Boxing Parson' and 'Christopher Caudwell', an assiduous writer of detective stories, poetry and marxist tracts. The brigades were poorly trained, badly equipped and subject to endless communist interference and persecution. Many quickly became disillusioned, like the volunteer who said 'they told me this was a revolution, but it's nothing but a – war'. The brigades never had more than about 20,000 men and thus never played a really decisive part in the war, and they left 10,000 dead; testament both to their bravery and to the poor quality of many of the officers. Their courage was considerable and in time they became effective soldiers who inspired the Spanish to fight harder. The propaganda effect of the International Brigades was considerable, for here was proof of international solidarity with the just cause of the Spanish people and with the struggle to stop fascism. The nationalists also made use of the brigades as proof that the republic was controlled by international communism. The nationalists were unable to attract anything like the same number of volunteers. 'General' O'Duffy led his Irish contingent of 'blue shirts' with such whiskey-sodden incompetence that he was probably an asset to the republic. There was an odd assortment of quasi-fascists, ultra-Catholics, White Russians and unemployed mercenaries who joined the nationalists, but their contribution was insignificant.

The Spanish Civil War has often been described as a dress rehearsal for the Second World War. In military terms this is far from the truth. Although some sophisticated equipment was tried in battle for the first time, both sides were starved of material, fighting with antiquated weapons on thinly held fronts with inadequate communications, little armour and poor air support. Civilians were bombed to an extent that caused grim foreboding of things to come, but morale held and shelters proved most effective. The overextended fronts meant that tanks and airpower were decisive, and it was nationalist superiority in both which ultimately decided the war.

The nationalists' aim at the beginning of the war was to seize Madrid, Mola advancing from the north with two other forces from Saragossa and Valladolid converging on the capital. The troops from Saragossa were diverted to Barcelona which Goded had failed to take, the other two were held in the mountains around Madrid by republican troops and militia who fought with great tenacity. The task of taking Madrid was now left to Franco who advanced from the south, having taken Toledo. The attack on the capital began on 7 November but came up against the determined resistance of the communist Fifth Regiment, Durruti's anarchist column from Aragon and the first units of the International Brigade. There were some 12,000 men on the nationalist side, tired after their long march and some heavy fighting in the previous month. It has been estimated that the republicans could muster at least 23,000 men, equipped with Soviet tanks, fighter planes and advised by Soviet experts.

In the initial attack the republican forces were disorganized, there were large numbers of desertions and the military junta headed by General Miaja was unable to impose an effective command over the different militia units, but they were able to stop the nationalists. The nationalists reached the university city but were beaten back, and Franco decided to halt the attempt to take the capital by frontal assault. Franco blamed his failure on the 'shock troops of international communism', but there is little supporting evidence for this assertion. The communist troops fought bravely, but they were poorly trained, inexperienced, inadequately supplied and poorly organized. The defence of Madrid depended on the units of the regular army and security forces which remained loyal to the republic, the efforts of regular officers who were appointed to the Mixed Brigades, and the tremendous spirit of the people of Madrid who were determined that the city would not fall.

The nationalists' next move was to attempt to isolate the city. In the encounters of December and January the republican forces fought with much greater skill and the nationalist offensive ground to a standstill. Troops on both sides dug themselves in and amid the winter rains fought limited battles of position. Madrid had been saved, although it was hardly the 'tomb of fascism' which the communists loudly proclaimed. Nevertheless the defence of Madrid was a tremendous boost to republican morale and the other great slogan of the day, 'They shall not pass', was much more than an empty boast.

Elsewhere the war went badly for the republic. The Basque region was cut off from France and from republican Spain. In the east the anarchists were more intent on orchestrating their social revolution than they were in fighting the nationalists, and little progress was made even though the rebels were hopelessly outnumbered. The CNT uncharitably blamed their failure on the refusal of the government to give them the arms they needed to do the job. A fundamental weakness of the republicans was that although they were determined in defence, as the battle for Madrid had shown, they were ineffective on the offensive. Lacking strategic skill or tactical cunning they tended to believe that courage was all that was needed. The suicide charges of the singularly inept Hungarian communist General Gal were typical of this approach, and the casualty rate in the International Brigades he commanded were intolerably high. Stalin did not approve and Gal was shot on his return to the Soviet Union.

In the south Malaga fell to the Italians in February 1937 without offering much resistance. Once again the republicans devoted most of their energy to burning churches and squabbling among themselves, their leaders both civil and military were inept, and little help came from nearby republican areas such as Valencia. The Italians celebrated the seizure of Malaga as a heroic victory, showing scant regard for truth and much to the annoyance of Franco. The nationalists established a reign of terror in Malaga which was effectively used by republican propagandists as a warning to inspire the defenders of Madrid.

The Italians pressed on to Guadalajara in the hope of another easy victory. The republicans were hopelessly outnumbered and fell back, but the Italians mounted their offensive on a very narrow front in foul weather and were unable to resist the republican counter-attack which was launched almost as soon as the reserves were in place. The Italians were routed, and among the victors were their anti-fascist compatriots in the Garibaldi Battalion. It was a terrible humiliation for Mussolini, but Franco was relieved that the Italians had not had another victory which might have undermined his claim to be the true saviour of Spain. The republicans celebrated a great victory and Ernest Hemingway, an unerringly poor judge of men and events, proclaimed it to be one of the truly decisive battles of all time. The propaganda value of the battle was enormous, for now the whole world, even Anthony Eden, realized the extent of Italian involvement in the war. The myth of 'non-intervention' was exposed, and the republicans could claim to be fighting against vicious foreign invaders.

After their defeat at Guadalajara the nationalists realized that Madrid could not be taken except at very great cost, and therefore decided to concentrate their efforts on the north, to deny the republicans access to the sea and use of the considerable industrial resources of the region. General Mola launched his attack at the end of March and made effective use of heavy artillery and aerial bombardment which had a devastating effect on republican morale. On 25 April the Condor Legion attacked the small Basque town of Guernica. High-explosive bombs were dropped first, then the incendiaries which created the fire which destroyed the town. Civilians were machine-gunned as they fled. The armaments factory and the bridge, the only military objectives in the town, survived as did the Tree of Guernica, a potent symbol of Basque nationalism.

The destruction of Guernica sent shockwaves of horror throughout the world. Here was a vivid and ghastly example of the destructive capability of bombers. Here too was a reminder of the savage brutality of the Germans. The nationalists claimed that Guernica had been destroyed by 'red separatist incendiaries', an absurd lie that was taken up by the British Catholic press. Most of the world knew that it was the work of the Germans, and this denial simply made them appear even more perfidious. Casualties were insignificant by later standards, but were greatly exaggerated by the republicans. This did much to discredit the nationalists but it did nothing to strengthen civilian will to resist as Mola's troops continued their advance.

In June Bibao fell, having been beseiged, blockaded and bombarded. In the course of the summer the remainder of the north fell into the hands of the nationalists. No compassion was shown towards the Basques, their language and culture was suppressed, and the victorious Christian crusaders treated their co-religionists with singular brutality. Priests who had sympathized with the republic were shot and no attempt at reconciliation was made. Asturias, a happy hunting-ground for anarchists and violent anti-clericals, had refused to bow to a unified command and was thus isolated and collapsed in October.

The republicans seized the opportunity offered by the enemy's concentration on the north to launch diversionary attacks. The first two attempts, at Segovia and Huesca, were disappointing failures. The major offensive was planned with considerable strategic skill against the nationalist forces to the west of Madrid around Brunete. Initially the attack was a success but the republicans lacked the training, discipline and organization to exploit their overwhelming numerical advantage. Franco threw in his reserves and the republicans were halted. Casualties were terrible: an estimated 25,000 on the republican side, and 17,000 nationalists. Strategically the battle ended in a stalemate, and the republicans found themselves in a large salient which needed a skilful defence if it were to hold.

The republicans attempted another offensive towards Saragossa in August. The Popular Army proved incapable of fighting a battle of manoeuvre, the deployment of tanks was ineffectual, and communications between armour and infantry were seriously deficient. The communists blamed this failure on the incompetent and treacherous anarchists and trotskyites, who in turn accused the communists for deliberately starving them of arms and equipment. Such accusations disguised the fact that the nationalists had a better trained and better equipped army under an effective central command. The republicans had lost the advantage, were dropping behind and had yet to master the difficult art of the offensive.

The republic was also fighting a war in the midst of a political crisis, whereas the nationalists could concentrate on winning the war. Largo Caballero, envious, suspicious and brooding, still refused to accept that the revolution was over and that the conservative communists should determine the future of Spain. He resisted the communist attempt to unite the communist and socialist parties. He opposed communist control over the armed forces and tried to curb the influence of the Soviet experts, and their meddlesome ambassador, Marcel Rosenberg. Largo Caballero was now on a collision course with the communists who were to use the crisis in Catalonia to engineer his downfall.

By early 1937 the quarrel between the Catalan Stalinists in the PSUC (*Partido Socialista Unificado de Cataluña*) and the 'trotskyites' in the POUM had become so serious that it only needed a small incident to trigger off violence on a large scale. On 3 May the police, who were controlled by the PSUC, seized the Barcelona telephone exchange which was a CNT stronghold. POUM, who in spite of many serious differences sympathized with CNT as fellow militants, took to the streets in protest. The communists in Valencia, where the republican government now resided, saw this incident as a golden opportunity to destroy POUM, put an end to Catalan autonomy, and strengthen their hold over Catalonia. They were able to win a majority for the proposal to suspend the Catalan Statute and to send Assault Guards to Barcelona. At the same time the communists unleashed a scurrilous press attack on Largo Caballero and demanded that POUM should not only be banned, but that its leaders should be tried for treason. The prime minister refused to treat a workers' party as a criminal organization, but was in no position to withstand the communist attack. He was forced to resign, his post taken by Dr Juan Negrin.

The communists pursued POUM with their customary determination and brutality. Andrés Nin, the highly respected leader of POUM, was murdered by the NKVD. An attempt to emulate Stalin's show trials and accuse POUM of being fascists, traitors, bukharinites and trotskyites misfired. Largo Caballero defended them against such absurdities, and George Orwell praised them lavishly in *Homage to Catalonia*, although the book remained virtually unread. POUM were absurd not to support the Popular Front and accept that a strong government was needed in time of war. They were misguided and mistaken, but they were not 'in the pay of European fascism', nor were they 'allies of the Gestapo' or 'beasts of prey'. Even the communists had to be content with seeing the leadership convicted of the lesser charge of rebellion, for which they were given fifteen-year sentences.

Negrin, a professor of psychology of some distinction, an intellectual who was also an effective administrator, was a passionate believer in individual liberty who knew that this could only be achieved if the war was won, and that this would necessitate centralization and discipline. His position was thus close to that of the communists, but he was far from being the uncritical fellow traveller his critics claimed him to be. With Largo Caballero's supporters and the CNT no longer in the government, Negrin had little choice but to hope that the Soviet Union would continue to support the republic, and that the British and French would realize the folly of appeasement and come to the defence of Spain. He could not afford to antagonize the communists, but he was determined not to capitulate to them. That he came perilously close to doing so was due to the overwhelming force of circumstances, not to any fundamental weakness of character.

Negrin's government followed up the attack on Catalan autonomy with the dissolution of the CNT-dominated Council of Aragon. For Negrin this was essential for efficient government, for the communists it was a means of settling a political score. Communist commanders carried out this task in a manner which greatly exceeded their instructions. CNT leaders were thrown into jail, the collective farms were forcibly dissolved, and industry was de-collectivized. Meanwhile Catalonia was brought under even closer control from Valencia, and the new secret police force SIM (*Servicio de Investigación Militar*) set about its task of hunting down subversives and traitors with a frenzy which bordered on the manic. To many who were used to the chaotic factionalism of earlier times it seemed as if behind the fig leaf of the Popular Front was a highly centralized communist police state. The republic was certainly better organized to fight a war, but an increasing number of Spaniards asked themselves whether such a regime was really worth fighting for. The chaos had gone, but so had the enthusiasm.

Negrin and his minister of defence, Indalecio Prieto, were convinced that the Popular Army had to go on the offensive to wrest the initiative from the nationalists. General Rojo selected Teruel, a thinly held salient, for an attack which would divert Franco's troops away from Madrid which he was determined to seize after his successful campaign in the north. The attack began on 15 December 1937 and was initially successful, and a sudden spell of freezing weather brought the nationalist counter-attack to a virtual standstill. On 8 January the Teruel garrison surrendered. But at the beginning of February Franco launched an offensive to the north of the town which broke through the republican lines after a massive aerial bombardment and an old-fashioned cavalry charge. On 22 February Teruel fell to the nationalists.

The Popular Army had not fought well at Teruel. Commanders refused to obey orders, troops mutinied and morale was pitifully low. Franco decided to follow up this victory with a drive south to the sea and the river Ebro in order to divide republican Spain in two. The Popular Army never recovered from the defeat at Teruel. Faced with overwhelming air superiority and with punishing artillery barrages morale collapsed and whole divisions deserted. The International Brigades were brought up to stiffen the front, but they too had lost much of their effectiveness and were helpless against the nationalists. Franco reached the sea with little difficulty and the republicans again began a frantic search for culprits, the communists accusing their political rivals of cowardice and treachery and being accused in turn of deliberately staging a disaster to discredit their opponents, particularly Prieto.

After these disasters Prieto was convinced that the war could not be won and that the only hope lay in a negotiated settlement. Negrin and the communists did not share this defeatism, the former because he still believed that France would come to the rescue of the republic, the latter because they were determined to tighten their grip on the republic and its army. All was illusion. Franco would never negotiate, France would not help, and the communists' ambitions infuriated many army commanders and further undermined morale. Communist optimism, although it was beginning to sound increasingly hollow, was every bit as damaging to the army as Prieto's pessimism. The division between the communists and their orthodox socialist allies and the *Caballeristas* and their sympathizers in the CNT was as serious as ever, in spite of frantic efforts to paper over the cracks. Prieto's resignation in April 1938 was taken as further evidence that the communists were virtual dictators in Valencia and it was even suggested that they were 'fascists'. The communists replied with wit and originality that the CNT were 'fascists' and 'agents of the Axis'.

All did not seem quite lost in the Spring of 1938: the French opened the border, giving supplies and renewed help to the republicans and Franco made the serious mistake of marching against Valenica rather than seizing the industrial base of the republic in Catalonia. Republican troops put up an impressive defence as the nationalists advanced towards Valenica, and at the end of July they launched a sudden offensive on the Ebro. It was a well-executed attack, the river was crossed at night and Franco's troops were caught by surprise, but the follow through was bungled. The nationalists recovered to build strong defensive positions and to launch a series of counter attacks which halted the republicans' advance. Franco then allowed the battle to degenerate into a bloody slogging match which was to last until November. He threw wave after wave of men on a wide front against strongly held positions and they were beaten back at terrible cost. But with overwhelming superiority in the air and in artillery he was bound to win this battle of attrition. Franco's defenders argue that although the cost was high, the battle of the Ebro destroyed the Popular Army. About two-thirds of the army was lost as casualties, prisoners and deserters. The Munich Agreement at the end of September put paid to any hope of help from Britain and France. Franco, his advance towards Valencia halted, decided to attack Catalonia in the final campaign of the war.

Franco's advance towards Barcelona turned into a rout. The republican army fell apart, Barcelona fell with scarcely a shot being fired, and Negrin escaped into France. He returned to Spain shortly afterwards to be with the Army of the Centre which was still intact. In Madrid Colonel Casado made a *pronunciamiento* against Negrin, having been assured by Franco's agents that there would be no reprisals if the republicans laid down their arms. Casado was supported by the CNT and by anti-communist marxists like Julian Besteiro and his National Council was welcomed by the majority of Madrid's half-starved population. Negrin left again for France, this time for good. In Madrid fighting broke out between communists and Casado's 'traitors'. Franco stood aside from this final and bloody internecine feud. It left Casado without a card to play, for Franco had no need to accept anything other than unconditional surrender. The nationalists had little difficulty in taking Madrid at the end of March where they were given a loud if somewhat forced welcome by a shattered populace. By 1 April he was master of all of Spain, his victory was total and he was in no mood to forgive or forget. For the republicans the future offered nothing but exile, death, imprisonment, or silent submission.

Franco had won the war and none disputed his leadership. The nationalists had not been plagued by the political divisiveness that beset the republicans. CEDA collapsed without a parliamentary forum and the monarchist *Renovación Española* disbanded. Only the Falange and the Carlists remained as small factions with some popular support. Neither liked the unideological authoritarianism of Franco and the generals. The Carlists dreamed of the day when a Prince of Bourbon Parma would ascend to the throne of Spain, the Falange entertained inchoate and confused ideas of a 'national revolution'. Franco and his brother-in-law, Ramón Serrano Suñer, had no sympathy with such nonsense and forced the Carlists and the

Falange to amalgamate into a new party which was given the convoluted but wide-ranging name *Falange Española Tradicionalista y de las Juntas de Ofensiva Nacional-Sindicalistas*. Manuel Hedilla, a crude and illiterate former dock worker who was head of the Falange, led a singularly inept coup attempt against Franco. The ring leaders were arrested and condemned to death, their sentences later commuted to life imprisonment partly because of a plea for clemency from the German ambassador. The Carlists were even easier to crush. Their leader, Fal Conde, was exiled, and Franco let it be known that he was lucky not to be shot.

Franco's Spain was dull, repressive and old-fashioned. His vision of society was that of a soldier: officers gave orders and men obeyed. No questions were asked. The Falange, or *Movimiento* as it was known for short, was simply a means of transmitting such orders and its unattractive ideologues were silenced for ever. Ideology was provided not by the party but by the Church and its stern Catholicism was heavily laced with nationalism. Their outriders among the laiety, Opus Dei and ACNP (*Asociación Católica Nacional de Propagandistas* – an organization dating back to the early seventeenth century) grew in power and influence. At the same time opposition to this crusading mission was slowly growing among Catholics who were concerned with reconciliation and with fundamental spiritual values. But they had to wait until the pontificate of John XXIII before they won the support of the heirarchy.

Hundreds of thousands of refugees left their homeland rather than live in Franco's miserable state. They were treated contemptibly, like all others facing a similar plight in this the century of the refugee. Even the left disowned them as failures and nuisances. Interminable political squabbles between communists and anarchists continued to make these years of exile even more wretched. Many fought and died for the allied cause in the vain hope that the defeat of fascism would entail the fall of Franco. There was only one country which helped these unfortunates. Mexico, which had generously supplied the republic with arms, in spite of its problems of poverty, overpopulation and unemployment, allowed any refugee who could meet the travel expenses to settle and work in peace. It was an exceptional act of charity at a time when men's hearts had turned to stone. It was amply repaid, for the Spanish refugees made an enduring contribution to Mexican life and culture.

CHAPTER ELEVEN
Nazi Germany

At first those who had helped to bring Hilter to power felt that they had good reasons to congratulate themselves for skilfully using the Nazis to overcome the political crisis while they remained in control of the situation. Hitler's position was far from secure. In the 'cabinet of national concentration' there were only two Nazi ministers, Goering and Frick, and in the governments of the larger German states they were not even represented. Hindenburg was clearly identified with the conservatives, as were the armed forces, the judiciary and the upper echelons of the civil service. But the two Nazi ministers held key positions: Frick was minister of the interior, and Goering was commissioner for the Prussian ministry of the interior, as well as being responsible for air transport. But their power was limited. Goering was formally answerable to Papen as reich commissioner for Prussia. The state secretary for the ministry of the Interior, Hans Pfundtner, although sympathetic to the Nazis, was not a party member and the minister of justice, Gürtner, was a nationalist, and his state secretary had been in office since 1924.

The parties of the left also shared the illusion that Hitler was an employee of the traditional right, their analysis of the situation clouded by their ideological obsession that this was merely a reshuffling of power within a monopoly capitalist state apparatus.

Hitler's first moves were to demand the dissolution of the Reichstag, and to strengthen his hold over Prussia, Germany's largest state and a socialist stronghold. By dissolving the Reichstag he silenced his opponents who might be tempted to use it as a forum to attack his policies, and he hoped to make significant gains in the forthcoming elections which would free him from the control of his coalition partners. They in turn unwisely agreed to new elections, having been promised by Hitler that the government would be unchanged, even though he had previously promised not to call an election in which the DNVP was unlikely to be able to improve its position. The government had a safe majority in the Reichstag provided that they had the support of the Centre Party, but Hitler turned his back on them by refusing to give a guarantee that fundamental constitutional rights would be respected. The nationalists thus gave their full support to Hitler's efforts to destroy parliamentary democracy, crush the left-wing parties and establish a permanent authoritarian regime, even though their own standing in the polls was unlikely to improve.

The Reichstag was dissolved on 1 February and three days later the president issued the emergency decree 'For the Protection of the German People'. Using as an excuse a call by the KPD for a general strike, the decree enabled the police to silence the press and forbid public meetings and thus to control the election campaigns of the opposition parties.

Meanwhile, Goering managed to push Papen into the sidelines and to gain effective control over Prussia. On 6 February the Prussian Landtag was dissolved in clear violation of the constitution, for it was contrary to a judgement in the Supreme Court, which had ruled after Papen's coup in 1932 that the duly elected social democratic government of Prussia should remain in office, even though its powers were drastically curtailed. The Prussian Landtag had rejected a Nazi motion for dissolution, as had the three-man executive board, President Braun and Konrad Adenauer voting against the Nazi president of the Landtag, Kerrl. Goering acted swiftly to rid the Prussian police of 'unreliable elements' and to bring it firmly under his control. In addition, the SS and the SA were employed as auxiliary police to deal with 'excesses by left-wing radicals, and particularly by communists'. Goering instructed the police to forget their political neutrality and to use their weapons whenever necessary against the 'enemies of the state'.

It was virtually impossible for the SPD and the KPD to fight an election campaign. Their meetings were forbidden, or violently disrupted by Nazis while the police stood aside. Their press was silenced and propaganda material seized. In some instances successful appeals were made to the Supreme Court against these practices, for even in extreme nationalist circles there was still a lingering belief in the rule of law; but the bourgeois parties were so cowed that they voiced their criticisms in such circumspect language that Hitler's image was hardly tarnished. The general mood was one of resignation, and there was still a faint hope that the ancient president would somehow restrain the government and keep it within the bounds of the law. Hitler was careful to avoid making any election promises, particularly on economic policy; instead he harped on the horrors and humiliations of the past and spoke in glowing but deliberately vague terms of a 'national awakening'. Even the more sceptical industrialists were delighted and Krupp, Vögler of the Vereinigte Stahlwerke and von Schnitzler of IG Farben helped to chip in several million marks to the Nazis' election fund.

On 27 February a simple-minded Dutchman, Marinus van der Lubbe, set fire to the Reicshstag. Hitler, Goering, Goebbels and Frick promptly announced that this was designed as a signal for a communist insurrection which was to be supported by the social democrats. With the almost paranoid belief in a vast communist conspiracy, which was widely held among the parties of the right, many Germans became trapped in their own propaganda and believed this to be true. It is certain that the KPD had no plans for an uprising, and almost equally certain that had they had any they would not have been supported by the SPD. Both the Nazis and the KPD made the maximum use of the situation. The communist propagandist, Willi Münzenberg, mounted a skilful campaign from Paris which attempted to prove that the Nazis had organized the fire themselves in order to destroy the KPD, and recent evidence that has been uncovered suggests that this version of events may indeed contain more than a grain of truth, even though the evidence produced at the time was almost entirely fraudulent. The controversy over who was responsible for the Reichstag fire still continues, and it is no longer possible to assert with absolute certainty that van der Lubbe acted alone.

On the day after the fire, Hindenburg signed another emergency decree 'For the Protection of the People and the State'. The decree abolished at one stroke all the fundamental rights of a democratic state: freedom of speech, the right to privacy and the protection of property. It allowed the government to interfere directly in the affairs of the individual states whenever it deemed necessary. Frick, as minister of the interior, was given plenipotentiary rights to implement the decree. He decided to give the states a free hand, and then promptly set about banning the KPD's press, meetings, and party organizations. Thousands of party functionaries were arrested, particularly in Prussia where Goering used these exceptional powers to the full. The Nazis decided not to ban the KPD outright, for fear that the SPD would pick up a large number of extra votes. The decree was also used to step up the persecution of the SPD, in spite of Foreign Minister von Neurath's suggestion that this might be harmful to Germany's image abroad. Hitler took no notice of such objections, assuring the foreign press that these measures were purely temporary and were designed to meet a specific danger from the communists. In fact, the Reichstag fire decree was to be one of the most important steps towards the creation of the Nazi dictatorship. It enabled the party to ignore the normal process of law and to destroy fundamental rights and freedoms.

In spite of these measures the NSDAP only succeeded in winning 43.9 per cent of the popular vote in the elections of 5 March 1933, the government parties winning a narrow majority of 51.8 per cent. The KPD got 1.1 million votes, which was remarkable under the circumstances, but a disastrous result compared with the 5.9 million votes in November 1932. The SPD managed to hang on to most of their voters, the DNVP and the Centre made modest gains. Although the election results were far short of the 'revolution' which Hitler proclaimed, they were sufficient for his purposes. There could be no question at all that the NSDAP was the senior coalition partner, and by arresting all the communist deputies in the Reichstag and the Prussian Landtag the Nazis had an absolute majority in both houses.

In those states where they did not yet dominate the government open terror was now used. The SS and SA no longer acted as an auxiliary to the police and beat up, humiliated and arrested countless opponents of the regime. Jewish civil servants, judges and prosecutors were summarily dismissed along with other 'unreliable' officials. Jewish businesses were boycotted. In Prussia alone some 25,000 arrests were made in March and April. Frick appointed Nazi police commissioners in many of the more important states, and special commissioners were sent throughout the country to complete the process of *Gleichschaltung* – the centralization of power under Nazi control. The Nazis made carefully co-ordinated demonstrations which very often led to violence, and these were used as pretexts to curtail the authority of the states under the terms of the Reichstag fire emergency decree. This was flagrantly unconstitutional, for the decree was specifically aimed against 'Communist acts of violence harmful to the state'. Non-Nazi state governments were warned that if they did not resign to make way for Nazi governments there would be no possibility of guaranteeing that law and order would be preserved. Under such threats the governments one by one gave

263

way. On 16 March 1933 this process was completed when the Bavarian government, which had tried hard to preserve its independence, finally resigned, having been stripped of most of its powers by the appointment of various commissioners. Perhaps the most important of such appointments was that of Heinrich Himmler as head of the Munich police force. This was be to the start of a remarkable career in law enforcement.

There were some complaints from the nationalists about the SA's use of terror, and the rowdy and lawless behaviour of the party activists. Even Papen complained to Hitler, only to be told to mind his own business and then treated to a diatribe about the feeble bourgeois world which prefered the kid glove to the mailed fist. But Hitler realized that something had to be done to placate the nationalists and to draw people's attention away from the violence, the newly built concentration camps, and the illegality of the *Gleichschaltung*. To celebrate the opening of the new Reichstag a ceremony was held in Potsdam at which Hitler paid homage to Hindenburg, the SA marched in step with the Reichswehr, and the young idealists of the movement showed their respect for the traditions of the past. It was made to seem that the days of Weimar were over, and that Germany had returned to the glorious traditions of Potsdam. Goebbels cynically described the event in his diary as a 'sentimental comedy'.

The Reichstag had only one task to perform: to pass a bill which would end parliamentary government in Germany. This Enabling Act was debated on 23 March, the Reichstag meeting in its temporary home in the Kroll Opera House in Berlin, ominously surrounded by units of the SS and SA. Hitler had difficulty in getting the necessary two-thirds majority for a constitutional amendment which would allow the government to pass any laws, including further constitutional changes, without consulting the Reichstag or the Senate (Reichsrat), and without asking the president to issue the necessary decrees. Among the bourgeois parties there was a widespread belief that the Enabling Act was a necessity, and that the violent excesses of the last few weeks were due to the very real threat of a communist uprising. It was felt that the government had been perfectly justified in acting decisively and harshly at such a time of national danger. The incessant propaganda campaign, and the muzzling of the liberal press, had helped people turn a blind eye to the real purpose of the law, to its unconstitutional origins and illegal implementation. The social democrats managed to convince themselves that the law was directed solely against the communists and that their party and their Free Trades Unions would survive. When the Free Trades Unions were declared illegal the Christian Trades Unions imagined that they had been spared. When they were banned it was hoped that it might be possible to keep the organization going under the umbrella of the German Labour Front (DAF). Similarly, the parties believed that Hitler would only ban the KPD, then that the SPD would be the last party to be outlawed. Soon only the NSDAP remained.

The Centre Party held the key to the necessary majority for the Enabling Act, and they were easily won over by Hitler's repeated assurances that he wanted better relations with the Vatican, respected the importance of the Christian churches, and would listen to the Centre Party's views on how the law would be implemented. Brüning, to his credit, was one of the few party members who realized that the law was exceedingly dangerous and could be easily abused. The SPD was alone in their courageous opposition to the bill, but even they hinted that negotiations were still possible, and they were not totally free from the widespread illusion that Hitler would respect the rule of law.

Hitler decided to tolerate the political parties for a little while, for he needed them to decorate the Reichstag when he gave a major speech on foreign policy on 17 May, in which he made repeated professions of his dedication to the cause of peace. The Free Trades Unions (ADGB) had been banned on 2 May, and the SPD knew that it was only a matter of time before they would be outlawed. Part of the party left for Prague where at least for a while they could enjoy freedom of speech; others decided to attend the foreign policy debate. On 22 June the party was banned, its assets seized, and its members treated as enemies of the state. On 5 July the Centre Party was dissolved. The Catholic Hierarchy had already decided to abandon the Centre Party and to support the Nazi regime, so that in spite of this ban negotiations for a Concordat with the Holy See continued, and they were completed on 8 July. The Catholic Church was guaranteed full rights to administer the sacraments, and her property was protected. Pastoral letters could be published, and Catholic schools would still be tolerated. Cardinal Secretary Pacelli (the future Pius XII) agreed that all political and social organizations of the Church should be disbanded and that the Church would support the regime. The DNVP had already disappeared, many of its members having joined the NSDAP in the mad rush to jump on the bandwagon in March, and Hugenberg had been forced to resign from the cabinet having hastened his own downfall by his singularly undiplomatic behaviour at the World Economic Conference in London. On 14 July all political parties other than the NSDAP were forbidden, and Germany became a single-party state, with Adolf Hitler its unchallenged dictator. On 12 November elections were held for the Reichstag in which the voters were asked to acclaim the 'Führer's list'. Terrified that they would be punished for not turning out to vote, and doubting that the secrecy of the ballot box would be respected, more than 95 per cent of the electorate cast their votes, and 92.2 per cent voted for the list.

The new Reichstag was a mockery, being little more than a servile audience in front of whom Hitler could make some of his more bombastic speeches. It did, however, serve a more practical purpose. It was needed at times to pass certain pieces of legislation which would not quite fit under the umbrella of the Enabling Act, or which had to be passed quickly. The most notorious of these were the Nuremberg Laws of 1935, which marked a new and terrible stage in the German persecution of the Jews.

The process of *Gleichschaltung* did not merely affect the states, it also touched organizations which were not under direct state control. Between March and July 1933 the Nazis, using their commissioners, party functionaries and the 'Combat League of Middle Class Businessmen', purged all business associations, farmers' clubs and professional organizations of opponents of the regime and of Jews, ensured that all leading positions were held by Nazis, organized them strictly according to the 'leadership principle', and amalgamated them into single national organizations. With the abolition of the Free Trades Unions all manual and clerical workers were forced to join the 'German Work Front' (DAF). The farmers' associations were combined to form the Reich Food Corporation, and lawyers were forced into the 'Legal Front'. All these organizations were closely supervised by the NSDAP. The 'Combat League for German Culture' tried to Nazify the museums, cultural organizations and academies of the fine arts, but their efforts resulted in chaos. In September 1933 a 'Reich Chamber of Culture' was formed which brought all the cultural activities of the country under party control.

The Catholic Church had decided to make its peace with Hitler's regime and in these early years gave him little cause for concern. The situation was somewhat different with regard to the Protestants. One group, the 'German Christians', fully supported the Nazis and even called themselves 'Evangelical National Socialists'. Those whose found National Socialism and the gospel message irreconcilable joined Pastor Martin Niemöller's 'Pastors' Emergency League' which formed the basis of the Confessing Church. Hitler publicly supported the German Christians and their leader, Ludwig Müller, was appointed Reich Bishop after considerable pressure had been brought to bear on the Church. The Confessing Church was a centre of opposition to the regime, and since its members were mostly solid conservative bourgeois this was something new and troublesome to the regime. Its spokesmen were to suffer terribly in the hands of an increasingly repressive regime. Dietrich Bonhoeffer was hanged, Niemöller was arrested in 1937 and mercifully survived the war.

Big businessmen and bankers were virtually exempt from this process of *Gleichschaltung*. The Nazi programme's strictures against cartels and monopolies, chain-stores and the 'slavery of interest' were studiously ignored, as Hitler had promised. The Reich Association of German Industry had its name slightly modified to make it sound more ideologically respectable, but it remained unchanged in essence. Krupp stayed in the chair and did not have to suffer undue interference from party officials. Hitler needed the support of big business, and it was not until 1936 that political pressure was increasingly brought to bear on this sector of the economy.

Hitler was determined to avoid discussing the economy in the campaign for the elections in March 1933 for, as he pointed out, no solution he might suggest would be acceptable to all of the millions of voters he hoped to attract. The appointment of Schacht as President of the Reichsbank was greeted with sighs of relief on the Rhine and Ruhr, for an impeccably orthodox financier with excellent connections throughout the business world had been appointed, rather than some party exotic like Gottfied Feder with his bizarre economic theories and questionable background. Schacht's appointment was most unpopular in the Nazi Party. They wanted to see some dramatic changes made, even if they were not quite sure what, and Schacht was a typical representative of the old regime which they hoped to destroy in the white heat of a National Socialist revolution.

Hitler and his circle had only the vaguest notions of economics and were uncertain how to tackle the problem of unemployment which was still by far the most serious problem facing the country. They were fortunate that Schleicher's job-creating programme began to have some effect, but in spite of pumping considerable sums of money into public works and housing projects, unemployment remained unacceptably high. The industrialists were somewhat critical of these early efforts to reduce unemployment. The encouragement of labour-intensive projects, the attempts to move women out of the work force and back into the home, the reduction of working hours and tax concessions to small businesses were not seen as serious efforts to stimulate production, and were subject to ideological bias and favouritism. Even Kurt Schmitt of Allianz Insurance, who succeeded Hugenberg as minister of economics, was critical of many aspects of the programme.

Gradually these criticisms waned, for the programme did bring down the number of unemployed, and leading businessmen were reassured that Hitler's government was responsible in economic matters and was not the prisoner of the extremist ideologues of the movement. Certain sectors of industry also profited considerably from larger armaments orders, and this also had some effect on the reduction of unemployment. Schacht was in favour of a modest degree of rearmament as a means of overcoming the economic crisis, and encouraged it by providing the necessary credit by means of 'Mefo' bills. These were drawn on the *Metall-Forschungs-GmbH*, a government-owned company with limited capital, and armament manufacturers could discount them at the Reichsbank. Schacht fondly imagined that this programme would be slowed down or stopped once the economy had recovered, and seems to have been unaware that Hitler had no such intentions and was convinced that a war of conquest and plunder was the most satisfactory way of paying for rearmament.

Even the limited rearmament programme of these early years caused severe dislocations. There was soon an acute shortage of foreign exchange to which rearmament contributed, but which was also caused by foreign investors being reluctant to leave their money in a country which still seemed to have a very uncertain future, by the export trade being damaged by the fact that Germany was seen abroad as a repressive and unjust state, and by rising tariffs which were designed to make the country less dependent on foreign markets. Schacht tried to deal with this problem by directing German trade towards countries which would pay for German goods by sending foodstuffs and raw materials. Blocked credit accounts were used to encourage exports. German importers offered handsome prices for foreign goods, but the money could only be spent in Germany. This worked quite well in the Balkans, but Germany's traditional trading partners were not attracted by the scheme. Similar attempts to substitute credits in marks for interest payments on foreign currency accounts were even less successful, and damaged Germany's credit rating. By the end of 1933 exchange controls were further tightened. All these measures harmed Germany's export industries and made the foreign exchange problem even more serious.

In September 1934 Schacht unveiled his 'New Plan' to deal with these problems. It imposed import quotas, encouraged barter agreements and directed German foreign trade towards eastern Europe and the Balkans. In these measures there were elements of a planned economy, but there was no fundamental conflict of interest between Hitler and the industrialists. Industry had to accept allocations of foreign currency and of raw materials and also price controls, but fundamental property relationships remained unchanged. The state invested heavily in industry, but without nationalization. Thus the state provided the capital for IG Farben to build large factories for the production of artificial petrol and rubber and bought guaranteed amounts of these commodities without demanding any direct control over the company. But this increasing level of state intervention did reduce entrepreneurial control over investment and production strategies, and even though industrialists were amply represented on state planning boards, their political influence was considerably less than it had been during the Weimar Republic.

The essentials of a market economy were thus preserved, and industrialists were greatly assisted. This was in marked contrast to the treatment of the workers who lost virtually all their political and economic power. When the Free Trades Unions were destroyed they were not incorporated into the National Socialist Factory Cells Organization (NSBO) but into the German Labour Front (DAF), which was created in May 1933 and headed by a foul-mouthed drunkard, Robert Ley. Questions relating to wages and industrial disputes were handled by Trustees of Labour who acted almost exclusively in the interests of the employers. This was the source of considerable conflict because the NSBOs, like the SA, were centres of 'left wing' Nazi activity. Their members voiced strident pseudo-socialist and revolutionary demands, complained of the rapacity of the capitalists, and at times even had the temerity to speak up on behalf of the workers. The DAF was not entirely free from such elements, and many of its functionaries hoped that it would play a leading role in the Nazi state by influencing social and labour policies. In November 1933 the DAF was reduced to being a purely propagandistic organization devoted, in the words of its 'Appeal to All Productive Germans', to 'the education of all working Germans for the National Socialist State and for the National Socialist way of thought'. To sugar the pill a large travel company was formed under the aegis of the DAF to provide cheap holidays and leisure activities. This imitation of the Italian Fascist *Dopo Lavoro* was given the absurd name 'Strength through Joy' (*Kraft durch Freude* – KdF). The Corporation of Germany Industry expressed its hearfelt approval of all these changes by promising to collaborate fully with the DAF.

In January 1934 the Law for the Ordering of National Labour established the *Führer* principle in the workplace and destroyed the last vestiges of worker participation. This marked an end to the left-wing Nazis' hopes for some form of partnership between capital and labour and for a radical modification of capitalism. The NSBOs now had virtually no influence and did little except organize beer and skittles evenings for old party comrades. After the 'Röhm putsch' in the summer of 1934 they were purged of 'anti-capitalist' activists and ceased to play anything other than a propaganda role, although Ley did use some of the old activists in an attempt to enhance the importance of the DAF and to create a sense of community (*Volksgemeinschaft*) and thus to emphasize his own significance as one of Hitler's leading paladins. But it had long since given up its attempts to represent the interests of the workers.

The first important step towards controlling and even conscripting labour was taken in February 1935 with the introduction of work books. These enabled the authorities to direct workers into industries which were suffering from labour shortages now that massive unemployment no longer existed and the rearmament programme absorbed large numbers of workers. Freedom of the workplace was further eroded with the introduction of labour conscription in 1938–39.

Although the *Volksgemeinschaft* was largely a sham, there can be no doubt that the Nazi state did restore a degree of social harmony. Unemployment, which had caused so much suffering and unrest in the final years of the Weimar Republic, was virtually ended by 1935. Although the workers had lost their fundamental rights and wages had been frozen at depression levels, at least everyone had a job. KdF, even if somewhat short on the joy, was popular and offered holidays which previously had only been enjoyed by the middle classes, and provided savings schemes designed to enable workers to buy a 'people's car' (*Volkswagen*). The Volkswagen works was opened with great pomp and ceremony in 1938 and was run by the DAF, but not a single car was delivered to the unfortunates who had saved up for one.

Even the burdens of this oppressive regime appeared to be shared equally by all social classes. Theoretically everyone had to serve in the compulsory Labour Service (*Reichsarbeitsdienst* – RAD) which was introduced in June 1935. There were new avenues opened up for social advancement through an emphasis on vocational training, and also within the swelling ranks of Nazi organizations. The DAF, for example, employed some 40,000 full-time workers. Nazi officials regarded themselves as forming a new class, drawn from all walks of life and self-consciously different fron the old exclusive elite. After 1936 there was a marked improvement in many workers' living standards which helped to reconcile many of them with the regime.

Endless propaganda about the 'ennobling' effect of labour had some effect in giving the workers a new sense of self-worth, as did pathetic proclamations of the end of the class war and the creation of a new community based on uniquely German virtues, rather than class distinctions. But most important of all, the people were reconciled to the regime because it was so strikingly successful. Once unemployment was solved there were a series of triumphs which gave the Germans a feeling of strength and power. The military restrictions of the Treaty of Versailles were thrown off in 1935, and the Saar returned to Germany in the same year. In 1936 the Rhineland was occupied. In 1938 Austria and the Sudetenland were incorporated into the Reich. Although the 99 per cent 'yes' votes in the plebiscites of 1936 cannot be taken as a serious test of public opinion, there is no doubt that the regime was immensely popular and that Adolf Hitler was respected, revered and even loved by a majority of the people.

Although Nazi support was strongest in the rural areas there was considerable discontent with the government's agricultural policies. At first the agricultural sector was delighted with the change in government, for the higher tariffs on foodstuffs and assistance for endebted farmers were very popular measures. When the government made its first moves towards agricultural self-sufficiency, as part of the policy of autarky, criticism became widespread. The Reich Food Estate (*Reichsnährstand* – RNF), although some of its functions were decentralized, was a vast bureaucratic apparatus which, by fixing prices, production quotas and marketing boards, set about destroying the free market for agricultural products. Farmers found this state intervention in their affairs very irksome and complained about time-consuming paper work and insensitive officials. The much publicized entailed farms (*Erbhöfe*) which were the Nazis' special form of land reform, granted inalienable rights to farmers of impeccable racial provenence on medium-sized farms.

This was frequently seen as a new form of serfdom, for the farmers could not sell their land which had to remain within the family. Although the entailed farmers, who eventually made up one third of all those with agricultural holdings, enjoyed certain economic advantages, they deeply resented their loss of freedom, and easy credit was not as freely available as had been promised. The great estates of the Junkers were virtually unaffected by the *Erbhof* scheme.

Attracted by industrial expansion and higher wages, large numbers of agricultural labourers began to leave the land to seek employment in the freer and more prosperous industrial sector. Between 1933 and 1938 some 800,000 people left the land, showing clearly that agriculture was lagging behind industry and that the Nazi ideology of 'blood and soil', and the attempt to preserve the peasantry as the 'life-source of the Nordic race', was having disastrous economic consequences. Robert Ley was sharply critical of Walter Darré, the minister of agriculture, suggesting that the RNF was at least partially responsible for this flight from the land and proposed that DAF should have sole jurisdiction over agricultural workers. The enthusiasm to create more entailed farms waned considerably, and the relative failure of National Socialist agricultural policy was acknowledged, giving rise to such power struggles within the Nazi elite as that between Darré and Ley. Hitler remained steadfastly committed to his vision of 'blood and soil', insisting that if it could not be realized within the existing boundaries of Germany it might be possible to create vast colonies in eastern Europe. The fundamental drive for *Lebensraum* was thus further reinforced by unresolved political and economic difficulties. The more pragmatic and opportunistic policies adopted towards industry, with the emphasis on a 'defence economy', could not be reconciled with this ideologically motivated agricultural policy. As a result of the conflicting social and economic interests between the two sectors, it was impossible to create the national community of which there was such endless talk. It was therefore hoped that a successful war of conquest would make it possible to overcome all these difficulties by imposing on the conquered territories a 'New Order' in which all these dreams would be realized.

Radical Nazis had always insisted on the implimentation of the sections of the party programme dealing with the destruction of the chain stores, co-operatives and impersonal big business enterprises. In the heady days immediately after Hitler became chancellor, party activists terrorized Jewish businesses, boycotted the department stores and consumer co-operatives and secured far-reaching personnel and organizational changes in trade associations and chambers of commerce. These activities had a disastrous economic effect, and the National Socialist leadership accepted that the long-term goals of the party could not be achieved by rejecting modern business methods. When the Jewish-owned chain of department stores, Hertie, faced bankruptcy and the dismissal of 14,000 employees, Schacht pointed out that if all similar stores were to vanish it would have a serious effect on employment figures. Hitler reluctantly accepted this argument, and the party was instructed to desist from any further attacks on the department stores. In the following years certain restrictions were placed on the department stores such as the closing of restaurants and book departments, and additional taxes were imposed upon them. In spite of these difficulties the department stores steadily increased their turnover, but were never able to reach the record levels of 1928, but this was due more to the general reduction in consumption than to a reduction of their share of total retail sales.

Nothing was done to help small businessmen, even though they had been among the strongest of the party's early supporters. The number of retail stores declined significantly and they were more than ever subject to the monopolistic practices of the manufacturers. The Reich Corporation of Handicraft, which like all similar organizations was soon completely under Nazi control, closed about 180,000 small concerns (about 10% of the total) between 1936 and 1939 in the interests of increased efficiency. The ideological commitment to small business gave way to the prerogatives of economic efficiency, and those who felt cheated by this abandonment of party policy were able to give vent to their spleen by destroying Jewish businesses in 1938. The anti-Semitic outrages of the 'Night of Broken Glass', in which 7,500 shops were destroyed and looted, was thus in part a surrogate for the failure to implement the party programme and a sop to the frustrated radicals. The destruction of 'Jewish capitalism' was a substitute for an attack on those aspects of contemporary capitalism which the Nazi left had for so long wished to see modified or abolished.

The 2 million members of the SA regarded themselves as the 'watchdogs of the revolution', and although they had no clear idea what should be done, they refused to submit to bureaucratic control, demanded the removal of the old elites from positions of power and influence and swore to continue the struggle for the creation of a new and specifically National Socialist Germany. These feelings were summed up in the call for a 'second revolution' which would realize the ambitions of the Nazi left.

The SA had done much to help bring Hitler to power. Their devotion to Hitler was unquestioned, they had done much to destabilize the Weimar Republic by their street fighting and by terrorizing their opponents. They were an impressive testament to the party's strength and determination. When Hitler became chancellor their support was no longer needed and they became a liability. He had distanced himself from revolutionary Nazism and had secured the support of the traditional elites who in turn were appalled by the excesses of the SA both in word and deed.

Ernst Röhm, the leader of the SA, hoped to create a National Socialist army in which the Reichswehr with its reactionary old-fashioned officers would play a subordinate role. As he put it, in a singularly unattractive phrase: 'The grey rock must be drowned in the brown flood'. This was all part of the rhetoric of the radical Nazis who wanted a National Socialist version of a peoples' militia, along with the destruction of chain stores and co-operatives, the abolition of all cartels and monopolies, and a drastic restructuring of banking and industrial corporations.

The Reichswehr was appalled by such talk and Hitler went to great pains to reassure them that the army would be the 'sole bearer of arms in the nation'. Industrialists were similarly concerned by the activities of the SA, but Hitler calmed them down by telling a meeting of Reich Governors in July 1933 that 'The ideas in our programme do not oblige us to act like idiots and overturn every thing.' By contrast, virtually nothing was done to appease the SA. Big business had survived the depression far better than smaller enterprises which were less able to make economies of scale and which found it far more difficult to get credit. Increasing levels of public investment caused interest rates to rise, which further hurt the small businessman, and postponed the day when 'interest slavery' would be abolished. The rise in prices and the wage freeze further exacerbated the situation. On his appointment as minister of economics, Schmitt guaranteed that business would not have to put with any 'interference by the NSDAP'. Coming from the director general of Germany's largest insurance firm this infuriated the Nazi radicals, and the special commission on banking which was established to appease them had the opposite effect. The commission was chaired by Schacht and was made up mainly of bankers and sympathetic academics. Although they did recommend a greater extent of state control of banking, this resulted in even greater profits for the banks.

Similarly the great estates of the Junkers, which were the object of particular criticism by the radicals, were untouched by the law on entailed estates.

Hitler was thus in a tricky situation. He saw the logic of Schacht's dictum that spinning wheels and folk dancing were very nice and pretty, but only big business could produce guns and submarines. But he could not risk an open break with the SA and its supporters, and still had some residual sympathies for their views. For the first few months he did little but issue statements that the revolution was over and that evolution was the order of the day. Goering and Frick hinted at 'concealed bolshevik elements' within the Nazi movement. Steps were taken to punish some of the SA and SS men who had committed criminal acts in their enthusiasm for the cause, and some of the 'irregular' concentration camps into which the SA had herded their enemies in the early weeks of the Hitler's government were closed down.

Hitler took the opportunity of an address to the general staff on the occasion of Schlieffen's birthday on 28 February 1934 to assure the army that he supported them in their opposition to the SA and the radical Nazis. He told the generals that Nazi economic policies had been successful, but added that the boom would be over in eight years. Therefore living space would have to be found in the east. This would be achieved by a lightning campaign in the west followed by a swift strike eastwards. For such a campaign a highly professional army was needed, and Röhm's militia was clearly unsuitable for anything other than providing pre- and post-military training and for political indoctrination.

Hitler felt that he had to move quickly against the SA because it was obvious that Hindenburg did not have long to live and he was determined to combine the offices of chancellor and president. The conservatives and nationalists were still critical of many aspects of the new regime, and there was much talk of restoring the monarchy when Hindenburg died, so as to have some check on National Socialist excesses. On 17 June 1934 von Papen delivered a speech in Marburg in which he attacked the excesses of the Nazis from a conservative perspective. This prompted Hitler into action. Confident that the army supported him, he decided to crush the SA before the conservatives became too disenchanted with his government and became a threat to his position. On 22 June Himmler and the Gestapo chief, Heydrich, called the SS leaders together and told them that they would soon have to work with the Reichswehr to destroy the SA. A fabricated list of the SA's intended victims, which included several prominent generals to encourage the army to support their joint venture, was produced to prove that the SA was planning a putsch. The Reichswehr co-operated closely with the SS in preparing this coup and all the army leaders were kept informed of the plans. The Reichswehr provided the arms and transportation for the SS units, including the SS *Leibstandarte Adolf Hitler* commanded by Sepp Dietrich.

The coup was planned for 30 June 1934 and was primarily directed against the SA leaders who were meeting in Bad Wiesee, but murders took place against sundry opponents of the regime throughout Germany. Among the hundreds killed were the ex-Chancellor Schleicher with his right-hand man, General von Bredow. Two conservative critics of the regime who were associates of von Papen, Edgar Jung and von Bose, were killed, as were Hitler's old rival in Bavaria, von Kahr, and Erich Klausener who was the head of Catholic Action in Berlin. Many old scores were settled, and some unfortunates were shot by mistake.

The coup against Röhm was a triumphant success. Hitler made much of his treachery and his homosexuality and repectable Germans were appalled as the lurid and partly fabricated story unfolded. The army, although two distinguished generals had been brutally murdered, was delighted. Reichswehr Minister von Blomberg extolled the Führer's 'soldierly determination and exemplary courage' in destroying these 'traitors and mutineers' and issued an order that no officer should attend the funeral of their murdered colleagues. Papen congratulated Hitler, but was rewarded by being dismissed from his post as vice chancellor and was sent on a diplomatic mission to Vienna. Germany's leading legal expert, Carl Schmitt, argued that in a state of emergency the 'true leader' could use virtually limitless power to destroy the enemies of the nation. The will of the Führer was thus the supreme law.

After this National Socialist Saint Bartholomew's Night the SA dwindled into insignificance. Röhm's successor, Victor Lutze, was a pliable nonentity and the once powerful organization became little more than a sporting and social club. In the 'Night of Broken Glass' the SA was unleashed once again in a carefully planned pogrom and their vestigial radicalism found an outlet in wilfully destroying property and terrorizing helpless people.

The real winners on 30 June 1934 were not the conservative forces but the SS. This organization was founded in 1925 as Hitler's bodyguard. From the outset it was distinct from the other paramilitary organizations of the time in that it saw itself as a sort of party police. In 1931 Himmler's closest associate, Heydrich, founded the Security Service (*Sicherheitsdienst* – SD) which served as a Nazi secret police force. When Hitler became chancellor, Himmler quickly gained control over the secret police forces of all the German states, with the exception of Prussia. In April 1933 Goering created the Gestapo as the political police force of Prussia and he did not want to hand it over to Himmler. Himmler eventually agreed to serve nominally under Goering in Prussia, and by 1934 amalgamated all the secret police forces of Germany into a single Gestapo which was given the task of 'investigating and countering all activities within the entire territory of the state which endanger the state'. Their activities could not be questioned in the courts, and the Gestapo was thus a law unto itself under the command of Heinrich Himmler. In June 1936 Himmler was made chief of all the police forces in Germany and the police, which had been under the control of the individual states, was now placed under a single Reich authority. Himmler was given the title of *Reichsführer SS* and Chief of the German Police, and henceforth appears in the exotic alphabet soup of the Third Reich as RFSSu.ChdDtPol. As a policeman, Himmler was formally subordinate to Frick in the Ministry of the Interior, but in practice he was fully independent, in spite of the rivalry of the two men.

Himmler divided the police into two main sections: the Order Police (*Ordnungspolizei*) under Daluege which was responsible for more conventional police activities, and the Security Police (*Sicherheitspolizei* – Sipo) under Heydrich, which included the Gestapo and the detective branch (*Kriminalpolizei*). Shortly after the beginning of the war Heydrich amalgamated the Security Police with the SD to form the Head Office of State Security (*Reichssicherheitshauptamt* – RSHA). The definition of 'state security' within the SD was extremely broad for it included institutes of 'race research' as well as one section (II S) devoted to the struggle against homosexuality and abortion. The concentration camps which previously had been run by the SA were now controlled by the SD.

As a gesture of his gratitude for the part they had played on 30 June, Hitler constituted the SS *Leibstandarte Adolf Hitler* as a proper regiment independent from the Reichswehr. Two further regiments were formed shortly afterwards. Hitler permitted further expansion of these SS military units in August 1938. The Army thus found that they had got rid of one rival only to find themselves faced with another. There was fierce rivalry between the army and the SS, the army resisting every move to increase the size of the military units of the SS. The SS denounced the army as reactionary and lukewarm in its National Socialism and hinted that it was planning a putsch. By the end of 1938 there were about 20,000 men in the military and Death's Head units (*Totenkopfverbände*), but during the war the *Waffen-SS* was to become a vast military organization.

The police functions and the military units were two of the main pillars of Himmler's SS empire. A third was provided by the Death's Head units who manned the concentration camps. The SS had considerable experience in running such institutions, for they had set up Dachau in Bavaria as a model camp. After 30 June 1934 all concentration camps were taken over by the SS. The experiences gained at Dachau were now put into practice all over Germany. The chaotic and somewhat random brutality of the SA was now replaced by the systematic and cold-blooded methods of the SS. At the beginning of the war there were about 25,000 prisoners left in German concentration camps, but Death's Head units were ready for the great task that lay ahead of them to purify Europe politically and racially. Millions were to die in this dreadful enterprise, in which the combination of organizational complexity, unbridled brutality and ideological insanity, which was so characteristic of the SS, reached its climax. The firm foundations for the SS state were laid in the years before the war, but it was not until the war began that it became a state within a state and National Socialism's terrible apogee.

On 2 August 1934 Hindenburg died. Hitler promptly combined the offices of chancellor and president and proclaimed himself 'Führer and Chancellor of the Reich'. On the the same day the Reichswehr was obliged to make an oath of allegiance to Hitler personally rather than to the country or its constitution. Ministers were also required to swear a similar oath of loyalty and obedience to Hitler. Leading Nazi jurists proclaimed the end of a state based on the articulation of 'many wills' and its replacement by the single will of the Führer. This 'Führer state' in which Hitler's will was the supreme law resulted in endless confusion, for it was frequently difficult to find out exactly what Hitler wanted. The cabinet seldom met, and many ministers found it virtually impossible to get access to Hitler, especially during the summer when he was at Berchtesgaden. Hitler not infrequently contradicted himself, ministers fought with one another in his absence, and the government divided into those ministers who had easy access to the chancellor and those who were excluded from the magic circle. Hitler tended to ignore the routine of government so that ministers had to carry on the mundane business of the state without his intervention. Ministerial bureaucracies therefore initiated laws without the cabinet or the Führer being involved. The 'Führer state' in this respect meant that Hitler played a less direct role in government than he had done before, and authority was delegated to a much greater extent.

In these changes after Hindenburg's death the authoritarian aspects of the state were of greater significance that the ideologically motivated National Socialist component. The radicals in the SA and the NSBOs had been brutally destroyed or shunted aside. The commissioners, who had imposed the party will on the states, had been given alternative employment, and even the local party bosses, the *Gauleiter*, had far less authority as power was centralized and the federal structure demolished. So many of the party offices were hopelessly amateur and could not be entrusted with the affairs of state. Thus the Foreign Office professionals continued in their traditional role while such party organizations as the Foreign Organization of the NSDAP under Bohle, the Ribbentrop Bureau, Rosenberg's exotic Foreign Policy Office, and Goering's own Research Bureau, along with a host of similar smaller organizations, squabbled with each other and unsuccessfully attempted to influence the course of Germany's foreign policy according to National Socialist principles. The Nazi Party now played a totally subordinate role, and only some outstanding figures such as Himmler, who owed their careers to the party, had any real authority.

The exact relationships between the party and the state, between the reich and the individual states, between the states and the communes, and between the absolutism of the Führer and the traditional organs of government were never clarified. A project of 'Reich reform' was mooted, but Hitler showed no interest in it and it was soon dropped. Frick proposed that the process of the promulgation of laws should be examined, but Hitler preferred to continue to use the Emergency Laws, and he showed a similar lack of enthusiasm for proposals to codify criminal and labour law.

This emphasis on the authoritarian rather then the ideological aspects of the regime between 1934 and 1938 did not mean that the long-term goals of National Socialism had been abandoned. The Catholic Church complained about endless breaches of the Concordat, particularly the attack on Catholic schools after 1935. Nazi policies on compulsory sterilization, abortion and on the treatment of the handicapped met with strong opposition from the Church. In March 1937 the Pope issued the encyclical *Mit brennender Sorge* in which he spoke of the sufferings of the Church in Germany and of the 'battle of annihilation' which was being waged against it.

In the Evangelical Church the 'German Christians' remained utterly loyal to the regime, but the criticisms of the 'Confessing Church' were courageously outspoken. At the Dahlem Synod in October 1934 they spoke of the 'ecclesiastical emergency right' to speak up against the totalitarian regime. The following year the Confessing Christians condemned Nazi philosophy as anti-Christian and false, and suggested that limits were placed on a Christian's obligations to obey the state. The appointment of the Reich Minister for Church Affairs, an old Nazi, Hans Kerrl, did not improve the situation. Part of the Confessing Church agreed to co-operate with the committees he established to examine the problems of the churches, but many refused to have anything to do with the regime. In 1937 some 800 ministers of the Confessing Church were arrested. Had the Nazi regime survived it would undoubtedly have stepped up its attacks on the churches, but with the outbreak of the war it was decided to be a little more tolerant of them in order to avoid anything that might endanger national unity.

In his first few weeks as chancellor it seemed almost as if Hitler had forgotten that anti-Semitism was one of the central doctrines of National Socialism. At this time his energies were directed largely against the left-wing parties which, as part of the 'Jewish-bolshevik world conspiracy', were admittedly doubly sinister. But curiously enough his coalition partners in the DNVP were more enthusiastically *völkisch* in their anti-Semitism. It was they who brought in legislation which stopped the immigration of Jews from eastern Europe, a group that was particularly detested because of their orthodoxy and their poverty. It was not until after the Enabling Act that the Nazis really went into action against the Jews. Goebbels and the odious *Gauleiter* of Nuremberg, Julius Streicher, formed a 'Central Committee' to organize the boycott of all Jewish businesses in Germany. Most Germans treated the whole incident with thoughtless indifference, and the more traditional anti-Semites continued to shop at Jewish stores when prices seemed attractive.

After three days the regime had to call off the boycott. Public reaction had not been as positive as they had hoped, and it had caused an uproar abroad. Discrimination against Jews in the civil service and the professions and the 'arianization' of important publishing houses like Mosse and Ullstein were the most notable examples of the anti-Semitic policies of the government up until the Nuremberg laws. There was not a little opposition to these laws

within the civil service, largely because of the absurd 'racial' classi-
fication system of 'Arians', 'Full Jews' and 'Miscegens' grades 1 and
2, which was based on religious affiliation over three generations.

Until the 'Night of Broken Glass' in November 1938 about
170,000 German Jews emigrated. The remaining 375,000 preferred
to stay, reassured by Hitler that the Nuremberg Laws was the final
piece of legislation that would be passed on the 'Jewish question'.
Henceforth the Jews in Germany were without rights, unable to
practise their professions and trades, stripped of much of their property, subjected to special taxes and forbidden to enter most public
places. Immediately after the pogrom some 30,000 Jews were sent
to concentration camps. The Jewish self-help organization which had
been founded by Leo Baeck (*Reichsvertretung der Juden in Deutschland*)
was brought under direct state control and headed by one of the
most murderous of anti-Semites, Reinhard Heydrich. Its basic
function was now to look after the funds from the emigration tax
which was imposed on wealthy Jews who wished to leave the
country. Those who could afford to do so took advantage of this
scheme, so that by the time the war began there were about 180,000
Jews left in Germany. The vast majority of the victims of the Final
Solution were thus foreign Jews.

In August 1936 the Four Year Plan was announced. More than
ever before economic interests were subordinated to preparations for
war. The aim was now to achieve autarky by building up stocks of
important raw materials and by the synthetic production of others.
This placed a further strain on foreign exchange reserves, and a
furious export drive to South America and to the Balkans was
launched in an attempt to overcome this problem. The resulting
trade rivalry with the United States, Britain and even with Italy
greatly increased international tension.

Although big business still remained relatively autonomous and
profits were still most satisfactory, it was now subjected more than
ever to state control and to the imperatives of Nazi war preparations.
These caused further dislocations, and in November 1937 Schacht
resigned as minister of economics, although he remained as the
president of the Reichsbank until September 1939. Hermann
Goering, as Plenipotentiary for the Four Year Plan, became a *de facto*
minister of economics, although Funk had been appointed to that
post. Goering was torn between his devotion to Hitler's policy of
rearmament and war at virtually any cost, and the advice of his more
conventional subordinates who were in agreement with Schacht that
economic considerations should come first. Thus he harangued the

industrialists in December 1936 that political needs were paramount and that a victorious war would pay for the entire rearmament programme. Yet at other times he appeared to be a moderating influence on Hitler, and to be in favour of a great power policy which would not involve war or fanatical schemes for the New Order.

Hitler had little sympathy for the belief that lengthy preparations for war were necessary, and he also wished to maintain levels of civilian consumption in order to bolster his immense popularity and prestige. This attempt to combine a massive rearmament programme with the maintenance of satisfactory levels of consumption would only be possible by planning for a series of short, limited wars and by avoiding 'armament in depth' for a protracted war of attrition. But even so, the economic crisis persisted, and there was an increasing shortage of manpower. Economic planners began to look at Austria and Czechoslovakia as reservoirs which could be used to overcome the deficiencies of the domestic market, thus lending expert support to Hitler's ideologically inspired desire for territorial expansion.

These economic tensions and contradictions gave rise to signs of unrest among the workers and the rural population. Goebbels' propaganda machine churned out endless material on the need for Germany to improve its defence capability, but workers in the armaments factories refused to work overtime and there was an unusual degree of absenteeism. The extent to which this was a typical consequence of the effects of full employment in an industrial society, or whether it was a specific protest against the Nazis is certainly open to debate, but although the situation in 1939 was hardly one of crisis, considerations of these growing social tensions may well have contributed to the decision to go to war in September 1939. Yet here again there is a curious paradox. Hitler never tired of claiming that Germany was a 'people without space', yet chronic labour shortages, particularly in the armaments industries, showed that it was in fact a 'space without people'.

Schacht complained bitterly as president of the Reichsbank about the unbridled spending of public money, and pointed out that the deficit had risen from 12.9 billion marks in 1933 to 31.5 billion in 1938. The printing press was once again used to finance the ever increasing expenditures, but the resulting inflation convinced many that the country faced a choice between war and bankruptcy. The attempt to rearm in defiance of economic reason threatened to undermine the much-trumpeted Community of the People, and a regime which depended on success to keep it going was threatened with failure unless it dared to leap into the unknown of war.

It was hoped that indoctrination could overcome some of these difficulties. Goebbels made skilful use of the radio, which was already under state control, to get vast audiences for important speeches by party leaders. 'People's radios', the VE 301s (*Volksemfänger* followed by the date of Hitler's accession to power) were introduced in August 1933. In that year only 25 per cent of households had radio sets, but by 1939 it increased to 70 per cent.

It was somewhat more difficult to achieve a monopoly control of Germany's 3,400 daily newspapers. There was a party newspaper, the *Völkische Beobachter*, and a small newspaper was produced in each *Gau*, but these local papers were of very poor quality. The sizeable communist and social democratic press was confiscated in 1933. In the following years the Nazi press chief, Max Amann, took over a large number of newspapers, so that by 1939 two-thirds of the daily newspapers were controlled by the party. The liberal *Frankfurter Zeitung* was the only newspaper of note which was untouched, partly because it enjoyed a considerable reputation abroad, and partly because IG Farben was the majority shareholder. It was also absorbed just before the outbreak of the war.

As was typical of the Third Reich, there were three bodies responsible for the press and there was frequent friction between them. Goebbels as propaganda minister claimed responsibility for the content of the German press and had a considerable say in personnel questions. Max Amann directly controlled the press and was responsible for the business side, and although he was not particularly concerned with the content of his newspapers there were some conflicts between him and Goebbels. The propaganda minister's greatest rival, however, was not Amann but the 'Press Chief of the Reich Government', Otto Dietrich, who acted as spokesman for the government and who was part of Hitler's immediate entourage. His press conferences, which amounted to little more than a series of instructions to the press on what to print, were seen by the minister of propaganda as an encroachment on his prerogatives.

A tremendous effort was made to indoctrinate German youth with National Socialist ideas. The Hitler Youth (HJ), which was established in 1933, became compulsory by 1936. The equivalent organization for girls was the League of German Girls (BdM). Compulsory labour in the RAD, which later also included girls, became increasingly a propaganda institution, for unemployment had long since been overcome. All these institutions were designed to break down class and educational differences and to create a sense of common purpose based on ideological and racial purity. The strongly anti-intellectual bias of this enterprise can most clearly be seen in the special Nazi schools (*Ordensburgen*) and Adolf Hitler Schools with their emphasis on unquestioning obedience and blind faith in the cause.

These institutions did much to obscure the enduring class divisions within German society. There were opportunities within the vast state apparatus for those who had been largely excluded in the Wilhelmine Empire and even under Weimar. Thus the landed aristocracy was not quite as powerful as it had been, but it was still a privileged elite. Small inefficient firms were closed down, but big business, for all the restrictions and controls placed upon it, was fundamentally untouched. If there was a 'social revolution' in Germany it came with the total defeat of 1945, and was largely the work of the red Army, not of the National Socialists.

Although fundamentally in agreement with the aims of the Nazi regime, the army tried to preserve a degree of independence. The officer corps was unsympathetic to the attempt by the Nazis to have an absolute monopoly over the ideological training of German youth. Relations between the army and the SS were becoming increasingly strained. The army felt menaced by the activities of the Gestapo and the SD and disliked the radicalism of their great rivals. The SS felt that the army was stuffy, conservative, snobbish and reactionary. There was also some concern in the upper echelons of the army that Hitler was prepared to risk a war before the country was adequately prepared.

The attack on the army leadership was mounted by Himmler, Heydrich and Goering, all of whom had their reasons for revenge. Goering resented the army for opposing the expansion of his Luftwaffe and had ambitions to become commander-in-chief of the armed forces. Himmler and Heydrich were determined to increase the armed units of the SS and to challenge the conservative army's position as the sole bearer of arms in the Third Reich. Hitler dismissed the war minister, von Blomberg, who had unwittingly married a woman who had once posed for pornographic photographs, the file on this delicate matter having been carefully prepared by Himmler and Goering. They also secured the resignation of von Fritsch, the commander-in-chief of the army, by fabricating evidence that he was a homosexual.

Hitler now assumed direct control of the armed forces. General Keitel, a subservient bureaucrat, was appointed to head a new organization, the High Command of the Armed Forces (OKW). Von Brauchitsch was appointed to the High Command of the Army (OKH). Although not a party man like Reichenau, who was Hitler's first choice, he was a pliable subordinate with a fanatically Nazi wife. He was thus acceptable both to the army and to Hitler. The result of this reorganization was further confusion at the top, with endless duplication of work and lack of co-ordination between OKW, OKH and the staffs of the Luftwaffe and navy. Hitler always got his way, but it was not an efficient and harmonious command structure.

The army which had accepted the murder of Schleicher and Bredow was in no mood to defend the unfortunate Fritsch. The younger officers tended to identify with the regime. Most of the generals seemed to be mesmerized by Hitler, or terrified that if they criticized him their careers would be ruined. In August 1938 the chief of the general staff of the army, Ludwig Beck, resigned in protest at Hitler's warlike policies and Brauchitsch's refusal to stand up against the Führer, even though he had said that a war would mean the end of German culture. He was replaced by Franz Halder, a brilliant and witty staff officer but a man who was incapable of standing up to Hitler.

A similar reshuffle took place in the Foreign Ministry. Von Neurath, a career diplomat of impeccably conservative views, was replaced in February 1938 by von Ribbentrop, whose diplomatic skills as Ambassador in London had earned him the nick-name 'von Brickendrop'. Although Hitler had made all the major decisions in foreign policy without consulting the Foreign Ministry, he wanted to remove any possible opposition to his increasingly aggressive policy.

Thus from 1936 the country was reorganized to prepare for war and to further strengthen the dictatorship. The Four Year plan of 1936 brought industry under the control of the state and the rearmament programme was stepped up. In 1938 the military High Command was reorganized and the Foreign Ministry brought under tighter control, being placed in the hands of one of Hitler's most fanatical followers. The pogrom of November 1938 showed that racialist terror was not simply a sop to radical Nazis, or an unfortunate side-effect of the seizure of power, but an integral part of 'mature' Nazism. By the end of 1938 the way to war and mass murder was wide open as Hitler prepared to realize his dream of a racially pure Europe, subordinated to Germany and controlled by a National Socialist elite. Thus *Lebensraum* and the racist utopia were inseparable in Hitler's mind, and it is this above all which distinguishes his radical brand of revisionism from that of the Weimar Republic.

CHAPTER TWELVE
The Origins of the Second World War

On 7 March 1936 Hitler informed the governments of France, Britain and Belgium that he considered that the Franco-Soviet Pact, which was signed on 2 May and ratified by the French Chamber of Deputies on 27 February, was a violation of the Treaty of Locarno and that he had ordered German troops to occupy the Rhineland. Hitler would hardly have risked this move if the Stresa front had not collapsed during the Abyssinian war. Italy was isolated, was beginning to feel the effects of the sanctions and sought rapprochement with the other great revisionist powers. On 7 January Mussolini informed the German ambassador that he greatly appreciated Germany's benevolent neutrality over Abyssinia and that he had no objections to Austria becoming a German satellite provided that there was a fundamental improvement of German–Italian relations. At the end of February Mussolini told the Germans that he would not side with Britain if Germany chose to violate the Locarno Treaty, even though he did not know exactly what Hitler had in mind.

Mussolini's change of sides in 1936 is still something of a mystery. The Germans were still sending arms to Abyssinia and wanted to prolong the war so as to divert Britain and France's attention away from Europe. Once the war was over the Stresa front could almost certainly have been revived and Abyssinia need not have caused a fundamental realignment of Italian foreign policy. It would seem therefore that Mussolini acted largely out of pique at Britain and France's efforts to negotiate a settlement and their half-hearted support of sanctions, and saw Germany as a dynamic and forceful power which was prepared to stand up against what appeared to him to be two feeble and declining states.

The French would not respond to Hitler's move without a British guarantee of support and Eden would not to take any action without full consultation. Negotiations between Britain, France and Belgium were inconclusive. Staff talks on the appropriate response to a German attack on France and Belgium resulted in Britain promising to send two divisions to France in the event of war. Although this hardly affected the military balance, it was Britain's first commitment to the defence of continental Europe since the war. The Council of the League met in London and condemned Germany's violation of the treaty. Hitler's cynical response was to suggest a new western non-aggression pact, a demilitarized zone on both sides of the Rhine and Germany's return to the League.

Hitler's move was generally approved by the right in Britain and France, for they disliked the Franco-Soviet pact and felt that Hitler had a right to do what he wanted in his own back garden. Hitler was quick to exploit this situation by unleashing a massive anti-communist campaign in the summer and by signing the Anti-Comintern Pact with Japan in November. Most important of all, on 25 July he agreed to Franco's request to intervene on behalf of the rebels in Spain. His motives were almost entirely political and strategic, for he was determined that Spain should not become part of the Franco-Soviet anti-German bloc and thus seriously weaken Germany's position in the event of war in the east. That such thoughts were uppermost in Hitler's mind can be seen in his memorandum on the Four Year Plan of 1936, which marked the beginning of the intensified rearmament programme, in which he reaffirmed his absolute conviction that war between Germany and the Soviet Union was inevitable. German intervention in Spain must be seen in the context of this anti-Soviet policy and the vigorous economic activity of the Germans in Spain was a result and not the cause of this decision, as was the testing of military equipment, the positive results of which should not be exaggerated.

The reoccupation of the Rhineland was accompanied by a large-scale programme of fortification which meant that France was even less likely to invade Germany in support of its allies in eastern Europe. Poland and Czechoslovakia had expressed their determination to stand by France when Hitler marched into the Rhineland, and were stunned when France did nothing. The system of alliances was further weakened when Austria, pushed by the Italians, signed an agreement with Germany in July by which the Germans promised to respect Austria's sovereignty and the Austrians announced that they were a 'German state'. Finally, the Belgians, fearing that

Locarno was more of a menace to their security than a guarantee and feeling that the Franco-Soviet pact made war with Germany more likely, announced that they were now neutral. Britain and France both expressed their determination to defend Belgium against upro-voked aggression, but this did not disguise the fact that the Western Pact was in ruins. The French could not afford to extend the Maginot Line to the Channel and it was an open question whether the Belgians would ask for help if the Germans attacked. Politicians who favoured military talks with the Soviet Union as a means of overcoming this weakness were stalled by the General Staff in Britain and France. The British government was strongly opposed to any such discussions and asked the French to desist.

The Spanish Civil War did much to confirm political prejudices, create new suspicions and realign the European alliances. Hitler and Mussolini were confirmed in their view that France would never move without British support and that the British would always prefer compromise to confrontation. Stalin looked at Britain and France's feeble response to Germany and Italy's intervention in Spain and began to have second thoughts about collective security. If the western democracies could not be trusted to stand up to the dictators would it perhaps be prudent to come to terms with them? In both Britain and France the Soviets' motives in Spain were regarded with suspicion, the murderous activities of the NKVD and the OGPU were seen as an extension of the brutal show trials in Moscow, and they were only saved from total condemnation by the civilized world by the spectacular brutality of the nationalists, particularly the bombing of Guernica, which was exploited by brilliant propaganda. The Soviets also enjoyed the skilfully manipulated endorsement of their policies by countless gullible intellectuals. French opponents of their own popular front, with their slogan 'better Hitler than Blum', found the Spanish version of left unity even more distasteful and felt that the fascist powers were distinctly preferable. The left shared this view that the fight over fascism would be won or lost in Spain, not in Germany or Italy. When it was lost their boundless enthusiasm gave way to a resigned pessimism which sapped their will to fight the dictators. Others combined an unfortunate combination of revul-sion against fascism with a passionate belief in pacifism. Even the conviction that fascism had to be stopped in Spain was probably mistaken. A republican Spain dominated by the communists might well have pushed the British to reach an agreement with Hitler, the champion of anti-communism, and France could well have joined such an alliance. Perhaps most important of all Spain was a frightening portent of the war to come. It was widely felt that the 'bomber always gets through' and that London and Paris would go the way of Guernica. It was also generally accepted that the Civil War and the fresh round of Japanese hostilities in China in July 1937 were incontrovertible evidence that the next war would be long and bloody and therefore should be avoided at all costs. Far from strengthening the determination to resist the dictators, the Spanish Civil War strengthened the convictions of the appeasers that war was the greatest imaginable disaster. In France fear of Germany was also coupled with fear of war, so that some sort of an agreement with Germany, probably at the expense of eastern Europe, seemed increasingly desirable.

Neville Chamberlain, who was appointed prime minister in May 1937, felt that appeasement was an urgent necessity and he followed this policy with a single-minded determination lacking in any of his predecessors. War had to be avoided at all costs because he believed that the money should be spent on social welfare programmes rather than armaments, and he felt that if his ambitious vision of Tory democracy was not realized the Labour Party was likely to win the next election. He strongly disliked the Soviet Union, had no faith in the French and believed that the United States was unshakably isolationist. The service chiefs warned him that Britain was in no position to fight Germany, Italy and Japan, thus confirming his own fears which were intensified when Italy joined the Anti-Comintern Pact in September 1937. He was not prepared to appease Japan, but this made it even more desirable to come to terms with Germany and Italy. Chamberlain prided himself on being a pragmatist and imagined that Hitler and Mussolini were at heart equally practical men with whom it was possible to negotiate in good faith. This belief in himself as a practical man was combined with a strong sense of mission resulting in a rigidity, an inability to adjust to unpleasant facts and a narrowness of vision which in the end proved disastrous. Hitler was able to exploit these weaknesses to the full to win a series of cheap victories which in turn stimulated his lust for further triumphs.

1937 was a year of uncertainty and foreboding. Stalin continued the mass murder of his myrmidons and decimated the officer corps. France rejected the Popular Front and Chautemps and Daladier were determined to reach a *détente* with the fascists as part of a plan to extirpate the left and win the approval of the propertied classes. Italy demanded a share of the control of the Suez Canal, laid claim to Tunis and complained stridently of British rearmament and Eden's refusal to reach an agreement. Eden found himself arguing with Chamberlain over whether to negotiate with Mussolini or whether to do nothing but express moderate disapproval of Italy's activities in Spain. This rather trivial dispute led to Eden's resignation in February 1938. The Germans and Italians fondly imagined that they had hounded him out of office and Eden won an undeserved reputation as a strong man and a principled opponent of appeasement. Hitler told the German people that his 'Germanic Reich' was a bulwark against bolshevism and Jewry and in November told pupils at a special Nazi training centre (*Ordensburg*) that he intended to create a nation in arms to secure *Lebensraum* in the east.

Hitler had already discussed these ideas on 5 November 1937 with von Neurath, the foreign minister, the war minister, Blomberg, and the service chiefs. The record of this conference, which was used as a key prosecution document at the Nuremberg trials, was kept by Colonel Hossbach from memory, and the document which survives is a copy of a copy; but there is no serious reason to doubt its accuracy for it accords with many similar remarks made by Hitler at that time. He was clearly growing impatient with Blomberg and Neurath, representatives of the conservative old guard who were soon to be replaced, and treated them to a long tirade on the need for conquest in the east, a crusade against bolshevism, the role of force in politics, the enmity of Germany's two 'hate inspired antagonists', France and Britain, and the need for him to play the role of a Frederick the Great or a Bismarck. The problem of finding space for the German 'racial community' would have to be solved by 1943–45 otherwise the strain on the economy would be too great, the armed forces would become obsolete and the Nazi movement might lose its vitality. Hitler then insisted that if France faced a severe domestic crisis or went to war with Italy, Czechoslovakia and Austria should be seized to protect Germany's flank, but both countries could probably be invaded even without such eventualities. Hossbach minuted that 'the Führer believed that almost certainly Britain, and probably France as well, had already tacitly written off the Czechs and were reconciled to the fact that this question would be cleared up in due course by Germany'. He added that Italy would not object to the annexation of Czechoslovakia and that if the Duce was still alive there would be no problems about an *Anschluss* with Austria. Poland and Russia were unlikely to intervene if the campaign was swift and decisive. Blomberg and Fritsch urged caution, stressing the strength of the French army and the impressive fortifications in Czechoslovakia and Neurath argued that a war between France and Italy was not as likely as Hitler seemed to think. Hitler replied that he expected a conflict in the summer of 1938.

The change of emphasis in German planning as a result of this conference can be clearly seen in Jodl's amendments to 'Operation Green', the plan for an attack on Czechoslovakia, dated 7 December 1937. The document, signed by Blomberg and issued to the armed forces, stated that: 'When Germany has achieved complete preparedness for war in all spheres, then the military conditions will have been created for carrying out an offensive war against Czechoslovakia, so that the solution of the German problem of living space can be carried to a victorious conclusion even if one or another of the Great Powers intervene against us.' If France and Italy went to war then 'Operation Green' could be mounted without Germany first being fully prepared. This offensive strategy was now given absolute priority over 'Plan Red' which was designed to counter a French attack while going on the defensive in the east.

In November Halifax visited Hitler at the Berghof and assured him that the British government had no objections to Germany's revisionist ambitions towards Austria, Czechoslovakia and Danzig provided that they could be settled without 'far-reaching disturbances', by which he meant a war. In return he asked Hitler to guarantee a permanent peace settlement. Hitler, who planned to annexe the whole of Czechoslovakia, would make no such undertaking and wanted nothing less than that Britain should give him a free hand in the east. This was much further than the Chamberlain government was prepared to go and Hitler began to listen more attentively to Ribbentrop's arguments that an agreement with Britain was impossible and that Germany should therefore build up an anti-British front with Japan and Italy. Hitler was still convinced that an agreement with Britain was the most desirable solution and he did not entirely give up the hope that this might be achieved. In the course of Anglo-French conversations in London, held immediately after Halifax's visit to Germany, Eden asked the French to persuade the Czechs to 'demonstrate their good will' towards Germany and Chamberlain would not give any assurance that the British would do anything to support the French guarantee if Germany invaded Czechoslovakia.

The more aggressive nature of German foreign policy was underlined by a series of personnel changes which took place at this time. In November 1937 Schacht, who was opposed to the pace of rearmament and the emphasis on autarky at almost any price, was replaced as minister of economic affairs. In January and February

Blomberg and Fritsch were dismissed, Hitler becoming minister of war, Keitel made chief of the armed forces high command (OKW) and Brauchitsch appointed chief of the army high command (OKH). Ribbentrop returned from the German embassy in London to become foreign minister. All these moves strengthened Hitler's position by giving him personal command over the armed forces; they also virtually ended the disagreements at the top over major policy issues, and there was little discussion of how these decisions were to be implemented.

Austria was now the first item on the foreign policy agenda, although as late as December 1937 Hitler was still opposed to the idea of an invasion. But he was pressed by Ribbentrop and Goering while the Austrian Nazis were straining at the leash. At the end of January 1938 the Austrian police discovered evidence of a Nazi plot to murder the German ambassador, von Papen, and to provoke such a degree of repression that the Germans would be obliged to intervene. Papen persuaded the Austrian chancellor, Schuschnigg, to visit Hitler at the Obersalzberg in Bavaria. Schuschnigg told one of his associates that a psychiatrist would make a more suitable visitor but, encouraged by the invitation, began to make some significant concessions to the Nazis, appointing them to the Council of State, ending discrimination against 'moderates' in the party and promising to improve relations with the Reich. Hitler, encouraged by such obvious signs of weakness, agreed to talk to Schuschnigg.

The meeting took place on 12 February. Schuschnigg was treated to an extraordinary performance by Hitler who modestly described himself as 'perhaps the greatest German in all of history' and surrounded by his generals for maximum effect gave the unfortunate Austrian a couple of hours to accept an agreement whereby the Nazis would enter the government and be given the ministry of the interior. Schuschnigg lamely protested that he could not act on behalf of the president, but he signed a protocol and was given three days to deliver a signed agreement.

Schuschnigg did little to win support for Austrian independence in Britain and France and let it be known that he did not want anything to be done which might provoke Hitler. The French felt powerless, the British ambassador in Berlin, Henderson, implied that his government would not object to an *Anschluss*. Hitler hoped that further concessions could be wrung from the Austrians without armed intervention and told his impatient followers in Austria that he wanted the 'evolutionary course to be taken'. Schuschnigg's announcement on 9 March that there would be a plebiscite for 'a free, German, independent, social, Christian and united Austria' with the voting age raised to twenty-four so as to exclude a large number of youthful Nazi sympathizers prompted him into immediate action. Hitler was almost hysterical with rage when he heard of this move and, convinced that the plebiscite would result in a major victory for Schuschnigg, ordered the military to prepare for an invasion, although he still hoped that violence could be avoided. Seyss-Inquart, the Austrian Nazi minister of the interior, was ordered by Hitler to resign if Schuschnigg would not call off the plebiscite. When the chancellor gave way under this pressure Seyss-Inquart was then ordered to demand Schuschnigg's resignation and his own appointment as chancellor. Schuschnigg appealed to Britain and France for help, but none was forthcoming and he resigned. President Miklas refused to appoint Seyss-Inquart in his place and on 11 March Hitler ordered the invasion of Austria. In the course of that night Miklas capitulated, but it was now too late to stop the invasion. Goering provided the pretext by dictating a letter on behalf of Seyss-Inquart asking the German government for help. The German government had been informed that neither Britain nor Italy would support Austria and that France, which was without a government during the Austrian crisis, was less likely than ever to move without British backing. Schuschnigg, who stayed on as a caretaker chancellor, broadcast to the nation on the evening of the 11th announcing that the army would not resist and that Austria was giving way to force.

The hastily improvised invasion, which began in the early morning of the 12th was bloodless. The German troops were enthusiastically welcomed by the Austrian people and on the 13th Hitler returned in triumph to Vienna. While Nazi thugs terrorized their opponents and looted their property Hitler decided to reduce Austria to a province of the Reich and even its name disappeared to be replaced by the unattractive appellation 'Ostmark'. In a further plebiscite 99 per cent of those voting supported Hitler's revenge on his native country. This cheap and spectacular victory silenced the critics of Hitler's change of course and of personnel in the previous months, particularly in the armed forces, and was a triumph for Goering who had goaded the hesitant Hitler into action.

The *Anschluss* made Czechoslovakia extremely vulnerable to German economic pressure and to attack from the dangerously exposed southern flank. In a crisis the 2 million Slovaks, 750,000 Hungarians, 90,000 Poles, and 500,000 Ruthenes would welcome the opportunity to overthrow the existing order. Most dangerous of all were the three and a quarter million Sudeten Germans. Nazi propagandists had been skilful at fanning the economic discontents and the feelings of cultural superiority of the Germans in Czechoslovakia and from 1935 Konrad Henlein's Sudeten German Party was generously financed by Berlin. The *Anschluss* triggered off such a frenzy of enthusiasm for the return of the Sudetenland to the Reich that the German foreign office felt obliged to advise the Sudeten German Party to moderate their demands. On 28 March 1938 Hitler received Henlein and told him to keep making demands which were unacceptable to the Czech government, assurring him that he would settle the Sudeten German problem in the not-too-distant future and that he had complete confidence in him as the future governor (*Stadthalter*). The Czech government, who began a fresh round of negotiations with the Sudeten Germans, acted on two false assumptions. The first was that the Germans genuinely wanted a solution to the outstanding problems, the second that French and the British would stand by them if it came to a crisis.

Any assurances that Chamberlain might have given to the Czechs, such as the prime minister's speech in the House of Commons on 24 March, were so hedged about by conditions to be worthless and it was made plain that Britain's vital interests were not at stake in Czechoslovakia. Privately he announced that there was nothing that the British could do to save Czechoslovakia, a view that was strongly endorsed by the service chiefs. This being so, the Czech government should be persuaded to give way to German demands and the British minister in Prague, referring to Czechoslovakia as if it were a terminally sick dog, reported that 'it would be no kindness in the long run' to preserve the country in its present state. The prime minister let Canadian and American journalists know that he did not object to Germany grabbing the Sudetenland and refused to deny this story when questioned in the House.

Léon Blum's second government seemed willing to honour the commitments to Czechoslovakia and to encourage Britain to stand firm, but it got no encouragement from the military and it soon fell from office. His successor, Daladier, had no intention of defending Czechoslovakia and his foreign minister, Bonnet, began frantically looking for ways to avoid the obligations of the 1925 treaty. Daladier was delighted when the British provided him with ample excuses not to act and thus to rescue him 'from the cruel dilemma of dishonouring her agreements or becoming involved in war'. For domestic political reasons he could not afford to appear to betray Czechoslovakia, but he would not risk war with Germany without

British support, and Britain was only obliged under Locarno to fight alongside France if Germany attacked in the west. His aim was therefore twofold: not to appear solely responsible for Czechoslovakia's plight and also to get a firm commitment from Britain. At the same time he was basically sympathetic to the German complaints about Czechoslovakia and agreed with the view that the country was too prone to Jewish and bolshevik influence.

Czechoslovakia could also expect no help from the Soviet Union. The treaty of 1935 between the two countries only obliged the Soviet Union to go to Czechoslovakia's aid if the French moved first. Neither Poland nor Romania would tolerate Russian troops on their territory and thus even if the French acted the Russians would have been unable to offer any direct assistance. The British government was appalled at the thought of the Soviets becoming involved in Czechoslovakia and the French, particularly in military circles, had a similarly low opinion of Soviet intentions and belittled their military effectiveness.

Hitler therefore had every reason to believe that France and Britain would not stand by Czechoslovakia if he were to provoke a crisis over the Sudetenland. During his visit to Rome in April he was assured by Mussolini of his full support, although the attempt in early May to form a military alliance with Italy failed. Sure of their benevolent neutrality, Hitler decided to tighten the screws without the Italians becoming directly involved. On 19 May there were provocative German troop movements along the Czech frontier. The following day the Czechs mobilized, fearing that the German were about to attack. Bonnet warned the Germans that France would provide Czechoslovakia with 'the utmost help' if they attacked, and the British, although alarmed that the French were exacerbating the situation, warned that they might not be able to stand aside. Hitler was furious at this response and felt that he might appear to have backed off in the face of such threats. On 28 May he told a group of military, state and party dignitaries that Czechoslovakia would have to disappear as the first step towards an attack on the west. Convinced from their reactions to the Czech crisis that the British would eventually go to war with Germany he ordered a massive naval programme, to be known as the Z-Plan, to be set in train. On 30 May a further revision to 'Plan Green' proclaimed the Führer's 'unalterable intention to smash Czechoslovakia by military action in the near future'.

Meanwhile the French government, urged constantly by London, began a hasty retreat, warning the Czechs not to continue their mobilization and telling the British that they might not stand by the treaty if the Czechs were 'unreasonable'. Daladier told the German ambassador that he was unhappy about the Czech alliance and later implied that he had no intention of honouring it. The British government felt that although Hitler had behaved badly the Czechs should be encouraged to come to terms with him and appeared almost to cringe before the Germans, Halifax even suggesting how nice it would be if the Führer were to visit Buckingham Palace. In Berlin the odious Henderson complained about the pigheaded Czechs, told the Germans that Britain would not risk one life for such an unreasonable country and acted as a willing conduit for Nazi propaganda on the justice of their cause.

Throughout the summer of 1938 the tension between Czechs and Germans in the Sudetenland grew more intense. The British decided that an impartial mediator could settle the crisis and, the British ambassador in Prague having headed off the patronizing suggestion of sending an 'ex-governor of an Indian Province', suggested Lord Runciman, the Liberal leader and a former president of the Board of Trade who was known as a heartless opponent of strikes rather than as a conciliator. President Benes was insulted by this proposal and horrified at the choice of Runciman but had no choice but to give way, sending a request couched in words that made it appear that it was a purely Czech initiative. No one was deceived by this palpable deception, nor by the British government's assertion that Runciman was a completely independent observer.

Runciman went to Czechoslovakia at the end of July, his hatred of that 'accursed country' heightened by troublesome bouts of insomnia. He enjoyed the lavish entertainment provided by German landowners and came to the conclusion that 'Czechoslovakian rule in the Sudeten areas for the last twenty years has been marked by tactlessness, intolerance and discrimination'. On his return to England he told the Cabinet that he had no solutions for the Czech problem, but four days later he presented his report which supported Chamberlain's promise to Hitler that the Sudetenland should be separated from Czechoslovakia. This would mean that 1 million Czechs, Jews and anti-fascist Germans would be transferred to the Reich.

At the beginning of September 1938 Basil Newton, the British ambassador in Prague, told Benes that his government would support Henlein's demand for a Sudeten German parliament. The *New Statesman* and *The Times*, for once in complete agreement, went further than this and called for self determination. Four days after he received this note from the ambassador, Benes announced that he would accept the Sudeten German request. Henlein was terrified that this might end the crisis and therefore provoked a series of incidents, including violence against Jews, which led to negotiations being broken off and martial law being imposed. Hitler did his part by whipping up the crowds at the Nuremberg rally into frenzied support of their persecuted racial brethren in Czechoslovakia. On 15 September Henlein fled to Germany with grim tales of brutal repression of the Sudeten Germans and announced, with blissful disregard for the fact that the area had never been part of Germany, that his followers' greatest wish was for the Sudetenland to return to the Reich. Chamberlain reacted to these events by informing Berlin on 13 September, without first consulting the French, that he wished to discuss the Czech problem with Hitler. Many saw this as a statesmanlike gesture by a man determined to save Europe from war. Mussolini was one of the few who thought that it would save the peace but would also be the end of British prestige.

Chamberlain visited Hitler at the Berghof on 15 September. His private talk with Hitler lasted for three hours with only Hitler's interpreter, Dr Paul Schmidt, as a witness. Hitler launched into a lengthy tirade about Czech atrocities against the hapless Sudeten German and the sorry fate of thousands of refugees and announced that he would risk a world war to bring the Sudetenland back into the Reich. Chamberlain agreed to Hitler's demands in principle, protesting rather lamely about his threat to use force, and said that he would have to consult his Cabinet colleagues, Runciman and the French. No mention was made of the unfortunate Czechs and Hitler agreed not to use force for the moment, but made no commitments that would have changed his deadline of 30 September for a military solution.

Chamberlain had little difficulty in getting the Cabinet to accept the German demand to annexe the Sudetenland, although some junior ministers protested. Runciman's report was carefully tailored to support Chamberlain's arguments. On 18 September Daladier and Bonnet came to London and were brought into line. Daladier expressed the fear that Hitler's real aim was the destruction of Czechoslovakia and a war of conquest in the east and asked Britain to join in a guarantee of what was left of Czechoslovakia when Hitler had wreaked his will. Chamberlain, who had argued that Hitler was a man whose word could be trusted, was trapped by his own argument and agreed. Thus the British government, which had resolutely refused to guarantee Czechoslovakia when it had the formidable defences of the Sudetenland, now agreed to stand by an enfeebled and defenceless country.

On 19 September Benes was told by the British and French governments to hand over those parts of the Sudetenland where the Germans were in a majority. The following day he rejected this note, having been informed by the Soviet Union that they would stand by their guarantee, although the Soviets were covered by the stipulation that they only had to act in co-operation with the French. The British and French ambassadors discussed the situation with the Czech premier, Hodza, who was anxious to negotiate a settlement, and Benes was told that he would not be able to count on British or French support. On 21 September Benes changed his mind and gave way, and the following day Hodza's government resigned, making way for a Government of National Concentration under General Syrovy.

On 22 September Chamberlain met Hitler again at Bad Godesberg only to be told that his solution was unacceptable and that the Sudetenland would have to be immediately occupied by the German army. Plebiscites would then be held in as yet undefined areas, and the claims of Poland and Hungary on Czechoslovakia would have to be respected. Chamberlain protested at this ultimatum and decried the threat of force. Hitler solemnly declared that this was his last territorial demand, adding somewhat threateningly 'in Europe'. The meeting ended in what appeared to be a deadlock, and the prime minister returned to London.

Chamberlain was in favour of accepting Hitler's demands, but public opinion was beginning to demand a firm stand against this attempt to destroy a decent little democracy. Trenches were dug in London parks, anti-aircraft guns were placed in some strategic points and 38 million gas masks prepared for distribution. At the Foreign Office Cadogan persuaded Halifax to stand up to the prime minister who eventually decided to send Sir Horace Wilson to see Hitler.

In Berlin on 26 September Wilson was treated to a demonic tirade from Hitler who swore he would destroy Czechoslovakia and that any further talk was useless. That evening Hitler repeated his ultimatum to the Czechs in a speech to an enraptured audience at the *Sportpalast* which even *The Times* described as 'rather offensive'. Wilson saw the Führer the following day who told him that Britain and France could go to war with Germany over Czechoslovakia if that was what they wished. Wilson undid any effect his threats might have had by promising to 'try and make those Czechos sensible'. On his return to London Wilson proposed that the Czechs should immediately evacuate those areas where the Germans were in a majority and on 27 September Chamberlain sent a message to Benes warning him that there was nothing Britain and France could do to help. That evening he broadcast to the nation insisting that this 'quarrel in a far away country between people of whom we know nothing' was not a matter over which the British Empire was prepared to go to war.

On 28 September Chamberlain addressed the House of Commons giving a lengthy and dreary account of the negotiations. In the middle of the speech he was handed a note which informed him that Hitler had agreed to a four-power conference at Munich, a proposal put to him by Mussolini at Chamberlain's prompting. The House cheered wildly at the news that at the last moment war had been avoided. Very few members did not share this sense of relief, among them Churchill, Eden, and Amery but only Gallagher, a communist, spoke up against Chamberlain's acceptance of the invitation.

The conference began the following day at the Nazi headquarters, the Brown House. Hitler travelled to Munich with Mussolini, who had accepted a set of proposals drafted by the German Foreign Office, which he was to put forward on his own in his implausible role as impartial mediator. Hitler told him that sooner or later they would have to fight Britain and France, and that they might as well do it whilst they were still young, but his opponents were not in a warlike mood. Chamberlain and Daladier had left their foreign ministers at home and their feeble objections were ignored by Hitler and Mussolini. An agreement was signed in the early morning of 30 September by which the Germans were to occupy the Sudeten-land between 1 and 10 October and the four powers were to be joined by Czechoslovakia to form a commission which was to supervise the takeover. When the Polish and Hungarian claims had been settled the rump state of Czechoslovakia was to be guaranteed by the four powers. Later that day Chamberlain, without consulting the French, signed an agreement with Hitler that their countries would never go to war again and would consult one another over any matters of mutual concern. Benes, fearing that his country might well be plunged into civil war and with only the Soviet Union as an ally, had no alternative but to accept the Munich ultimatum and on 4 October he resigned.

Chamberlain returned to London in triumph, waving the Anglo-German agreement at the delighted crowd and later comparing himself to Disraeli and the Treaty of Berlin in 1878 when he said: 'This is the second time that there has come back from Germany to

Downing Street peace with honour. I believe it is peace for our time.' The vast majority of the British public was grateful that war had been avoided, but many were uneasy that Hitler had gained his victory by the threat of force. The press was far from unanimous in support of the government. The *Daily Worker* and *Reynolds' News* were strongly critical, but so were the *Manchester Guardian*, the *News Chronicle*, and the *Daily Herald*. On the right the *Daily Telegraph* shared the general relief that war had been avoided, but also argued that the government should have taken a far firmer stand against Hitler's excessive demands. Some Conservatives abstained from voting for the Munich agreement, but there was only one resignation, by Duff Cooper, the First Lord of the Admiralty, who felt that Britain should have gone to war. The French were equally enthusiastic about Munich and Daladier's welcome home was as rapturous as Chamberlain's. This public response in both Britain and France was due in part to relief that war had been averted, satisfaction that honour had been satisfied and the conviction that Germany's legitimate grievances had been redressed. No one wished to appear as a war monger and all were ignorant of the pressure which their governments had exerted on the Czechs. Very soon this feeling of relief was to give way to one of shame when the *Kristallnacht* of 9 November showed up the full barbarity of the Nazi regime, and when Hitler's speeches were full of crowing about Munich as a victory of force and his contempt for the pusillanimity of Chamberlain and Daladier became abundantly clear.

Immediately after Munich the dismemberment of Czechoslovakia began. The International Commission rubber-stamped German demands to such an extent that even Henderson was embarrassed. Poland and Hungary were awarded substantial tracts of land. Czech defences were dangerously weakened and the country lost 70 per cent of its iron and steel capacity, 70 per cent of its electric power and 86 per cent of its chemicals; 800,000 Czechs were delivered over to foreign powers. Hitler had won a cheap victory and he could bide his time to absorb what was left of Czechoslovakia.

Although disturbing news reached the west of Hitler's determination to invade Czechoslovakia the appeasers still emphasized détente rather than rearmament and even Halifax, who was becoming increasingly uneasy and tried unsuccessfully to persuade Chamberlain to include some critics of appeasement in the government, argued that German conquests in the east would be 'normal and natural'. Halifax also told the French that since there was nothing Britain and France could do to help the Czechs its was best to do nothing that might provoke them to antagonize the Germans. After some rather lame protests the French accepted the British argument that the four-power guarantee should only apply if three of the powers agreed to act. Since the Germans refused to ratify the guarantee this made little difference. By November the Nazi leadership was becoming increasingly belligerent. On the eve of the *Kristallnacht*, Himmler told his henchmen that their Führer was about to create the greatest empire ever seen on earth and extolled the virtues of the armed forces. Two days later Hitler told representatives of the German press that the country had to be psychologically prepared for war and that they should therefore cease writing about the need for peace. The pogrom on 9 November occurred within the context of these intensified preparations for war and in January 1939 Hitler spoke to the Reichstag of the final solution of the Jewish problem as the 'radical, racial-ideological objective of the coming war' which would result in the 'destruction of the Jewish race in Europe'. In October Hitler sent Ribbentrop to Rome with a message for Mussolini which said that Germany would be in an excellent position to fight the 'great democracies' in September 1939.

While OKW was ordered to refine plans for the liquidation of Czechoslovakia, attempts were made to get Poland to join the anti-Soviet alliance, but the Poles tried to remain independent of both Germany and the Soviet Union. Eventually in March 1939, with the Germans already in Prague, the Poles refused the German offer, which included promises of compensation in the Ukraine, and it became obvious to all but the most purblind of appeasers that Poland was next on Hitler's list.

German pressure on rump Czechoslovakia began with demands for an extra-territorial road from Breslau to Vienna and an extra-territorial canal linking the Oder to the Danube. This was granted. Then in January 1939 the Germans demanded complete neutrality, withdrawal from the League, drastic disarmament, a large degree of German control over foreign policy and the economy, and the adoption of anti-Semitic legislation as the price of a guarantee of the continued existence of an independent Czechoslovakia, a country which had already been reduced almost to the level of a German province. The Germans found useful allies against the government in Prague in the Slovaks who were demanding autonomy, and whose leaders were welcomed in Berlin, addressing Hitler as *'Mein Führer'*.

Britain and France were relatively unconcerned about developments in Czechoslovakia in the winter of 1938. British intelligence, based on reports from German opposition groups, came to the conclusion that Hitler would first attack in the west, invading the Low Countries as the first step towards an invasion of Britain and an attack on France. Only then would Hitler move east in the pursuit of *Lebensraum*. The British drew the conclusion that staff talks with the French should begin at once and that a field force would have to be committed to the Continent. The French were absorbed with the threat from Italy, and in February 1939 Chamberlain extended the Locarno undertaking to include a threat to France's vital interests 'from whatever quarter'. Yet in spite of these fears the general feeling in London and Paris was that the dictators were likely to behave themselves. The Spanish Civil War was over, British and French rearmament programmes were producing satisfactory results and were likely to have a deterrent effect, and both Hitler and Mussolini were making some conciliatory noises, their expressions of utter contempt for the western powers being reserved for their familiars. Reports of Hitler's hostile intentions towards the west were often attributed to war-mongers in the Foreign Office and to like-minded politicians. On the other hand the French realized that the loss of the Sudetenland made Czechoslovakia militarily worthless and that a firm Anglo-French alliance was the only way that France could restore the strategic advantage. The French were determined not to give way any longer and for this reason resisted any British suggestions for further appeasement of Mussolini in North Africa.

The determination to stand by Locarno and even to extend its scope did not imply an equally strong will to resist Germany's ambitions in the east. The Franco-German declaration of 6 December 1938, modelled on the Anglo-German agreement at Munich, was a tacit gesture of acceptance of German expansion eastwards which the French felt was inevitable. The British government got soothing reports from Henderson to the effect that all would be well if the British maintained a friendly disposition towards Germany. Even the news that President Hacha of Czechoslovakia had dismissed the government of the Carpatho-Ukraine and Slovakia, had proclaimed martial law and had imprisoned the Slovak premier and deputy-premier, Monsignor Tiso and Durcansky, and that the Germans were demanding independence for Slovakia, did not change Chamberlain's confidence. Immediately after these events he told the press that Europe was 'settling down to a period of tranquillity'.

Tiso, after his brief spell in jail, was ordered to Berlin, told to appeal to Hitler for protection, and a declaration of Slovakian independence was virtually dictated to him. It was adopted by the

Slovakian Diet on 14 March. The Hungarian government issued an ultimatum demanding the withdrawal of the Czechs from Ruthenia. President Hácha and his foreign minister Chzalkovsky went to Berlin to save what they could. They were admitted to Hitler's presence at 1.15 a.m. on the 15th, treated to a vicious tirade and told that their country would be invaded at 6 a.m. Hácha collapsed and had to be revived with an injection and then signed a document entrusting 'with confidence' the fate of his people to the Führer. Czechoslovakia offered no resistance, there was no question of Britain or France lending assistance. Thus on 15 March the Protectorate of Bohemia and Moravia was established and shortly afterwards Slovakia was reduced to vassal status by a treaty creating what was euphemistically termed a 'protective relationship' with the Reich.

Chamberlain was reticent in his speech to the House of Commons on the 15th but two days later, prompted by Halifax, he gave a speech in Birmingham which sounded a note of slightly peevish annoyance. The British and French ambassadors were withdrawn from Berlin for consultations. Protest notes were sent by both governments and by the Soviet Union and the United States deprecating this blatant aggression. Public opinion in both Britain and France hardened against Germany for there was now no question of justice for German minority groups or the rectification of an unjust peace settlement. Hitler was now seen as bent on the domination of eastern Europe, possibly of the whole continent.

None of this had any effect on Hitler. On 20 March the Lithuanian foreign minister was summoned to Berlin and was issued an ultimatum by Ribbentrop that Memel must be handed over to the Reich. By the 23rd the Lithuanian government gave way and Hitler arrived in Memel on the *Deutschland* after an uncomfortable voyage during which he was much troubled by sea-sickness. The story was a familiar one: local Nazi fanatics had got completely out of hand and could no longer be controlled by their more moderate leader, Dr Neumann, who had been threatened with summary execution if he could not impose order on his unruly followers. Much of this was bluff, for Hitler was determined to seize Memel at the earliest convenient moment, and encouraged by his success in Czechoslovakia he decided to act. This in turn gave Mussolini further incentive to pursue his ambitions in Albania. Assured by Ribbentrop at the end of March that the Germans had no interest in Yugoslavia, Mussolini ordered the invasion of Albania to take place on Good Friday, 7 April, claiming that he was acting merely to restore 'peace, order and justice'. The British government protested mildly, but the Italian foreign minister, Ciano, was reassured by Lord Perth, the British ambassador in Rome, that this was largely for domestic consumption and he expressed the hope that the invasion would not affect the Anglo-Italian agreement.

It then appeared that Romania was likely to be Hitler's next target. On 17 March the Romanian minister in London, Tilea, informed the British government that Germany had issued an ultimatum demanding that the Romanian economy should be subordinated to the interests of the Reich, and he urgently asked Halifax what his government would do if Hitler made good his threat. London immediately informed Paris, Moscow, Warsaw, Athens, Ankara and Belgrade, asking what they would do. The replies were all much the same – it would all depend on what the others did. The following day the Romanian foreign minister announced that there was not a word of truth in Tilea's alarmist tale. This was a somewhat optimistic gloss on the German–Romanian trade negotiations which were designed to secure German control over the oil of Romania and a dominant position in the economic life of southeastern Europe. Even if Tilea was being unnecessarily alarmist, the mere suggestion that Germany might corner the Romanian oil supplies was enough to cause grave concern in Paris. The French Foreign Office began to imagine a sinister plot against Romania in which Poland would try to stop Hitler from pressing his demands over Danzig and the Corridor by encouraging him to go for the riches of Romania which would provide the fuel for the German armed forces which could then be unleashed against the rest of Europe.

Prompted by the French and by a Soviet suggestion for a meeting with Britain, France, Romania and Poland to work out a common strategy, the British government proposed a joint declaration with the Soviet Union, France and Poland that discussions would be held about the appropriate action to take if the political independence of any European state was threatened. This suggestion took on a certain urgency when King Carol of Romania spoke of threatening troop movements in Hungary and Bulgaria and the possibility of war. For the British the key to the whole situation was Poland, a country which was considered militarily far more significant than the Soviet Union, and without which no help could be given to Romania, since neither the Poles nor the Romanians wished to have anything whatever to do with the Russians.

The Polish foreign minister, Colonel Beck, disliked the suggestion that the Polish government should sign a joint declaration with the Soviet Union and countered the British proposal with the suggestion that there should be a secret Anglo–Polish agreement. The Poles had every reason to look for allies. German pressure on Danzig was a constant irritant, the annexation of Memel threatened its security and raised the possibility that Danzig might be for Poland what the Sudetenland was for Czechoslovakia. The Foreign Office began to think that Hitler had serious designs on Poland and that he had to be stopped by offering a guarantee to Poland, a view that was strengthened when Ian Colvin, the Berlin correspondent for the *News Chronicle*, told them that Germany planned to attack Poland and that Beck was probably in Germany's pay. The conclusion was that Poland and Romania would go the way of Czechoslovakia and that Hitler would attack in the west unless Britain and France took decisive action to stiffen both countries.

On 31 March Chamberlain announced in the House of Commons that if Poland's independence was threatened and if she offered armed resistance Britain and France would 'lend her all support in their power'. It seemed that Britain had undergone a minor revolution in foreign policy and Chamberlain's critics were momentarily silenced. Four days later Beck visited London where he downplayed the threat from Germany, refused to consider closer relations with the Soviet Union and remained silent over Danzig. The British extended the interim guarantee to Poland, encouraged by Beck's assurances that it was unlikely ever to be invoked, and expressed their determination to press ahead with the finalization of a pact which would include France.

Beck did not see the British guarantee as a reversal of his previous policy of negotiating with Berlin, and managed to convince himself that Hitler was a 'timid Austrian' who would not risk alienating Poland and thus drive her into an alliance with Russia. The British were annoyed at the Poles for refusing to divulge the full details of the German demands and felt that Beck was duplicitous in his attitude towards them. The French were alarmed at the way that Poland had followed in Hitler's train at Munich and had profited from Czechoslovakia's humiliation, and there was disgust in some quarters at the fresh outbursts of virulent anti-Semitism in Poland. There was therefore an increased disinclination to be dragged into a war by Poland under the terms of the 1921 treaty. Nor was the British guarantee very reassuring, for if it were to work effectively the French would clearly have to do most of the fighting. The French eventually made promises to attack in the west, but they had no intention whatever of carrying them out. The prevailing sentiment was expressed by the French fascist Marcel Déat who asked the famous rhetorical question: 'Why die for Danzig?'

From the outset there was a question whether the guarantee of Poland would involve dying for Danzig. *The Times* was quick to point out that the guarantee was of Poland's independence not its territorial integrity, and that it therefore did not mean that Poland could not be required to make certain territorial concessions, presumably in Pomorze and Danzig. Since Geoffrey Dawson, the editor of *The Times*, was close to Chamberlain this was seen as a quasi-official statement. Assurances by the Foreign Office that this was not the case were not particularly convincing since the prime minister largely ignored their advice. He hoped that the guarantee would convince Hitler to moderate his demands, which seemed to be even more justified than those against Czechoslovakia, that it would oblige the French to take a tougher stand, and would make a negotiated settlement possible.

The British government was now under mounting pressure to give a guarantee to Romania. On 10 April the secretary-general of the Romanian Foreign Ministry visited London and asked for an undertaking to defend his country which could be used to strengthen the hand of the foreign minister, Gafencu, on his forthcoming visit to Berlin. Daladier announced that he would offer a guarantee to Romania and Greece and asked the British government to join him. Chamberlain and Halifax tried to stall, but they were pushed by the Admiralty, who wanted to secure Romanian oil, and also by the Labour Party. On 13 April Chamberlain announced in the House of Commons that the British government would lend all the support in its power to Romania and Greece if they decided to fight in defence of their independence.

Chamberlain and Halifax still felt that Mussolini could be persuaded to exercise a restraining influence on Hitler, but Daladier was convinced that Italy was now completely under Germany's control. The new British ambassador in Rome since May 1939, Sir Percy Loraine, unlike his predecessor, Lord Perth, supported the French reading of the situation and insisted that the only way to deal with the dictators was for there to be a solid Anglo-French alliance against them, that further concessions would be unrequited and that the only argument they understood was brute force. But in London Halifax told the Italian chargé d'affaires not to heed the government's somewhat harsh words about Italy, for they were designed to placate public opinion.

While the British government pursued the chimera of an understanding with Italy they overlooked the importance of the Soviet Union. On 10 March Stalin gave an address to the Eighteenth Party Congress in which he accused the west of appeasing the 'aggressor states', Japan, Germany and Italy and of rejecting the policy of collective security. Stalin warned that he would not allow the Soviet Union to be 'drawn into conflict by warmongers who are accustomed to have others pull their chestnuts out of the fire', and announced that he wished to concentrate on the 'strengthening of business relations with all countries'. The precise meaning of these remarks remains obscure, but it would seem that it was designed as an invitation to the west to improve relations with the Soviet Union, although it did include the accusation, subsequently taken up by Soviet historians as an article of faith, that the west wanted Germany to become embroiled in a war with the Soviet Union and the speech did not close off the possibility of improving relations with Germany.

The British and French guarantees to Poland and Romania greatly strengthened the Soviet position and Stalin could wait to be approached by both Germany and the west to see who would make the better offer. His greatest concern was to improve the defence of Leningrad by expanding into the Baltic States, a demand to which the British government could hardly accede. Many observers felt that the Soviet demands were such that a rapprochement with Germany was on the cards; others felt that the very idea of such an alliance was absurd. Neither in Britain nor in France was there much enthusiasm for an agreement with the Soviets. It was agreed that their armed forces were unlikely to make much contribution to the common effort, that the price of their friendship was ludicrously high, that an alliance would only provoke the Germans and would be viewed with singular displeasure by Italy, Japan, Spain, Yugoslavia and the Vatican to name but a few of the stalwart anti-communist states. It was also a matter of concern that the Soviet Union might get Britain and France involved in some adventure in which their own vital interests were not at stake.

On 14 April Maisky, the Soviet ambassador in London, sounded out the possibility of a Soviet guarantee to Romania, but three days later tentative steps commenced towards an understanding between Hitler and Stalin. To make the situation even more complicated the Germans, principally Goering but also Hitler, examined the likelihood of Britain acquiescing to German ambitions in the east. On 17 April Litvinov formally proposed a pact with the Soviet Union which would oblige Britain and France to take military action in defence of the eastern European states. No reply was forthcoming by 3 May when Litvinov, a champion of collective security and a Jew, was replaced by Molotov. The Soviets had ample reason to doubt the west's determination to stop Hitler, and dissension between London and Paris on the susceptibilities of Poland and Romania about an understanding with Russia did nothing to persuade them otherwise. Molotov harped on the differences between the French and the British position, and by the middle of May he upped the ante, rejecting the British proposals as inadequate.

A somewhat modified Soviet proposal was still on the table which anti-appeasers like Churchill and the Labour Party felt should be accepted, as did the French, but still the British government dragged its feet. On 27 May the British presented a counter-proposal designed to make sure that the Soviet Union would only become involved if the state which was the object of aggression actually wanted their help. Molotov replied two days later saying that some states would have to be guaranteed whether they liked it or not, and repeated this in a speech on 31 May, in which he also mentioned that trade talks with the Germans might soon be reopened. On 2 June the Soviets named those countries which would have to accept a guarantee regardless of their own wishes, a list which included Belgium, Poland, Romania and Greece, but neither Switzerland nor Holland.

A British counter-proposal was presented to the Soviet government on 15 June by a relatively junior Foreign Office official, William Strang, which was obviously unacceptable to the Russians and which omitted the Russian clause that there should be no separate peace. Some concessions were made, mainly at the prompting of the French government, and fresh proposals were given to Molotov on 1 July. Britain and France now agreed to a list of states, if they included Switzerland and Belgium and if they were only mentioned in a secret protocol. The Soviets wanted to include a paragraph which would enable them to interfere in a state which underwent a 'reversal of policy in the interests of the aggressor' which was seen as 'indirect aggression'. The British would only accept this if the state in question agreed to such action and if there was a threat of force. Molotov replied that cases where there was no threat of force would also have to be included. Halifax thought that this would enable the Soviet Union to engage in 'naked, immoral interference' in the affairs of its neighbours, but it was agreed that military talks should commence before the 'indirect aggression' issue was resolved.

Strang was recalled from Moscow, trade talks between the Soviet Union and Britain were postponed, and Admiral Reginald Aylmer Ranfurly Plunckett-Ernle-Erle-Drax, a man whose name was somewhat more impressive than his military importance, was sent by the slowest possible route to Moscow to head the military discussions with instructions to stall until a political agreement was reached. Talks began on 12 August and two days later Marshal Voroshilov asked the only really pertinent question, one which hitherto had been studiously avoided: would Poland and Romania allow Soviet troops on their territory? Britain and France put all the pressure they could on the Poles to accept, but Beck replied that this amounted to a new partition of Poland, adding: 'With the Germans we risk losing our liberty. With the Russians we lose our soul.' On 21 August the military talks were adjourned and that evening it was announced that Ribbentrop was to visit Moscow. Two days later he signed a pact with the Soviet Union.

Hitler had at first been wary of Soviet approaches in April and May, when it was suggested that trade talks could be combined with political discussions. It was felt that Soviet terms might be exorbitant and that an understanding would harm German relations with Japan. On 23 May Hitler told his service chiefs that he intended to destroy Poland by force of arms. He had been told by Mussolini the day before, on the occasion of the signing of the 'Pact of Steel', that Italy would not be ready for war until 1942 and therefore needed to ensure that the Soviet Union did not combine with the western powers to defend Poland. It seemed unlikely that the Japanese would become involved in a European war and, since it was plain that negotiations between London and Moscow were going badly, cautious moves were made towards the Soviet Union by the end of the month.

Throughout June and July the Germans and the Russians sounded one another out, but it was not until the end of July that the Germans made a definite move. Dr Julius Schnurre, the Wilhelm-strasse's economics expert, invited Astakhov, the Soviet chargé d'affaires and Babarin, a senior trade official, to a fashionable Berlin restaurant and let it be known that Germany saw no real reason why there should not be an understanding between the two countries since Britain, not the Soviet Union, was the main enemy. Astakhov agreed that such an understanding was desirable and added that the Soviet Union accepted Germany's claim to Danzig and the Corridor. These sentiments were repeated a week later to Astakhov by Ribbentrop, who was a little concerned that the Moscow talks between Britain, France and the Soviet Union might make some progress. By the middle of the month the Germans offered a twenty-five-year non-aggression pact, which Ribbentrop said he would sign any time from 18 August. The Soviets demanded a definition of spheres of influence and stressed the need for thorough preparation. On 20 August Hitler sent a telegram to Stalin almost begging him to receive Ribbentrop by the 23rd at the latest. Twenty-four hours later Stalin's reply came, to the immense relief of the Germans.

The signing of the pact was accompanied by a mammoth banquet. Stalin told Ribbentrop that Britain should not be allowed to rule the world, but warned him that she would be a formidable adversary. Ribbentrop told Stalin that the anti-Comintern Pact was aimed against Britain and not the Soviet Union. Stalin reassurred his guest that he would never betray his new partner.

The pact did not contain the usual escape clause found in other Soviet non-aggression pacts and thus applied in the event of German aggression against Poland. Soviet claims to Polish territory, to the Baltic States and to Bessarabia were acknowledged. Germany and the Soviet Union would thus meet face-to-face on the Narev, Vistula, San and in a subsequent agreement on the Pissa.

On the day before the pact was signed Hitler harangued his generals at the Obersalzberg, telling them that the Nazi-Soviet pact would make it impossible for Britain and France to give any assistance to Poland and that the Poles would have to give way. The following day orders were given for the invasion of Poland to begin on 26 August. On 24 August the Polish–German customs talks, which resulted from a series of provocative incidents, were broken off when the Germans put forward totally unacceptable demands. Both Britain and France still hoped that the Poles would negotiate and that war could be avoided. Chamberlain sent a message to Hitler on 22 August urging discussions between Germany and Poland to end the crisis over Danzig. Hitler's reaction was one of unmitigated delight and there was much chortling and thigh-slapping as the wretched Henderson left his presence. The ambassador sympathized with Hitler's point of view and later told Halifax that the Poles were 'utterly foolish and unwise' and informed Hitler that 'Jews and enemies of the Nazis' were undermining Anglo-German relations and that a war would only benefit the 'lesser races'.

On 24 August the House of Commons passed the Emergency Powers Act and on the following day the Anglo-Polish Treaty was ratified. The French government desperately tried to avoid their commitment to Poland but the Chief of the General Staff, General Gamelin, insisted that the army was ready and would have to fight, although no plans were drawn up for an offensive against Germany in support of Poland. Daladier hoped that the Poles would be prepared to sacrifice Danzig, and he suggested to Hitler that the French might mediate between Germany and Poland.

On 25 August Hitler made Henderson a 'large, comprehensive offer'. Germany was to have a free hand in Danzig and the Corridor and in return he would agree to co-operate with the British Empire and reach an agreement on disarmament. On the same day he postponed the attack on Poland. He had been told that Italy was not yet prepared to fight, he was impressed by the signing of the Anglo-Polish pact and decided to continue with his war of nerves to secure another Munich rather than go to war the next day.

The following day Hitler was introduced to Goering's friend, the Swedish industrialist Birger Dahlerus, who was treated to a long tirade on Germany's military might and then told that Germany would guarantee Poland's frontiers in return for the seccession of Danzig and the Corridor. Dahlerus began his frantic but futile effort to keep the peace by going straight to London where he met Chamberlain, Halifax and Cadogan. The prime minister suggested that Poland might agree to the German demand for Danzig but not to the Corridor, and suggested an extra-territorial corridor under international guarantees. Hitler still hoped that he could drive a wedge between Britain and Poland, but on 28 August he ordered the attack on Poland to begin on 1 September. His mistake was the belief that the British and French had hardly changed since Munich. Both were still determined to avoid war, but they were now negotiating from a much stronger position. Their armed forces had been greatly strengthened in the last year, and they were convinced that Hitler had now placed himself in a tricky situation, was threatened by a revolt from moderates, led it was fondly imagined by Goering, whose brutality was hidden behind layers of vulgar *gemütlichkeit*, and that his bluff could be called.

On the evening of 28 August Henderson downed half a bottle of champagne and went to deliver the British reply to Hitler. He confirmed that the Poles had agreed to negotiate, but insisted that his government would only accept a settlement which respected Poland's vital interests. Much to the dismay of the anti-appeasers in the Foreign Office the ambassador dangled the prospect of an Anglo-German treaty in front of the Führer's nose, but all to no avail. Hitler demanded Danzig, the Corridor, parts of Silesia and vowed to destroy Poland. Hitler was now convinced that he could win a easy victory in the east and had clearly given up the idea of a rapprochement with Britain, but it was an idea which he never entirely discarded and was one to which he would return during the war.

The Poles decided to mobilize on 29 August but were persuaded by the British and French ambassadors to put off this action, which was felt to be dangerously provocative. This proved to be a fatal mistake which left the Polish armed forces not fully prepard to respond to the German invasion. Hitler's reply to the British offer was so insulting that even Henderson lost his temper with him, although on reflection he still hoped, as did Halifax, that negotiations were possible. But the Poles would not negotiate. The Corridor was theirs, their rights in Danzig were clear and there was simply nothing to discuss. Joseph Lipski, the Polish ambassador in Berlin, was pushed from all sides to reach an agreement with the Germans, but the most he could say was that his government was 'favourably considering' the suggestion that talks should begin.

Mussolini told the British that he would remain neutral and on 31 August he proposed a conference, which looked ominously like a second Munich, to discuss revisions of the Treaty of Versailles and which was to be held on 5 September. Both the British and French ambassadors in Rome were enthusiastic but the proposal was over-taken by events. Hitler told Attolico, the Italian ambassador, that the die was cast. The attack on Poland began at 4.45 the following morning.

The British government still wavered, although they did not accept the German tale that they wee responding to Polish aggression. The French still hoped that something might come of Mussolini's proposed conference. By the evening both the British and the French issued warnings that the Germans must withdraw from Poland, but no time limits were set and it was made clear the following day that these were not ultimata. After lunch on 2 September the British Cabinet unanimously agreed to issue an ulti-matum that would expire at midnight, but Halifax still hoped for a conference and Chamberlain willingly dragged his feet to keep in step with the French. In the Commons that evening Chamberlain said that he would welcome a conference if the Germans agreed to withdraw their forces. The House was outraged, for this was not the same as insisting on the actual withdrawal of the German forces. When Greenwood as acting leader of the Labour Party rose to speak Amery called out from the Conservative ranks 'Speak for England, Arthur!' Back at Number 10 members of the Cabinet told Cham-berlain and Halifax that the time for prevarication was over. 'Right, gentlemen', the prime minister replied, 'this means war'. A well timed clap of thunder heightened the dramatic effect of this statement. Henderson was instructed to deliver the British ultimatum at 9 a.m. to expire by 11 a.m. and the French, once more following the British lead, delivered theirs at noon. It expired at 5 p.m.

Ribbentrop refused to receive Henderson, who handed the British note to Dr Schmidt. At the chancellory Hitler, Goering, Ribbentrop and Goebbels waited for the news to come. It was not a happy gathering. Hitler was angry that his gamble had failed and Britain and France had stood by their guarantee to Poland. Goering contemplated the consequences of defeat and Goebbels was lost in gloomy thoughts. This pessimism was misplaced. The campaign in Poland was a spectacular success, and Britain and France did virtually nothing to help their ally. Hitler did not get quite the war he anticipated and may not have got it at exactly the time he had planned, but it was his war. That the phoney war became a major war in May the following year was the result of his decision, as was the continuation of the war against the Soviet Union in June 1941. The invasion of Poland need not have led to a world war; that it did has nothing to do with the selfishness and timidity of the British and French or the perfidious callousness of the Soviet Union. Hitler and those who followed him bear the responsibility for that war. Thus the 25 million Europeans who died in Hitler's war did not 'die for Danzig' as some historians and their radical right-wing admirers still insist they did: they died as a consequence of Nazi Germany's insatiable lust for conquest. Debate will continue about the extent and consistency of Hitler's aims, the degree to which he planned the war and the kind of war he intended to fight, the extent to which it was due to the polycratic power structure of the Nazi state or the impact of social and economic forces, but there can be no doubt that Hitler was prepared to risk a European war and that he doubled and redoubled the stakes. The ultimate responsibility was his that the war became one for German hegemony, whether continental or global, that it was fought with unmatched brutality and was fuelled by visions of a pathological and immoral utopia.

Select Bibliography

CHAPTER ONE

R. Albrecht-Carrié, *Italy at the Peace Conference*. New York 1938.

Francis Deák, *Hungary at the Peace Conference: The Diplomatic History of the Treaty of Trianon*. New York 1942.

Michael L. Dockrill and J. Gould, *Peace Without Promise: Britain and the Peace Conferences, 1919–1923*. London 1981.

Howard Elcock, *Portrait of a Decision: The Council of Four and the Treaty of Versailles*. London 1972.

Sir James Headlam-Morley, *A Memoir of the Paris Peace Conference*. London 1972.

Ivo J. Lederer, *Yugoslavia at the Paris Peace Conference: A Study in Frontier Making*. New Haven 1963.

David Lloyd George, *The Truth about the Peace Treaties*. (2 vols). London 1938.

Arno J. Mayer, *Politics and Diplomacy of Peacemaking: Containment and Counterrevolution at Versailles 1918–1919*. London 1968.

Harold Nicolson, *Peacemaking 1919*. London 1966.

H. M. V. Temperley, *A History of the Peace Conference of Paris*. (6 vols). London 1920–1924.

John M. Thompson, *Bolshevism, and the Versailles Peace*. Princeton 1966.

Marc Trachtenburg, 'Reparations at the Paris Peace Conference', *Journal of Modern History*, 1979.

F. P. Walters, *A History of the League of Nations* (2 vols). London 1952.

Gerhard L. Weinberg, 'The Defeat of Germany in 1918 and the European Balance of Power', *Central European History*, 1969.

CHAPTER TWO

D. H. Aldcroft, *From Versailles to Wall Street 1919–1929*. London 1977.

I. T. Berend and G. Ranki, *Economic Development in East Central Europe in the 19th and 20th Centuries*. New York 1974.

C. Bresciani-Turroni, *The Economics of Inflation: A Study of Currency Depreciation in Post-War Germany*. London 1937.

T. Kemp, *The French Economy, 1919–39: The History of a Decline*. London 1972.

C. P. Kindleberger, *The World in Depression 1929–1939*. Berkeley 1975.

D. S. Landes, *The Unbound Prometheus: Technological Change and Industrial Development in Western Europe from 1750 to the Present*. Cambridge 1977.

W. A. Lewis, *Economic Survey, 1919–1939*. London 1939.

S. Pollard and C. Holmes, *The End of the Old Empire 1914–1939*. New York 1972.

G. Rees, *The Great Slump: Capitalism in Crisis, 1929–33*. London 1970.

F. K. Ringer, *The German Inflation of 1923*. New York 1969.

CHAPTER THREE

E. H. Carr, *International Relations Between the Two World Wars, 1919–1939*. London 1947.

E. H. Carr, *The Twenty Years' Crisis, 1919–1939*. London 1946.

Denis Mack Smith, *Mussolini's Roman Empire*. London 1976.

Hans Gatzke, *Stresemann and the Rearmament of Germany*. Baltimore 1954.

Jon Jacobson, *Locarno Diplomacy*. Princeton 1972.

George Kennan, *Russia and the West under Lenin and Stalin*. Boston 1961.

Charles S. Maier, *Recasting Bourgeois Europe*. Princeton 1975.

Sally Marks, *The Illusion of Peace: International Relations in Europe 1918–1933*. London 1976.

F. S. Northedge, *The Troubled Giant: Britain Among the Great Powers, 1916–1939*. London 1968.

Piotr S. Wandycz, *France and Her Eastern Allies, 1919–1925*. Minnesota 1962.

CHAPTER FOUR

POLAND

Norman Davies, *God's Playground: A History of Poland*, Vol. II (1795 to the Present). New York 1982.
Oscar Halecki, *A History of Poland*. New York 1976.
Hans Roos, *A History of Modern Poland: From the Foundation of the State in the First World War to the Present Day*. London 1966.
Richard M. Watt, *Bitter Glory: Poland and its Fate, 1918–1939*. New York 1982.

HUNGARY

István Barta and others (ed. Ervin Pamlényi), *A History of Hungary*. Budapest 1973.
C. A. Macartney, *Hungary: A Short History*. Edinburgh 1962.
Rudolf L. Tókés, *Béla Kun and the Hungarian Soviet Republic*. New York 1967.

CZECHOSLOVAKIA

Victor S. Mamatey and Radomir Luza (eds.), *A History of the Czechoslovak Republic 1918–1948*. Princeton 1973.
Vera Olivová, *The Doomed Democracy: Czechoslovakia in a Disrupted Europe, 1914–1938*. London 1972.
R. W. Seton-Watson, *A History of the Czechs and Slovaks*. Hamden, Connecticut 1965.

SPECIALIZED AND GENERAL STUDIES

Gregory F. Campbell, *Confrontation in Central Europe: Weimar Germany and Czechoslovakia*. Chicago 1975.
Antony Polonsky, *The Little Dictators: The History of Eastern Europe since 1918*. London and Boston 1975.

Hans Rogger and Eugen Weber, *The European Right: A Historical Profile*. Berkeley and Los Angeles 1966.

Hugh Seton-Watson, *Eastern Europe Between the Wars, 1918–1941*. Cambridge 1946.

Peter F. Sugar (ed.), *Native Fascism in the Successor States 1918–1945*. Santa Barbara 1971.

Elizabeth Wiskemann, *Czechs and Germans: A Study of the Struggle in the Historic Provinces of Bohemia and Moravia*. London 1967.

CHAPTER FIVE

E. H. Carr, *A History of Soviet Russia*, 14 vols, London 1952–1979.

E. H. Carr, *The Russian Revolution from Lenin to Stalin, 1917–1929*. London 1979.

W. H. Chamberlain, *The Russian Revolution*. (2 vols). London 1935.

Stephen F. Cohen, *Bukharin and the Bolshevik Revolution. A Political Biography, 1888–1938*. New York 1973.

Isaac Deutscher, *The Prophet Armed. Trotsky: 1879–1921*. London 1954.

Isaac Deutscher, *The Prophet Unarmed. Trotsky: 1921–1929*. London 1959.

Sheila Fitzpatrick, *The Russian Revolution 1917–1932*. Oxford 1984.

Jerry F. Hough and Merle Fainsod, *How the Soviet Union is Governed*. Cambridge, Mass. 1979.

T. H. Von Laue, *Why Lenin? Why Stalin? A Reappraisal of the Russian Revolution, 1900–1930*. Philadelphia 1964.

Roy A. Medvedev, *Let History Judge. The Origin and Consequences of Stalinism*. New York 1971.

Robert C. Tucker, *Stalinism. Essays in Historical Interpretation*. New York 1977.

Robert C. Tucker, *Stalin as Revolutionary 1879–1929*. New York 1973.

Adam B. Ulam, *Stalin. The Man and his Era*. New York 1973.

CHAPTER SIX

G. Carocci, *Italian Fascism*. London 1974.

F. L. Carsten, *The Rise of Fascism*. Berkeley 1967.

A. Lyttelton, *The Seizure of Power: Fascism in Italy 1919–1929*. New York 1973.
D. Mack Smith, *Mussolini*. New York 1982.
G. Salvemini, *Under the Axe of Fascism*. London 1936.
G. Salvemini, *The Origins of Fascism in Italy*. New York 1973.
R. Sarti, *Fascism and the Industrial Leadership in Italy 1919–1940*. Berkeley 1971.
R. Sarti, *The Ax Within: Italian Fascism in Action*. New York 1974

CHAPTER SEVEN

V. R. Berghahn, *Modern Germany*. Cambridge 1982.
R. Bessel and E. J. Feuchtwanger (eds.), *Social Change and Political Development in Weimar Germany*. London 1981.
F. L. Carsten, *Reichswehr and Politics*. Oxford 1966.
T. Echenburg *et al.*, *The Path to Dictatorship: 1918–1933*. New York 1967.
E. Eyck, *A History of the Weimar Republic* (2 vols). London 1962
H. Lebovics, *Social Conservatism and the Middle Classes in Germany*. Princeton 1969.
A. J. Nicholls, *Weimar and the Rise of Hitler*. London 1968.
A. J. Nicholls and E. Matthias (eds.), *German Democracy and the Triumph of Hitler*. London 1971.
A Rosenberg, *A History of the German Republic*. New York 1965.
A. J. Ryder, *The German Revolution of 1918*. Cambridge 1967.
B. Weisbrod, 'Economic Power and Political Stability Reconsidered', *Social History*, 1979, pp. 241–263.

CHAPTER EIGHT

Maurice Cowling, *The Impact of Labour, 1920–24*. London 1970.
Maurice Cowling, *The Impact of Hitler. British Politics and British Policy 1933–1940*. London 1975.
Sean Glynn and John Oxborrow, *Interwar Britain. A Social and Economic History*. London 1976.
Robert Graves and Alan Hodge, *The Long Weekend: A Social History of Great Britain, 1918–1930*. London 1940.
W. N. Medlicott, *Contemporary England 1914–1964*. London 1967.

C. L Mowat, *Britain Between the Wars 1918–1940*. London 1955.

G. A. Phillips, *The General Strike. The Politics of Industrial Conflict*. London 1976.

Sidney Pollard, *The Development of the British Economy 1914–1967*. London 1969.

L. C. B. Seaman, *Post-Victorian Britain 1902–1951*. London 1966.

A. J. P. Taylor, *English History 1914–1945*. Oxford 1965.

CHAPTER NINE

Denis W. Brogan, *The Development of Modern France, 1870–1940*. New York 1940.

Daniel Brower, *The New Jacobins: The French Communist Party and the Popular Front*. Ithaca, New York 1968.

Alfred Cobban, *A History of Modern France. Vol. 3: 1871–1962*. London 1965.

Joel Colton, *Léon Blum: Humanist in Politics*. New York 1966.

Nathaniel Greene, *From Versailles to Vichy: The Third Republic, 1919–1940*. New York 1970.

Nathaniel Greene, *Crisis and Decline: The French Socialist Party in the Popular Front Era*. Ithaca, New York 1969.

James Joll (ed.), *The Decline of the Third Republic*. London 1959.

John T. Marcus, *French Socialism in the Crisis Years, 1933–1936*. New York 1958.

Eugen Weber, *Action Française*. Stanford 1962.

Alexander Werth, *The Twilight of France: 1933–1940*. New York 1966.

CHAPTER TEN

B. Bolloten, *The Grand Camouflage: The Communist Conspiracy in the Spanish Civil War*. London 1968.

Franz Borkenau, *The Spanish Cockpit*. London 1937.

Gerald Brenan, *The Spanish Labyrinth*. London 1943.

Pierre Broué and Emile Témime, *The Revolution and the Civil War in Spain*. London 1972.

Raymond Carr, *Spain 1808–1975*, Oxford 1982.

Raymond Carr, *The Spanish Tragedy*. London 1977.

Noam Chomsky, *American Power and the New Mandarins*. London 1969.

Ronald Fraser, *The Blood of Spain*. London 1979.
Richard Herr, *An Historical Essay on Modern Spain*. Berkeley 1971.
George Hills, *Franco, the Man and his Nation*. London 1967.
Gabriel Jackson, *The Spanish Republic and the Civil War 1931–39*.
  Princeton 1965.
Hugh Thomas, *The Spanish Civil War*. London 1977.

CHAPTER ELEVEN

W. S. Allen, *The Nazi Seizure of Power*. Chicago 1965.
K. D. Bracher, *The German Dictatorship*. London 1970.
M. Broszat, *The Hitler State*. London 1981.
A. Bullock, *Hitler*. London 1974.
J. S. Conway, *The Nazi Persecution of the Churches*. London 1968.
K. Hildebrand, *The Third Reich*. London 1984.
F. Neumann, *Behemoth*. New York 1966.
R. O'Neill, *The German Army and the Nazi Party*. London 1966.
E. N. Peterson, *The Limits of Hitler's Power*. Princeton 1969.
D. Schoenbaum, *Hitler's Social Revolution*. London 1967.
A. Schweitzer, *Big Business in the Third Reich*. New York 1972.

CHAPTER TWELVE

Anthony P. Adamthwaite, *The Making of the Second World War*.
  London 1977.
Anthony P. Adamthwaite, *France and the Coming of the Second World
  War*. London 1977.
P. M. H. Bell, *The Origins of the Second World War in Europe*.
  London 1986.
Wilhelm Deist, *The Wehrmacht and German Rearmament*. London
  1982.
Keith Eubank, *The Origins of World War II*. New York 1969.
Klaus Hildebrand, *The Foreign Policy of the Third Reich*. London
  1973.
W. Hofer, *War Premeditated*. London 1962.
Gordon Martel, *The Origins of the Second World War Reconsidered: The
  A. J. P. Taylor Debate After Twenty-Five years*. London 1986.
Simon Newman, *March 1939: The British Guarantee to Poland*.
  London 1976.

Esmonde M. Robertson (ed.), *The Origins of the Second World War.* London 1971.

William R. Rock, *British Appeasement in the 1930s.* London 1977.

A. J. P. Taylor, *The Origins of the Second World War.* London 1963.

Christopher Thorne, *The Approach of War 1938–39.* London 1967.

Gerhard Weinberg, *The Foreign Policy of Hilter's Germany, vol. 1, Diplomatic Renolution in Europe, 1933–1936*, Chicago 1970; *vol. 2, Starting World War II.* Chicago 1980.

Maps

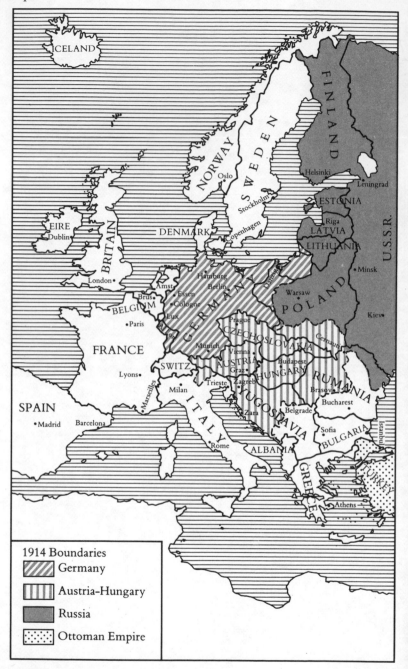

Map 1 The peace settlement of 1919.

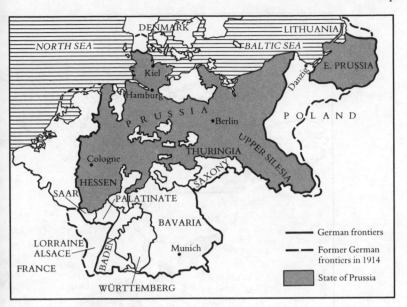

Map 2 Germany after the peace settlement.

Map 3 The League of Nations, 1931.

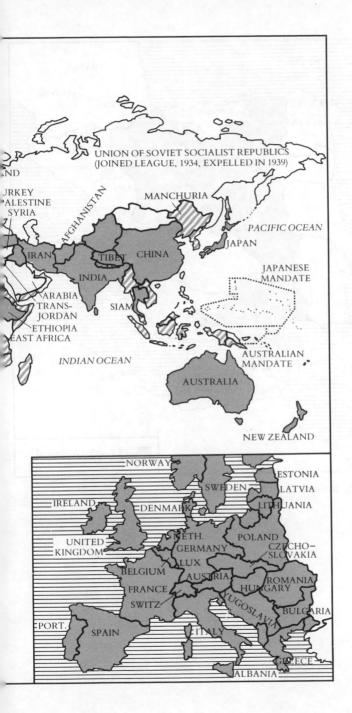

UNION OF SOVIET SOCIALIST REPUBLICS
(JOINED LEAGUE, 1934, EXPELLED IN 1939)

ND

URKEY
PALESTINE
SYRIA

AFGHANISTAN

MANCHURIA

PACIFIC OCEAN

JAPAN

IRAN

TIBET

CHINA

JAPANESE
MANDATE

INDIA

ARABIA
TRANS-
JORDAN

SIAM

ETHIOPIA
EAST AFRICA

INDIAN OCEAN

AUSTRALIAN
MANDATE

AUSTRALIA

NEW ZEALAND

NORWAY

ESTONIA

SWEDEN

LATVIA

IRELAND

DENMARK

LITHUANIA

UNITED
KINGDOM

NETH.

POLAND

GERMANY

CZECHO-
SLOVAKIA

BELGIUM

LUX

AUSTRIA

FRANCE

HUNGARY

ROMANIA

SWITZ

YUGOSLAVIA

BULGARIA

PORT.

SPAIN

ITALY

GREECE

ALBANIA

Map 4 The Spanish Civil War, 1936.

Map 5 The expansion of Germany 1933–39.

Index

330

Index